COMMUNITY PLANNING
FOR HUMAN SERVICES

COMMUNITY PLANNING FOR HUMAN SERVICES

By BRADLEY BUELL and ASSOCIATES

GREENWOOD PRESS, PUBLISHERS
WESTPORT, CONNECTICUT

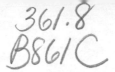

The Library of Congress has catalogued this publication as follows:

Library of Congress Cataloging in Publication Data

Buell, Bradley.
    Community planning for human services.

    Based on a project conducted by Community
Research Associates, inc.
    Bibliography: p.
    1. Community organization. I. Community
Research Associates. II. Title.
[HM131.B75 1973]   361.8   72-9588
ISBN 0-8371-6585-7

The basic research for this volume was made possible by appropriations from THE GRANT FOUNDATION, INC., *New York.*

DEDICATED TO THE VISION OF

JULIA C. LATHROP, EDWARD T. DEVINE, MARY BEARD,

MILTON J. ROSENAU, WILLIAM T. SEDGWICK, ADOLPH MEYER,

MARY E. RICHMOND, THOMAS MOTT OSBORNE, JOSEPH LEE,

JANE ADDAMS, SHERMAN C. KINGSLEY, AND ALL OTHERS

WHOSE PIONEERING ENTERPRISE LAID THE FOUNDATIONS

FOR THE AMERICAN COMMUNITY'S PRESENT-DAY

PROGRAMS OF HUMAN SERVICE

PREFACE

IN OUR CENTURY, and especially in this country, man's conscious resentment of his own suffering has exploded into a great diversity of activity in behalf of human welfare. Medical and social science are following the path of specialization so productively pursued by those whose concern has been with the physical forces that surround us. Along this same road practitioners of the humanitarian professions are now marching. Specialists in medical practice, social casework, public assistance, probation and parole, public health, group work, hospital administration, nursing, psychiatry and mental hygiene, rehabilitation, correctional administration, and recreation minister increasingly to different manifestations of human needs and ills. It has been mainly in this century that local communities, and the larger state and national communities of which they are a part, have undertaken to assure that agencies and organizations will make these services available to those in need of them.

Materials from these and other professional, occupational, and organizational specialties are presented in this volume. Our purpose is not, however, to provide a compendium of information about a series of separate activities, but to create the framework of a coherent program of community well-being. Thus, good teamwork has been vital to this research. The outcome is, in fact, the result of a joint undertaking, participating in which have been the board of directors and staff of Community Research Associates, Inc., consultants from the principal fields who have served continuously during the course of the project, and many others who contributed particular knowledge and experience at special points.

Of great value was the fact that our corps of project consultants had behind them prior association in local community studies and surveys —which for the most part extended over a decade and a half—with a strong thread of continuity in experience and thought. The main foci of our research, together with the principal classifications of problems and services around which our materials are organized and much of the analysis and interpretation of the new materials from the St. Paul project were wrought from working sessions in which all participated. More than anything else, perhaps, did the capacity of these men and women to pool specialized knowledge and thought assist in creating purposeful directives for the synthesis of our materials. While not officially a member of the group of consultants, Miss Olive Johnson gave valuable assistance and provided liaison with the United States Public Health Service in establishing the ill-health problem and service classifications.

To our headquarters staff, each member with specialized experience in his own right, there had accrued the advantage of more or less continuous association during the same decade and a half, focused upon practical problems of community organization and planning. In this present work Madeline Berry's particular assignments have included supervision of the field study in St. Paul; assembling, checking, and editing the materials of the section on ill-health; and the processes of final editing and preparation of the entire manuscript for publication. Caroline Wagner Robinson has been primarily responsible for the collection of materials for the sections on dependency and maladjustment, and the revisions and checking of these chapters of the manuscript. Reginald Robinson was responsible not only for the collection of the materials for the recreation section, but also for the initial draft of these chapters. All members of the staff have participated in the development of the thought and the framework of the total project.

In the final stages of the project, each consultant reviewed and advised regarding the use and presentation of the materials in the section of his chief concern. In addition, we must acknowledge our debt to many others who read and gave thoughtful criticism of all or special sections of the manuscript. We should be negligent if we did not mention: Dr. Paul Stevenson, National Institute of Mental Health; Mrs. Francisca Thomas, Associate Director of the Hospital Council of New York; Richard Chappell, Chief of the Probation Service, United States Courts; Charles K. Brightbill, School of Physical Education, University of Illinois; D. Paul Reed, Director of the National Information Bureau; Mrs. Frederic R. Kellogg, Milton H. Glover, and the late Cecil Smith, members of the board of directors of Community

Research Associates, Inc. Marion O. Robinson gave valued assistance in shaping the final form of the first and summary chapters. Inevitably, responsibility for any final accounting for the basic approach and for particular interpretations in the ensuing pages must rest upon my own shoulders.

All associated in the project take pleasure in joining to express our sense of appreciation to Mr. W. T. Grant and the Board of Directors of The Grant Foundation, whose sympathetic interest and support made the undertaking possible. Given without stint during the entire period have been objective counsel and stimulating encouragement from Perrin C. Galpin and Adele W. Morrison of the Foundation staff.

The materials in these pages give eloquent testimony to the contribution made by Charles J. Birt, Executive Director of the Greater St. Paul Community Chest and Council, Inc.; Frank M. Rarig, Jr., Executive Secretary of the Amherst H. Wilder Charity; Ruth L. Bowman, Executive Secretary of the Ramsey County Board of Public Welfare; and a host of others who made the St. Paul project possible.

Tribute should be made to Margaret Otto, Head Librarian of the New York School of Social Work; Eva R. Hawkins, Head Librarian, and Anna Cabral, Assistant Librarian of the National Health Library, for their cheerful aid in ferreting out elusive materials. To Matilda L. Berg, of the editorial staff at Columbia University Press, we are grateful for sympathetic and perceptive treatment of the editorial problems as a whole.

We should be remiss if we did not acknowledge our debt to all the authors and publishers whose works have provided the basis for our systematic search of the literature for expert knowledge of the many different facets of problems and services it was our task to synthesize. Special acknowledgment is made to the following publishers for permission to quote from the works cited: Association Press, New York, for David F. DeMarche, *The Relative Effectiveness of Y.M.C.A. Branches with Various Types of Buildings,* 1947; Harvard University Press, Cambridge, and The Commonwealth Fund, New York, for The Commission on Hospital Care, *Hospital Care in the United States,* 1947; D. C. Heath and Company, Boston, for Harold D. Meyer and Charles K. Brightbill, *Community Recreation,* 1948; Houghton Mifflin Company, Boston, for Gertrude Wilson and Gladys Ryland,

Social Group Work Practice, 1949; McGraw-Hill Book Company, New York, for Paul V. Lemkau, *Mental Hygiene in Public Health,* 1949; The Macmillan Company, New York, for Wilson G. Smilie, *Public Health Administration in the United States,* 1947; Public Affairs Committee, New York, for Sir William Beveridge, *Social Insurance and Allied Services,* 1942; Russell Sage Foundation, New York, and United Charities of Chicago, for Joanna Colcord, *Cash Relief* (quoting from the United Charities Sixteenth Annual Report), 1936; University of Chicago Press, Chicago, for Harold C. Ostertag, "New York Revises and Simplifies Its Social Welfare System," *The Social Service Review,* XX, No. 1, March 1946.

It is a source of deep personal sorrow that Carlton Matson and Cecil Smith, two of our trustees who from the first gave so generously of thought and time to the creation of this work, did not live to see its conclusion. The memory of their discerning concern for the welfare of human beings is symbolic of the inspiration which has come to us from privileged association with many leaders in local communities in every section of this country.

BRADLEY BUELL

New York
October, 1951

CONTENTS

xiv Contents

COMMUNITY PLANNING
FOR HUMAN SERVICES

Chapter I

THE PROBLEM AND
THE SETTING

FROM PIONEER DAYS, the spirit of America has been in protest against anciently conceived ideas about the inevitability of human trouble. The rights of the individual to life, liberty, and the pursuit of happiness have been linked inextricably with a common duty to "promote the general welfare." During 300 years of our history we have been constructing a vast network of community-supported services whose purpose affirms this intent.

Many of these services, originally founded for the benefit of the disadvantaged, have now become indispensable to everyone, regardless of his means. Almost all the services have the intent to provide protection for anyone upon whom life's hazards may fall too heavily. The early pauper lists and poor farms have grown into a system of public assistance and insurance. From the first institutions for the sick poor has come the modern community hospital. The ideas which found expression in the gaol, the stocks, and the whipping post have been supplanted by quite different notions of criminal justice and correction. For the mentally abnormal of an early day there were only a few institutions, and these were to protect the community against the so-called "criminally" insane. Today a host of mental hygiene, casework, and other agencies strive to aid those whose circumstances and behavior handicap their adjustment to society. Not so long ago, abundant nature surrounded nearly every doorstep. Now, in urban America, carefully planned parks and playgrounds must serve a common purpose for many thousands of city dwellers. Today we pay through taxes, contributions, and fee payments about $13 billion annually to support a gigantic, sprawling, and complex network of community-provided services that we have welded into the structure of our society to protect ourselves as best we can against the historic inevitabilities of human trouble.

THE CHALLENGE OF COMPLEXITY

The structure of community services was built largely without benefit of blueprint. Different parts were constructed at different times to meet different needs. Moreover, because their foundations were fitted to particular communities, they differ widely in surface appearance from one community and one section of the country to another.

In the last three decades all of the parts have expanded rapidly, sprawling out in many directions. The prosperous 1920s encouraged great private philanthropic expansion. The depressed 1930s demanded large-scale additions to governmental service. Both of these phenomena accelerated the natural growth of community-provided services to meet the pressures and complexities which accompanied the change from the social independence of a rural agricultural society to the necessary interdependence of an urban industrial society.

Out of this turmoil of rapid expansion and social pressure has emerged a large-scale enterprise, progressively specialized in its professional personnel and in the organization of its many separate agencies and units. At this turning point of the twentieth century it presents a picture of such complexity that it can scarcely be comprehended as a whole. The authors of this book are convinced, however, that it must be so comprehended.

Community welfare has deep meaning for Americans. In the scores of communities studied during the past twenty years by those who participated in the preparation of materials for this volume, there was found an abundance of sincere citizen belief in the importance of services designed to contribute to the common welfare. But everywhere we discovered confusion and mounting frustration about what that design should be and why. The vital spirit of America's protest against the inevitability of human ills is in danger of becoming lost among protests against irrationalities in its organized expression. The phenomenal growth of voluntary and public services has compounded bafflement with bewilderment. The truth is that many facets of community administrative machinery are separate in origin, purpose, and tradition. Professional and agency specialization now pose problems of service relationships that are only slightly less confusing to professional leaders than to the citizen leaders of their communities.

One who peers beneath the complex structural surface will see that the sources of confusion are profound. Public policy regarding our community services has its roots in a welter of misconceptions, fears, and conflicting traditions, complicated by great gaps in precise knowledge. But to the present authors a more important reason for this incoherence is that in the past three decades these services have been increasing rapidly in volume, variety, and cost, without corresponding gains in purposeful direction. As more people are served at more cost in connection with more manifestations of trouble, the heart of the problem to be attacked becomes obscured, and the organization and administration of service functions move dangerously close to becoming ends in themselves.

Analysis of the community-wide characteristics of the problems creating the need has not kept pace with the promotion of resources for their remedy. Study of methods to reduce the prevalence of certain problems has been neglected. Research into the causes of problems, a move which might produce the key to their prevention has, in many areas, taken a minor place. Scientific evaluation of the results of service has been by-passed. On the other hand, matters of auspices, administration, financing, and professional techniques have risen in importance.

THE ROAD TO PREVENTION

This book is based on the premise that our historic duty to promote the common welfare carries not only the intent to care for people with problems but to prevent their occurrence and protect the community against their deteriorating consequences. It has been written out of a deep belief, engendered by three decades of intimate knowledge of American communities, that the prevention and reduction of these ancient ills is a realistic possibility. Further, it is believed that the very pursuit of this aim can begin to dispel the frustration arising from the present complex pattern.

Our thesis is that the vast networks of health, welfare, and recreation services can and should be more effectively planned and organized to prevent and reduce these community-wide problems. The task is to set this great community enterprise on the road leading in this direction, and to shift gears for more efficient travel.

The research project upon which this volume is based was designed to produce a definitive treatise on the major issues underlying community organization efforts in four large interrelated areas of community service: dependency, ill-health, maladjustment, and recreational need. It was carried out by Community Research Associates, Inc., and underwritten by The Grant Foundation. The approach was threefold: (1) extensive research into the history and literature of each field; (2) careful analysis of the problems and organization of the community services, in consultation with experienced specialists; (3) a comprehensive statistical study of the four areas of service in a typical urban American community.

The statistical study, made in St. Paul, Minnesota, was an attempt to measure, for the first time, the shape, size, and interrelatedness of these problems on a community-wide basis. With the cooperation of 108 public and private agencies in the four service fields, data were obtained about the problems presented by and the services rendered to every family under care in the month of November, 1948. Cross-tabulations established reliable unduplicated figures for the numbers of families being served simultaneously by agencies in the same and different fields of service, and the specific problems for which they were being served.

Those who participated in the research project are well aware that the size, although not the form of human problems, differs from community to community, from section to section, from region to region. We believe, and in these pages attempt to show, that much of the necessary knowledge of cause and method of treatment is at hand. We recognize, too, that there are great gaps in learning and have tried to show where they are, and how they handicap our purpose. But after three years of intensive study and analysis of this gigantic community phenomenon, we are convinced that our communities have much more knowledge than is being effectively put to work; that we are allowing inherited ideas to interfere with common sense and scientific fact; in short, that we know better than we do.

A PROBLEM OF LOGISTICS

Planning and organizing the community's services for an attack upon the major problems of dependency, ill-health, maladjustment, and recreational need is essentially a matter of logistics. In terms of what is known about the characteristics of these enemies, their methods of community infiltration, and the nature and disposition of their forces, the right services in sufficient amount must be brought to bear at the right places at the right time with a maximum of efficiency and economy. The fruits of victory are the preservation and enhancement of individual and family capacity for social self-maintenance and self-sufficiency.

We believe that comprehension of this problem of logistics can come only with a philosophy which encompasses the following understandings:

1. The community is in truth the battle area.

2. Systematic community-wide knowledge about the characteristics of these problems and the total resources available to meet them is a necessity.

3. There are active interrelationships between the major human problems.

4. Within the family group these destructive forces move continuously to reinforce each other.

THE COMMUNITY-SIZE PATTERN

It is always well to remind ourselves of the simple truth that it is in the community that people have troubles and seek solution for them. The community is the place where people benefit much or little from services provided in their behalf. Here must converge all the particular ideas about what these services should be, what degree of protection they should afford against the hazards of modern living, and what enhancement they should bring to family and personal well-being. This is true even when the services are paid for out of a federal or state pocket and carried out by a hierarchy of ascending administrative levels.

Today some measure of the welfare of two thirds to three quarters of the families in a community may depend in a single year upon the manner in which its health, welfare, and recreation services are provided. The St. Paul study showed that in a single month 41,000 families, 40 percent of all the families in the community, were being served by the city's 108 public and private agencies. A previous study, made in Syracuse, New York, established with considerable accuracy that about 100 community agencies and administrative units had collectively rendered services to approximately 70 percent of the city's families during the year 1941.

Finally, there is the compelling fact that about three quarters of a community's service cost is met directly from local funds. In St. Paul, for instance, the annual cost for community services is about $17 million. Over half of this is local money paid in fees or in voluntary contributions and over half the tax money comes from city-county taxes. About $1.5 million, mainly money for public assistance, comes from federal sources.

THE COMMUNITY-WIDE PICTURE

The intent to promote the common welfare, by very definition, does not distinguish among different segments of the community population. Neither are human problems, especially under the pressure of modern living, respecters of particular persons. The nature of the problem and its volume, the segments in the population which it attacks with greatest ease, the measure of serious social fatalities flowing from it—these and many other matters of knowledge concerning its community-wide characteristics are essential to a sound strategic plan for prevention and control. An effective program, then, will be community-wide in nature. Before it can be designed, both the problems and the services set up to meet them must be seen and comprehended on a community-wide scope. The parts of neither problems nor services can be seen in perspective until they are seen in relation to the whole.

THE VICIOUS CIRCLE

It is a matter of common observation and experience that one trouble leads to another. Professional health and welfare workers have long been aware that human problems set up a vicious circle within individuals and family groups. In the strategy which underlies the plan of logistics, it is of the greatest importance to see the interrelatedness of these problems in measureable terms. For it is in this relation that the person comes back into true perspective. We see what we have always known, but forgotten in the specialized complexity of our times, that his life's success or failure stems from a composite of his assets and his liabilities.

Modern psychiatry teaches us that many of our human problems grow out of faulty family soil. Moreover, professional workers of all kinds know that family strengths and weaknesses constitute powerful assets and liabilities in the treatment and cure of many different kinds of problems. But strangely enough they sometimes forget or overlook the family in preoccupation with a part of its problem. It is not that particular troubles do not enlist their sympathies. The caseworkers, doctors, psychiatrists, nurses, public welfare workers, probation officers, prison wardens, club leaders, recreation directors, and the rest whose services will pass in review in this volume, all draw upon great wellsprings of sympathy and understanding in dealing with human problems and human suffering. Indeed, without these qualities of spirit such workers would be unable to perform their daily tasks. But the mind is sometimes prone to forget that in most cases this difficulty has arisen in a *family* where each member is dependent on the others, each looking to the family as a whole for the strength with which to solve his own problems.

Among the 41,000 families under care of St. Paul agencies in November, 1948, about 7,000—7 percent of the community's families—were dependent, nearly 11,000 had problems of maladjustment, well over 15,000 had problems of ill-health, and almost 19,000 were being served by public and private recreation agencies. It can be seen at a glance that some families had more than one kind of problem. Seventy-seven percent of the dependent families also had problems of ill-health or maladjustment. Fifty-eight percent of the families with problems of maladjustment were known to agencies in the other service fields. Thirty-eight percent of the families with health problems also had other problems. The most dramatic evidence of the vicious circling of problems in St. Paul's families came with the discovery that a group of 6,600 families, about 6 percent of the city's families, were suffering from such a compounding of serious problems that they were absorbing well over half of the combined services of the community's dependency, health, and adjustment agencies.

The troubles of humanity and the particular things professional workers seek to do to help are now divided into such small segments that the family framework fades quietly from view. We believe that

Community Planning for Human Services: Frame of Reference

PROBLEMS	SERVICE FUNCTIONS	SERVICE SYSTEMS
DEPENDENCY		
Economic dislocation (unemployment)	Determination of need	The insurances
	Provision of maintenance	Assistance programs
Personal disabilities	Economic rehabilitation	
ILL-HEALTH		
Communicable disease	Community-wide disease prevention and control	Public health
Hazards of maternity, infancy, and childhood	Diagnosis and treatment	Organized medical care (hospitals and clinics)
Chronic disease	Nursing	
Chronic handicaps	Control of the environment	Private medical practice*
General morbidity		
Environmental hazards		
MALADJUSTMENT		
Behavior disorders: Mental defect Mental disease Antisocial behavior Social failure	Diagnosis and treatment of behavior disorders	Correction
	Situational treatment	Mental health
Situational difficulties	Community-wide prevention and control of behavior disorders	Social casework
RECREATIONAL NEEDS		
Recreation satisfactions: Sports and games Social occasions The arts Informal education	Provision of facilities for public use	Municipal recreation
		Private youth agencies
	Organization of activity interests	Federal-state parks and preserves
Group association	Organization of friendship interests	Religious-social-fraternal organizations *
		Commercial recreation *

* Not community-organized systems with financial support from taxes or community-wide campaigns.

in the forefront of sound strategy must be a realistic concept of the family's relationship to the particular problems which the community program must attack.

FRAMEWORK FOR STUDY

From the start, the conduct of the research project which produced materials for this volume posed a basic problem of classification. Some framework for study and analysis was needed to bring order out of the complexities of our health, welfare, and recreation operations. Its devising was not easy. The whirlwinds of expansion and specialization, almost within a single generation, have scattered widely the seeds from which our present multiplicity of welfare activities have grown. The working tool which we finally produced is a relatively simple classification of problems, functions, and structure (see p. 10). We would be the last to proclaim its enduring perfection. But it has enabled us to search coherently for widely scattered materials about the strategic characteristics of the problems toward which the different facets of our community programs are directed. It has assisted us in critical analysis of the functions indispensable to prevention of these problems and protection against their consequences. It has guided our evaluation of the structure most appropriate to the administration of these essential functions. From this composite of basic factors has come stimulation to precise thought about the avenue for productive movement toward coherent community-wide planning and action. It is within this framework that we attempt, in the final chapter of this work, to synthesize the results of this assembly as it is presented in the four sections of the book.

FOUR MAJOR HUMAN PROBLEMS

The foundation for this classification rests on four major types of human problems toward which our community-supported services are directed. Three of these—dependency, ill-health, and recreational need—are self-descriptive and have long been terms in common usage. The fourth, maladjustment, serves a purpose for this project which is new in the annals of health and welfare. For here are grouped together symptoms of crime, delinquency, child neglect, mental and emotional disturbances that traditionally have been regarded as separate entities. The term maladjustment comes into usage in tacit recognition of psychiatry's teaching that the roots of these disorders lie deep in the same teeming soil. Correctional, mental health, and casework agencies are putting this teaching into practice by increasingly requiring some combination of the same three professional skills—psychiatry, psychology, and casework—to diagnose and treat the basic problems which underlie these several symptoms of disturbance.

The reader will note that we have characterized these problems negatively, or as one might say "according to their pathology." Some no doubt would prefer a phraseology couched in terms of more affirmative human aspirations—economic security, health, social adjustment, recreation.

Our own use of the pathological terminology is deliberate, however, because we believe it is conducive to more precise thinking. Pathological conditions exist; it is possible to get data about them, study their causation, observe and test efforts to correct them and prevent their occurrence. The practical danger of using more optimistic sounding phrases lies not only in the fact that the concepts may be more vague, but also, and more importantly, in the fact that a program which does not accept ultimate responsibility for the prevention or protection against pathological conditions is removed from the compulsion to measure specific results. The essential difference is not in goals, but in the degree of realism in methodology.

THE HUMAN PICTURE

In the pages of this book, the problems of people are dealt with in the aggregate, as they must be to serve the interests of community-wide planning. But we should remind ourselves that the very form and substance of such terms as dependency, ill-health, maladjustment, and recreational need are drawn from the troubles of the people who live side by side in all the communities of America.

Here is Joe Jones whose troubles started when he lost his job and became dependent when he had to go on relief. But if we lived next door we would also see the slow growth of strain and irritability in his home atmosphere, his 13-year-old daughter's gradual withdrawal from the normal social life of the adolescent, his 11-year-old son's association with a gang of older boys who daily skirt the edge of delinquency. Since the day Joe began to be unable to maintain his family, these consequences have been compounding.

Tom Brown, on the other hand, probably never will have to depend on the community for money to buy his food and pay his rent. But today a chronic illness has stricken his wife. He will invest as much as may be needed in modern medicine and its battery of modern hospital services. Yet he is desperately worried about his three small children, their nightmares and their eating problems. One may hope indeed that medical science and its community facilities will be successful and return Tom's wife to her all-important family role. Otherwise his youngsters, and perhaps he himself, may be headed for real trouble.

Since the sudden death of her husband, Mrs. Green had kept a jealous hold upon her only son. The long battle to maintain his exclusive devotion has changed him into a rebellious, now a delinquent, youngster. Today she has learned that he must appear in juvenile court on theft charges. Her inability to adjust to the loss of her husband had impinged upon her relationship with her son so that he begins to show symptoms of maladjustment to the society in which he must live and grow up. Her worries are spreading in other directions, too. Medical treatment for stomach ulcers has begun to eat into her financial reserves. The operation which her doctor advises is yet an extra cost for which she must plan. One wonders, on the basis of her past experience, if she will be able to manage these new burdens.

Antonio Pastro, aged 10, lives with his grandparents down in the Irish Channel of his town. There isn't much there except pavements and sidewalks, old bricks and mortar. A tree is seldom to be seen. When he's out of school, he can hang around the warehouses and alleys with his gang. On hot days his grandparents can sit on the front stoop and fan themselves. Here is very little real fun for the young, or lift or inspiration for the old. Neither Tony nor his family, nor any of the rest of us, thrive on wasteful and unsatisfying leisure.

Mr. Jones, Mr. Brown, Mrs. Green, the Pastros, and their families are simple friendly people. So are their neighbors. It is their general welfare, and our own, which communities seek to promote by organizing services to deal with the problems of dependency, ill-health, maladjustment, and recreational need. We trust that in the ensuing pages of this book, the human realities of their need will never become obscured by the intricate task of executing the community's intent.

THE AGENCY SYSTEMS

The reader will note that the community-supported services which are today at the disposal of these community neighbors have been classified in broad groupings for the purposes of this project.

The use of the phrase "agency systems," however, is for generic and descriptive characterization rather than to define a precise structural or administrative unity. In fact, there is very little of the latter. An exception is found in the federal-state program of relief for the aged, the blind, and dependent children, which does have a good measure of organic and administrative unity. In our characterization of the "public assistance system," however, we also have included "general assistance," which is not part of the federal-state program, as well as the small amount of private relief which communities now provide. These agencies, separately administered and financed though they may be, are, nevertheless, part of the "system" through which communities provide for people who are in need of food, clothes, and shelter.

The degree of organic and administrative unity among the other "systems" of our classification is much less, and in some cases, entirely nonexistent. Nevertheless, some device is necessary to achieve orderly thought about the literally thousands of different agencies, departments, and service units that are serving the people of this country. The groupings in our framework have behind them a good deal of rule-of-thumb usage. In all instances they deal with a common basic problem. In many of these systems large segments meet in common conferences and conventions. In most, although not all, a profession or a basic program philosophy supplies a cementing factor.

SOURCES OF MATERIALS

The materials in this volume are drawn from many sources. Our own staff and most of our consultants have been variously associated in the study of community services since the early 1930s through times of great import in the development of health, welfare, and recreation services. Each has had a continuing interest in pooling special knowledge to give form and substance to the common product, the community welfare. The combined practical experience on which we have drawn embraces general and special surveys and studies in more than 150 communities throughout the United States. That experience has been mainly with urban America. Human suffering from poverty, ill-health, social unadjustment, monotonous leisure, is intrinsically the same wherever people live. This volume contains much data about the country as a whole, but its prime focus reflects the particular experience of its authors with the more elaborate community service structure that has grown up to meet the complexities of city life.

Each of the major fields and the special fields within them, has an authoritative literature of its own, built upon the knowledge, study, and experience of the field practitioners. Our second source of material for this volume emerged from a systematic and selective search of this literature for materials of value and significance for the task of better community planning. We have tried to put these diverse materials into a common framework which would enable the reader to gain a better understanding of the responsibilities now assumed by the community, and of the strengths, weaknesses, and gaps in its program for prevention and protection.

But the existing literature, voluminous as it is, does not give all the data needed to complete this assignment. There is abundant information about separate parts of the present community program, and there are some facts about the way these parts should be set up and planned. But facts on which to base planning for efficient relationships between the parts are mostly missing. Missing, too, are tested patterns and procedures for assembling such facts.

The St. Paul study, an integral part of the research of this undertaking, was an attempt to break ground in this area. It was designed to produce new statistical facts of practical significance, to test procedures for classifying materials from all fields in a manner which would enhance their utility for community-wide planning. The results have been integrated with materials from other sources.

The St. Paul study was carried out under the joint auspices of the Greater St. Paul Planning and Research Council, and Community Research Associates, Inc. The direct costs of processing the data, including IBM tabulations, were met locally through contributions from the Greater St. Paul Community Chest, the Amherst H. Wilder Charity, and the Ramsey County Board of Public Welfare.

The basis for the study was a detailed schedule, calling for data about problems presented by and services rendered to the families and individuals receiving service in Ramsey County agencies during the month of November, 1948. The reporting agencies included not only all of the local health and welfare agencies, but state and regional agencies and administrative units that had Ramsey County people under their care. A unique feature of the reporting process was that each of the 108 agencies filled out a schedule on every case known to it, giving identifying information about the whole family, even though the agency might be serving only one family member. Thus it was possible to consolidate data from different agencies into a composite picture of the problems presented by a given family and the constellation of services being rendered to the family.

The results of the entire study were presented to a special Conference on Appraising Family Needs, held in St. Paul in the fall of 1949 and attended by a hundred leaders from the fields of social science, public health, public welfare, recreation, mental health, social casework, corrections, and others of special interest. The comments and discussions growing out of this conference played a considerable part in creating the form and substance of the materials which follow.

THE "WHAT" AND THE "WHY"

In this volume we have offered no manual of precise instructions. Many necessary parts of the community welfare programs are still on the drawing board. No attempt has been made to throw light on those dynamic processes through which communities become persuaded to improve the pattern of their community services. This research was exclusively concerned with the "what" and "why" of the best directions for those changes, not "how" communities make up their minds to pursue the course.

We have presented, in as orderly a fashion as we could, the knowledge and experience underpinning this great community enterprise. We have pointed out the weaknesses in the application of that knowledge to the purposes of community-wide prevention and protection, as we see them. In each section we have tried to bring out, as precisely as possible, the points at which the four principal segments of the community's program should be related, as well as the issues of planning and method which must be resolved in bringing about this relationship.

It is our hope that the facts will speak as eloquently to the reader as they do to us, bearing witness to the importance of planning this program so that its several parts may converge to strengthen the capacity of people to achieve more satisfaction and self-sufficiency in modern life. It is our belief that each step in this direction will bring us closer to genuine fulfillment of our traditional American intent to promote the general welfare.

DEPENDENCY

Chapter II

ACCEPTANCE OF RESPONSIBILITY

FOR MANY YEARS, communities have accepted certain responsibilities for dependency, defining the term according to their lights. By *dependency* we mean the problem facing families who would be without the sheer necessities of life unless the community made some provision for them. What the community may regard as necessary varies greatly with time and place—how much food, how warm the clothes, how dry and well ventilated the shelter. Nonetheless, from very early times society has recognized that at some point people who are unable to provide food, clothes, and shelter for themselves become a social, or community, responsibility.

Among the "needs" of people which communities undertake to meet, these essentials always have had priority. One of the few "instincts" which scientists identify with confidence is the urge to satisfy hunger. In our society, this powerful personal instinct has its counterpart in a community urge to see to it that people do not starve no matter what else we may, or may not, be willing to do for them.

A very practical test of this essential priority came in the United States in the early 1930s. In 1932 unemployment had risen to over twelve million [1] people, with resultant increases in the need for relief. The large government programs were still to come, and private social agencies, financed primarily by community chest drives, were swamped with relief demands. In the face of falling incomes, these drives were failing to meet their goals, and budget reductions were the order of the day. But large cuts seldom were made in the allocations to agencies which gave relief. Substantial reductions, amounting to from 10 to 25 percent or more, occurred two and a half times as often in allocations to recreation agencies and half again as often

[1] Stanley Lebergott, *et al.*, "Labor Force, Employment, and Unemployment, 1929–39: Estimating Methods," *Monthly Labor Review*, LXVII, No. 1 (July, 1948), 51.

in allocations to health agencies as in allocations to agencies dispensing the necessities of life.[2]

From a practical standpoint we may say that the amount of dependency at any given time or place depends ultimately on community judgments as to who would lack these minimum necessities if they did not receive aid. In 1949 almost $2.2 billion of government money was spent to provide the essentials of living for people in need, while various types of government insurance and compensation—designed at least in part to protect against the hazards of dependency—accounted for nearly $8 billion. In January, 1950, between five and six million persons were dependent, while some nine million were recipients of government insurance or compensation payments,[3] for which are now spent from 10 to 15 percent of all money disbursed by local, state, and federal units of government.[4]

TWO MAIN SYSTEMS

This substantial responsibility for dependency is undertaken through two principal systems of programs and agencies. The *assistance system* provides direct assistance or relief to people in actual need, whatever the phrase "necessities of life" is interpreted to include. The *insurance system* insures people against, and compensates them for, loss of income due to various causes, and thereby seeks to provide an economic security which will help to make direct assistance unnecessary. The assistance system is largely a governmental system and the insurance system is wholly so. The pattern of participation in both varies from state to state.

THE ASSISTANCE SYSTEM

Assistance is the older type of program. An important part of the present assistance program belongs to a national system, jointly operated by the federal government and the states. In any particular community other parts may be included in a system operated by the state.

[2] Association of Community Chests and Councils, *Community Chests and Appropriations to Their Member Agencies* (Bulletin 71), p. 3.

[3] These are estimates based on "Current Operating Statistics," *Social Security Bulletin,* XIII, No. 3 (March, 1950), 19–26; No. 4 (April, 1950), 20.

[4] Community Research Associates, Inc., "Estimated Expenditures for Economic Security, Welfare, Health and Recreation Services by Public and Private Non-profit Agencies for 1947," based on available data.

Almost everywhere there will be certain public and private agencies purely local in their administration and finance.

Nearly every local community has public agencies providing the following types of assistance:

Categorical assistance.—Since 1935, assistance to aged people, to blind persons, and for children one or both of whose parents are dead, incapacitated, or continuously away from home, has been provided through community agencies which are part of the federal-state system. The programs directed to these "categories" of needy people are now well known as Old Age Assistance (OAA), Aid to the Blind (AB), and Aid to Dependent Children (ADC). State participation in any or all parts of this system is entirely permissive. As this is written, all 51 states and territories are included in OAA, all but four in AB, and all but one in ADC.

The principles behind the general plan under which this federal-state system operates are relatively simple. The state is the administrative unit responsible to the federal government. To participate in any one of the three federal programs, the state must have prepared a plan that has met the approval of the Federal Security Agency. According to requirements set forth in the Social Security Law, every such plan must provide for:

1. State-wide coverage of the program
2. Financial participation by the state
3. The establishment or designation of a single state agency either to administer or supervise the plan ("plan" here refers to any one of the three categories, not to a consolidation of the three)
4. An opportunity for a fair hearing before this state agency in any case in which assistance is denied
5. Efficient methods of administration (including selection of personnel on a civil service or merit system basis)
6. Submission of the reports called for by the federal agency
7. A procedure for determining need which takes into account the other income and resources of the applicants for assistance
8. Safeguards against misuse of confidential information concerning persons applying for or receiving grants

It will be seen that these requirements say little or nothing about the administrative structure within the state, nor about the division of responsibility between the state and its political subdivisions for financing the nonfederal share of the cost. To all intents and purposes, however, federal law and administrative practice in respect to federal financial participation define precise boundaries within which people may become eligible for categorical assistance. The law defines old age assistance merely as aid to "needy aged individuals." But federal reimbursement is available only in cases where the needy aged individual has passed his sixty-fifth birthday. A state wishing to set a younger age limit can do so, but only by financing the entire cost of all cases of persons under 65 years old. As this is written, only one state, Colorado, makes payments to persons between 60 and 65, and then only if the person has been in continuous residence for 35 years.[5] However, quite a number of states have provisions for lowering the eligible age to 60 when and if the age minimum for federal financial participation is lowered in like manner.

The Social Security Law defines a dependent child as:

A needy child under the age of sixteen, or under the age of eighteen if found by the state agency to be regularly attending school, who has been deprived of parental support or care by reason of the death, continued absence from home, or physical or mental incapacity of a parent, and who is living with his father, mother, grandfather, grandmother, brother, sister, stepfather, stepmother, stepbrother, stepsister, uncle or aunt, in a place of residence maintained by one or more of such relatives as his or their own home.[6]

Although federal funds can be spent only on behalf of children who meet this definition, several state ADC programs have an unqualified upper age limit of 18. Such an arrangement not only is acceptable to the Social Security Administration but is specifically recommended by them "even though Federal matching is not available." [7]

The Social Security Act, in authorizing "aid to needy individuals who are blind," did not define blindness. But the federal administrative regulations require a definition of blindness in terms of ophthalmic measurement, and prescribe a series of procedures to insure proper diagnosis by competent personnel.

[5] Jules H. Berman, "State Public Assistance Legislation, 1949," *Social Security Bulletin,* XII, No. 12 (December, 1949), 6.

[6] Social Security Administration, Federal Security Agency, *Compilation of the Social Security Laws,* p. 35.

[7] Federal Security Agency, *Handbook of Public Assistance Administration,* Section 3255, Part IV (April 24, 1946).

All these programs were set up to aid "needy people." But when it comes to determining who is needy and who is not, it is the state and not the federal government which sets the standard. According to the federal definition, "a needy individual . . . is one who does not have the income and resources sufficient to assure economic security, the standard of which must be defined by each state." [8] The only federal demand is that there be a state standard which is applied uniformly to all cases.

The aggregate annual cost for 1949 was $1,904 million distributed as follows: OAA, $1,380 million; ADC, $476 million; AB, $48 million.[9]

In January, 1950, there were 2,749,049 persons throughout the country receiving old age assistance; 610,443 families, representing 1,550,203 children, were receiving aid to dependent children; aid to the blind was being given to 93,109 blind persons.[10]

General assistance.—If a needy person does not happen to be a child deprived of a parent, blind, or over 65, he must rely mainly on another type of government program, called "general assistance," or sometimes "home relief" or "direct relief."

General assistance is not a part of the federal system. If the community has such a program, the state or the community itself or a combination of the two is responsible for it. According to the best available data, there are 23 states and territories in which from 50 to 100 percent of the money spent for general assistance comes from state funds. At the other extreme are 11 states which spend no state money, but leave financing of general assistance entirely to the local community. In between are 17 states which put up some money, but less— frequently very much less—than 50 percent.[11]

In January, 1950, there were over one million people in the United States whose needs were met through this type of program; the annual expenditure during the year 1949 was $282 million.[12] When aggregate numbers served and money spent are compared with the federal-state categorical system, it will be seen that this wholly state and local

[8] *Ibid.*, Section 3120.

[9] "Current Operating Statistics," *Social Security Bulletin,* XIII, No. 3 (March, 1950), 26, Table 14.

[10] *Ibid.*, XIII, No. 4 (April, 1950), 30, Table 16.

[11] Federal Security Agency, *Social Security Year Book, 1948,* p. 56.

[12] Estimates based on "Current Operating Statistics."

government program is of considerable importance, accounting for almost a fifth of the total number of assistance recipients, and about 13 percent of the total expenditures.

In a number of places, resources for general assistance are extremely meager. In some areas, for all practical purposes, there is no such program, and public assistance is available only to those eligible for categorical aid. A recent study of policies in a representative number of cities found that in many of them general assistance was not providing even the "bare essentials for existence" and that all too often its administration did not measure up to accepted standards.[13]

Almshouses.—One estimate has it that in the United States there are some 2,000 almshouses, county poor farms, and infirmaries housing about 85,000 people.[14] Fifty years ago such responsibility as government assumed for the care of dependent families was mainly discharged by putting people in the poorhouse. Now, these institutions are used chiefly to house aged persons who are chronically ill and incapacitated, and others with mental and physical infirmities. Administration and financing are always wholly local, usually by the county unit of government. In 1925 it cost $28,740,535 a year to operate 2,183 almshouses which were valued at something over $150 million.[15] More up-to-date figures are not available.

Private agencies.—In almost every urban community there are some private agencies giving direct relief to the needy. Such agencies may include a Red Cross chapter, sectarian or nonsectarian family societies, the Salvation Army, the Travelers Aid Society, old folks homes, and other organizations peculiar to the locality. Financial assistance, however, is no longer their main purpose. Even in urban communities where these agencies are most strongly organized, they now account for only about 6 percent of all expenditures for direct assistance.[16]

THE INSURANCE SYSTEM

Social insurance is the newer type of program designed to relieve the community's problem of dependency. At present there are five

---

13 Felix M. Gentile and Donald S. Howard, *General Assistance*, p. 35.

14 Louis Evans, "Providing Institutional Care for Recipients of Public Assistance," *Public Welfare*, III, No. 11 (November, 1945), 250.

15 Estelle M. Stewart, *The Cost of American Almshouses*, p. 7.

16 Community Chests and Councils of America, Inc., *Expenditures for Community Health and Welfare, 31 Urban Areas, 1948*, p. 39.

separate government plans for protecting different groups against loss of income. The Old Age and Survivors Insurance (OASI) program, which was established by the Social Security Act of 1935, provides payments to retired workers who have reached the age of 65, or to their survivors, regardless of the worker's age at death. The Unemployment Insurance program, established by the same Act, provides payments to workers who suffer income loss because of unemployment. In four states the unemployment insurance program has been extended to cover wage loss due to temporary sickness or disability. Special insurance plans for railroad workers, which went into effect at approximately the same time as the other social security legislation, provide for payments in case of retirement, death, unemployment, and both temporary and permanent disability. Under a program dating from the First World War, and considerably extended during the Second World War, veterans of the armed forces and their survivors are compensated for disability or death incurred in connection with military service, and under certain limited circumstances for disability or death due to other causes. All states and territories have laws providing for compensation payments to workers injured in the course of employment, or to survivors if a worker is killed. All but four of these state workmen's compensation plans were in effect before 1930.

Before the 1950 expansion of the OASI, it was estimated that government insurance (exclusive of the veterans programs) gave about three fifths of the labor force—mainly workers in business and industry—some measure of protection against various types of income loss.[17] Agricultural workers, those in domestic service, and self-employed persons were among the groups who were not covered. The 1950 amendments to the Social Security Act extended OASI coverage to some ten million additional persons, including the self-employed, those in domestic service and in certain other occupational groupings.

CONFLICTING PUBLIC POLICY

In the local community the separate pieces of these two systems make up a variegated mosaic of agencies and activities. Each particular piece is an expression of a particular public policy adopted at a particular time by some level of local, state, or national government,

[17] A. J. Altmeyer, "Old Age, Survivors and Disability Insurance," *Social Security Bulletin*, XII, No. 4 (April, 1949), 4.

by a combination of these levels, or by private enterprise. The mosaic reflects the substantial responsibility for dependency which our communities have assumed. But it also reflects great confusion and conflict about the purposes for which they have undertaken this responsibility, and the methods by which it should be discharged. The confusion and conflict stem from two distinct but closely related sources. The one comes out of contemporary history, the other from long centuries of the past.

IMPROVISATIONS OF THE THIRTIES

Prior to the depression of the thirties, workmen's compensation was the only form of insurance for which government had assumed any general responsibility. This was a state system, directed to a type of income loss that occurs to relatively few people. Special benefits for veterans of the First World War also touched a comparatively small number of people.

However, there had long been an established government relief system. It is estimated that this system spent about $21 million in 1913.[18] In 1949, the public assistance system was spending almost $2.2 billion,[19] an increase of more than 10,000 percent.

In 1913 the largest part of the money was spent for the care of people in poorhouses, which by state laws were the responsibility of local government units. Relief recipients were officially "paupers," and it was deemed "conducive to economy and public morality to make relief so disagreeable to the recipient that he would be persuaded or forced to devise some means of self-support to remove himself from the relief lists as soon as possible." [20]

This basic system had not greatly changed by 1929. Some forty cities had established public welfare departments. Social reformers had battled with fair success for mothers' aid programs, and some states cared for the needy aged and the needy blind. By 1930, legislation provided for mothers' aid in 45 states, old age pensions in 12, and pensions for the blind in 20. Most of this legislation was permissive rather than mandatory upon the local communities. State supervision was rare and state financial participation meager. Still,

[18] National Resources Planning Board, *Security, Work and Relief Policies* (report of the Committee on Long Range Work and Relief Policies), p. 7.
[19] Estimates based on "Current Operating Statistics."
[20] *Security, Work and Relief Policies,* p. 26.

these laws did represent the first break with the tradition that assistance was purely a local concern.

During the twenties, the rapid organization of community chests greatly increased the resources of private agencies. However, even in 1929, there were probably not more than four hundred cities with any important private relief agencies, and government disbursed some 76 percent of all relief expenditures.[21]

On this almost wholly local combination of relief and charity, the depression descended with terrific impact. By 1932 the valiant efforts of local government and private philanthropy to care for the unemployed had everywhere broken down. Three years later, the Social Security Act created our national systems of social insurance and categorical assistance.

It is well to recall the turbulent sequence of emergency improvisations leading up to the Social Security Act. In the fall of 1931, and as the depression deepened, some states took on responsibility for assisting localities with relief funds; by the middle of 1933 about half the states had appropriated emergency funds, and the majority had established temporary emergency relief administrations. Meantime, the federal government was lending money to states for direct relief, work relief, and "self-liquidating" projects through the Reconstruction Finance Corporation. These never-to-be-repaid "loans" amounted to $300 million.

In March of 1933, the first federally operated agency, the Civilian Conservation Corps, was established. In May, creation of the Federal Emergency Relief Administration (FERA) brought the federal government openly into the administration of direct relief. FERA appropriated money to states; helped to reorganize state emergency relief agencies and to set up new ones; and laid down rules and regulations regarding use of its funds. In June, the national government launched its first effort to provide work in lieu of relief—the Public Works Administration, which increased expenditures for major public construction projects. The short-lived Civil Works Administration, with funds for light public construction and repairs, followed in November. Many of its projects were continued by the Emergency Work Relief Program, under FERA.

In October of 1933 came the Federal Surplus Relief Corporation,

21 *Ibid.*, p. 26.

which distributed certain commodities to needy families—mainly through FERA. In 1934, two new programs were created under FERA, one for rural rehabilitation and the other for transients.

FERA was discontinued in 1935. Its successors were WPA (the Works Progress Administration—later the Work Projects Administration), wholly national in administration and financing of direct relief except for locally sponsored projects, and the programs embodied in the Social Security Act of 1935. Within another five years war production began reducing the relief load even below normal, and the confusion and controversy over the nature of the dependency problem and government's responsibility were soon forgotten in our compelling preoccupation with the Second World War.

We are among those who believe that, in their broad results, the improvisations of the 1930s successfully met a condition which otherwise might have had disastrous consequences to our way of life. But it should occasion no surprise that our communities still mirror a profound confusion of public purpose as a result of the rapid imposition of these new systems upon the traditional systems which they only partially replaced.

DEEPER ROOTS OF CONFLICT

The basic conflict which the depression fanned into heated controversy and emergency action is the conflict in the public mind about the causes of dependency. The present varied programs for dealing with dependency, their differing purposes and methods, in reality reflect current and historical differences of opinion about the reasons why people become dependent, and the relative importance of these reasons to public policy.

For over five centuries in the history of English-speaking peoples, the organization of relief was guided by the belief that defects in the individual were the sole cause of dependency. For about half of this period a belief in the reluctance of impoverished people to work to sustain themselves far outweighed all other considerations. This belief was at the foundation of the English poor relief system. The purposes and methods of that system gave this country the foundations for the public relief system with which it entered the depression of 1930. Traditions carried over from English poor relief methods still exercise an important influence upon issues affecting the present assistance and insurance systems.

Welfare historians date the English poor relief system [22] by the Statute of Laborers of 1349. The Black Death in 1348, killing a third or more of Britain's population, had created a great labor shortage; the feudal system was breaking up and "beggars, vagabonds, thieves and knaves" roamed the country. This statute, prohibiting begging and restricting freedom of movement so that people would be forced back to the land and again become the responsibility of the lord of the manor, marked the community's first attempt to deal with dependency, although it was an attempt to escape responsibilities.

The endeavor failed, and by the 1500s there were "great and excessive numbers" of "vagabonds and beggars" throughout England. In 1596–97, when people were dying of starvation in the streets, Parliament enacted the Elizabethan Poor Law, formally accepting public responsibility for the poor and thereby inaugurating the public pauper relief policy which England and the United States were to follow for three centuries. During this entire period, "rogues, beggars, paupers and lusty vagabonds" were generally conceived to be to blame for their condition.

In a new approach to the problem, the Act of Settlement of 1662 empowered local justices to return to his former residence any person coming into a parish who in the opinion of the overseers of the poor might at some future time become in need. The belief that the evils deriving from personal shiftlessness can somehow be cured by localizing responsibility for them also inspired the American settlement laws. At the present writing, all but two states prohibit general assistance to persons who have lived within the state for less than a specified number of years, and nearly all states have similar restrictions for OAA, ADC, and AB.

The year 1722 marked the official adoption of the workhouse as a means of forcing relief recipients to work. Their management was farmed out to contractors who could use the inmates' labor for their own profit. Relief in England was truly a "racket" until the Act was repealed in 1782. In repealing it, Parliament officially recognized the

22 For a fuller account of the history of English poor relief see Karl de Schweinitz, *England's Road to Social Security.*

distinction between the poor who are able to work and those who are not, for in the workhouse the aged, sick, crippled, insane, and able-bodied had all been treated alike.

This distinction was made in the United States by the two federal programs in 1935—WPA for the able-bodied; categorical assistance for the aged, the blind, and dependent children. In England, however, in 1782, Parliament decided that the ill and the aged indigents, as well as orphan children, should be cared for in poorhouses, though not under a contract system. These poorhouses and the workhouses are the direct ancestors of the almshouses and county poor farms which were the principal foundation of our own public assistance system prior to 1930.

The Act of 1782 devised a plan which was in fact the first attempt to provide outdoor work relief for the able-bodied. In practice, the parish supplemented insufficient wages out of tax funds, or farmed out the labor of an unemployed man for whatever it could get and supplied the balance required for his subsistence. Actually, therefore, pauper labor was competing with ordinary labor to the latter's detriment. The contemporary criticisms of this policy call to mind the controversies which raged hotly over WPA wages and the going wage rate.

The next fifty years in England demonstrated the viciousness of this system, which lowered wages, destroyed initiative, and increased the numbers on relief. By the 1830s the poor had turned to riotry, burning and destroying crops, and there was a very real fear of revolution.

A famous Royal Commission of inquiry ensued in 1834, when poor relief had long been entirely a parish responsibility. The recommendations of the Commission, enacted into law, provided for larger local units and national supervision of the reestablished workhouses. But the only recognized causes of dependency among the able-bodied were still those inherent in man's moral imperfections, and the only remedies proposed were measures to pressure relief recipients to remove themselves from their low estate.

By 1853, relief expenditures were 20 percent less than in 1834, despite a 25 percent increase in population.[23] But the misery and degradation of the poor under the new system poured fuel on the flames of labor's revolt against the rapidly expanding industrial system, and

23 *Ibid.*, p. 137.

stimulated the great reform movements with which the names of Charles Booth, Joseph Chamberlain, Sidney and Beatrice Webb, and many others will always be associated.

Out of the great changes of the Industrial Revolution, the thinking of early economists and political philosophers, and the reform movements of the latter half of the nineteenth century grew the conviction that "imperfections in the economy" were a contrasting cause of the condition of the poor. This conviction first found public expression in another Royal Commission, appointed some seventy years after the first, to study the operation of the Poor Law. The Commission's recommendations, published in 1909, overhauled the poor relief system and sanctioned outdoor relief, to which it gave the name "public assistance." Even more significant were the measures recommended for correcting the effect of an imperfect economy upon the fortunes of the individual. Subsequently adopted by Parliament, these included a national system of labor exchanges and a system of unemployment and health insurance. In 1908 Parliament had authorized noncontributory old age pensions for aged persons whose income was below a certain level. The depression which began in England in the twenties witnessed a great expansion both in assistance and insurance measures, each of them marking a further departure from the philosophy of the Poor Law.

The conviction that dependency may also be caused by imperfections in the economy had little direct effect upon public relief policy in the United States until the 1930s. But the idea exerted a powerful influence upon the new policies of the 1930s, and the whole concept of a social security system stems directly from it. The OASI and unemployment insurance plans were designed specifically to put varying degrees of responsibility upon the economy for protecting people against the hazards which its imperfections create.

This conviction has exerted a powerful influence upon the administration of the assistance programs. After so many centuries of harshly conceived relief policies, the pendulum has swung vigorously in the other direction. Many believe that, in an "imperfect" economic setting which subjects the individual to hazards over which he has no control, a person in need has a "right" to adequate assistance. This concept is the direct antithesis of the theory of "personal responsibility" which so largely ruled public policy up to twenty years ago.

Thus, what converges in the community is more than a confusing mosaic of agencies concerned with different aspects of the dependency problem. There also converges a bewildering conflict of ideas about the causes of dependency, about methods for dealing with cases due to these causes, and especially about the relative importance of different causes and different methods. Those with responsibilities toward the economy tend to stress the importance of personal defects and what should be done to correct them. Those with responsibilities for assisting people tend to stress the importance of economic imperfections and demand that something should be done about them. This conflict of opinion emerges into public view most clearly in debates over the expenditure of public money. Both assistance and insurance programs are expensive.

It is when money has to be appropriated that there is a public airing of divergent opinions about the relative responsibility of the person and of the economy for the conditions of dependency; about the level of individual payments—whether they should represent a "compulsion" to income-producing initiative, or a "right" to a reasonable standard of subsistence; about the importance of the distinction between those who are aged, sick, and infirm and those who are able-bodied.

It is at the point of adoption of every local, state, and federal budget that issues about the kind of assistance or insurance programs we are willing and able to finance are resolved pragmatically. We must hope that debates of this kind, constructively guided, eventually will result in a clear-cut, community-wide program for preventing dependency and for protecting the community against its consequences.

Unfortunately, we now lack one important tool needed in clarifying the outline of such a program. There are at present few methods for the systematic collection and study of facts about the dependency problem that have practical relevance to planning an attack on it. Statistics are kept by the various agencies of the various systems to serve their own administrative needs. It is extremely difficult to establish an accurate rate of dependency for the community; to relate the problem to the community's total population; and to analyze the circumstances affecting the rate's rise and fall. Methods for distinguishing between dependency caused by personal disabilities and dependency due to economic imbalance have yet to find their way to acceptance in community practice. There are few procedures for gaining accurate knowledge about the constellations of personal disabilities which converge to undermine family economic capacity, or about the comparable constellations of employment hazards which may be producing much of the community's need for assistance. In short, there has been as yet very little systematic thought or practical experiment directed toward determining what a community ought to know in order to plan a concerted attack upon its total problem.

We believe that the materials of our St. Paul project are indicative of the importance and utility of better tools for this purpose. This project established, with considerable accuracy, the fact that over 6 percent of the families in that community were dependent in November, 1948, the month of the study. This was a period of high employment. In a total of 6,640 dependent families, there were only 277—approximately 4 percent—in which unemployment was the sole reason for the inability to provide for themselves what that community regarded as the minimum necessities of life. In all other cases there were one or more serious personal disabilities which either destroyed completely, or handicapped seriously, the family's income-producing capacity: old age, a broken home, chronic disease, chronic handicaps, mental deficiency, mental illness, or some type of behavior disorder. As we shall see, St. Paul data about the constellations of these serious personal handicaps throw much light on the basic problem of preventing the dependency which stems from personal and family incapacity, as well as on the methods appropriate for doing so.

COMMUNITY-WIDE PROGRAM ISSUES

The logic of what we understand to be the causes of dependency dictates that one part of a community-wide program for prevention and protection should be directed to the reduction and the control of unemployment, the principal by-product of economic imperfections. But even a theoretical analysis of what this phase of such a program might offer is outside the competence of our research.

The literature of economics deals at length with types of unemployment—casual unemployment; seasonal unemployment; labor reserve unemployment; frictional unemployment; and the cyclical unemployment which produces our nationwide depressions. The causes of these last affect conditions in all communities and are the subject of many, often conflicting, theories which deal with the perplexing relationships of a variety of factors, such as prices, wages, profits, savings, investments, interest rates, taxes, monopoly and competition, federal fiscal policies, and international trade.

Speculation about, and experimentation with, the practical application of such theories has been confined almost wholly to the question of how to manipulate these complex variables at the national level in order to prevent the violent downswings of productive employment which come from major dislocations of the economy. As one of the few studies of the local community relationship between dependency and employment points out:

It is possible that too much of the effort devoted to labor market research has emphasized gross, nationwide effects and results—the synthesis of what happens in a myriad of local labor markets—and that too little research is directed at these individual market phenomena. . . . Communities . . . need to know more about their local labor markets, rather than more about a nationwide composite of such markets.[24]

A brief exception to the traditional approach may be noted in the early programs of the National Committee on Economic Development. Organized in 1942, it aimed to stimulate local planning for a high level of industrial production, in order to provide plenty of employment opportunities for returning servicemen. However, when the shift from wartime to peacetime production was accomplished without great economic disturbance, the Committee's interests shifted to a preoccupation with the national economic scene. Local activities now are limited primarily to the efforts of chambers of commerce to bring new and diversified industries into their communities, and of individual corporations and unions to stabilize employment within their own ranks. Aside from such unrelated efforts, there has been little practical consideration of an over-all program to prevent dependency by means of community-wide industrial stabilization.

Our research and the materials of the present volume are concerned with issues about which there is experience that can be directed to a better community-wide attack upon the dependency problem. These issues, the subject of the succeeding chapters of this section, have to do with: (1) The administration of the assistance functions, by which

[24] Dale Yoder and Donald G. Paterson, *Local Labor Market Research,* p. 5.

(*a*) need is determined and dependency defined realistically on the community's behalf; (*b*) maintenance is provided out of community funds. The manner in which these assistance functions are discharged determines the community method for protecting people against the ultimate consequences of dependency, whatever its cause. (2) The structure of community agencies, through which these functions are administered. There are few communities in which this structure could not be improved. (3) The community-wide plans for the prevention and rehabilitation of the personal disabilities which cause dependency. Present community thinking assigns a growing importance to steps in this direction. (4) Protection by insurance against both economic and personal hazards. The issues here will be settled at the national and state levels, but the community's concern with the manner of their settlement is obvious.

Chapter III

ADMINISTRATION OF THE ASSISTANCE FUNCTIONS

WE CAN REMEMBER when the office of any local relief agency was a sorry affair: battered desks, chairs, and files cast off by a succession of more prosperous users; applicants crowded into hallways or a meager waiting room. Misery was presumed to feel at home only in miserable surroundings.

Now, in any well-ordered community, a public welfare office will be conveniently placed; clean, with good light and ventilation; modestly, though not luxuriously, equipped with modern appurtenances; the general atmosphere like that of any normal place of business dependent on the good will of its customers. The applicant for assistance proceeds to a designated desk behind which a worker listens courteously to his story. If apparently eligible, he is handed an application blank, and helped to fill it out. The required information includes his name, address, and age, with similar information about other members of his family, employment history if any, and other standard items set by the rules and regulations of the office. With the signing of the blank, his application for assistance is formally filed, and he is entitled to a formal report as soon as the office has decided what to do about it.

The staff then undertake what authorities agree to be the first main function of every public assistance agency—to determine whether there is a need which warrants assistance.

DETERMINATION OF NEED

The truth is, however, that need is a relative matter.

We accept as axiomatic that people must eat to live. But there is no axiom to tell us how often and how much they must eat. We accept also that people must have clothing, at least if they are to live with decent regard for the conventions of organized society. But the graphic depictions of ragged paupers give historic testimony that this regard for decency can be quite minimum even in this country. We accept, too, that shelter of some kind is a necessity of life. After this fashion, the workhouse, the almshouse, and the poor farm automatically supplied this want. But payment of an indigent person's rent in the early days of the century was rare even among private agencies, and almost nonexistent in public relief.

Thus a family may seem to you to be in need, but someone else will think that it is suffering no more than the proper hardships of its lot. If you give the family money out of your own pocket, this difference of opinion will not matter. But a public welfare agency must take both opinions into account in fixing the point at which it will spend community money.

Public welfare authorities agree that this—fixing the point at which suffering begins—is the crux of the problem in determining need. One may safely predict, as did Raymond Hilliard, while he was director of the Illinois Public Aid Commission, that "just what is a level of aid sufficient to provide health and well-being remains, and probably will continue to remain, one of the basic problems of public aid administration, [and one on which] we will continue to find differences in opinion." [1]

METHODS OF THE EXPERTS

As we have seen, when it passed the 1935 Social Security Law, Congress decided what types of needy people would be eligible for categorical assistance. In order to be eligible they had to be old, or blind, or dependent children, and for all practical purposes either the law or the federal regulations relating to reimbursement now specify within narrow limits how old, how blind, and, in the case of the children, on whom they have to be dependent. Congress also specified that all needy persons in each state should be treated alike; that their own income should be taken into account in determining whether or not they were needy; that confidential information about the na-

[1] Raymond M. Hilliard, "Basic Principles in Public Assistance," *Public Aid in Illinois* (March, 1948), p. 9.

ture of their need should not be misused; and that when it was decided that a person was not in need, he should have a fair opportunity to object to this decision. Congress also decided, but in a very general way, that a needy person was one who did not have enough income to assure economic security for himself.

Congress did not decide the "point of suffering" at which a person lacked that assurance of security. This crucial problem is left up to the states. In passing laws and adopting plans, the state legislators did not decide that point either. All states adopted general directives instructing the administrators of assistance programs to provide "a reasonable subsistence, compatible with health and decency" or "with the essentials of living." But only five states put any dollar-and-cents value on those phrases in any of the three categories.[2] Thus the people's representatives, both in Congress and in the state legislatures, have passed on to their administrative experts the thorny responsibility for deciding how little money a family must have to qualify as "in need."

Although the final determination of this point of suffering rests with the state, the federal administrative personnel exercise a good deal of authority over the basic methods used in the process. Throughout the entire federal-state assistance system, therefore, there are now in use three tools for determining need, hard-wrought by the experts out of the experience of the past half century.

First, nutritionists, dietitians, and the medical profession have accumulated extensive knowledge about the kind and amount of food necessary to enable the human animal to function properly and efficiently. They consider a daily consumption of 2,650 calories the average minimum requirement for health (the actual average consumption in the United States is over 3,300 calories),[3] and they set 2,200 calories a day as an emergency subsistence level, that is, "the minimum necessary to prevent serious undernutrition leading to disease and the danger of civil unrest."[4] The war and postwar experience of Europe provided a mass demonstration of the validity of these standards. Serious physical effects of the food shortages were

2 Eveline M. Burns, *The American Social Security System*, p. 300.

3 Fred A. Hoehler, "What is UNRRA Doing?" *Survey Midmonthly*, LXXXI, No. 4 (April, 1945), 99.

4 J. W. Evans, "The Facts in the Case," *Survey Graphic*, XXXVII, No. 3 (March, 1948), 109.

reported from those countries where the average caloric intake fell substantially below the 2,200 level,[5] and these effects became more apparent as time went on.

The second tool is the standard family budget. Studies of how much it cost people to live have been made for many years and for various reasons. In order to create a "standard" budget for a family someone must decide (a) what items shall go into it; (b) how much of each item; (c) what it will cost. There are several methods of arriving at these decisions. The method now generally in use was perfected during the present century and is based on a combination of fact and expert opinion. It uses the average of what a number of families do spend, supplemented by a recognition of nutritional needs and decent housing requirements, and sometimes by common-sense judgments of what is necessary. Once the content of such a budget is agreed upon, the amount of money needed to maintain it is ascertained by pricing the constituent items in the current market.

In this manner the United States Bureau of Labor Statistics arrived at its "City Workers Family Budget" for a family of four. Here the food item is based on the recommendations of the Food and Nutrition Board of the National Research Council, which take into account calories and essential minerals and vitamins. Age, sex, and occupational activity then determine the allowance for each family member. The rent allotment represents a compromise between actual practice and standards developed by the American Public Health Association's Committee on the Hygiene of Housing. Allotments for other items are based solely on actual average expenditures among city workers and their families.

In the early years of the century the better private agencies recognized the budgeting process as a means of giving assistance on a more equitable and scientific basis. They adopted the practice of setting standard quantities of goods and services for needy people and calculating a budget for every family to which they gave help. Since then, social agencies, public and private, not only have kept abreast of budgeting developments but have contributed much to the application of budgeting techniques to this particular purpose.

To keep a standard budget up to date there must be a periodic check on the constantly varying cost of the articles which it includes.

[5] Ibid.

This is where our third tool comes in. It consists of tested procedures for studying and measuring fluctuations in the retail price level—the cost of living. The best known and most extensive study of this type is the cost of living index which has been maintained continuously by the Unites States Bureau of Labor Statistics for more than a quarter century. This is a barometer of the price rise and fall of specific items of food, clothing, rent, and other family expenditures in a representative number of cities throughout the United States.

Taken together, the knowledge of the home economist, the techniques of the family budget expert, and the procedures for measuring price fluctuations give the modern public welfare administrator a systematic process by which to fix "a point of suffering" or, in the Social Security Act terminology, a point of "income and resources" sufficient to "assure economic security."

Every state public welfare administration has experts skilled in the use of these tools, to provide the basic processes by which the local welfare office determines the need in each case. The federal agency also has on its staff experts who assist and supervise the state in this task.

THE BUDGETARY PROCESS OF ESTABLISHING NEED

At the base of this process is a simple form used by the worker to calculate the budget needed for each family which she investigates. Each state welfare department prepares for all the local public units a list of the items which this form should include. These vary from state to state, but they usually include food, fuel (heating and light), shelter, household supplies, clothing, and personal incidentals.

Prior to 1930, rent or shelter was seldom included in the calculation of a person's need, even by private agencies. The reason was that the figure for rent is inevitably large, and its inclusion substantially increases relief costs. On the one hand, therefore, landlords "carried" families without payment; on the other, families lived in continual fear of eviction. The inclusion of rent in relief budgeting was a burning issue during the evolution of the emergency relief program of the 1930s, and even after federal money was available in 1933 many localities held to their traditional practice.[6]

6 Benjamin Glassberg, "Rent Policies under Emergency Relief," *Social Service Review,* XI, No. 3 (September, 1937), 419-33.

Similarly, clothing was seldom included in cash allowances on the assumption that "hand-me-downs" and gifts would somehow meet the need. Even today the practice in many places is to give clothing on an "as-needed" basis.

In addition to listing the consumption items which the budget should include, the state office also sets up standards for use by local public welfare agencies in determining the amount of each item necessary according to the age, sex, and specific circumstances of the recipient. These standards may be expressed in terms of money, or in terms of the quantity and quality of the article or articles which a particular budget item covers.

With the standards as a guide, the local agency can calculate the amount needed for each item on the budget form, in terms of the number of members, age of each, and the general circumstances of every family applying for assistance. The total is the amount of the family budget, expressing in dollars what the agency believes to be necessary to maintain that particular family at a reasonable level of subsistence. If the family's income is below that amount, then in the agency's judgment it is in need of assistance. If the income is above that amount, the family is considered to have no need for aid.

The all-important process of investigation is partly to determine how much, if any, of the family income should be credited against this budget. Such information comes in the first instance from the application blank signed by the person who applies, and from the worker's interview with him. The investigation may include a series of steps, such as a check for possible bank accounts, verification of employment income, interviews with family members and perhaps with other persons familiar with the situation. Standard routines for this investigation vary considerably with the staff available for it, the size of the load they must carry, and experience with the results obtained in relation to the expense and staff effort involved.

As we have seen, the Social Security Act requires that the states take into consideration the other resources of applicants for categorical assistance. In practice, this means that all current income of an OAA or AB recipient or of an ADC mother must be credited against the standard budget. There are, however, wide variations in state policies in regard to income received by other members of the household.

An applicant's ownership of real property presents a particularly difficult problem. In most states, if the upkeep exceeds a "reasonable" amount for rent, his application is denied. If the charges for taxes, interest, and so on, constitute a reasonable rental allowance and the application is granted, a public welfare department may take various measures to protect its own interests. In some instances the local public welfare district acquires title to such property; in others, liens equal to the amount of assistance granted are filed against it periodically. And when the person receiving aid dies, the department generally seeks to recover as much as possible of the total assistance he has received. New York State, for example, recovers about $2 million a year in this way.

Then there is the whole perplexing matter of the ability and willingness of relatives to support or to contribute to the support of a needy person. So difficult is this question of relatives' responsibility that during the 1949–50 Congressional hearings on the extension of social security, the House Ways and Means Committee ordered the Federal Security Agency to make a special study of it. At present some states have very restrictive regulations on this point, refusing assistance to anyone whose relatives (wherever they may live) are able to support him, whether or not they are willing to do so; other states are extremely lenient. Whatever the policy, it is during the investigation that the possibility of support from relatives is explored.

The investigation must seek also to produce documentary evidence substantiating the applicant's eligibility for the type of categorical assistance for which he applies: a birth or baptismal certificate to show that a person is over 65 or that a dependent child is below 16 or 18 (whichever the state has set as its upper age limit for ADC); confirmation from the school that a child between 16 and 18 is still in attendance; and in the case of an applicant for AB, a signed report from an approved ophthalmologist or optometrist to show that the person qualifies according to the state's definition of blindness. If the needy person is not able to establish eligibility for categorical assistance, that is, if he is over 18, under 65, and not "officially" blind, he must fall back on general assistance—for which he may or may not qualify, depending on the restrictions governing the local program.

Finally, the investigation must check on whether or not the applicant meets the residence requirements which, as already noted, most states still have both for categorical and general assistance.

It should be clear that the key point in this entire process is the standard used by the state agency to guide the local worker in determining the amounts (expressed in money costs) of food, rent, heat and light, clothing, and miscellaneous items regarded as necessary to minimum subsistence. For it is this standard which fixes the point, expressed in income, below which the community accepts responsibility for need. Even so, this "point of need" often proves to be an academic one, as we shall see.

CONTRASTING METHODS OF GENERAL ASSISTANCE

In the administration of general assistance there are no such standards which have been adopted throughout the country. In some places the administrators of general assistance use the methods prescribed for categorical assistance. But in many places they do not. Instead, they follow the methods which reflect the traditions of public pauper relief that were in effect prior to the establishment of the federal-state categorical assistance program.

The use of a standard family budget has no place in such procedures. Practices of determining need may be guided by whims, prejudices, or even the political advantage of the person administratively responsible. In describing a situation in which general assistance was administered by township overseers of the poor, Grace Browning pointed out that "applications for aid are subjected to the varying attitudes of men who have no special knowledge or understanding of social problems." [7] Similarly, Gentile and Howard, in a study of general assistance, report that officials give some cases special consideration and treat others harshly, according to their personal predilections.[8] We have known of instances where it helped greatly to be related to the relief administrator, and some where the relief worker received her instructions about many cases directly from the mayor.

The practice of publishing officially in the local press the names of all recipients of town relief was in vogue as late as the 1930's and probably still persists in some places. Howard and Gentile reported

[7] Grace Browning, "Public Administration and Human Welfare," *Social Service Review*, XXII, No. 1 (March, 1948), 11.
[8] Felix M. Gentile and Donald S. Howard, *General Assistance*, Chapter I.

three states in which applicants "were usually required to present their requests in person and at public meetings of the local county court or at public town meetings." [9]

PROVISION OF MAINTENANCE

After deciding that a family is eligible for assistance, the agency has the function of providing it with maintenance. In the federal-state system of categorical assistance this maintenance must be in the form of money—monthly checks which the recipients can cash anywhere and spend at their own discretion.

Logically, the amount of this monthly check should be the difference between the total budget needed and the income, if any, which has been credited against it. But in many states the check is rarely for this amount. If there are more applicants for aid than there is money to pay them, the agency is faced with a problem. Some welfare departments have established waiting lists of eligible persons to whom no payments can be made until further funds become available, but the Social Security Administration frowns on this practice as inconsistent with the principle of equal treatment for all eligible people in the state. Instead, the federal authorities recommend that the money be spread among all who are eligible even though individual payments are reduced well below need as determined by the budgetary process. And, as we shall see shortly, all too often this is what happens.

CONTRASTING METHODS OF GENERAL ASSISTANCE

Many agencies administering general assistance follow this same method of giving "cash relief," but in certain sections of the country many still follow the traditional policies of public pauper relief and provide maintenance in kind. As recently as 1943, a study of 182 local welfare offices showed that grocery orders or commodities were being given in about one third of all the general assistance cases, and that this type of grant predominated in over 40 percent of the agencies.[10] In December, 1934, when FERA was spending over $100 million a month, three quarters of it was in kind and only one quarter in

[9] *Ibid.*, p. 13.
[10] "Local Council Notes," *Public Welfare*, I, No. 3 (March, 1943), 93.

cash grants.[11] In fact, it was over this issue and the payment of rent that old and new concepts clashed most audibly in those fast-moving days when about a fifth of the country's population was on relief.

There are two methods of administering relief in kind. One is by giving a written order for a specified quantity of food, fuel, or clothing, which will be honored by certain merchants. The order may list the articles, or it may give only a top figure and permit considerable choice among a standard list of items. The recipients use these orders in lieu of money, and the merchants bill the agency. The older method is for the agency to operate a commissary with a stock of staples from which the relief recipient is supplied. Both methods were used before 1930, and both were tried out again, on a large scale, during the emergency regimes of 1930–35. At present most agencies which give relief in kind use the order system.

The policy of giving relief in kind always has seemed logical to those who see as the primary reason for dependency the moral culpability, shiftlessness, or untrustworthiness of the individual. In the light of that concept, relief in kind not only places the recipient in a deservedly unfavorable light with his neighbors and his merchants, but guarantees that he and his family will eat the groceries instead of squandering the money for them in more riotous pursuits.

In 1873 the annual report of the Chicago Relief and Aid Society, which had tried first the commissary and then the grocery order plan, told why it had discarded both. To meet the emergencies created by the great fire, the commissary plan was adopted because the Society thought it "could purchase in large quantities at lower rates" but was abandoned after two years because of the "expense of keeping up several large storehouses, the inevitable waste and loss in handling, and numerous complaints as to quantity and quality."

As for the order system:

This soon proved less satisfactory than the first, complaints were very frequent of ill treatment and of neglect in delivering, and the old charge of fraud in quantity and quality of goods ordered was no less frequent than before. We could not investigate and correct every possible error. . . . In view of all these facts, we concluded to abolish the whole system of relief in kind, excepting only fuel, blankets and shoes, and for all other purposes give money.

Whatever objections may be urged against this policy, we think that it

11 Joanna Colcord, *Cash Relief*, p. 42.

is justified by experience. The applicants can in most cases make as good or better use of the money in providing only that which they most need. . . . The principal objection to the cash policy is the possible abuse of money by some. The proportion of such cases is small, and any kind of goods can very readily be diverted by the intemperate. The mass of worthy, honest and economical poor should not be treated as thieves and paupers, because large numbers of these last classes attempt to defraud us or because a few of them may possibly succeed in doing so.[12]

Seventy-five years can add little to this analysis of the uneconomy and inefficiency of relief in kind.

RECONCILING EXPERT AND PUBLIC OPINION

During the years in which this research was undertaken a rash of public welfare investigations and exposés broke out in many communities throughout the country. For the first time since the turbulent thirties, public welfare became front-page, and apparently unsavory, news. Lurid examples of "chiseling" and "hotel" cases created the impression that relief had become a luxurious way of life.

As this is written, the urge to "investigate" seems to have abated. Indubitably, some of this community probing pointed a finger at ineptness in the administration of what has become a large-scale enterprise, and at the irrationality of certain practices. But in most instances, it is doubtful whether the amount of sheer abuse which was disclosed justified the money and effort expended on the investigations. Nevertheless, they left in their wake convincing evidence of the prime importance of reconciling expert opinion about the administration of the assistance functions with the realities of public opinion and public finance. And in this respect, unfortunately, the investigations generated much more heat than light.

It is clear, we believe, that expert opinion and public opinion as reflected by ultimate public policy now tend to diverge at two principal points. The first is over the minimum standard of living which should define the need for assistance. The second is over methods of administering the assistance functions. As we have seen, divisions of opinion at these points have their roots in deep-seated attitudes and traditional beliefs. The task of public welfare and community statesmanship should be so to clarify the issues and guide the processes of

12 *Ibid.*, pp. 9, 10.

decision that attempts at reconciliation will be accompanied by a maximum of light and a minimum of heat.

THE STANDARD OF DEPENDENT LIVING

Standards for assistance, resulting from the budgetary process described, tend to be higher than public policy, as expressed in money appropriated, is willing and able to support. This situation reflects something more than the natural and universal divergence between the administrator's wish to expand activities and the caution of sponsors who must pay the piper. It is a disagreement stemming from confusion and conflict about *what* each party wishes to pay for.

Two kinds of information seem to us to be important to any objective examination of this divergence. Unfortunately, neither kind is readily available.

Missing facts.—No published national data show the relief family living standards, expressed in money, which result from the budgetary criteria adopted by the different states. Present procedures are well suited to the technical processes of administration. As we have seen, the state offices adopt standards regarding the amount of food, clothing, and other necessities believed to be essential to the maintenance of one person, with suitable differences based on age and other circumstances. These items then are priced, and the local offices use them as a guide in determining the budget needed by each family, in accordance with its size and other variables. The broad result, however, is to conceal rather than publicize the basic average standard of family living which the composite of these specific criteria supports. Certainly, few standards are as high as the $1,974 estimated by the New York City Department of Welfare as the annual minimum for a family of four.[13] But there are no assembled data from which either "experts" or the public can study the comparative standards reflected by various state and local criteria.

Neither, so far as we know, are there any easily available data to show the proportion of cases in which the amount of money actually provided from the public treasury falls short of meeting the need estimated in accordance with the state standard. The data most commonly used to illustrate this lag have to do with the meagerness of the

[13] "Comparison of Monthly Estimated Needs," *The Welfarer*, II, No. 1 (December, 1949), 12.

average grants made by the several states. Such data are published regularly by the Federal Security Agency.

The average OAA grant, made individually, was $44.66 in January, 1950—less than $1,100 annually for an elderly couple receiving assistance. Varying with the state, the annual income of this couple would range from approximately $1,770 in Colorado to little more than $450 in Mississippi. The average family on ADC received less than $900, with California granting less than $1,400 and Mississippi, about $320. Unless there was more than one blind person, an average family on AB would have received about $570; the same family in California would have received a little less than $1,000 and in Kentucky, about $270.[14]

In many states the "money need" of people who receive general assistance is not estimated at all, by any standard. In some it is, however, and in general the average grant tends to be less than the usual categorical grant. In some sections, if there is any general assistance at all, the grant is almost negligible. In five states, for example, the last available data show that the average grant was only 35 percent of their comparatively low grants for ADC.[15]

At face value, therefore, these data about "average" grants, as regularly reported by the Federal Security Agency, show average expenditures per family which are almost bound to be below need as estimated by any reasonable standard compatible with the minimum essentials of living. Unfortunately, however, such data cannot be taken at face value in any precise sense. Averages include payments made to families who require only a few dollars to balance their "needed" budget. They also include families with no income at all, whose total budget must be met from assistance funds.

Two reasons make it unlikely that many large grants are included in the categorical assistance averages. The first is the fact that the rate at which the federal government reimburses the states decreases after the first $20 of the average monthly payment per recipient in OAA and AB, and after the first $12 of the average monthly payment per child in ADC. There is *no* federal reimbursement for payments over $50 a month for OAA and AB, or beyond $27 a month for the first child and $18 for all others in ADC. States and localities tend

14 Based on "Current Operating Statistics," *Social Security Bulletin,* XIII, No. 4 (April, 1950), 30, 31, Tables 17 and 19.
15 Gentile and Howard, *op. cit.,* p. 43.

to be more chary about spending their own money, and in the poorer states, that is, those with a low per capita income, grants amounting to more than these federal maximums are made infrequently or not at all.

The second reason is that some of the states have set limits on the total monthly payment per recipient, although the Federal Security Agency frowns on this practice on the ground that state maximums often prevent need from being met. As this is written, there are 25 states with no maximums for OAA, 30 with none for ADC, and 36 with none for AB. However, where state maximums do exist, they are usually the same as the maximum that can be matched by federal funds, although they go considerably higher in a few cases, as for example $80 for OAA in Alaska and $84 for AB in California. A new law in Illinois, while setting $65 and $60 as the present top payments for OAA and AB respectively, provides for semiannual reconsideration and adjustment of maximums in the light of the Bureau of Labor Statistics cost of living index for Chicago.[16] But any maximum usually means that need, as estimated by the budgetary process, cannot be met in full when there is no other income.

There are no such practical restrictions on the purse strings in wealthier states where general assistance is administered liberally. While the national averages for general assistance seem extremely meager, in certain sections quite large amounts may be paid in individual cases to meet unusual needs. In these sections, also, general assistance funds may be used to supplement the amounts given to families receiving categorical aid, when the maximum allowed by categorical restrictions is below the estimated need. Reports from about one third of the states in 1947 indicated that this practice accounted for about 15 percent of all general assistance cases.[17]

Thus, although these data present a picture which is far from accurate, there is no doubt that a great discrepancy exists between needs as estimated by administrative standards and by the public's current willingness and ability to meet them. Dr. Eveline Burns quotes various studies and computations made by the Social Security Board between 1944 and 1946 which showed that assistance payments *plus* family income were failing to meet the estimated need in one third of

[16] Jules H. Berman, "State Public Assistance Legislation, 1949," *Social Security Bulletin*, XII, No. 12 (December, 1949), 5.
[17] *Social Security Year Book*, 1947, p. 52.

the OAA cases, two fifths of the AB cases, and three fifths of the ADC cases.[18] These figures were based on data from a number of states. In 1946 some states were giving as little as 40 to 50 percent of the amount they had estimated as necessary to meet their own budgetary standards.[19] Although legislation in 1948 increased the federal share in categorical payments, on occasion even the wealthier states meet only 85 to 90 percent of their standard budgets. Among public assistance workers everywhere this inability to meet recognized needs arising out of administrative restrictions is the source of common complaint and great frustration.

Uncertain objectives.—The budgetary process—knowledge about nutritional needs; facts about average consumption of essential items; facts about prices—has resulted in systematic procedures for arriving at precise estimates. But concepts about the kind of living standard to be upheld by assistance grants governs the direction of their use. Undoubtedly, there is considerable uncertainty on the part of the public about the objectives of their administrative experts.

The differences in objectives to which budgetary criteria may be put is well illustrated by the City Worker's Family Budget, proposed by the Bureau of Labor Statistics, to which we referred earlier. According to the Bureau, the standard of this budget is neither subsistence nor luxury. It is modest but currently adequate to provide family health, worker efficiency, nurture of children, and social participation by all members of the family. The point at which items are selected for inclusion

is in general the point where the struggle for more and more things gives way to a desire for better and better quality. Above this level, for example, the family is likely to be more interested in escaping from an endless round of cheaper cuts of meat, than in increasing the number of pounds. Below this level people find it harder to economize, being unable to shift to cheaper commodities and therefore forced to do without.[20]

At prices in June, 1947, this budget cost $3,004 in New Orleans, and $3,458 in Washington, D.C.[21] At the same time in Washington, 34 percent of the families composed of husband, wife, and two children

18 Burns, *op. cit.*, pp. 317, 331, 339.
19 *Ibid.*, p. 312, quoting from the 1946 Annual Report of the Social Security Board.
20 Lester S. Kellogg and Dorothy S. Brady, "The City Worker's Family Budget," *Monthly Labor Review*, LXVI, No. 2 (February, 1948), 133–70.
21 *Ibid.*, 137.

under 18 were living on incomes of less than $3,458, and by the Bureau's criteria were "forced to do without" some of the items provided by this budget.[22]

Another illustration of possible differences in budgeting objectives is found in the variety of standards prepared by the Heller Committee for Research in Economics of the University of California. This committee regularly prepares standard budgets for people in different income and occupational groups.

LIVING COSTS FOR FAMILY OF FIVE, 1946 [a]

Executive's family	$11,591
White collar worker's family	4,661
Wage earner's family	3,576
Dependent	1,695

[a] Heller Committee for Research in Social Economics, *Quantity and Cost Budgets for Three Income Levels, Priced for San Francisco, and Budget for Dependent Families.*

The phrases "essentials of living," "minimum subsistence," "minimum comfort," "minimum standard of living," "minimum economic security," a "fair standard of living," so frequently used to express the objectives of public assistance standards, thus give no clear guide to the standard of living concepts behind them. We think it possible, nevertheless, to distinguish at least three low-income budget levels, regardless of what they are called, among which public welfare administrators generally have to make some choice:

1. The lowest is the minimum subsistence level, which covers the bare essentials of living (food, clothing, shelter, fuel, and light). Probably the emergency budget of WPA would be considered "minimum subsistence." According to the National Resources Planning Board, "The diet at the 'emergency' level provides the probable minimum requirements for adequate nutrition, but the margin of safety is less than is desirable. . . . It is believed, moreover, that families forced to live at this level for any extended period of time may be subject to serious health hazards." In June, 1940, this budget cost about $930 for an urban family of four.[23] At present prices it would cost considerably more.

[22] Abner Hurwitz, "D.C. Income in Relation to BLS Family Budget," *Monthly Labor Review,* LXVI, No. 6 (December, 1948), 622–23.
[23] National Resources Planning Board, *Security, Work and Relief Policies,* p. 162.

2. The second level is harder to identify but seems to be intermediate between bare subsistence and a fair and adequate standard of living. Some home economists call it a "moderate standard." It has been referred to as "minimum comfort," but that term seems a misnomer since the comforts it provides are few and far between. This level probably is illustrated by the basic maintenance budget of WPA, which in June, 1940, cost $1,347 for a family of four in contrast to $930 for the emergency budget. The maintenance budget gives "some consideration to psychological needs," but the food is simple and the clothing meager. "This level is certainly not high," comments the National Resources Planning Board, "nor does it permit families to enjoy what Americans like to think of as 'the American standard of living.' " [24]

3. The third level, that of an adequate standard of living, is reflected in the City Worker's Family Budget, the cost of which averaged $2,700 in 1946 for our typical family of four, and $3,200 in 1947.

Although actual standards are set by the states, the Federal Security Agency's broad view is that they should provide a "basic content of living," a phrase which connotes more than minimum subsistence and seems to refer to "basic maintenance" at a "minimum comfort" or "moderate" level. In so far as they are relevant, the foregoing data on present payments suggest that the public takes the view that assistance budgets should be at the "minimum subsistence" level.

One reason for this undoubtedly is based on the widespread opinion that the standard of living of families receiving assistance ought not to exceed that of any sizable group of families in the community who maintain themselves by their own effort. In discussing the basic maintenance budget of WPA days, the report of the National Resources Planning Board recognized this dilemma:

. . . the known fact that many urban families maintain themselves somehow on incomes which are below the money equivalent of the basic "maintenance" level suggests that it is not very practical to assume that all families of the defined size whose incomes fall below this level are in need of public aid. Nor is it practicable public policy for governmental authorities to attempt to supply a level of living to recipients of public aid which exceeds that attained by many families who live upon their own earnings or property.[25]

24 *Ibid.*   25 *Ibid.*, p. 163.

A proposal by the Welfare Council of New York City that the typical family of four should receive a relief allowance of $60.50 a week, or $3,346 a year, was derided publicly on the ground that it would disqualify the recipients for the benefits of the city's low-cost housing.[26] Similarly, a study in Monroe County, New York, computes that according to the present assistance standards a family of four with no income of its own would receive $2,130 for basic requirements plus special allowances for health care and transportation. Pointing out that the average local weekly wage amounts to a gross income of $29.90 before pay-roll deductions, the report comments that "the level of assistance for a moderate-sized family group appears to have drawn alarmingly close to the average net income for workers in the community." [27]

Another reason for the position taken by the public is, of course, to be found in the practical exigencies of public finance. Resources vary widely from state to state—and even from community to community, when local funds are used to pay part of the categorical assistance bill. While it is true that the cost of living varies somewhat from one section of the country to another, the spread is nothing like that between assistance payments in rich states and those in poor states. In 1948 the cost of the City Worker's Family Budget was $3,230 in New York City and $3,064 in Birmingham, Alabama.[28] But in January, 1950, the average monthly ADC payment was $100.91 in New York, the state with the second highest per capita income, and only $33.95 in Alabama, the fourth state from the bottom.[29] And since Alabama cases averaged almost three children per family whereas the New York average was somewhat less, the discrepancy is even greater than these figures indicate.

The public's point of view in the poorer states thus poses two practical obstacles to the adoption of anything more than a minimum subsistence level of assistance standards. Large sections of their population now maintain themselves at this level from their own earnings.

26 New York *Times*, February 24, 1950, p. 44.

27 *A Study of the Public Welfare Program in Monroe County*, a report to the Board of Supervisors from the Special Citizen's Committee on Social Welfare, p. 21.

28 *Social Security Act Amendments of 1949, Hearings before the Committee on Ways and Means, House of Representatives, 81st Congress, on H.R. 2893*, p. 182.

29 "Current Operating Statistics," *Social Security Bulletin*, XIII, No. 4 (April, 1950), 32, Table 20.

The states have relatively less public money to subsidize families at any higher level.

Missing procedures.—Finally, it seems clear that we need new procedures which can be used as effective guides in reconciling expert and public opinion about the all-important standards which are at the basis of modern public assistance methods. According to the present procedure, such standards are determined by the administrative experts of the public welfare system, who have been given this responsibility by the Congress and by their respective state legislatures. Except for a few people serving on small welfare boards at the local or state level, the community in general has little knowledge of the money value the standards represent and little voice in determining the basic level of family living which they support. The community, therefore, makes its weight felt at a later stage by wielding the time-honored power of the public purse and by conducting investigations which usually miss this central point of issue. In our opinion, public participation should take place when standards are adopted, and it is here that community views and expert judgments should share in the formation of policy.

ABOUT GENERAL ASSISTANCE METHODS

We have seen that within the federal-state system of categorical assistance, communities everywhere have accepted the methods developed both for determining need by budgeting the requirements and offsetting income of each family that applies, and for providing maintenance in cash instead of kind. Community acceptance of these methods is, in fact, a condition of participation in the financial benefits of the federal-state system.

In many sections, communities have not accepted these methods in the administration of their general assistance programs, which are governed wholly by local or state policy. It is this underlying fact of nonacceptance which now so frequently makes general assistance the weak link in the community's program to protect itself against the consequences of dependency. For, whatever their shortcomings, the systematic investigations and budgetary practices of modern assistance programs have marked a notable advance from the prejudices and callousness inherited from the English poor relief system.

As this is written, the state pays some portion of general assistance costs in 40 of the 51 states and territories, although in five instances the amount is inconsequential. On the other hand, in 22 the amount is more than 50 percent. In nearly half the states, the administration of general assistance is combined with the administration of the categories as a matter of state-wide policy. In some of the rest there is state supervision by a separate agency; in others, local integration of general and categorical assistance in the larger urban communities. By June, 1947, there were only 11 states where general assistance was administered by appointed or elected local welfare officials, entirely without state supervision or with supervision limited to units or classes of persons for whom state funds were provided (for example, nonresidents).[30]

The fact that general and categorical assistance are administered by one agency or that general assistance is subject to some measure of state supervision does not mean that the same standards and procedures necessarily apply to both programs. The same basic procedures for family budgeting are likely to be followed throughout the agency; relief usually is given in cash in both instances; but the standard of "determined need," the amount of the grant, and the rules of eligibility may be quite different. Gentile and Howard, for example, report one state granting only 40 percent of "determined need" to general assistance families, as against 50 percent to ADC and 100 percent to OAA; another state where one large city appropriated local funds to pay 95 percent of "determined need" to OAA cases in contrast to a 55 percent policy throughout the rest of the state; and still another state where the budgets of general assistance families were calculated on only 9 of the 15 items used in determining need for the categories.[31]

Nevertheless, the trend is clear. Twenty years ago no states provided money for general relief or took any action concerning it other than to pass laws placing the entire responsibility for paupers upon the local towns and cities.

ACHIEVING ADMINISTRATIVE EFFICIENCY

It is no part of the purpose of this volume to delve into the internal techniques of public welfare administration. But the issues relating

[30] Burns, *op. cit.*, p. 393.   [31] Gentile and Howard, *op. cit.*, p. 31.

to policies and methods can be seen in true perspective only as one recognizes the rapidity with which public welfare has become a large and complex enterprise.

The depression of 1930 found the country almost totally lacking in the administrative competence required to handle the volume of relief business thrust upon its hastily created emergency relief systems. A few welfare departments in the larger cities had had some experience with large-scale administration; and private agencies had been giving relief on a budgetary and casework basis for a long time, though always in relatively small volume. But the task of ministering to one fifth of the country's population, with any degree of efficiency, was wholly outside the bounds of past practice.

To illustrate the complexity of modern relief giving, we may cite the state of Florida, which has a state-administered categorical assistance system. Florida is not one of our richest or most populous states, but in 1948 it spent approximately $39 million for categorical assistance alone, approximately $16 million of which was from state funds, the remainder a reimbursement from the federal government. Altogether in the month of December of that year 83,557 cases were given assistance ranging from a few dollars to a maximum of $99 a month for an ADC family. These funds were spent through 48 unit offices in different localities and communities. On the pay roll of these offices and on the state supervisory staff there were some 862 people, 548 of them classified in professional social work capacities.[32]

To make the system work is a sizable task. Directives, covering the rules and regulations of state and federal policy, must go from the state office to all these local units. They must be clear and concise, and must not conflict with one another. A state staff must see that they are carried out, and a federal staff must see that state operations are in line with federal policy and requirements.

Each month the local offices must compile lists of cases which are to receive payments. Authorizations go first to the State Welfare Department, where they are recorded, and thence to the State Comptroller's Office, which prepares the necessary checks and mails them to the recipients.

All of this involves efficiency in the basic process of administration —planning, accounting, uniform personnel policies, interoffice com-

[32] *A Survey of the Florida State Welfare Board,* p. 5, Part I; *ibid.,* pp. 20, 21, Part IV.

munication, uniform records and statistics, and public relations. Public welfare administration has made great advances in the fifteen years since the Social Security Act created the programs of categorical assistance. Perhaps its greatest forward step is the recognition that it is now a big business, requiring business methods and business efficiency.

Chapter IV

THE ASSISTANCE
STRUCTURE

IN PASSING THE ASSISTANCE PROVISIONS of the Social Security Act, Congress delegated to the states the responsibility for setting up the administrative structure to carry them out, as well as the responsibility for determining who is "needy." The social security legislation stipulates that the state must help to finance the program; that its methods of administration must be such as are necessary for proper and efficient operation, specifically including the selection of personnel on a merit basis; and that a single state agency must have administrative responsibility for the plan. But since the Act refers to a "plan" for each category, a state may administer the three categories through more than one state agency, and half a dozen states now do so.

The administration of general assistance follows many different patterns. It may be the responsibility of the town or township, the city, county, or state, or of a combination of these governmental units. It may or may not be combined with the administration of the federal-state categorical system. In addition, there are everywhere other separate public agencies whose business it is to give aid to the needy, and also certain private agencies which still have as their primary purpose the relief of economic need. Private relief agencies most commonly include: homes for the aged; agencies dealing with transients or nonresidents, such as the Salvation Army and Travelers Aid Societies; casework agencies, such as the Red Cross, sectarian and nonsectarian family service societies, and other casework agencies organized for special purposes.

No matter how many administrative units a community may have, each performs the same basic assistance functions: it determines that the applicant is in need, and it provides him with maintenance. Each unit, however, makes its own choice of methods.

Seldom has the resulting waste been described better than by Harold C. Ostertag, chairman of the legislative committee which achieved a notable reorganization of New York State's public welfare structure:

1. A person in need may have to go from one agency to another to find the program for which he is eligible.
2. As his circumstances change, a person may be shifted from one agency to another, involving a new application, a new investigation, another set of records and perhaps a different standard of assistance . . .
3. A given family may require investigation and service from two or more agencies, with the result that several workers visit the home, aid comes from several sources, and a separate record is made in each of the separate agencies.
4. The present system of overlapping agencies means futile duplication . . . the territory of a given town may be covered at the same time by workers from the town welfare department, the county department of public welfare, and the county board of child welfare.[1]

SIMPLIFYING THE LOCAL STRUCTURE

It should be obvious that in any community the interests of efficiency would be served (1) by consolidating all the public assistance services in a single administrative unit, or at least in the smallest possible number of units; (2) by defining clearly the areas in which private service is needed to supplement the public program.

CONSOLIDATING THE PUBLIC SERVICES

On few matters are public welfare authorities more generally agreed than upon the desirability of consolidating all community provision for public assistance regardless of the sources of financial support for the individual program. In general, also, they agree that the consolidated agency should be a county unit, except in sparsely settled rural areas and large metropolitan centers not coterminous with county lines.

Great progress toward administrative consolidation has been made during the past fifteen years. Integration of general assistance and categorical assistance is now in effect on a state-wide basis in about half the states and territories. In about one fourth, consolidations have taken place in many localities, particularly in larger urban centers, where such steps can be taken without special legislation.

[1] Harold C. Ostertag, "New York Revises and Simplifies Its Social Welfare System," *Social Service Review*, XX, No. 1 (March, 1946), 14.

In the remaining fourth of the states and territories, according to the best available information, there has been no consolidation of these services. It is doubtful whether consolidations could be effected in some places purely on local initiative. Approval by the state agency responsible for the categories and, in some instances, action by the state legislature would be necessary. But the Social Security Administration itself has recommended administrative unification of all the assistance services, and urged legislative action where necessary.[2]

In our experience too little attention has been paid to the desirability of consolidating the administration of the special state relief programs for veterans with the local public welfare department. After every war, states have provided special relief funds for ex-soldiers, along with other special privileges such as tax and license exemptions, employment preferences, land settlement privileges, educational benefits, and so on. Twenty-six states now appropriate some special funds for the relief of veterans of the First World War, and by 1945 twenty-four states had made similar provision for the veterans of the Second World War.

It has been estimated that, in 1943, state cash benefits to veterans of all kinds, including confederate pensions, amounted to about $20 million. The amount of such money earmarked for direct relief is relatively small, especially in comparison with present general expenditures for public assistance, to which veterans, of course, also are entitled. According to the best estimates, $6.5 million was spent by states for veterans relief and pensions, heavily weighted by confederate pensions in some states, and sometimes including burial and educational benefits. The amount ranged from a high of $854,000 in Texas to a low of $1,000 in Oregon, with five states reporting no expenditures of this type. These relief funds are administered by state veterans welfare commissions, occasionally by one of the veterans organizations, or they may be administered by the local departments of public welfare, as in New York and a number of other states, with accompanying advantages in administrative economy and in quality of service.[3]

Somewhat different considerations are involved in integrating the

[2] Social Security Administration, Federal Security Agency, *Public Assistance Goals*, 1947, p. 21.

[3] Franklin Aaronson and Hilda Rosenbloom, "State Aid to Veterans," *Social Security Bulletin*, VIII, No. 2 (February, 1945), 18.

county home or poor farm into a unified local public welfare setup. For one thing, some communities could save money with no loss in service by liquidating these institutions. Few old-fashioned county homes are used to capacity, most of them are ill-equipped, and many are poorly run. Yet, typical of many states is Missouri, where only two almshouses have been closed since passage of the Social Security Act in 1935, and an almshouse population of 2,585 in that year had risen to 3,048 by 1944.[4]

On the other hand, an increasingly large number of the people who receive assistance, particularly those on OAA, are chronic invalids. Many of these bedridden persons need institutional care, but hardly anywhere are there enough buildings equipped to care for them. Recent studies in Maryland, Illinois, and New York showed that about four fifths of the present inmates of public homes were ill (in most cases, chronically ill), though usually the institution did not provide adequate medical or nursing care.[5]

For this reason some state public welfare administrators have been trying to persuade counties to convert almshouses into nursing homes for chronic invalids. The Illinois Public Aid Commission, for example, some years ago adopted the policy of granting OAA and AB payments to eligible inmates of the county homes cooperating in such a program, although at the time the Federal Security Agency did not allow federal participation in such payments. By the end of 1946 twelve county homes had been reconstructed for this purpose.[6] At the same time, fourteen counties in New York State were planning institutional alterations or replacements at an estimated cost of over two and a half million dollars.[7] Similar trends have been reported in other states. In both Illinois and New York, the state policy encouraged a type of reconstruction and program which would appeal to patients paying all, some, or none of the cost of care. The New York law specifically permits the care of paying patients, provided their admission does not keep out some needy person.

Indeed, most authorities are agreed that well-run public institu-

[4] Edgar M. Moorman, "Public Institutions and Public Assistance," *Public Welfare*, V, No. 6 (June, 1947), 131.
[5] New York State Health Preparedness Commission, *A Program for the Care of the Chronically Ill in New York State*, p. 79.
[6] Raymond M. Hilliard, "The Emerging Function of Public Institutions in Our Social Security Structure," *Social Service Review*, XX, No. 4 (December, 1946), 481.
[7] *A Program for the Care of the Chronically Ill in New York State*, p. 80.

tions providing care for chronic invalids would help to do away with the evils of low-grade commercial nursing homes which have sprung up everywhere. The 1950 amendments to the Social Security Act, taking cognizance of the whole problem, not only made possible federal reimbursement for categorical assistance payments to the inmates of public institutions, but also stipulated that a state authority must be responsible for establishing and maintaining standards in all public and private institutions housing recipients of such payments. An improvement in both types of institution may, therefore, be expected.

When a county home is converted into a public nursing institution for the chronically ill, administrative responsibility in a generalized county welfare department should help to insure its efficient use as part of the total assistance program.

AREA OF PRIVATE SERVICES

In the ordinary urban community, as we have pointed out, private agencies seldom account for more than 5 to 10 percent of the total funds spent for assistance. The structure of this private program, that is, the number and particular identity of the agencies which comprise it, will vary greatly from community to community, and each agency will have its own special purpose and constituency. The central problem is to relate these special purposes so that they will supplement and not duplicate the larger program of public aid.

The first general area of present usefulness for private service is created by the same basic community need which is moving some states to make better use of their county homes. Chronically ill persons now comprise a substantial bulk of the total dependency load, and the combined public and private institutional facilities are almost never adequate.

Private voluntary, or nonprofit, homes for the aged have a long history in this country. Few urban communities are without one or more. In 1939 the Bureau of Labor Statistics found that there were 1,428 homes for the aged, with those under private auspices constituting 96 percent of the total and accounting for about 83 percent of a combined institutional capacity of over 100,000.[8]

A quarter century ago these homes were almost the only community

[8] Louis Evans, "Providing Institutional Care for Recipients of Public Assistance," *Public Welfare*, III, No. 11 (November, 1945), 248.

resource available for needy elderly people. Now, however, we have two programs, OAA and OASI, both well designed to meet the need of old people whose problems are purely financial. At present about one in every four persons 65 years of age and over is receiving old age assistance and approximately one in six is receiving old age and survivors insurance.[9]

It is logical, therefore, for the community to urge its private old folks homes to reorient their policies so that they may utilize their plants in order to meet the increasing demand for chronic nursing care. But to our knowledge there has been little trend in this direction. Many homes still prohibit the admission of persons who are ill at the time of application. The requirement of an admission fee ranging from $500 to $1,000 is common, as are other specific but widely differing requirements in respect to church affiliation, residence, nationality background, membership in the sponsoring fraternal order, and the like.

A second field for private service is among those ineligible for relief because of state or local laws stipulating periods of residence or settlement. On November 1, 1949, all but five states had a residence requirement for OAA, all but seven for ADC, and all but nine states for AB.[10]

The length of the period during which the state (or community) will take no responsibility varies greatly from state to state. In ADC this period is limited by federal law to one year, but for the other two categories it may be—and frequently is—as long as five years. Restrictions are even more complicated in respect to general assistance, for which there are often both state and local residence requirements. So far as we know, there are only two states, Rhode Island and New York, where residence requirements for general assistance have been abolished, along with all other restrictive settlement laws.

One may hope, but not overconfidently in the light of historical precedent, that the considerations which led New York State to do away with its settlement laws ultimately will be accepted by legislative policy-makers elsewhere. A study in New York in 1941 disclosed that determination of settlement required 11.6 percent of the total

[9] *Social Legislation Information Service Bulletin,* 81st Congress, Issue 56, February 27, 1950.

[10] Jules H. Berman, "State Assistance Legislation, 1949," *Social Security Bulletin,* XII, No. 12 (December, 1949), 6.

time spent by the social worker on investigation of eligibility, and 18 percent of the over-all time of the entire staffs of local welfare offices.[11] This caused the study committee to conclude "that if localities would pay for their needy, where found, they would come out financially at least as well off as they are now, whereas the saving in clerical work, investigations and legal proceedings would be a total gain." [12]

During normal times the potential need for assistance among this "ineligible," nonresident group varies between different cities and different sections of the country, principally in terms of two kinds of population mobility. Cities on the main line of traffic, particularly at railroad or highway junctions, are likely to have a steady flow of itinerants, although few cities escape altogether the problem of transients, living "off the country" more or less intentionally. The professional hobo of earlier generations was this type of transient, but travel by thumb or by ancient jalopy is no longer the prerogative of any one special class.

Another type of nonresident group is to be found for the most part in those sections of the country which rely upon migratory labor to meet seasonal variations in their need for manpower. Every year thousands of migrants supply the extra hands needed for the wheat and sugar-beet harvests of the West, for fruit picking in California and the middle Atlantic states, for the fish canneries of both coasts, and for the cotton fields of the South. This type of mobility is more likely to be rural than urban, but in some cities the nonresident relief problem is influenced substantially by the annual flow of migatory labor.

In abnormal times, mobility greatly accelerates. The tragic trek of the unemployed and dispossessed during the thirties had its counterpart in reverse in the later war years when it was estimated that over fifteen million people moved from one place to another, half of them across state lines.[13]

As long as restrictions prohibit public assistance to nonresidents, needy transients must have recourse to a private agency. In our experience, however, communities are often as unwilling to provide systematically for the nonresident needy through their private agencies as through their public relief programs. The traditional belief

11 Myron Falk, *Settlement Laws*, p. 13.   12 Ostertag, *op. cit.*, p. 16.
13 Arthur J. Altmeyer, "People on the Move: Effect of Residence Requirements for Public Assistance," *Social Security Bulletin*, IX, No. 1 (January, 1946), 3.

that nonresidents should somehow be the responsibility of the place whence they came still governs the private as well as the public relief policies in most communities.

There is, finally, in almost every community a group of private casework agencies that use relief as "a tool of treatment"—to quote the technical phrase. Family agencies and other casework agencies which deal with adjustment problems work with many cases in which the family is trying to get along at a very low income level. In such circumstances relief or assistance often is essential to a constructive plan for rehabilitative treatment. These agencies frequently prefer to meet this need from their own funds, particularly if it is of a temporary nature; although in other instances, the relief may be given by the public agency and the service by the private. Among 51 nonsectarian members of the Family Service Association of America, the median proportion of active cases receiving financial aid from the agency runs about 18 or 19 percent. The median number of cases carried cooperatively with the public agency was 17 percent in 1947.[14]

As these figures indicate, in a well-organized community private casework agencies no longer are concerned primarily with the functions of assistance. Their present primary concern is, or should be, with the diagnosis and treatment of problems of maladjustment.

In contrast, twenty years ago the private agencies, although found mainly in urban communities, were caring for an estimated 25 percent of all the people in need, as determined by the standards of that day. And almost everybody, including the agencies themselves, thought they were carrying an even higher proportion of the total load. The sudden and rapid organization of the public assistance program necessitated equally sudden and rapid shifts in private agency policy. These shifts, community by community, and agency by agency, have not been easy, but today there are few private casework agencies which are still in the relief business.

IMPROVING THE FEDERAL-STATE STRUCTURE

The federal-state structure of categorical assistance has been in operation for fifteen years, and during that time there has been little

[14] According to Family Service Association of America.

basic change in it. The numerous efforts made to change it, however, reflect a series of issues related to its improvement and adaptation as a more effective mechanism. About some of these issues there is considerable unanimity in administrative circles, with the principal resistance coming from the makers of legislative policy. About other issues there is a divergence of expert opinion. Practically always the questions must be settled at national and state levels, but they are nevertheless of obvious concern to the local community. For it is there that aid is given to needy people, through whatever structure national and state policy-makers may devise.

THE ADDITION OF GENERAL ASSISTANCE

The Federal Security Agency, the American Public Welfare Association, public welfare administrators, special agencies, and social workers generally are practically unanimous in recommending that general assistance be incorporated into the federal-state system. "The Social Security Administration," to quote one of its typical statements, "strongly urges that federal grants be authorized for general assistance as well as for the three special types of public assistance. Only if this gap is bridged will the nation have a strong and flexible public assistance system able to meet changing demands." [15]

Those who back this proposal have two cogent reasons for doing so. In the first place, average general assistance grants in about one third of the states, in January, 1950, were below $30 a month.[16] Federal subsidy would raise this level and put general assistance on a parity with categorical assistance. In the second place, public welfare leaders desire to improve and standardize the policies and methods of general assistance. Participation in the federal system would be conditioned upon budgetary determination of need; upon payments in cash instead of relief in kind; upon state supervision; upon a nonpolitical merit system for personnel; and upon the recognized right of any needy person to a "fair hearing." For nearly fifteen years responsible public welfare leaders have hoped for Congressional action in this respect. While this volume was in preparation, the 81st Congress considered this as well as other recommended changes in our social se-

15 *Annual Report of the Federal Security Agency, Section I Social Security Administration, for the Fiscal Year 1947,* p. 113.
16 "Current Operating Statistics," *Social Security Bulletin,* XIII, No. 4 (April, 1950), 31, Table 18.

curity laws, but the legislation adopted in the summer of 1950 did not provide for federal participation in general assistance. Instead there was created a new category—aid to the permanently and totally disabled—and it is expected that state plans for the new category will be authorized promptly by the various legislatures.

In general, there seem to be three basic reasons why Congress is not yet ready to add general assistance to the present structure. The first reason is the cost. The Federal Security Agency estimated that the general assistance provisions of the expanded program recommended to the 81st Congress would cost the treasury $144 million a year, on the basis of December, 1948, assistance levels.[17] This is no great amount in comparison with expenditures for other assistance programs, but December, 1948, was a month of high employment. One must not forget that general assistance is now the only aid available to people whose sole reason for need is unemployment. General assistance case loads immediately reflect changes in the condition of the labor market and are subject to greater fluctuations than those in any of the categories. By agreeing to share in the responsibility for general assistance, the federal government would be taking on future commitments of unknown magnitude in the event of a substantial economic downswing.

The second reason is fear of the ramifications in relief practice to which the vague phrase "assistance to any needy person" may lead. The traditional poor law distinction between the able-bodied and the aged, sick, and infirm still worries the legislators. They fear that ready access to relief will undermine the initiative of self-sustaining workers. Poorer states, which currently give general assistance only to the unemployable handicapped, fear that a relief standard comparable to that set for the categories would compete with wage income.

The third reason why the federal-state system never has been completed is political, both in the broad sense and in the sense of practical party politics. The nature and degree of responsibility which the federal government should take in relation to various aspects of our economy is without doubt one of the fundamental issues of our times. One may doubt that either of our principal political parties has ar-

---

[17] *Social Security Act Amendments of 1949, Hearings before the Committee on Ways and Means, House of Representatives, 81st Congress, on H.R. 2893,* p. 28.

ticulated the real essence of this issue. Nevertheless, conflicting party views undoubtedly contributed to Congressional reluctance to include general assistance under the Social Security Act and to make certain other proposed changes.

There is another factor that may have some significance in this respect. In contrast to the developments in the other major fields of health and welfare, large-scale federal involvement in the public assistance field came before the states themselves had accepted any measure of responsibility for public aid except on a brief emergency basis. To a considerable degree the pressures for change in state and local relief practices have come from the top down. During the depression, policies initiated at the national level were necessary if the country was to meet the exigencies of the period with any measure of adequacy. Against the background of the crises, reform from above was relatively easy. Once the crisis had passed, it was easy no longer. Congress seldom legislates much beyond the solid support of its respective political home fronts. At least such has been our observation.

It has seemed to us, therefore, that public welfare strategy has tended to overlook the fact that while it was failing to convince Congress of the wisdom of including general assistance in the federal structure, the states themselves were proceeding steadily to incorporate this program into their own assistance systems. To be sure, individual state action has been taken with little regard for uniformity on a nationwide basis, and in many instances without serious regard for modern relief standards and methods. It is possible that many states never will give adequate support to the general assistance efforts of their communities without the incentive of a federal reimbursement. Nevertheless, we believe that this home front recognition of state responsibility is likely to spread. At some point, though it would be folly to predict just when, federal legislation to incorporate and extend these inclusive state systems into the present federal-state system should follow naturally. At that point also, the necessary Congressional action may be backed by considerable public conviction.

THE PRINCIPLE OF VARIABLE GRANTS

At present, the Federal Security Agency reimburses each state for the amount it actually spends up to a certain maximum in each category, in accordance with formulas which are uniformly applicable to all states and territories. States, however, differ in wealth, and conversely in need for assistance. The less wealthy states frequently appropriate a larger percentage of their tax dollar for assistance, but are able to put up less money than the richer states. Hence they receive less federal money in proportion to their case loads, "despite the fact that these states often make the greatest fiscal effort in proportion to their total aggregate income." [18] In January, 1950, for example, the average per capita grant made possible by Mississippi's appropriation for OAA was $18.98, and Mississippi ranks lowest in per capita income among the states. The average grant in New York was $54.50, and New York ranks second.[19] According to the existing formula, the federal reimbursement would be $14.24 to Mississippi and $30 to New York.

The proposal to equalize the situation by making the federal contribution greater to those states with greater need and less resources is endorsed by the Social Security Administration, the American Public Welfare Association, and most students of the American social security system. Congress, however, has been unwilling to apply this principle to the federal assistance system.

Through the variable grant formula proposed to the 81st Congress, the federal government was to pay from 40 to 75 percent of the costs, depending on the relationship between the per capita income of each state and that of the United States as a whole. The state with the highest per capita income could claim only 40 percent reimbursement; the state with the lowest would get 75 percent; and the other states would receive intermediate percentages.[20]

Although this formula involved a reduction in the present categorical grants to the wealthier states, supporters of the bill pointed out that the losses would be offset in some measure by the proposed federal participation in general assistance and medical care. Nevertheless, the wealthy states opposed the variable grant provision since it would mean an increase in their assistance expenditures. They also expressed the fear that the poorer states would substitute federal dol-

[18] *Ibid.*, p. 233.
[19] "Current Operating Statistics," *Social Security Bulletin*, XIII, No. 4 (April, 1950), 30, Table 17.
[20] *Social Security Act Amendments of 1949, Hearings*, p. 13.

lars for present state expenditures and that the needy would reap no benefit from the proposed change. The legislation finally adopted did not include a variable grant formula.

Thus the Congress, in shaping assistance policies, has refused consistently to authorize differential treatment in determining the states' need for federal subsidy. As we shall see in a subsequent section, it has taken an almost opposite position in respect to the distribution of federal subsidy for programs protecting the public's health.

ABOLITION OF THE CATEGORIES

If Congress does complete the federal-state system by adding general assistance, will it and should it at the same time do away with the categorization of relief? The majority of public welfare administrators probably would like to abolish the categorical approach in favor of a single flexible administrative plan for everyone in need.

Undoubtedly, the categorization of aid makes for inequities because of the relative political pressures exerted by the special recipient groups. Aged people vote, children do not. The aged on OAA account for over 2.5 million of the estimated 5 million people who are receiving assistance, and they get the lion's share of the money: in 1949 it was $1,380 million out of a total of $2,187 million for all types of assistance.[21] Since they are such a large group, in many states they have been able to exert powerful political pressure and to obtain preferential treatment quite out of line with that accorded to other assistance recipients.

ADC, on the other hand, is the stepchild among the categories. Not only do many states favor the aged, but the federal matching maximums are on a much lower scale for ADC than for OAA and AB. Largely for this reason, it is most often the ADC grants which are cut below determined need.

Critics of the present system point out that many needy people who are handicapped by personal disabilities are neither aged, blind, nor children with an absent or incapacitated parent. Even with the addition of new categories, such as the newly authorized one for the permanently and totally disabled, there would still be large gaps in our total assistance program for persons with employment disabilities.

21 "Current Operating Statistics," *Social Security Bulletin*, XIII, No. 3 (March, 1950), 26, Table 14.

When the categorical structure is buttressed by an adequate general assistance program, these gaps may not be serious. But when there is no general assistance program, or only a meager one, the rigidities of the categorical philosophy are a constant source of frustration to the public welfare administrator. "In both OAA and AB," says the *Social Security Year Book* for 1947, "more than ¼ of the cases added to the rolls represented persons who were approximately as needy six months before, but did not meet some requirement for eligibility." [22]

As a practical matter, the three categories of the federal-state system probably are here for some time to come, since no policy once established is easily changed. Equally practical is the consideration always used by proponents of the categorical approach that it has proved easier to get tax appropriations, both federal and state, for people with obviously appealing needs, such as the aged, the blind, and fatherless children, than to get funds for needy people in general. Finally, categorization is an easy way of effecting a compromise between those who wish to spend enough money to meet total assistance needs in terms of relatively high standards of adequacy, and those who fear extensions of this policy.

WORK RELIEF

In contrast to the proposal to abolish the present categories are the arguments concerning what would be in effect the addition of another category—the "employable unemployed," whose needs would be met by work relief rather than by direct assistance. As far as we know, work relief is not considered a vital issue at the present time in either administrative or legislative circles. After ten years of high employment, both legislators and administrators are well satisfied to hope the present happy condition is permanent, and that the controversies which raged in the WPA days are over forever.

We do not venture to predict the course of national policy in the event of another great depression. But if and when a work relief program is deemed necessary as a matter of public policy, we believe that it should be administered through the machinery of the federal-state categorical system, and that the states should contribute a fair portion of its cost. We should point out that we do not refer here to expanded public works programs, for which labor is hired in the open market.

[22] *Social Security Year Book,* 1947, p. 52.

Such programs have long been advocated as the best means by which a government can deal with severe unemployment, though they failed to meet the situation in the early 1930s. Programs of this type are outside the scope of the present volume.

We are talking about work relief for employable persons who need assistance during the less catastrophic downswings of the economy. General assistance is now the only recourse for these people. It measures the community's ability to assist them after their unemployment insurance has run out, and even earlier if they are not covered by insurance. In most sections of the country, this ability is quite limited. In times of high employment almost all families on the general assistance rolls include the aged, sick, and infirm. But in any economic downswing, these unemployables are greatly outnumbered by the able-bodied.

For whatever it may be worth, we should like to record our view that the primary issue is whether there should be a work relief program under any circumstances. The crux of this issue is whether work relief as administered by WPA was more effective in keeping up the morale of its recipients and their capacity for self-support than was direct relief, as administered under other auspices. The country accepted WPA mainly on the basis of the traditional hypothesis that work relief is more effective than direct relief in this respect.

Unfortunately, eight years of WPA with its ten-billion-dollar expenditure left us with no objective or systematic evidence about the validity of this assumption. A few limited studies, mainly by university professors who did remember that this was the basic hypothesis, are inconclusive. The principal evidence left by WPA itself is simply that when the program was launched, a good many people thought work relief was better than direct relief and that a good many—especially WPA administrators—still thought so when it ended.

It may be, as some writers imply, that we do not yet know enough about psychological motivation either to prove or to disprove the case for work relief. Research to produce facts relevant to this issue admittedly presents many difficulties. But one cannot help but marvel that among so many projects so ingeniously devised to spend so many billion dollars to aid so many million people, no one devised a project to throw light on the validity of the primary hypothesis which accounted for the enterprise itself.

LOCAL PARTICIPATION AND AUTONOMY

A final issue regarding the federal-state assistance structure relates to the degree of community autonomy and local participation in policy-making which is most desirable in a federal-state structure. Any state welfare administrator would agree that it is important for the local administrators to be sensitive in their general community relations and cooperative with other community agencies; and that, in general, the state program must have local support from both citizens and professional workers in allied fields. Any administrator also would agree, perforce, that basic uniformity in assistance policies as well as in administrative practice throughout the state is of primary importance.

To attain these two objectives, the individual states have set up a wide variety of structural patterns of state-local relationships, ranging from almost complete state control to almost complete local independence. The Pennsylvania Department of Public Assistance, a state agency with local units in every county, illustrates one extreme. There are local county boards of assistance, but their members are appointed by the governor with the advice and the consent of the State Senate. The assistance budget comes entirely from state and federal funds. This state agency administers both the categories and general assistance. In other words, this is a completely state-administered and state-financed assistance program with all ultimate authority vested in the state. Arkansas has the same kind of setup, and a similar degree of state control is quite common in the administration of the categories; the programs in Florida, Idaho, Kentucky, and Michigan are examples. The Federal Security Agency will not approve a state plan for categorical assistance unless sufficient state supervision is provided to insure its execution, but there are many states where this supervision is at a minimum. Similarly in states which put up considerable money for general assistance, the expenditure of this money may be governed to a large extent by local policy and practice.

New York State illustrates a middle policy between complete state control and complete local autonomy. In principle, the relationship between the state and the localities is very much like the relationship between the federal government and the states in the federal-state system. Each local "public welfare district" in New York must submit to the State Department of Social Welfare an administrative plan, conforming to certain state standards. Reimbursement for local assistance expenditures is conditioned upon an annual review and approval of the local plan by the state. The state, out of its own funds and the federal money available for the categories, contributes 80 percent of the amount spent for all types of assistance; the county or city, 20 percent.[23]

In states where the localities share in financing assistance and exercise a considerable degree of administrative autonomy, this local participation is believed to insure a program which is adapted to local needs and attitudes and which will command community support. States with central financing and administration attach less importance to community participation; they feel that any loss in the local sense of responsibility is more than offset by increased efficiency and state-wide uniformity. Especially do they contend that centralization makes it easier to assure equal treatment in all parts of the state.

Unfortunately, so far as we know this is one of those issues, so common in welfare organization and administration, to which objective research has never been directed. One must rely instead on opinions growing out of individual experience. Our experience leads us to believe that local community influences and pressures can be brought to bear upon actual practices in local public welfare administration just about as easily under one system as under another. It seems to us, however, that state offices are more likely to keep close to local community attitudes when the state structure provides for some measure of local administrative autonomy and financial sharing. Although some authorities on administrative practice undoubtedly prefer a certain degree of remoteness from local influence, our own bias quite naturally favors the maximum of local control consistent with state-wide uniformity.

23 Richard T. Gilmartin, "From Planning to Action: New York State Integrates Its Welfare Services," *Public Welfare*, IV, No. 6 (June, 1946), 133.

Chapter V

THE PREVENTION OF
DEPENDENCY

WHEN THEY PASSED LAWS setting up machinery to administer the federal categories, most states declared their intent not only to provide assistance for needy people, but also to prevent the occurrence of such need. What was meant by "prevention" was no less uncertain than what was meant by "needy." Methods by which to "determine need" have been hard-wrought out of accumulated experience in administering relief. Practical methods by which to carry out the instruction to "prevent" dependency have still to be wrung from experience.

During the depression, those who used the term "economic security" undoubtedly were referring to measures to stabilize industry and provide insurance against unemployment, and to protect people against its consequences. By far the largest number of persons then on relief were in need because of "imperfections in the economy," and it was natural that remedial measures should be a primary concern. As we have indicated, there has been little experimentation with community-wide methods for stabilizing employment. Consideration of more general measures for economic stabilization is outside the competence of this volume.

The last ten years have been years of high employment and high production. Public welfare administrators spend a great deal of time trying to explain why, in this situation, there continue to be 5 million people on the relief rolls at an annual cost of $2 billion. Economists, on the other hand, generally agree that during most of the decade unemployment has been no more than must be expected in any private enterprise system.

Those who now speak of "prevention" are likely to be concerned with how to rehabilitate the residual group of families who apparently are unable or unwilling to earn their own living even in a pe-

riod of high employment. The present chapter, therefore, is concerned with that part of the community-wide program which should
be directed to the prevention, reduction, and control of the residual
relief load.

STRATEGIC CHARACTERISTICS OF THE RESIDUAL LOAD

The national figures make it clear that caring for this residual load
is expensive. Data such as those from the St. Paul project should help
to focus community attention on the load's local size and cost. In
November, 1948, out of every 1,000 families in St. Paul 67 were receiving assistance, at an annual cost of $3,952,944—amounting to
$11.09 for every person in the population. Assistance accounted
for almost a quarter of the city's total expenditures for community
welfare, health, and recreational purposes. All but 6 percent of this
money was from tax funds—35 percent from city-county taxes, 22 percent from state taxes, and 37 percent from federal funds. This was a
substantial financial burden upon the community and its contributory partners, the state of Minnesota and the federal government.

CLASSIFICATION OF THE LOAD

During the later 1930s many attempts were made to classify relief
loads into "employables" and "unemployables." In fact, this type of
classification became essential after WPA was organized, for only
"employable" persons were eligible for its work relief. Some states
and communities now prescribe that their general assistance money
shall go only to "unemployable" families.

The trouble with this classification is that both "employable" and
"unemployable" are relative terms. For example, "unemployable"
blind or crippled persons, for whose labor industry often has little
regard during normal times, were in demand during wartime labor
shortages. At one time during the depression it was estimated that
about 5 million people on the relief rolls were "unemployable."
But during the war it was pointed out that "if we have reached the
peak of manpower utilization with an irreducible minimum of 2
million unemployed, then we must certainly have been mistaken
about the 5 million unemployables of the depression years." [1]

[1] Henry H. Kessler, *Rehabilitation of the Physically Handicapped*, p. 18.

The significant factor in a community-wide attempt to prevent and reduce that part of dependency not solely due to economic causes is the presence of inherent obstacles to family self-maintenance. No one can doubt that certain disabilities do constitute handicaps to self-sufficiency, no matter what the state of the labor market may be. Some of these disabilities may be overcome by certain families. Some of them may be much less difficult to overcome when the demand for labor is high. But that the presence of one or more of these disabilities among its members is an actual or potential handicap to a family in achieving self-sufficiency, no one can deny.

In analyzing the St. Paul data, we accepted the following as evidence of the presence of these inherent obstacles: First, the fact that there was some family member who (a) was over 65 years of age or was laboring under some physical or mental handicap; (b) had not been employed at any time during the month; and (c) in the judgment of the worker handling the case, was unemployed because of the condition specified. Second, the fact that the family was "broken," that is, either the father or mother or both were absent from the home, with the obvious handicaps to family economic self-sufficiency which such absence entails. Third, the fact that there was some "special" burden, such as an unusually large number of children, or the chronic illness or invalidism of some family member, which made the family's income insufficient to meet its maintenance needs.

One or more of these obstacles to the production of sufficient income for self-maintenance were present in all but 277 of the families who made up St. Paul's residual relief load in this period of high employment. These families with no intrinsic income-producing handicap accounted for only 4 percent of the 6,640 dependent families. In over three quarters of the dependent families there were unemployed aged, ill, or mentally disordered persons. About one sixth were broken families, and in the remainder there were special burdens too heavy for the family to finance without assistance from some community agency.

These data, as well as materials and experience of a more general nature, leave little doubt that any community attack upon the quasi-permanent or residual problem of dependency must be directed at the prevention and reduction of those disabilities which handicap a family's capacity to earn the "minimum essentials of living."

A NATIONWIDE BACKLOG OF DISABILITIES

There seem to be no data to show the number or proportion of families throughout the country whose capacity for self-maintenance is handicapped by such disabilities. But there are data which show, with varying degrees of accuracy, the extent and spread of specific disabling conditions.

Age is no absolute criterion of productive capacity. But as long as industry continues to set age limits in hiring labor, advanced age per se will constitute a definite obstacle to the maintenance of personal and family self-sufficiency.

In 1940 there were some 9 million persons 65 years of age and over in the United States. They constituted 6.8 percent of the population, in contrast to 4.1 percent in 1900, and an estimated 14.4 percent in 1980.[2] These figures reflect the steady increase in life expectancy which the generations of the twentieth century are enjoying as the result of steady advances in medical science and public health. In December, 1948, the proportion of the aged population in need of OAA ranged from a high of 791 out of every 1,000 people over 65 in Louisiana to a low of 47 per 1,000 in Washington, D.C., with an average rate of 228 per 1,000 for the country as a whole.[3]

Although the disadvantage of age per se is something which can be remedied only by a change in industrial practices, it is multiplied manyfold when the aged person also suffers from chronic illness or other disabilities. A study in Illinois estimated that 24 percent of the state's expenses for all types of public assistance were in behalf of persons who were chronic invalids, the great majority of whom were aged people receiving OAA.[4] The St. Paul data showed that age alone was a handicapping factor in only about one third of the families in which there were aged members. In the remainder, age was complicated by chronic illness, physical handicaps, mental disability, or serious emotional problems.

Chronic illness as a handicap to economic self-sufficiency is not solely an attribute of the aged, although it tends to increase with ad-

[2] Ollie A. Randall, "The Aged," Social Work Year Book, 1947, pp. 41, 42.
[3] Social Security Act Amendments of 1949, Hearings before the Committee on Ways and Means, House of Representatives, 81st Congress, on H.R. 2893, Part I, p. 56.
[4] Raymond M. Hilliard, "Chronic Illness Major Cause of Dependency," Survey Midmonthly, LXXXIII, No. 11 (November, 1947), 307.

vancing years. There are varying estimates as to the amount and incapacitating seriousness of chronic illness throughout the country, but a statement sponsored by the American Hospital Association, the American Medical Association, the American Public Health Association, and the American Public Welfare Association puts the over-all total at 25 million persons of whom some 7 million have appreciable disability and 1.5 million are chronic invalids.[5]

The principal physical handicaps to the production of family income are blindness, deafness, and orthopedic disabilities. Such handicaps may be congenital, or they may result from disease, industrial injuries, or other accidents.

It is estimated that there are more than 250,000 [6] persons in the United States suffering from blindness, as it is technically defined. Partially sighted persons who have a defect severe enough to require special attention are estimated to number another 450,000.[7]

The number of completely deaf persons in the United States— those born deaf, or deafened early in life before they acquired a vocabulary—is estimated at between 85,000 and 100,000.[8] A far larger number, estimated at between 6 percent and 10 percent of the population, suffer hearing loss later in life. Of the latter, those who cannot hear at all sometimes are called the "deafened," while the rest are known as the "hard of hearing."

Persons suffering from orthopedic handicaps have been estimated to number some 2,600,000, of whom 341,000 are incapacitated.[9] Accidents and injury account for almost two thirds of all cases; diseases, about one third; and congenital defects, only a small percentage of the total.[10]

Serious mental illness is another disability likely to produce or contribute to dependency. In recent years, hospitalizations for mental disease have been mounting steadily; by the end of 1945 there were 592,454 patients under permanent care in mental hospitals as opposed to 484,252 at the end of 1936.[11] Less serious mental and emotional

5 Joint Statement, "Planning for the Chronically Ill," *American Journal of Public Health*, XXXVII, No. 10 (October, 1947), 1256.

6 Robert M. Barnett and Helga Lende, "The Blind," *Social Work Year Book, 1951*, p. 63.

7 Kessler, *op. cit.*, p. 182.   8 *Ibid.*, p. 189.

9 House Committee on Labor, *Aid to the Physically Handicapped*, p. 4.

10 United States Employment Service, *Selective Placement for the Handicapped*, pp. 54–55.

11 Leon E. Truesdall, *Patients in Mental Institutions*, 1945, p. 52.

disorders which do not require hospitalization still may constitute income-producing handicaps, and the volume of such cases, though unknown, is certainly substantial.

Mental deficiency is another obvious employment handicap. It is estimated that at least one percent of the population, or roughly 1.4 million people, are mentally deficient—"characterized by a degree of intelligence so far below average or normal as to be seriously disabling for life adjustment." [12] Mental deficiency may be congenital, or it may be due to injury, brain tumors, or disease.

Antisocial conduct deprives many families of their potential breadwinners. During the course of a year over 200,000 persons serve sentences in state and federal prisons and reformatories,[13] while some 600,000 receive jail terms varying in length from one day to several months.[14] Over 90 percent of those incarcerated are men, about a third of whom are married and presumed to have family responsibilities; [15] and almost all of them are of an age when they normally would be a source of some support for the families from which they come.

Finally, as we have noted, in about 15 percent of St. Paul's dependent families need was due in part at least to the absence of one, or both, parents from the home. Bureau of the Census population estimates for 1947 revealed that in the country as a whole there are more than 2 million "broken" families in which there are children under 18, and that in about four fifths of these the woman was the remaining family head.[16]

In these figures there is a considerable, though unknown, amount of duplication. It is particularly high between the aged and those with certain physical and mental handicaps. The fact that a substantial number of those in correctional institutions are mentally subnormal indicates further duplication. Yet even when allowance is made for duplications, we estimate that the total number of aged and handicapped persons probably would run to 26 or 27 million.

12 R. E. Wyers and George Tarjan, "Administrative Practices to Provide Better Psychiatric Care of Mental Patients," *American Journal of Mental Deficiency*, LIV, No. 1 (July, 1949), 31–37.

13 U.S. Bureau of the Census, *Statistical Abstract of the United States: 1949*, p. 141, Table 168.

14 Committee on the Model State Plan, *Manual of Suggested Standards for a State Correctional System*, p. 81.

15 *Statistical Abstract of the United States: 1949*, p. 29, Table 39.

16 *Ibid.*, p. 23, Table 32.

It is thus clear that in the country as a whole there must be a large backlog of families who have to overcome or compensate for inherent handicaps in their attempt to produce income sufficient to maintain themselves at a reasonable standard of living. Although it is impossible accurately to estimate their number, we believe it is conservative to assume that handicaps to income production affect at least one fourth of the 39 million households in the country—perhaps some 10 million families.

DISABILITY CONSTELLATIONS

It would be a mistake to attempt to establish any precise relationship between this estimate of 10 million economically handicapped families and the 5 million people, probably representing some 2 or 3 million families, who were actually on the assistance rolls in the fall of 1949. Nevertheless, the data from St. Paul show clearly that almost all the families who needed assistance during that period of peak employment were handicapped by one or more of these disabling factors. Our general experience leads us to believe that a study of assistance loads throughout the country would reveal much the same situation everywhere.

We also know that many families with these disabilities are not in need of financial assistance and that many of them never will be. An accurate ratio between the total of disabled families and those who require assistance would be exceedingly useful for long-range planning purposes, since a significant proportion of the disabled families always are unable to overcome their obstacles, and as a result do become dependent.

We believe that the St. Paul project gave us a significant clue to the reason why some families are able to maintain themselves in spite of their handicaps, while others are not. The data suggest that a family is likely to become dependent when it must surmount not one, but several such handicaps. The data suggest, too, that constellations of disabilities tend to accelerate family deterioration, not only undermining the capacity to function as a self-sustaining economic unit, but also accentuating the specific disabilities which impair the competence of individual family members.

Among the 6,640 families dependent on the community for assistance in the month of the St. Paul study was one group of 1,526 cases, made up largely of people receiving old age assistance, in which there were apparently no other handicapping factors in the family situation.

More than three quarters of the families dependent in that month were part of a group of 6,466 families (6 percent of all the families in the community) whose life was complicated by constellations of the major problems of ill-health, maladjustment, and dependency. In 2,119 of these 6,466 families there was chronic disease; in 1,404, there were chronic physical handicaps; in 4,870 of the 6,466 there were serious problems of ill-health. In 1,919 families there was mental defect or mental illness; in 1,786 there was an official record of some type of antisocial behavior—crime, delinquency, or child neglect; 5,211 of the 6,466 showed some evidence of personal or family maladjustment. In 3,612 families there were persons who were "unemployable"; 5,114 of the 6,466 families were dependent upon the community for financial assistance.

Included in the total group of multiproblem families were 5,001 persons with behavior disorders (mental defect, mental disease, antisocial behavior, and the like), of whom 2,394 were either the male or female heads of their respective families. There also were 4,192 ill persons who were heads of families, and 983 family heads who were affected both by ill-health and some serious behavior disorder.

In other words, here was what we might call a group of "pathological families," each with its own constellation of serious problems and disabilities. Not all were dependent on the community for assistance during that particular month, but nearly 80 percent were, and it seems reasonable to predict that most of the others will be in similar need as time goes on. From this group as a whole came all those in the community who did require assistance during that month, except those families already noted, who were mainly aged persons with no known health or adjustment difficulties. These facts, we believe, help to explain the reasons for the residual load of relief recipients in a time of high employment. They help to explain why disabilities in one large group of families may produce a substantial proportion of the dependency load. Equally important, they illustrate certain characteristics significant to a community-wide program for the prevention of dependency.

COMMUNITY-WIDE PROCEDURES

A community-wide program for the prevention and control of a residual load of this kind calls for three main types of procedure: (1) prevention of particular disabilities; (2) systematic concentration on the most disorganized families; and (3) systematic use of the insurance services.

PREVENTION OF SPECIFIC DISABILITIES

Later sections of this volume will be concerned with considerations relevant to the community-wide attack upon many of the particular disabilities which handicap family economic capacity.

The public health system has to its credit during this half century not only substantial reductions in the tuberculosis death rate but also reductions in the consequences of this disease, long one of the worst of the economic disablers. Both trachoma and *ophthalmia neonatorum,* once principal causes of blindness, have been brought under control by public health measures. The control of such communicable diseases as syphilis, an important cause of blindness, and of scarlet fever, chicken pox, measles, meningitis, influenza, diphtheria, and other infections of the nose and throat which may affect hearing, is part of the basic public health disease control program. The prevention of accidents (the greatest single cause of orthopedic handicaps) is by no means the exclusive responsibility of public health, but it is being given special attention because of the high accident death rates. The causes of most chronic diseases and of many chronic handicaps are still obscure, and measures to prevent and control such conditions are not so well developed as those dealing with the infectious and communicable diseases which used to be the chief "killers" of mankind. But health authorities are directing more and more thought and experimentation to the development of measures and resources which would make possible a community-wide attack upon the chronic disorders.

Science is constantly adding to knowledge about mental illnesses, mental defects, and emotional disturbances, as well as about the relationship of these conditions to antisocial conduct. The principal community agencies which deal with evidences of maladjustment gradually are developing measures for the diagnosis, treatment, and rehabilitation of persons and families thus handicapped. And while these measures fall considerably short of a systematic community-wide program, there is no doubt that the trend is in that direction.

CONCENTRATION ON THE MOST DISORGANIZED FAMILIES

In our opinion, the various community-wide programs for the prevention and reduction of specific physical, emotional, or social disabilities, of and by themselves, even when perfected, will not be completely effective in preventing and reducing the residual load of dependent families. The constellations of disabilities which so undermine the family's basic capacity to function must be met by a coordinated attack upon them all.

The facts from St. Paul showed that the particular problems of such families already are receiving a great deal of specialized attention. In November, 1948, the month of our study, 46 percent of the health services of the special clinics, dispensaries, nursing agencies, and public hospitals went to the group of 6,466 families with two or more major problems. These families also absorbed 55 percent of all the adjustment services, including psychiatric service, casework, and protective supervision. At least two and often many more agencies were working currently with practically every family in the group.

Thus a vast amount of service, by over 60 different specialized agencies or administrative units, was channeled to this group of families. While the St. Paul situation may differ in detail from that in other cities, our general experience makes us confident that the picture in every urban community in the United States is basically the same. Everywhere the residual load of financially dependent persons is absorbing a high proportion of the total time and money devoted to specialized community welfare services.

On the other hand, the various agencies in St. Paul had no accurate knowledge that so much of their service was directed to this group of multiproblem families, because previously there had been no means of producing the necessary facts about such families. The public welfare department did not know the full complexity of the health and maladjustment problems of the families under its care, because no one had devised a means of assembling the knowledge contained in the records of the many agencies which gave specialized service to them. No one yet knows the extent to which the present substantial volume of service results in the rehabilitation of capacity for self-support. One must frankly admit also that there is as yet no generally accepted pattern or community-wide design for accomplishing this purpose.

There is great need for a methodological pattern, developed and tested to the point of demonstrable utility, which a community can use to concentrate its services upon the prevention and reduction of the underlying disabilities of the families in this group. Any such pattern, we believe, must include practical methods for implementing a series of five closely related procedures.

1. Procedures for the continuous identification of the families who give evidence of serious disorganization and for the systematic recording of data about them.

The St. Paul project illustrated one such procedure. In particular, we think that its classification of problems provides a valid basis for recording the family data significant to the four succeeding steps. However, the extensive reporting and elaborate statistical machinery required by the over-all project served many purposes besides the eventual identification of this particular group of families. A high proportion of them was known—and in any well-organized community would be known—to the Department of Public Welfare. We believe, therefore, that simpler methods of identification and recording could achieve the same practical result.

2. Procedures which will assure an integrated diagnosis of the whole family situation, taking into account the range of special problems and specific disabilities. Naturally, the resulting evaluation should form a part of the basic record set up by the procedures of the first type.

Lack of provision for an integrated diagnosis is without doubt one of the key weaknesses in the present organization of services. A number of agencies and many professional workers usually have diagnostic information and other data about the individuals in the family, but their data and their professional insight are seldom synthesized in relation to the family. What is needed is a definite assumption of community responsibility to assure that synthesis.

3. Procedures for developing a prognostic classification by which this group of families can be analyzed in terms of their rehabilitative

potentialities. Naturally, the results also would form a part of the continuing family record.

The need for this classification reflects another key weakness in the present organization of specialized services. In almost every community known to us, there are at best only limited facilities for the kind of medical, psychiatric, casework, vocational, and other specialized services necessary to fundamental rehabilitation. Our experience convinces us that the present method, under which each particular agency approaches a particular symptom, tends to result in an over-all concentration of the most service in families with the least rehabilitative potentiality. This is the fault of no one agency. Rather, the fault is inherent in a community program which has no way of classifying its agencies' soundly conceived prognostic judgments.

4. Procedures and policies which will assure continuity of the indicated treatment and rehabilitative service.

We doubt that this would present as many difficulties as might be imagined. The process merely involves methods by which the community can keep track of the families identified and recorded by the first procedure, can keep posted on what is happening to them, and on what services are being provided to them in accordance with the diagnosis and prognosis concerning the basic family situation. Experience with fairly simple methods and further experimentation should lead to systematic procedures bearing on both the appropriateness and the continuity of the total community effort to solve a family's problems.

5. Procedures for the periodic review and evaluation of the total program.

Primarily, these must involve an objective review of the status of each identified and recorded case; they must provide for an evaluation of changes in its situation, and of the apparent appropriateness and effectiveness of the services being rendered. Such procedures constitute practical tools to assure a continuity of the appropriate services.

We have noted the general absence of procedures for the collection and analysis of data about those characteristics of dependency which are significant to the organization of a practical community-wide program for its prevention and reduction. Such data and such analyses do not spring full-blown from the infertile soil of intermittent interest and casual curiosity. They grow slowly, out of a soil fertilized by a recognized responsibility for undertaking such a program and by persistent efforts to carry it through with some measure of demonstrable success. This fifth procedure, in other words, involves an objective research discipline to be used in illuminating, evaluating, and modifying all the others.

Specific principles and methods for the implementation of these procedures must come initially from the results of controlled experimentation and applied research. There has been little practical experience with the basic processes of diagnostic and prognostic classification. Experience is needed to establish sound lines of functional responsibility among the various agencies which provide the main types of treatment, as well as to clarify the nature of the necessary service agreements among agencies and to set up operational methods for supervising these agreements. Specific processes for assuring continuity of treatment to families with complex and deep-seated difficulties are still to be worked out. There are as yet no standard criteria for measuring rehabilitative results. In all these areas, methods must be developed and tested objectively, but in none of them do we anticipate insuperable difficulties. Indeed, investment in this kind of experimentation and research seems to us a logical and profitable next step in the long and baffling attempt to cope with those causes of dependency which are not exclusively of an economic nature.

THE INSURANCE SERVICES

Even before social security was extended by the 1950 amendments, considerably more than half of the working force in any ordinary industrial community was likely to be covered by one or more of the five types of governmental insurance: OASI; unemployment insurance; insurance for railroad workers; veterans benefits; and workmen's compensation. As of January, 1950, about 9 million people were receiving insurance or compensation payments, totaling two and a half times the amount paid out to the 5 million or more people receiving assistance.

Except for the unemployment benefits paid by the federal-state unemployment insurance program and by the Railroad Retirement Board, these payments are made on account of old age, physical handicaps or illness, or death of a family breadwinner. In other words, they are made to members of that large group of handicapped families from which comes the smaller group with constellations of continuing disabilities, who make up a substantial part of the residual dependency load.

Theory and logic dictate that it should be possible to incorporate the resources of this insurance system into a community-wide program in two principal ways:

First, the insurance agencies, taken together, have a great deal of data which should lend themselves to an analysis of the spread of these disabilities, the trends in respect to them, the effects of insurance as a cushion against the need for relief, and possibly certain other significant factors.

Secondly, the payment of an insurance benefit automatically identifies the incidence of a disability which in certain families under certain circumstances may set in motion a chain of consequences leading to family disintegration. Procedures for the skillful selection of such cases and for their referral to appropriate community agencies in accordance with planned service agreements seem a logical way to put the community's treatment resources systematically to work before rather than after serious consequences develop.

The various insurance and compensation systems, however, were not set up to serve the theoretical and logical purposes of community planning. An urban community of average size probably will have separate offices for unemployment insurance, OASI, and the Veterans Administration. Only a railroad center is likely to have an office representing the railroad insurances, and in all probability there will be no local office of the state workmen's compensation program. In the interests of efficiency in administering each system, records and data from the local community are kept at national, area, or state headquarters. Statistical tabulations showing the number of recipients, or the amount and type of benefits paid, are usually published only for the larger territorial areas. At present, therefore, the community cannot turn to its insurance units, either separately or in combination, as a source of much factual help in analyzing its dependency problems.

The agency administering unemployment insurance refers the applicant or recipient for employment. The Veterans Administration is responsible for providing medical and psychiatric service to its beneficiaries, and it may make special contracts or arrangements for the use of community facilities when it has no local services of its own. With these exceptions, however, the local offices of the various agencies function mainly as service and information centers to assist with the filing of claims and to handle other routine technical matters.

In our experience, insurance offices do very little to identify or refer for appropriate service those beneficiaries whose family circumstances indicate that the qualifying disability may have potentially serious consequences. This situation has been recognized by the director of the Committee on Social Security of the American Council on Education:

Pointing or opening the way to the use of the varied resources of the community is an inherent part of the work of the insurance interviewers. . . . People in the course of their contact with the organization indicate needs which other institutions can supply. A personnel adequately equipped with knowledge of these facilities can provide directions about where and how such services can be had, sometimes actually introducing the individual to appropriate representatives of the other agency.[17]

Our communities still lack considered plans for developing procedures that will fit efficiently into a community-wide program to prevent the serious family disorganization which produces so much of the residual dependency load. Experimentation with referral procedures as an integral part of such a plan would be fruitful.

ROLE OF THE PUBLIC WELFARE DEPARTMENT

Public welfare leaders were among the first to recognize their responsibility "for laying the groundwork of a sound system of community social services." [18] They are now aware of the necessity for a program which will focus on the rehabilitation of their assistance cases. To quote from a statement of the Welfare Policy Committee of the American Public Welfare Association:

Increasingly public welfare workers and the community at large are coming to recognize that the public welfare function is a dual one in which the rendering of service plays a role closely related to the relief of economic need. Moreover, the sharply rising financial burden of meeting needs caused by dependency, preventable illness, delinquency and similar con-

---

[17] Karl de Schweinitz, *People and Process in Social Security*, p. 41.

[18] Alice Scott Nutt, "The Responsibility of the Juvenile Court and the Public Welfare Agency in the Child Welfare Program," *Redirecting the Delinquent (1947 Yearbook, National Probation and Parole Association)*, p. 222.

ditions emphasizes the long run economy of an early investment of public funds in the preventive social services which help individuals and families to meet their own problems.[19]

In deciding upon their role in the prevention and reduction of dependency, both the local public welfare department and the public welfare movement as a whole are confronted with a choice between two courses. These courses are not mutually exclusive, but the distinction in the demands which they make upon public welfare leadership is quite clear.

We have been concerned with the first course in the immediately preceding pages. Planning, organizing, studying, and evaluating a program for identifying and classifying the seriously disorganized families and for assuring a continuity of appropriate services to them must involve much more than the services of one community agency no matter how strategic its location. In any urban community the organization of resources for the effective use of health, casework, psychiatric, and other adjustment services entails the cooperation of many people at many points. This task confronts the public welfare department or any other agency which assumes the role of organizer.

The effectiveness of the program will depend upon whether or not such services are available to a reasonable degree. If not, as its second course, public welfare may choose to invest money and effort to provide and administer them.

COMMUNITY ORGANIZATION

There are several reasons why the local public welfare department and the public welfare movement should assume leadership in this program. The public welfare agency has the profound responsibility for providing most of these families with their ultimate means of livelihood. No other single agency has as much basic information about their complex problems. No other single agency bears so much of the brunt of the end results of those problems.

As yet, public welfare leadership in community organization has been lacking. Instead, its primary concern has been the provision of direct services under its own administrative auspices. It has urged the need of more public money—federal, state, and local—so that

[19] Welfare Policy Committee, "Objectives for Public Welfare Legislation—1947," *Public Welfare Platform*, p. 4.

the public agency itself can provide the necessary preventive and rehabilitative services. This attitude is a natural outcome of developments over the past fifteen years, a period in which public welfare, of necessity, was intensely preoccupied with administrative mechanisms for an assistance system that was almost completely new.

Only meager formalized training is available for those who wish to become public welfare directors, and the qualifications for administrative positions are couched mainly in terms of general personal capacities. At the beginning of the depression, many assumed that technical competence in casework was essential to the effective administration of relief, a belief carried over from private agency practice. This belief soon broke down in the face of the overwhelming importance of administrative ability in operating large-scale relief programs. It is not surprising, therefore, that public welfare so far should have conceived of its role primarily in administrative and financial terms.

It seems to us that public welfare will play a vital and dynamic part in creating a community pattern for the prevention of dependency only if the leadership sees that it should occupy a community organization role and seeks to equip itself for that purpose. Signs are multiplying that leadership in the field recognizes this broader challenge.

The public welfare department is not the only agency which logically might assume the organizing role. Our St. Paul data showed that a high proportion of the multiproblem families was affected by chronic disease and chronic handicaps. Almost half of the community services for organized medical care were rendered to families with these serious conditions. Public health has had long experience in the community organization of systematic procedures for preventing and controlling illness and disability. If, as we believe, the extension of these procedures to the control of chronic conditions involves a full consideration of family circumstances, the public health program inevitably will find itself concerned with this group of seriously disorganized families. The same is true of the psychiatric, correctional, and other adjustment agencies which are beginning to think about systematic community-wide patterns for the prevention and reduction of mental problems and behavior problems. Our St. Paul data indicate that a substantial proportion of these problems is concentrated in this same disorganized family group.

The community, in short, should welcome leadership and experimentation on the part of any agency in systematic planning directed toward this group of families. If soundly conceived, such planning is bound to be concerned with dependency, ill-health, and maladjustment. The development of adequate procedures necessitates the cooperation of the community's principal assistance, health, and adjustment units.

DIRECT SERVICE

In practice, the contribution of public welfare to a preventive program has been limited mainly to the assumption of administrative responsibility for special services incidental to assistance. Practice varies greatly, depending principally on the adequacy of financial resources and the degree to which the various assistance services have been consolidated into a single public welfare department. But where preventive services have been developed as part of the administrative program they usually consist of generalized casework, foster home care, medical care, or some combination of these.

It may be well again to remind the reader that this volume, as well as the experience and materials on which it draws, is concerned primarily with the urban community. Usually urban resources exceed those of rural areas and towns both in volume and in variety. Although basic public health, medical, and correctional services are present in some measure everywhere, the urban community is likely to be better supplied than its rural counterpart. Specialized services under private auspices are concentrated almost entirely in the urban centers. Public welfare authorities obviously must take into consideration these differentials in determining the nature of the responsibilities they assume for providing services, other than relief, to the families of the community.

Casework service.—Since the federal-state system of categorical assistance was organized it has been the universal intent of public welfare agencies who participate in it to provide casework service. Authorities point out that the agency should formulate social plans for those incompetent to do their own planning—minor children, the feeble-minded, those with personality difficulties. This service ordinarily is rendered by the same staff members who perform the assistance functions of the agency.

It is well to remember that the first obligation of the public welfare department is to administer the assistance functions. We described in an earlier chapter the modern procedures regarded as essential to this task: the determination of need; the investigation of eligibility; the provision of money for maintenance. The development of skill in these processes is an elementary part of the training of social caseworkers. For this reason the field personnel of public welfare agencies are usually classified as "caseworkers."

On the other hand, the standards for professional caseworkers, as articulated by the professional training schools and by the American Association of Social Workers, call for a competence beyond budgeting and investigatory skills. These standards involve the possession of the professional discipline necessary to diagnose problems of personality and of family relationships and to treat them by skillfully assisting people to make the most satisfactory adjustments possible within their circumstances and capacities. Completion of a two-year course in a graduate school of social work, accompanied by an internship in supervised field work, is regarded as essential to the acquisition of this discipline.

The use of the term "casework" to denote skills at both of these and intermediate levels has created considerable confusion about the exact type of direct service which the public welfare department can and should attempt to provide. The first and most fundamental question is whether the skill necessary to discharge the basic assistance functions of determining need and eligibility and of providing maintenance constitutes a distinctive and valid occupational specialty. There is considerable opinion that it does and should. The laws, rules, and regulations are specific in setting forth eligibility requirements; before the individual can be granted assistance he must meet these requirements. It is impossible to act upon his application without giving some degree of service; for this, the workers who administer the assistance functions need special occupational training. At the present time, the great majority of public welfare staffs possess the equipment for this occupational specialty.

Agencies which provide a diagnostic and treatment service with the requisite complement of professional caseworkers have found that each should carry no more than 30 to 40 cases. On the other hand, some public welfare workers carry as many as 400 to 500 cases; loads

of 200 are not uncommon,[20] and even New York State, with a relatively well-organized and well-financed program, sets a maximum
standard of 100 cases per worker. Professional talent of graduate
school competence would be wasted under such circumstances. But
it is obvious that most of them have little need for the kind of intensive training and experience which the professional caseworker must
possess.

Local welfare departments employ few caseworkers with graduate
training, and these few mainly for supervisory positions. Instead,
public departments everywhere rely to a very great degree on workers
with a good general education and background, who gain their special
experience and skill through the agencies which employ them.

If the skills necessary to the performance of the assistance functions
do constitute a distinctive occupational specialty, the second question
is what additional adjustment services the public welfare department
can and should provide under its own administrative auspices. Data
from the St. Paul project throw considerable light on this question.
The 6,640 dependent families were composed of the two broad groups.
The first, consisting of 1,786 families, presented by far the more
complicated set of difficulties. In over 60 percent there was ill-health.
But in all of them were persons with serious behavior disorders:
mentally defective persons; mentally ill; persons convicted of crime,
delinquency, child neglect, or some other official form of antisocial
behavior; as well as persons diagnosed by social caseworkers as failing
in some major social responsibility. The age level of the adults in these
families was lower than in the second group, and there were more
children.

Many of the adults in the second group, 4,854 families, were recipients of old age assistance. The principal complicating factor other
than age or dependency was ill-health, with chronic disease and
chronic physical handicaps in high proportion. On the basis of the
data, the casework treatment needed was help in formulating their
social plans, for securing adequate medical attention, for budgeting,
perhaps for vocational assistance and employment, and in general
for making the most constructive adjustment to their situation. This
group represented problems due to situations which can be aided by

[20] Bureau of Public Assistance, "Personnel in State and Local Public Assistance Agencies, June 1949," *Social Security Bulletin*, XIII, No. 4 (April, 1950), 12.

the kind of workers, with the kind of training, and the kind of case loads now practical for a public welfare department.

On the other hand, it seems clear that the public welfare department could not adequately serve, and should not try to serve, the first group. Their difficulties presented a complex of mental, emotional, and behavior disorders which required either diagnosis and treatment by a psychiatric agency or a high-level type of family casework service which the public welfare agency at present is not equipped to give.

Thus the public welfare department is faced with perplexing questions in deciding what adjustment or casework services it can and should provide over and above those inherent in the performance of its basic assistance functions. Whatever the decision may be in any particular community, policies should be determined on the basis of data, systematically collected and classified, about the constellations of problems presented by the families in the assistance load; in other words, by the same basic procedures for diagnostic and prognostic classification which are essential to the organization of any community-wide program for preventing dependency.

Foster home care.—Most public welfare departments provide foster home care for dependent and neglected children. In many instances the families from which these children come are not receiving assistance and so are not "dependent" as we have defined the term. The child is removed from his home because his family is incapable of providing the care and training deemed necessary to his satisfactory upbringing. Since separation from his normal home and his relation to foster parents create problems of adjustment, these services are dealt with in our section on maladjustment. On the other hand, the economic problem, that is, the parents' lack of sufficient funds to support their children, is an important reason for foster care in some instances. Sometimes the family's release from the expense of caring for a child constitutes, in effect, a substitute for direct assistance.

The St. Paul data showed quite clearly that the families of children under public care are part of the stream flowing from a pool of physical, mental, emotional, and social disabilities. Many of the relatively small number of multiproblem families who were not on the assistance rolls in November, 1948, had children under the care of the Division of Child Welfare of the Public Welfare Department. Since the period during which children from seriously disorganized families must remain in foster homes is usually long, the total bill for their care is correspondingly large. Private agencies originally carried much of this burden and still carry a share of it, but the trend toward public responsibility is unmistakable. Almost everyone agrees that where the responsibility is public, the welfare department should administer the program.

Some welfare departments now provide juvenile probation and detention services. Also, a few local departments assume special duties such as the inspection and licensing of privately operated facilities.

Medical care.—This is the third type of direct service which many public welfare departments undertake to provide. The whole question of community responsibility for medical care is marked by considerable confusion. Prior to the depression:

Medical relief consisted as a rule of provisions made for the sick poor by small annual part-time stipends paid to city and county physicians and by hospital care at public expense. Public hospitals were rare, outside of the large cities. In the smaller communities, local governments provided a minimum amount of hospitalization for the poor in private hospitals, usually by paying for their care on a per capita per diem basis.[21]

Public welfare departments had little part in this program because there were very few of them in existence.

The great expansion in assistance programs during the thirties confronted public welfare administration with the importance of doing something about the medical needs, not only of families on the assistance rolls, but also of families who were "medically indigent," to use the phrase coined to describe those who could provide their own food, clothes, and shelter, but needed money for emergency medical expenses. As a result, public welfare agencies initiated a variety of undertakings to meet this need. According to a report issued by the American Public Welfare Association in 1938, welfare departments even then were accepting "wide responsibilities for administering medical care," and the consequent confusion, overlapping, and duplication of functions among the several governmental authorities active in this field, at both the state and local levels, were causing welfare administrators to regard medical care as "the worst headache of all." [22]

[21] National Resources Planning Board, *Security, Work and Relief Policies,* 1942, p. 27.
[22] American Public Welfare Association, *Report of the Committee on Medical Care,* pp. 9-13.

The actual responsibility taken by welfare departments for medical care at present runs the gamut from the operation of a complete program, including general hospital, outpatient service, and salaried physicians' service for home and office care, to practically no program at all. As might be expected, the more substantial programs are found in the states with the greatest resources and then usually in the larger cities. It is hoped that greater uniformity will result from federal participation in expenditures for medical care to assistance recipients, as authorized by the Social Security Act Amendments of 1950. Medical costs, however, must be included within the maximums on individual payments, and the new provision can have little practical effect except where present assistance expenditures are below the maximums.

For the country as a whole, public welfare responsibility for medical care is still almost as uneven and confused as it was in 1938. Nevertheless, we can distinguish several general types of policy followed when welfare departments assume some responsibility in this area. First, they may administer a medical service for needy people in any one of several ways. The department itself may operate a public hospital, with an outpatient service, or it may employ physicians to give medical service to those who are on the assistance rolls and perhaps also to others, or it may operate a clinic apart from a hospital, for the same purpose. Second, the department may pay all or part of the hospital and medical costs for any person on its assistance rolls. Also, although we believe this practice is less common, it may pay a physician's charge for service in the home. Third, the department may pay the same costs for people not in need of food, clothes, and shelter who are found to be "medically indigent." As a matter of general community policy, we believe it unwise for a public welfare department to operate direct medical services, that is, to administer hospitals or clinics or to employ a corps of physicians.

For reasons which are developed in greater detail in the section on ill-health, we believe it is a sound community policy for the public welfare department to meet the actual hospital costs both of assistance cases and medically indigent cases. Public welfare departments even in the richer states seldom pay full hospital costs. In poorer states this principle is admittedly unrealistic. Nevertheless, by diverse, confusing, and often inefficient methods our communities do pay the hospital costs of people presumed to be unable to pay for their own hospitalization. And it is only when the public welfare department determines need for assistance in meeting hospital costs that some measure of uniformity and order enters into the judgment of who is needy and who is not. It is only by centralizing the responsibility for such costs that the community can know what they actually amount to, and hence can adopt an intelligible fiscal policy in relation to them. In the last analysis, it is the community's dollar which is spent —whether the policy is intelligible or not.

Any community-wide program for the prevention and reduction of the residual dependency load must be built on certain basic services, including diagnostic and treatment services by caseworkers, foster home facilities, and diagnostic and treatment services by physicians with the aid of hospital and clinic facilities. To the extent that public welfare assumes leadership in designing and implementing any such program, it also must take as much responsibility as may be practical for assuring that these basic services are reasonably available. But we regard as mistaken any long-range view which assumes that money to provide these services can be substituted for a community plan to focus them at the strategic points dictated by the community-wide characteristics of the problem.

Chapter VI

PROTECTION BY INSURANCE

AS WE HAVE NOTED, the idea that the community (actually, the national community) should insure itself against dependency is relatively very new. A better understanding of our modern industrial economy, and of the hazards to self-maintenance which it creates, led to a revolt against the deeply embedded notion that man, as the sole arbiter of his economic fortunes, must accept entire responsibility for his economic failures.

The idea of comprehensive social insurance was born out of this new understanding. In allocating responsibility for financing, all our present systems of public insurance give the industrial economy a share at least equal to that borne by the insured individual. Except in two states all the financial burden for unemployment insurance is borne by the employer. All the state plans for workmen's compensation put the entire financial responsibility upon industry. In the case of veterans, a proper sense of patriotic obligation places complete financial responsibility upon the treasury of their employer—the federal government.

We have noted also that the application of the insurance idea in this country is of recent origin. It did not take substantial hold until the middle thirties, when the imperfections of the national economy became very evident and their disastrous consequences to the individual created profound anxiety in the public mind. Only workmen's and veterans' compensation preceded the several plans promulgated into legislative action by the impetus of the depression.

A considerable patchwork of insurance plans and devices results from the legislation enacted to date. Together, however, our existing programs are designed to protect a portion of the people against some of the hazards accruing from an imperfect economy and against some which arise from personal disabilities.

INSURANCE AND COMPENSATION SYSTEMS

It is not the purpose of this volume to delve deeply into questions of administration. Nevertheless, an understanding of the objectives and the principal methods of the present systems is essential to the formation of public policy. One may predict with confidence that issues regarding the extension and reorganization of the insurance systems will be matters of public thought and debate for many years to come.

OLD AGE AND SURVIVORS INSURANCE

The Old Age and Survivors Insurance program (OASI), as we have noted, is designed to provide retirement payments to workers, and their wives, who have reached the age of 65, and to the survivors of workers, regardless of their age at death. It is a wholly national system, uniform in all its policies, administered by the Bureau of Old Age and Survivors Insurance of the Federal Security Agency.

OASI covers well over half of the employed workers of the country—since January 1, 1951, an estimated 45 million of a labor force of over 60 million. The principal groups not covered are certain agricultural and domestic workers, railroad workers, and the rural and professional self-employed. Two million workers in nonprofit undertakings and public employees, formerly excluded, now may elect to come under the program.[1]

Money to finance OASI is collected by the Bureau of Internal Revenue in the form of a contributory tax on each worker's wages (up to an annual wage of $3,600) shared equally by the employer and the worker. Until 1950 the combined tax was 2 percent of the wages earned. It is now 3 percent and is to be increased gradually, to 4 percent in 1954 and finally to 6½ percent in 1970. The contribution of self-employed workers will start at 2¼ percent in 1951 and reach 4⅞ percent in 1970.[2]

Benefit payments are related to the previous monthly wage, although they are proportionately higher for lower paid workers and are further modified by the number of eligible dependents. (A new

[1] *Social Legislation Information Service Bulletin,* 81st Congress, Issue No. 85, September 11, 1950.
[2] *Ibid.*

formula to increase benefits for those retiring in the future will go into effect in May, 1952.) The maximum family payment allowed prior to the amendments of 1950 was $85 per month and average payments have run considerably lower. In 1948 the payments averaged $24.40 per month for a single person, $39.90 per month for a couple, and $52.60 per month for a mother with three or more dependent children.[3] The 1950 amendments provide an average increase in benefits of 77½ percent, with the lowest benefits doubled and the highest raised by 50 percent. The new maximum payment per family is now $150.

OASI is administered through six area offices and almost five hundred field offices. Consequently, there is likely to be a field office in almost every urban community of any size. The principal function of a local office is to handle the routines of administration. It assigns social security numbers, aids workers and employers in correcting wage records, assists workers and their survivors in filing claims, makes determinations as to entitlement, and in general serves as an information center on all matters relating to the program.

UNEMPLOYMENT INSURANCE

This program, also inaugurated by the Federal Security Act of 1935, is designed to provide payments to workers who suffer income loss through unemployment. It is a federal-state system (known as a "tax-offset" plan) which recognizes state plans if these meet federal specifications. To be certified, a state law must provide that:

1. All compensation be paid through public employment offices.

2. Contributions to the state unemployment fund, that is, the monies collected through state unemployment taxes, shall immediately be transferred to the Federal Unemploymnt Trust Fund.

3. Money withdrawn from the Unemployment Trust Fund shall be used only for the payment of benefits.

4. Benefits shall not be denied to otherwise eligible persons for refusing to accept work in vacancies due to labor disputes; where wages or working conditions are substantially below those prevailing in the locality; or where membership in a union is prohibited as a condition of employment.

[3] "Current Operating Statistics," *Social Security Bulletin*, XI, No. 10 (October, 1948), p. 24, Table 8.

The federal government pays the entire cost of administering these state programs and thus maintains a further measure of control over them. Money for this purpose comes from the general fund of the Treasury and is supplied by the remaining 10 percent of the original federal tax (0.3 percent of the taxable pay roll) which is collected by the Bureau of Internal Revenue.

The employer not only pays this federal tax, but almost everywhere he pays the entire state tax as well. In only two states (Alabama and New Jersey) is there provision for joint employer-employee payments such as are made for OASI. We should note, however, that the Senate Advisory Council on Social Security has recommended equal payments by employers and employees. The Council points out that among other advantages which would accrue, such an arrangement would "make employees more responsible in their demands for higher benefits. . . ." [4]

Unemployment compensation covers much the same types of workers as OASI did prior to the 1950 amendments, but the unemployment coverage is further restricted because the majority of state laws limit it to firms with a certain minimum number of employees. In January, 1950, 33 million workers out of an estimated labor force of over 60 million were in covered industries.[5]

Benefit payments depend on earnings during a "base period," prior to loss of the job—usually four quarters. Minimum payments vary from fifty cents to $15 per week, with $5 the most common provision. Maximums vary from $15 to $27,[6] with 41 states paying a maximum weekly benefit of $20 or more.[7] In January, 1950, the average weekly payment for the country as a whole was $21.17 and individual state averages ranged from $13.89 in Florida to $24.63 in Michigan, and $25.61 in Alaska.[8]

Each state fixes a maximum duration for the payment of benefits during a single year. This ranges from 19 to 26½ weeks under various

4 Eveline M. Burns, *The American Social Security System*, p. 155.

5 "Selected Current Statistics," *Social Security Bulletin*, XIII, No. 4 (April, 1950), p. 2.

6 William H. Wandel, "Insurance Against Unemployment in the United States," *Monthly Labor Review*, LXX, No. 1 (January, 1950), pp. 10–11.

7 Senate Advisory Committee on Social Security, "Unemployment Insurance: Recommendations of the Senate Advisory Council," *Social Security Bulletin*, XII, No. 1 (January, 1949), 16.

8 "Current Operating Statistics," *ibid.*, XIII, No. 4 (April, 1950), 28, Table 12.

plans, but in 1948 it was 20 weeks or more in 40 states and territories.[9] Eleven states permit additional allowances for dependents.

In three states—Rhode Island, California, and New Jersey—the unemployment insurance system has been used as a base for state programs of temporary disability or sickness insurance. In these plans the disability program is under the same state administrative agency as unemployment insurance, with identical coverage and the same general pattern as to eligibility and benefits. New York State, on the other hand, has made a different type of provision for temporary disability insurance, by placing it under the state workmen's compensation agency. All plans provide for employee contributions to finance the disability program, and these are supplemented by employer contributions in two states.

Every community is served by a local public employment office as part of what is now a state public employment system. This office receives applications for unemployment insurance and transmits them to the state agency administering the insurance program. The degree of administrative responsibility taken by the local office varies from state to state, although at present there is a strong trend toward making it completely responsible for decisions on eligibility and qualifications. In a few states the local office actually makes benefit payments also, but in most cases these are mailed from the state headquarters. In addition, the local public employment service is responsible for assisting the recipients of unemployment benefits to find new jobs.

INSURANCE FOR RAILROAD WORKERS

Original efforts of railroad workers to secure compulsory retirement annuities antedate the passage of other social security legislation. However, the first law enacted for their benefit—that of 1934— was declared unconstitutional by the Supreme Court, and the present Railroad Retirement Act dates from 1935. The Railroad Unemployment Act was passed in 1938. It is estimated that currently about 1,600,000 employees are covered by the railroad insurances, although a much larger number of former railroad workers have credits accrued to them.

[9] Senate Advisory Committee on Social Security, "Unemployment Insurance: Recommendations of the Senate Advisory Council," p. 16.

This is a wholly federal system, administered by the Railroad Retirement Board with headquarters in Chicago. In addition to its independent administration, we may note two other differences between this system and that set up originally under the Social Security Act. The first was in the size of retirement benefits. In January, 1950, some 242,500 persons were receiving an average monthly grant of $82.87,[10] only about $2 less than the maximum allowed under OASI prior to the 1950 amendments. As a consequence, railroad employers and employees each pay 6 percent of wages earned to finance the plan, and this amount is to be increased to 6¼ percent in 1952. The employer also makes an additional contribution for unemployment insurance.

The second difference is that the Railroad Retirement Act under certain circumstances provides payments to persons who are unable to continue working because of permanent disability. Eligibility depends on age, length of service, and current connection with the industry. The unemployment plan also provides payments to persons who are out of work because of sickness.

In any rail center there probably will be one of the 95 district or branch offices of the Railroad Retirement Board, which is administered through nine regional offices. Otherwise, local railroad employees must rely on part-time service supplied by the Board for help in making applications, filing claims, and so on. This process, which varies somewhat with the type of benefit, has been summarized as follows:

Unemployment applications are filed initially with a railroad officer designated as a claims agent. The application is forwarded to the appropriate regional office for determination of the claimant's eligibility for benefits and benefit rate. . . . Sickness applications and claims are mailed directly by the claimants to the regional office. Death and retirement claims may be filed at any Board office, but are adjudicated at the Headquarters Office, where the wage records are maintained.[11]

WORKMEN'S COMPENSATION

All states and territories have laws providing for compensating payments to workers injured in the course of their employment, or to

10 "Current Operating Statistics," *Social Security Bulletin*, XIII, No. 4 (April, 1950), 20, Table 1.
11 Burns, *op. cit.*, pp. 261–62.

their survivors if they are killed. These laws and the provision for their administration represent the first forms of public social insurance or compensatory payments to be introduced in this country. Prior to their passage, an employee could not collect damages unless he could prove in court that his employer had been negligent—a difficult and costly procedure beyond the resources of most workmen. By 1930, all but four states had compensation laws—usually administered by state industrial accident boards including representatives both of employers and of labor.

From its inception, workmen's compensation has been entirely a state system. State plans vary greatly in the occupations covered; in the compulsion upon employers to take out insurance; in the methods by which such insurance is handled—whether by private companies or by state funds; in the scale of compensation allowed for various injuries; in the methods of payment and adjudication of claims.

The most recent estimates available indicate that about 41 million workers [12] probably are covered in some manner by workmen's compensation, and annual payments for compensation and medical benefits are estimated at $536 million.[13] Payments in individual cases vary greatly from state to state and according to the type of injury. Maximum payments for disability, however, run from $20 to $25 per week, and minimum payments range from $3 to $18. Death benefits depend upon the survivor's status. Where aggregate maximum amounts for death benefits have been fixed, the payments range from $3,500 (Puerto Rico) to $12,000 (Missouri).[14]

One thing this state system has accomplished, or at least helped to accomplish, is the reduction of industrial accidents. It is significant that the private insurance companies carrying workmen's compensation insurance were among the principal sponsors of the National Safety Council.[15]

[12] *Ibid.,* p. 187.

[13] "Extent of Workmen's Compensation in the United States," *Monthly Labor Review,* LXXI, No. 4 (October,. 1950), 487.

[14] V. A. Zimmer, *State Workmen's Compensation Laws as of June 1, 1946,* Bulletin No. 78, Division of Labor Standards, 13, 30. See also Alfred Acee, "State Workmen's Compensation Legislation in 1947," *Monthly Labor Review,* LXV, No. 4 (October, 1947), 417; and, by the same author, "Workmen's Compensation Legislation, 1948," *Monthly Labor Review,* LXVII, No. 3 (September, 1948), 280.

[15] Burns, *op. cit.,* p. 205.

Unless the local community happens to be the state capital it probably will have no office of the state workmen's compensation agency. Hearings on compensation cases will be held in the locality either regularly or from time to time. The local physicians who provide the medical aid (now available to injured workers in all states) will be selected in one of the following ways: (1) by the employer or by the insurance company; (2) by the employee from a panel made up by the employer or the insurance company; (3) by the employee from a panel made up by the compensation agency and the local medical society; (4) by the employee's free choice. The Bureau of Labor Statistics reports that compensation agencies rarely have sufficient staff to devote adequate time to the medical aid aspects.

VETERANS COMPENSATION, PENSIONS, AND INSURANCE

Veterans who were employed in the armed forces during the First and the Second World Wars, during other wars, or between wars are the final group for whom the federal government provides protection against income loss. Benefits are of two types: compensation and pensions to which the beneficiaries have made no contribution; and government life insurance which covers only those veterans who agree to pay premiums.

It is estimated that in 1951 a total of 3,057,000 individuals and families will receive noncontributory benefits. The annual cost of this program, financed as part of the federal general budget, exceeds $2 billion. Annual expenditures for life insurance benefits account for another $400 million, but only $39 million of this amount is a charge against the government.[16]

A further word about these programs will clarify the differences and distinctions between them:

1. Compensation, by far the most important, is paid to a veteran in the event of a service-connected disability of more than 10 percent and to his survivors in case of a service-connected death. The present recipients number about 1,981,000 veterans and 344,000 surviving families.[17]

Payments are made as long as the disability exists and range from $13.80 per month for a 10 percent disability to $138 for total disability, with fixed additional amounts for such conditions as blind-

[16] New York *Times,* January 10, 1950, p. 21.   [17] *Ibid.*

ness or anatomical losses, and allowances for dependents in very serious cases.[18] In 1948 the average monthly payment for all Second World War cases was $39.50.[19] The amounts paid to survivors vary with the number and dependency status—$75 a month for a widow alone, $100 for a widow and one child; and so on.

2. Pensions totaling over $500 million now are going to some 732,-000 cases, two thirds of them living veterans and one third of them survivors. The term *pension* refers only to war service. As applied to the two world wars, it includes only amounts paid (1) to the dependents of deceased veterans whose death was not traceable to service-connected causes; and (2) to disabled ex-servicemen whose disability similarly is not service connected. In the latter case the man must be permanently and totally disabled, must meet certain requirements as to length of military service, and cannot have an income in excess of $1,000 per year if he is single, or of $2,500 if he has a wife and/or minor child. In the case of death, only the widow and children are eligible for pensions, the same limitations apply, and there are certain other qualifying conditions. Disability pensions start at $60 per month and are increased to $72 after ten years or when the recipient reaches the age of 65. Survivor pensions, which are lower than comparable compensation payments, vary with the number of survivors and with their relationship to the deceased.

Because of the present availability of other governmental security programs there is increasing question as to the desirability of making these "means test" payments to veterans for nonservice-connected causes. The plan, a sound one when first adopted for veterans of the First World War, was intended to forestall efforts of veterans' organizations to get pensions for all ex-soldiers, their widows and children, regardless of need, as similar pressure groups had done after earlier wars. In view of the new responsibilities the government has assumed for all types of people, the logical course seems to be the one recommended by President Truman in his budget message to Congress in January, 1950: "Our objective," said the President, "should be to make our social security system more comprehensive in coverage and more adequate. . . . We should provide through the veterans' pro-

[18] American National Red Cross, *Handbook of Information Concerning Servicemen and Veterans* (rev., September, 1947), Paragraph 1122, p. 11–9 (this page dated 10–8–48).

[19] Administrator of Veterans Affairs, *Annual Report for Fiscal Year Ending June 20, 1948*, p. 37.

grams only for the special and unique needs of veterans arising directly from military service." [20]

3. During both world wars the government enabled servicemen to purchase life insurance which covered them during the war and later was convertible to one of the standard forms of insurance. Both of these insurance plans provide benefits for death and for permanent total disability. The holders pay premiums, but the cost is less than for private insurance because the government pays all administrative expenses and assumes the special hazards of military service. Many men allowed these policies to lapse when they left the service, but there were 6,800,000 active policies in the two systems as of January, 1950.[21] Both systems are now on a dividend-paying basis.

4. One further veterans' program deserves mention, although it is scheduled to end on July 25, 1952. This is a system of federally financed unemployment compensation for veterans of the Second World War. It provides $20 for each week of unemployment up to 52 weeks occurring within two years after discharge or release from service, or after July 25, 1947—whichever is later. There are similar provisions for self-employed veterans whose net earnings fall below $100 a month. In this case, the amount of the monthly benefit equals the difference between actual earnings and $100 and is payable for a maximum period of 10.4 months. The Veterans Administration, though financially and administratively responsible for this program, has arranged to have the local public employment offices handle and pay claims in the unemployment cases.

The number of beneficiaries of the two unemployment compensation programs, which averaged 1.5 million a week in 1946,[22] had dropped to 67,300 in January, 1950,[23] and is expected to fall to an average of 59,000 during the fiscal year ending June 30, 1951.[24]

In 1948, according to the annual report of the Veterans Administration, full-time contact representatives were assigned at 781 locations, while itinerant contact service was given at 1,659 locations.[25] This means that even though a community may not be the seat of one of the VA's 70 regional offices, it almost certainly will have a field

[20] New York *Times*, January 10, 1950, p. 21.
[21] *Ibid.*   [22] Burns, *op. cit.*, p. 373.
[23] "Current Operating Statistics," *Social Security Bulletin*, XIII, No. 4 (April, 1950), 20, Table 1.
[24] New York *Times*, January 10, 1951, p. 21.
[25] Administrator of Veterans Affairs, *Annual Report, 1948*, p. 105.

office or contact representative to furnish information and assist veterans and their dependents in the preparation, development, and
presentation of claims. Whether or not the local office performs other
functions will depend upon its size and personnel. An office may have
a medical staff and conduct one or more clinics, but more likely it
will arrange for examination and treatment by local "fee-designate"
physicians and dentists, and perhaps for home nursing service by the
local visiting nurse association. Associated with the medical service
is a medical social work staff, working under the direction of the
regional office. A member of this staff may be assigned to a particular
local office or may visit it only periodically.

GAPS AND DUPLICATIONS

He who runs may read quite easily that the present pieces of our
insurance system do not fit together logically in terms of risks insured,
groups covered, type of administration, or method of financing.

The majority of those now covered by OASI are covered also for
unemployment; a somewhat smaller number, for industrial injuries;
and a few who happen to live in certain states, for temporary disability. Railroad employees are covered for everything except industrial
accidents. Some governmental employees, particularly those who
work for the federal government, have a fairly complete security system of their own; others are entitled to more restricted benefits under a variety of state and local plans; and still others are without any
coverage. A fairly large segment of the working population, including the professional and rural self-employed, most agricultural workers, and some domestic servants, still has no protection against any
risks. Veterans entitled to special benefits for nonservice-connected
causes are scattered throughout all types of employment.

Before the 1950 amendments were passed, people used to shuttle
back and forth between covered and noncovered employment, and
they are still likely to go from one program to another. This is one
explanation for the fact that while 80 million living workers (or
former workers) had some credits under the OASI program in 1949,
only 44 million were eligible for benefits.[26]

The 1947 report of the Social Security Administration gives a

[26] A. J. Altmeyer, "Old Age, Survivors and Disability Insurance," *Social Security Bulletin*, XII, No. 4 (April, 1949), 5.

good description of the practical effects of the illogical and duplicating setup:

It would be possible for an individual to work at some time during the course of his working life in jobs covered by Federal Old Age and Survivors Insurance, the Railroad Retirement Act, the Civil Service Retirement Act and the retirement plan of a state or locality. According to the length and timing of such employments he might become eligible to receive retirement benefits under one or more or all of these plans. Another man, with similar earnings under several of the programs, may go through a working life without ever acquiring retirement rights under any. Conceivably the survivors of a worker who dies might be eligible for benefits under the Federal Old Age and Survivors Insurance system as well as under a State Workmen's Compensation law and under general veterans legislation. Another family equally in need of income to replace the father's earnings may have had no opportunity to gain protection.[27]

A further inequity results from the fact that persons leaving employment covered by OASI before they have acquired fully insured status lose their contributions unless they subsequently return to a covered job. Their money, however, helps to pay benefits to the family of a man who dies after a relatively brief period in covered employment.

In view of the existing confusion, it is not surprising that the insurance experts of the Social Security Administration advocate a comprehensive basic national system of contributory insurance. This basic program, covering all major risks, would be designed:

to provide a consistent relationship, not only among the insurance provisions for the various risks covered but also between the provisions of the basic system and those of supplementary special systems in effect for particular groups. As compared with separate programs to meet particular risks, such a comprehensive system would reduce administrative costs and reporting burdens and simplify arrangements as they affect workers, employers, and public agencies.[28]

CONFLICTING OBJECTIVES

The fact is that until the amendments of 1950, the only change which Congress had been willing to make in the original Act of 1935

27 *Annual Report of the Federal Security Agency, Section I Social Security Administration, for the fiscal year 1947*, p. 7.

28 "A Comprehensive Social Security Program," *Social Security Bulletin*, XIII, Nos. 1–2 (January–February, 1950), 4.

was the addition of survivors as beneficiaries in OASI. The changes made in 1950 extended insurance against old age to certain previously uninsured groups and increased the specific benefits. The new legislation did not include coverage against other hazards, and it can hardly be said to lay the foundation for "a comprehensive basic national system covering all major risks." Although the amendments of 1950 ultimately were passed by large majorities in both Houses of Congress, drastic changes were made in the original proposals, and there is still a great conflict of opinion over the ultimate course which the country's insurance policy should take. The sources of this conflict are many, but in our opinion one important contributing factor is a lack of clarity about the proper objectives for any such comprehensive public insurance system as that proposed by the Social Security Administration.

REDUCTION OF THE ASSISTANCE LOAD

As articulated in these terms for the Finance Committee of the United States Senate, by its Advisory Council on Social Security:

Our goal is, so far as possible, to prevent dependency through social insurance and thus greatly reduce the need for assistance. . . . The Council looks forward . . . to the time when virtually all persons in the United States will have retirement or survivorship protection under the old age and survivors insurance program. If insurance benefits are of reasonable amount, public assistance will then be necessary only for those aged persons and survivors with unusual needs and for those few who . . . have been unable to earn insurance rights through work.[29]

Only since 1939 have unemployment benefits been payable everywhere. OASI began paying benefits in 1940, but the proportion of persons sixty-five and over who are insured is much smaller than it will be after an entire generation has lived out its working life under the program.

The past ten years have not subjected the system to any serious test of its capacity to prevent the need for assistance. High employment was the rule during practically the entire period, while the war inevitably was accompanied by serious labor shortages. Less than in almost any other decade of the twentieth century was there need for

[29] Advisory Council on Social Security, "Proposed Changes in Old-Age and Survivors Insurance," *Social Security Bulletin*, XI, No. 5 (May, 1948), 22.

protection against the risk of unemployment, or against the employment handicaps of old age.

Nevertheless, OASI and unemployment insurance cover more than half of the people in most communities, and they have been paying benefits for the past ten years. It should be possible to make some deductions regarding the effect which such payments have had upon the need for assistance. Unfortunately, no one has devised a method to measure precisely—or to estimate systematically—the degree to which the insurance systems are preventing, or controlling, the dependency rate. To do this, data would have to be kept continuously over a period of time, and related both to the proportion of the population covered by all the insurances, and to the proportion currently receiving payments.

On these points, the St. Paul data were inconclusive, and in any case the project covered only a single month. However, they did tend to show that only a very small proportion of the families who were dependent in November, 1948, were receiving, had previously received, or had applications pending for any type of social insurance. It was not possible to compare the insured and noninsured dependent people with the number of workers in covered and uncovered employment because, as we have pointed out, the insurance systems do not make these latter data available for community use.

A recent national inquiry as to the overlapping between OASI on the one hand and OAA and ADC on the other showed that only 6 percent of all OAA recipients were also in receipt of OASI benefits, and less than 5 percent of the ADC families were currently receiving the two types of payment.[30] Like our St. Paul data, the results seem to indicate that the bulk of the families who make up the assistance loads in these two categories are outside the coverage of the present insurance systems.

The Social Security Administration also makes certain deductions by comparing the industrial states where a majority of the labor force has insurance coverage with the agricultural states where they do not. Such comparisons show that the agricultural states have a much higher proportion of their aged population on OAA than do

---

[30] Bureau of Public Assistance, "Public Assistance Supplementation of the Income of Old Age and Survivors Insurance Beneficiaries," *Social Security Bulletin*, XII, No. 10 (October, 1949), 13, 18.

the industrial states, whereas exactly the reverse is true of OASI beneficiaries.

For the country over, the number of aged people receiving assistance in 1950 still exceeded by several hundred thousand those receiving insurance benefits. But whereas the number receiving assistance had remained fairly static (between 20 and 24 percent of the aged population during the period 1940–48), in many of the industrial states the proportion of aged people receiving assistance had decreased as the proportion receiving OASI payments increased (16 percent for the country as a whole in February, 1950).[31] In New York, New Jersey, Connecticut, Delaware, Maryland, the District of Columbia, and Virginia, aged assistance recipients made up less than 10 percent of the aged population in December, 1948, and they were outnumbered by insurance beneficiaries here as well as in several other states. On the other hand, in 27 states, most of them predominantly agricultural, assistance recipients were at least twice as numerous as insurance beneficiaries, and in eight states they made up over 40 percent of the aged population.[32] It is to be expected, however, that the present ratio between assistance and insurance recipients will be reversed in the years immediately ahead, because the 1950 legislation liberalized eligibility requirements for insured status on the part of elderly workers. An estimated 500,000 additional persons will be eligible for benefits in the first year of operation under the new program. In introducing the final compromise bill in the Senate, Senator Walter F. George pointed out that under its provisions OASI beneficiaries of all types would exceed 7 million by 1960.[33]

OASI pays benefits in the event an insured worker dies and leaves children under 18 years of age. In this respect the program corresponds to the assistance program of ADC, although the latter also makes payments to families whose breadwinner is incapacitated or absent because of desertion or institutionalization. Again, in the industrial states the insurance program carries a higher proportion of the total load, whereas ADC rates in many of these states are relatively low.

These comparisons show that, if we spend for insurance, we need

[31] *Social Legislation Information Service Bulletin,* Issue No. 56, February 27, 1950.
[32] *Social Security Act Amendments of 1949, Hearings Before the Committee on Ways and Means, House of Representatives, 81st Congress,* on H.R. 2893, pp. 56, 1171.
[33] New York *Times,* August 18, 1950, pp. 1, 14.

to spend less for assistance. But they leave considerable doubt about the ratio between the two rates of spending and the precise effect which increasing the cost of insurance will have upon lowering the cost of assistance. For example, in 1949 OASI and the Railroad Retirement Board together paid out nearly a billion dollars in benefits.[34] It seems certain that even a uniformly high standard of "determined need" would not have resulted in increased assistance expenditures at all commensurate with this amount if no insurance payments had been made.

It is even more difficult to relate the cost of unemployment insurance to expenditures for general assistance. During 1949, when unemployment averaged 3.4 million in contrast to the 2 million of the previous year, an estimated 7.2 million workers received benefits, at a cost of $1.7 billion,[35] more than double the amount spent in 1948. By the end of 1949, general assistance loads were climbing; cases in December, 1949, numbered 562,000 compared with 397,000 at the end of 1948. The statistics for 1949 as a whole show that most of the workers received payments for only about twelve weeks and that only a third of them completely exhausted their benefits.[36] But how many of the 7.2 million would have applied for assistance had there been no insurance program we have no way of knowing.

The data from the St. Paul project suggest another reason for devising a means to get more precise information about the degree to which present insurance payments are preventing dependency. We have seen that in a month of high employment the residual dependency load was made up very largely of families whose life was complicated by chronic illness, physical handicaps, mental illness, mental defect, emotional problems, and behavior disorders.

Such a group of families were least able to manage for themselves on the income provided by our present insurance payments, and least likely to have supplementary resources. We know that very few of these families were receiving any insurance payments, presumably because they were not covered by the present system. We admit frankly that we do not know whether, or to what extent, insurance would have prevented them from ultimately becoming a responsibility of the public assistance agency.

[34] "Current Operating Statistics," *Social Security Bulletin*, XIII, No. 3 (March, 1950), 19, Table 1.
[35] "1949 in Review," *ibid.*, p. 1.   [36] *Ibid.*

Thus the available evidence about the degree to which insurance accomplishes the objective of the Advisory Council on Social Security tells us little more than one might deduce by means of ordinary common sense: insurance against loss of income undoubtedly does reduce the need for assistance. But insurance is an expensive way to accomplish this objective. Indeed, another agency of the federal government, the National Resources Planning Board, although advocating better insurance coverage, came to this same conclusion about ten years ago:

Financially also, the risks of making any specific sum of money generally available as a right, with no test of need, are considerable. For, if the sum is to be large enough to provide basic security for those with no private resources, it will be more than is necessary for those with resources of some kind. Total expenditures will inevitably be much greater than if payments were graduated according to need.[37]

A GUARANTEED MINIMUM STANDARD OF LIVING

Of a different nature is the objective of the present British social security plan. As we have seen, this country throughout its history has tended to follow England in respect both to relief and insurance. Fear that it will continue to do so, to the ultimate socialization of our economy, is one source of present confusion.

The first thing one should know about the plan adopted by Great Britain after the Second World War is that it is complete.[38] It assumes responsibility for the full range of consequences of living: unemployment, sickness, disability, maternity and the economic burdens of parenthood, old age, death, and the ultimate need for assistance. Governmental measures cover everybody in Great Britain—the employed, the self-employed, and the non-employed—without regard to title or address. The second thing one should know is that the present plan consolidates into a single system under a single Ministry (of National

---

[37] National Resources Planning Board, *After the War—toward Security*, p. 25.

[38] For a detailed description of the various phases of the British program see John G. Hill, "Great Britain's New Social Security," *Survey Midmonthly*, LXXXIV, No. 8, 243–45; Elva Marquard, "Dependents in Social Security Systems of Great Britain, New Zealand, Australia, and Canada," *Social Security Bulletin*, XI, No. 9 (September, 1948), 3–15; John Moss, "The New English National Assistance Scheme," *Social Service Review*, XXII, No. 2 (June, 1947), 194–98; Carl Farman and Catherine Perrins, "The New British System of Social Security," *Social Security Bulletin*, X, No. 2 (June, 1947), 9–22; and John S. Morgan, "Some Recent Developments in Social Service in Great Britain," *ibid.*, No. 6 (February, 1947), 3–10.

Insurance) all the insurance programs which England had previously built up. This same Ministry is responsible for all assistance payments. The assistance program, known as National Assistance, is a single, consolidated program with but one standard of need and eligibility.

The employee pays a flat weekly amount, which varies with the age and sex of the contributor but is *not* related to his income. This single payment constitutes the individual's contribution to the entire system and entitles him to all the various types of benefits.

The employer pays a flat weekly amount for each employee, and the government supplements every contribution. In other words, this is not an employer-employee "actuarial" system but one which must be subsidized from general taxation.

Two important parts of the plan bear no relation to "insurance" as we customarily think of it. A sick worker not only is insured against income loss, but also receives without cost whatever health care he needs. Free medical, dental, optical, surgical, and hospital services (and in some cases even home nursing care and domestic help) are available to everyone. The government also makes to every family with more than one child under 15 years of age a weekly cash payment of five shillings (seventy cents) for each child after the first.

The most important thing to know about the British plan is that its objective is not to reduce the need for assistance, nor is the plan intended primarily to insure people against specific and particular risks. Its aim is to guarantee a minimum standard of living to everyone in Great Britain.

This aim is stated clearly in the following excerpts from Sir William Beveridge's report on "Social Insurance and Allied Services":

The aim of the Plan for Social Security is to abolish want by ensuring that every citizen willing to serve according to his powers has at all times an income sufficient to meet his responsibilities. . . . Want could have been abolished before the present war by a redistribution of income within the wage earning classes. . . . The plan for Social Security is first and foremost a method of redistributing income, so as to put the most urgent needs first, so as to make the best possible use of whatever resources are available. That is worth doing even if the resources as a whole are insufficient for the standard of life that is desired.[39]

The actual measures adopted in Great Britain fell short of this intent in at least two important respects: they made insurance pay-

[39] Sir William Beveridge, *Social Insurance and Allied Services*, pp. 165, 176.

ments per se too low to assure complete freedom from want, and they thereby gave the assistance program a larger place in the program than Sir William and his committee had advocated. There is no doubt that in spite of these modifications the British system still recognizes that its primary objective is to guarantee such a distribution of the national income as will raise permanently the standard of living, as expressed in money, of the lower income and marginal income population. Given that objective, a complete plan, covering everybody and including a subsidized health service and a family allowance system, becomes a logical necessity.

An understanding of this objective helps to explain an apparent paradox of the British plan, or of any plan which approaches such a measure of completeness. For while the financing of the plan at the desired living standard is conditioned upon the maintenance of maximum production and full employment, this is precisely the economic circumstance in which the need for protection against dependence upon the community is reduced to a minimum.

THE EXTENSION OF PROTECTION

The desire to protect people through insurance against specific hazards, may provide its own justification and need not be related to any ulterior objective. An extraordinary number of people in this country buy insurance. They buy it to protect themselves against loss by fire, storm, theft, accidents, and so on. They buy it to protect others who are dependent on them or toward whom they have economic responsibilities. This purchase of protection does not guarantee anything except a specified sum of money in hand. The amount depends upon what the responsible participants in the hazard are willing and able to pay for such protection.

It seems to us that the adoption of our present governmental insurance schemes has been grounded in the public acceptance of this concept of purchasing future protection. Except for veterans' compensation, which is a special case, all the present programs are paid for, or in effect purchased, by the parties who have responsibility for the hazards of income loss. None of the programs is subsidized from general tax funds, although some experts hold that OASI eventually should have a governmental subsidy, and in 1943 Congress actually passed an amendment authorizing appropriations from general revenues to the OASI Trust Fund, if that step should prove necessary. However, no such appropriation had to be made, the authorization was deleted from the Social Security Act in 1950, and the whole program is now on what it is hoped will be a paying basis. While we may lay small claim to prophetic vision, we are inclined to regard the rescinding of this authorization as indicative of the temper of Congressional opinion for some time to come. It seems to us that adoption of further governmental insurance programs will be grounded in the acceptance of this objective of buying protection and will depend in large measure on the willingness and ability of the responsible participants in the hazard to pay the costs.

Twentieth-century thought has brought us to see that the responsible participants in the hazard of income loss are employers and employees. It is beyond either our purpose or our capacity to attempt to reconcile conflicting opinions about the amount which our productive economy (in which both these parties have a considerable stake) can afford to pay for protection against this hazard. But it seems to us entirely natural that there should be conflict and controversy between the two interested parties as to their respective willingness and ability to pay. In our political system, these conflicts are reflected and ultimately composed by the Congress. There, after prolonged hearing and debate, a bill was passed by both Houses and signed by the President in the summer of 1950, covering both insurance and assistance. This bill (H.R. 6000) provided for somewhat more restricted old age and survivor coverage, excluded self-employed farm labor, but extended insurance benefits to some 11 million persons not covered under the old program. It increased the wage base and authorized a higher scale of benefits. Disability insurance was limited to protection against permanent total disability.

One powerful influence behind the increase in old age benefits was the pattern of industrial retirement plans negotiated by the Congress of Industrial Organizations during the summer and fall of 1949. These plans all called for retirement annuities paid entirely by the employer, usually at the rate of $100 a month, toward which OASI benefits (representing a contribution from both employees and employers) would constitute a credit. Labor always has been an ardent supporter of government insurance, and any further extension of this industrial retirement pattern seems quite likely to convince corporate management that governmental retirement insurance is a very good thing.

Another bill providing for insurance to cover the cost of medical care in case of illness also was introduced in the Senate in 1949. This proposal has aroused great controversy and opposition, especially on the part of the medical profession.

It should be noted that this type of insurance is not primarily for protection against loss of income. Rather it would offer protection against extra costs—those added expenses which physicians' fees and hospitals entail even when normal income is maintained. Procedures for organizing and providing services—the services of the physician and the hospital—also are essential to health insurance although they are not characteristic of programs providing insurance against income loss.

The details of the plan for medical care, however, are related more directly to the community's health program than to its program for the prevention of dependency, and therefore will be discussed in our next section.

The national insurance systems for protection against the hazards of dependency are still a patchwork. The inclusion of the railroad insurances within a single integrated administrative system would seem to be logical. So would the integration of the diverse state plans for insurance against disabilities from industrial accidents and injuries. But these issues of administrative order and efficiency tend to be obscured by the controversies arising from the different objectives of the protagonists of specific insurance measures. One may hope that in the course of time an increasing clarity of public purpose will permit more attention to such neglected opportunities for administrative improvement.

ILL-HEALTH

Chapter VII

ACCEPTANCE OF
RESPONSIBILITY

ACCEPTANCE BY THE COMMUNITY of some measure of responsibility for the protection of its members against the consequences of illness dates far back in historical times. Traditionally, the focus of this concern has been upon measures to prevent and cure specific diseases. The philosophy that "health is a state of complete physical, mental, and social well-being, not merely the absence of disease or infirmity," [1] is of more recent origin, and is only beginning to be translated into practical community programs. Yet none can deny that this concept has been furthered by measures designed to prevent, cure, and alleviate specific conditions of ill-health. These provide the solid foundation upon which any future programs to assure optimal health to the population must rest.

The most comprehensive data about the prevalence of illness come from the National Health Survey made by the United States Public Health Service,[2] which in 1935 undertook a house-to-house canvass in representative sections of the country. The purpose was to secure information about any physical conditions which had disabled individuals for seven days or longer during the preceding year. On the basis of the data secured, it has been estimated that every year 22 million people (172 out of each 1,000 of the population) suffer some illness which disables them for one week or longer. Or, to put it another way, there are 16 illnesses for every registered death.

The average person, the survey indicated, is incapacitated by illness for ten days each year. Healthiest persons are those in the 15-to-20-year age range, of whom only 2.5 percent were ill on the day of the canvass; the least healthy are those 65 or over, of whom 12 percent were ill at that time.

[1] From World Health Organization's definition of health.
[2] Public Health Service, *National Health Survey, Bulletin 1, Sickness and Medical Care Series*, pp. 1–3.

THREE PRINCIPAL SYSTEMS

Considering the importance which people attach to good health, it is not surprising that around $3.5 billion annually are spent in the United States for protection against certain health hazards, and for hospital, medical, and allied services.[3] This substantial sum is spent through three general systems which together protect and promote the health of the community: (1) the public health system, under governmental auspices; (2) the community-organized system of medical care under a variety of auspices, both governmental and voluntary; and (3) the system of private medical care, provided by the physicians and dentists of the community.

These systems, particularly the last two, are essentially local in character and very loosely organized; in no sense are they subject to any nationwide administrative authority, but each has special features which characterize it unmistakably as a distinct entity. The community undertakes both organizational and financial responsibilities for public health and for community-organized medical care. The private physician or dentist practices independently, but there is a high degree of interdependence between the system of private practice and the community-sponsored systems which protect and promote the community's general health.

THE PUBLIC HEALTH SYSTEM

By philosophy and tradition the public health system has been a local one. Its cornerstone is the public health department, locally administered and financed. Both state and federal governments, however, have long played important parts in developing this system, and they are now playing enlarged roles.

The minimum basic activities of public health departments reflect the broad purposes of the entire system: the control of communicable disease; protection of maternal, infant, and child health; environmental sanitation; public health education; the collection and publication of vital statistics; and the provision of laboratory facilities. In addition, nursing services and specialized health services sponsored by voluntary agencies may be regarded as integral parts. Taken to-

[3] Estimated by Community Research Associates, Inc., based on available data.

gether all these units of our general public health system spend in the
neighborhood of $250 million annually.

Local, state, and federal public health units.—The local health
department is an integral part of the government of the city, county,
township, village, or other political unit. There are, in fact, about
5,500 local official health units throughout the country, but not all
are staffed and organized to give the full range of basic health
services. According to an exhaustive study made by Dr. Haven Emerson, nearly forty million people in the United States live in areas in
which the public health services do not meet minimum standards.[4]

The efficient provision of basic public health protection requires
the services of a trained, full-time health officer and an adequate
complement of public health nurses, engineers, and sanitarians. A
substantial proportion of the population must be immunized against
certain diseases, particularly smallpox, diphtheria, and whooping
cough. There must be systematic reporting of individual cases of a
long list of diseases and appropriate measures to protect the community from them. Instruction, nursing, medical, and hospital facilities must be provided for pregnant women.

The public health officer is responsible for advising about and
enforcing the sanitary laws and regulations. He is the collector, analyst, and purveyor of facts about the community's health, and a principal instrument of instruction in how to keep well. Laboratory services enable him to check the diagnosis of diseases reported, and to
serve private physicians in connection with their diagnostic examinations. Moreover, health departments are beginning to assume specific
responsibilities in relation to chronic diseases, previously considered
unamenable to public health measures.

Local government action to control disease antedates action by
states, although local political units derive authority to organize these
services from the states. While all states have long since established
health departments to exercise general authority over public health
matters, ordinarily they undertake only limited direct health activities. Their role, like that of the federal department, is generally conceived to be one of providing consultation, technical service, and
leadership, except where activities are of such a nature that they can

[4] Haven Emerson and Martha Luginbuhl, *Local Health Units for the Nation,* p. 1.

best be conducted on a statewide basis. The regulation of milk, food, and water supplies is of such a character, since these are matters which transcend local, and even state, boundaries. In recent years, however, states have been assuming greater responsibilities for the promotion and financing of local health services, particularly in areas of low economic status.

The federal government traces its concern with public health back to 1798 when the Marine Hospital Service was organized in the United States Treasury Department to administer a prepayment plan for medical services for merchant seamen. Eighty years later inspection and quarantine powers in the nation's ports were added. In 1902 the Marine Hospital Service was reorganized into the United States Public Health and Marine Hospital Service. In 1912 it became the United States Public Health Service, with a program broadened to include interstate control of sanitation and water pollution, medical research, and the general improvement of public health administration.

Although federal grants for specific public health services began in 1918, it was not until the Social Security Act of 1935 that the flow of federal money assumed considerable proportions. By 1948 some $42 million was allocated to the states through the Public Health Service and the Children's Bureau. This accounted for about one fifth of the $202 million spent that year by all local and state health departments.[5]

The public health system is no longer an exclusively local one, although the local departments continue to maintain a high degree of autonomy. State and federal policies and standards, however, are having an increasing effect upon the extent and the quality of the local services. From a surface view, it seems that our public health system is emerging gradually into an integrated local-state-federal system. Consideration of the issues implicit in this trend will be discussed in a later chapter.

Public health nursing.—No characterization of the public health system would be complete without a description of the role of the public health nurse. On her shoulders falls the brunt of the program for maternal, infant, preschool and school hygiene, communicable disease control, and a variety of activities involving public health service to the individual.

In cases of communicable disease, the nurse may arrange for im-

[5] Unpublished estimates by Carl E. Buck, University of Michigan.

munization. If necessary she instructs the family in regard to the care of the patient. She must carry out all instructions relative to the protection of the sick person and of the community. She must visit regularly and give such aid as the health officer may determine to all tuberculosis cases in her district, keeping records of each case.

The nurse must try to get in touch with all expectant mothers in her district and give instruction in maternal and infant hygiene. If necessary, she must arrange for medical examination and supervision and for hospitalization. Her services are required in all public health clinics.

Public health nursing is thus a unique and indispensable concomitant of our present system for prevention of disease and protection of the public health. Nearly 80 percent of our public health nurses are employed by the official public health departments. The remainder are in voluntary nursing associations or other private agencies, or are on teaching staffs.[6]

Voluntary agencies.—Voluntary agencies contributed notably in pioneering many programs which gave impetus to the development of the modern public health movement. The programs formulated by the National Association for the Study and Prevention of Tuberculosis (organized in 1904), by the American Social Hygiene Association (1905), and the substantial research and experimentation of the Rockefeller, Commonwealth, Milbank, Kellogg, and other foundations are illustrative. More recently there have been established a number of voluntary national agencies concerned with the study and prevention of chronic and other diseases about which there is as yet meager scientific knowledge.

Primarily through demonstrations and educational programs, voluntary agencies endeavor to improve the quality of existing services and to establish new ones. A few provide clinics; some sponsor local services; others limit themselves to national programs of promotion and education, and of fund raising on behalf of these activities.

Local health departments have now absorbed most of the earlier public health services which private agencies were instrumental in developing, but Selskar Gunn and Philip S. Platt estimated that in 1944 national and local voluntary health agencies spent in the neighborhood of $48 million annually for a variety of programs. The

6 American Nurses' Association, *1949 Facts About Nursing*, p. 21, Table 1.

extensive public health services then provided through the American Red Cross chapters, particularly in rural areas, were not included in this estimate.[7]

Communities throughout the United States have organized, under both governmental and voluntary auspices, a number of services designed to assure medical and dental care for those who require it. Hospital facilities for inpatient care; hospital outpatient departments; independent dispensaries, clinics, and other direct medical facilities, together with bedside nursing service in the homes, constitute the community-provided system for medical care. It can be designated as a "system" only in broad terms, and cannot be considered as wholly coherent and integrated.

The confusion about its nature arises primarily from the fact that communities do not attempt to bear the cost of these medical services for all persons who use them, although undertaking to see that appropriate facilities are available. Furthermore, while such facilities originally were organized to provide free service to the poor, they are now used by patients from all economic levels. On the other hand, every community still pays, through taxes or voluntary funds, for a substantial amount of hospital, medical, and bedside nursing service for persons who can afford to pay little if any of the cost. Since the growth of the hospital and medical insurance plans, however, payments from patients have met an increasingly larger part of the expense of providing these services.

Hospitals.—According to the National Health Survey, 27 out of every 100 persons who were ill in 1935 received medical attention in a hospital.[8]

To care for illness requiring hospital care, some 6,000 hospitals provide over 700,000 beds [9] (exclusive of 705,423 beds in 606 hospitals for nervous and mental conditions). In 1949 these hospitals admitted nearly 16.5 million patients, and on an average day had 642,-194 persons under care. Of these hospitals, four fifths (4,761) are general, responsible primarily for short-term care. Long-term care of

[7] Selskar Gunn and Philip S. Platt, *Voluntary Health Agencies, 1945*, p. 208, Table 5.

[8] Rollo H. Britten, "Receipt of Medical Service in the Different Urban Populations," *Public Health Reports* (reprint 2213), LV, No. 48 (November 29, 1940), p. 8, Table 6.

[9] *Journal of the American Medical Association*, CXLIII, No. 1 (May, 1950), 25.

tuberculous patients is provided by 444 special hospitals; 559 hospitals specialize in the care of other specific types of illness, both chronic and acute. Hospital departments are also maintained by 202 institutions which provide a total of 20,920 beds.

Slightly over one fifth of all hospitals are proprietary; that is, they are owned and operated as private enterprises, with profits unrestricted. While these usually are not regarded as a part of the community-provided system of medical care, in many communities they constitute an important, and sometimes the sole, hospital facility. Most of the 1,308 proprietary hospitals (exclusive of those for nervous and mental diseases) listed by the American Medical Association in 1949 are for short-term general and specialized care, accounting for approximately 7 percent of the general hospital beds available in the country as a whole.

Three fourths of the nation's hospitals, and 93 percent of its hospital beds, serve the population on a nonprofit basis. Building funds have been provided either through tax funds or through voluntary resources, including individual contributions. Maintenance costs are met in various ways, including tax funds, voluntary contributions, insurance, or direct payments by people who use the services.

The hospital system is essentially a local one, although state and federal hospitals do provide some short-term general and specialized care. The greater number of the nonlocal hospitals, however, are for patients with nervous and mental conditions and for long-term care of the tuberculous. Local governmental hospitals, under city, county, or joint auspices, provide about 22 percent of the total number of beds. Nonprofit hospitals, under voluntary auspices, provide some 48 percent; proprietary hospitals, 6 percent; and state hospitals, about 8 percent.[10] While federal hospitals provide about 16 percent of all hospital beds (exclusive of those in hospitals for the mentally ill), the service is restricted to segments of the population and generally is not available for community use.

Since 1946 the federal government has become a participant in the construction of local hospitals. Concern with the maldistribution of hospital resources, typified by the range from 6.5 hospital beds per 1,000 of the population in the District of Columbia to 1.5 beds per 1,000 in Arkansas, culminated in 1946 in the Hill-Burton Hospital

10 *Ibid.*, p. 26.

and Construction Act. Under the federal hospital construction program, administered by the United States Public Health Service, $3 million was provided to states for hospital-planning surveys, and up to $75 million a year authorized for construction purposes for a period of five years. By the end of 1949 specific projects estimated to cost $669 million, of which federal funds will provide one third, had been approved for construction.[11] The original Act, which was for five years, was extended to a ten-year period by the 81st Congress. One may not predict with confidence how federal and state developments under this program may alter the essentially local nature of the hospital system.

Even this introductory characterization of the all-important hub of our general system of community-organized medical care cannot neglect the problem of paying for its operation. The maintenance of a hospital is expensive, and these costs have been increasing steadily. Many public hospitals are designed primarily for care of indigent or medically indigent patients and, where this is true, probably provide most of such "free" care. Operating budgets are met from city, county, or other tax funds, although these may be augmented by fees or insurance payments.

About three quarters of the budget of the average voluntary hospital is met by fees or insurance payments. The balance comes from a variety of sources—endowments, community chest or other contributions, per diem or lump subsidy payments for charity cases by public welfare departments and other governmental or voluntary community services. Notable within the last decade and a half has been the rapid increase of Blue Cross prepayment insurance plans. It is estimated that these and other plans now cover over one third of the country's population.

Hospital outpatient departments.—In 1945 some three thousand hospitals reported that they were operating outpatient departments for ambulatory cases, that is, for sick people who are not bedridden. The National Health Survey reported that in 1935 five out of every hundred ill persons received medical care from a public clinic.[12] In 1945 over 31.5 million visits were made to hospital clinics by an un-

[11] John W. Cronin, *et al.*, "Hospital Construction under the Hill-Burton Program," *Public Health Reports*, LXV, No. 23 (June 9, 1950), 744, Table 1.
[12] Britten, "Receipt of Medical Service . . . ," p. 8, Table 6.

recorded number of persons. Nearly 87 percent of this outpatient service was provided by the general hospitals. Those under voluntary private auspices accounted for 60 percent of the total; public tax-supported hospitals, 28.4 percent; and proprietary hospitals, 11.6 percent.[13]

We do not know how much these services cost, for hospitals tend to include outpatient service in the over-all cost of operation. We do know that a great deal of outpatient service is provided free or for a small fee. As long ago as 1939 a study of a group of voluntary hospital outpatient departments showed that nearly 40 percent of reported expenditures was met from patients' fees. Issues in connection with this and other phases of outpatient service will be considered in later chapters.

Other direct medical services.—Although hospitals and their outpatient departments now constitute the greatest part of the organized community medical services, in almost every urban community other agencies provide some medical service to certain people, under special circumstances. Some public welfare departments operate clinics for their clients, or pay physicians for their care. Public health departments sometimes operate independent tuberculosis, venereal disease, or other specialized clinics. Voluntary agencies may conduct special clinics for such diseases as tuberculosis, cancer, rheumatic fever, and heart conditions. Especially in older sections of the country, they still conduct comprehensive general clinical services and independently organized general dispensaries. It is not uncommon to find special, and detached, medical services for crippled children and other handicapped persons.

Bedside nursing.—The distinction made between "public health" and "bedside" nursing is traditional, although it is coming to have less meaning. Basic to it is the fact that in the past the public health system has been concerned primarily with communicable disease control and with maternal, infant, and child health, in which the need for bedside nursing has not been predominant. The visiting nursing associations, on the other hand, have had a concern with all manner of illnesses, many of which have required bedside care as well as instruction in public health and the care of the sick. At the present time, bedside nursing is provided mainly by staff nurses of visiting nursing

[13] Commission on Hospital Care, *Hospital Care in the United States*, pp. 322, 326.

associations, although at the same time they may also undertake substantial responsibilities in connection with the disease-control procedures of the public health system. The best data available indicate that slightly over one third of all the public health nurses in the country give bedside nursing care.

Although originally designed to serve the poor, visiting nursing services now are extended to many who pay a fee per visit. This type of service, however, must not be confused with that of "private duty" nurses who undertake full and continuous care of a particular patient. The average call of the visiting nurse lasts from twenty-five minutes to an hour, and rarely exceeds two or three hours per day for a single patient.

Great impetus was given to fee arrangements for visiting nursing when two large industrial insurance companies, Metropolitan Life (which will discontinue this service in 1953) and John Hancock, contracted to give this service to their policyholders. It is now estimated that insurance and other fees provide about 50 percent of the funds for the nursing services. The remainder comes from community chest and other community-contributed funds.

PRIVATE MEDICAL PRACTICE

The National Health Survey found that 81 out of every 100 cases of illness received medical attention, and that 75 of these were attended either at home or in the office of their physician.[14] On the basis of available data we estimate that it costs the American people about $1.75 billion annually for the services of physicians.

In 1950 the American Medical Association listed 201,277 licensed physicians, of whom 9,700 were retired or currently not in practice and 4,464 in the armed forces or other branches of government service. According to the AMA analysis, 73,079 physicians are in general practice, 55,049 limit their practices to one of the medical specialties, and 23,139 give special attention to one of the specialties.[15]

The distribution of physicians is uneven. More than half are in cities of 50,000 or over, representing 34 percent of the country's population. Thirty percent serve 22 percent of the population in cities of

14 Britten, "Receipt of Medical Service . . . ," p. 8, Table 6.
15 The American Medical Association, *1950 Directory of Physicians,* p. 9, Table 1, p. 11, Table 3.

2,500 to 50,000. Only 15 percent of the physicians serve rural areas, which represent 44 percent of the total population.[16]

No other profession with which this volume is concerned has such rigorous professional and educational standards. These standards are established and enforced by official bodies within the medical profession itself. Medical schools are routinely inspected and rated by the Council on Medical Education and Hospitals of the American Medical Association, and by the Association of American Medical Colleges. To be approved, a medical school must be affiliated with a hospital which has sufficient patients to guarantee ample opportunity for clinical instruction and experience. Each of the 19 medical specialty boards prescribes standards for certification of specialists, including the extent and methods of medical education and training. Hospitals approved for residencies in the specialties must guarantee a sufficient number of patients to provide the needed experience and must have a recognized specialist in charge of the service.

The private physician provides the solid foundation for the conservation of health. Yet the only official responsibility assumed by the community is to require that the physician be licensed to practice within the state borders. By establishing the qualifications which candidates must meet to be eligible for licensing, states assure the minimum quality, although not the extent, of medical care throughout the state.

COHESIVE PUBLIC POLICY

In the local community the three systems—public health, organized medical care, and private practice—together provide the framework of the present pattern for the prevention of disease and disability, and the promotion of health. There is considerable illogic in their manner of organization, or at points in the lack of it, and there are gaps in the total service. Yet, behind these services, individually and collectively, there is an extraordinary record of achievement in the reduction of disease and disability and the prevention of untimely deaths. It is fruitless to try to distribute the credit, but the fact is that the rate of death in this country was 17.8 per 1,000 of the population in 1900 and it is now 9.9.[17] The normal life expectancy, now nearly 70

16 *Hospital Care in the United States*, p. 250.
17 National Office of Vital Statistics, *Deaths and Death Rates for Selected Causes*.

years (65.2 for males, 70.5 for females), was only 49 in 1900. The average person may thus expect to live seventeen years longer than he could when the century began, and he can expect to escape entirely many of the diseases which earlier took a heavy toll in sickness and death.

Behind these benefits to mankind, one may see a mighty force exerting a cohesive power in the formation of public policy toward all matters affecting the community's health. This is the force and power of scientific thought.

However one may choose to articulate his concept of science, and of scientific thought, the truth is self-evident that the importance attached to the scientific view, to the value of objective evidence, to systematic and painstaking research, and to the testing of results has exerted great and accelerating impact upon the direction of conscious effort to protect and preserve our health.

It seems well to distinguish three main processes through which scientific thought has contributed its fertile and cohesive strength. One is through the pursuit of knowledge about the processes of cause and cure of disease. A second is through the pursuit of knowledge about the processes of organizing the community for its own effective protection. A third, resulting from these two, is through the clarification of priorities of problems demanding community action.

Upon none of the other human ills with which the community and this volume are concerned has this power as yet become so apparent and effective. But it may help the community, and the reader, in gaining perspective toward them, to be reminded that the cohesive influences of scientific thought upon the formation of policies in the interest of the public's health have hardly half a century behind them.

CAUSE AND CURE

In the Middle Ages scientific thought had no more penetrated the causes which disabled the sick man than it had those producing the "pauper," the "rogue," or the "vagabond." All human ills were regarded as the visitation of Providence. The great scourges of the times were attributed variously to "comets and the other astral influences, to storms, the failure of crops, famines, the sinking of mountains, the effect of drought or inundation," [18] and other equally irrelevant phenomena. During the sixteenth and seventeenth centuries, medical practice was bound up with "superstition, herb doctoring, and quackery." Popular prejudices discouraged post-mortem examinations to confirm diagnoses, and dissections required special papal indulgences. As late as 1793, Dr. Benjamin Rush, the best known American physician of his day, believed that all diseases were a single entity, with bloodletting and purging the basic treatment applicable to all the numerous manifestations.

It is well to remember the tragic results of this incomprehension. In the United States, for example, there were thirty-five epidemics of yellow fever between 1702 and 1800. The years from 1800 to 1850 were marked by epidemic after epidemic. Chief among these were smallpox, yellow fever, and typhus, but deaths from scarlet fever and tuberculosis were high on the list. New Orleans lost 8,000 of its population of 50,000 from cholera in 1832, and suffered high fatalities from yellow fever in 1853. The great pandemic of diphtheria was in 1872–76; cholera swept the land in 1873; yellow fever reappeared in 1878 and ran its final devastating course in New Orleans in 1905.[19]

It was not until the end of the last century that the long struggle to achieve a scientific discipline, sharp and powerful enough to pierce the impenetrable mystery of the causation of these great killers of mankind, began to pay the dividends which we now reap. Preoccupation with the soul of the sick man gradually had given way to concern for the various conditions of his illness. Medical scientists shifted their interest in symptoms to the task of distinguishing the specific diseases which caused them. The slow and painstaking study of normal anatomy, of morbid anatomy, of medical entomology and bacteriology, created a framework of knowledge within which to remove the veil of ignorance surrounding the "visitation" of disease.

It does not occur to the modern generation to fear the great epidemic diseases which killed their forefathers, nor to give undue regard to the hazards of birth. This country's last death from yellow fever was in 1924, and smallpox is seldom encountered. Typhoid fever now causes few deaths, and diphtheria causes less than one death per

[18] Fielding H. Garrison, *An Introduction to the History of Medicine*, pp. 14, 178.
[19] Ralph H. Major, *Fatal Partners in War and Disease*, p. 203.

100,000 population.[20] By 1946 the infant death rate had dropped from 161 per 1,000 live births to 34.6, and the maternal death rate had fallen from 13.4 per 100,000 population to 1.6.[21] These and many other specific eventuations of the scientific pursuit of knowledge have left their great stamp upon the welfare of mankind. Other diseases and conditions, about the causes of which we now know relatively little, compete vigorously for attention. New discoveries are eagerly awaited. The thought would enter no one's mind that future planning for protection against diseases about which little is yet known could be unaccompanied by investment in the scientific study of their cause and cure.

COMMUNITY ACTION FOR PREVENTION AND PROTECTION

One must go as far back as the Black Death in the middle fourteenth century to find the beginnings of community attempts to organize systematic measures for protection against the ravages of disease. In those years many European cities appointed "guardians of the public health" to exclude persons coming to them from afflicted areas. This was in fact a good idea, although it was not until over five centuries later that anyone knew exactly why.

Systematic pursuit of knowledge about community action for prevention and protection began with the collection and analysis of community-wide manifestations of death and disease. As early as the sixteenth century, some European towns collected and published pertinent records. At first it seemed that the principal result was that by watching the rise and fall of the death rates some persons were enabled to leave town ahead of the arrival of plague epidemics.

In 1657, in England, John Graunt found that 36 percent of all live-born infants died before reaching the age of six years. The heaviest tolls of life, it was observed, occurred in the congested slums of the larger cities and towns. Statisticians then began to collect facts which showed a correlation between epidemic fatality and filth, overcrowding, and unsanitary conditions, and sanitary engineers began to devise means for the better collection of garbage, for better water supply, for the removal of nuisances to decent living. These, as it turned out,

[20] National Office of Vital Statistics, *Deaths and Death Rates for Selected Causes, 1948,* (National Summaries, March 6, 1950).
[21] *Ibid.* (Special Report, November, 1948).

were sensible precautions. But years were still to follow before scientific inquiry into the causation of disease was able to tell why.

In this country Lemmuel Shattuck, not a medical man, analyzed the "Bills of Mortality" prepared by Boston's superintendent of burying grounds, the only official recordings of death at the time. His conclusions regarding the major reasons for deaths between 1810 and 1845, the prevalence of contagious diseases, and the periodicity of epidemics would have done credit to many a later analyst with far better tools at his disposal. They resulted directly in setting up the first state board of health in this country, in Massachusetts in 1869,[22] and they were a major factor in bringing about the establishment of the national death registration area in 1880. It may be well to remind any who may assume a self-propelling facility in scientific progress that the national birth registration area was not established until 1915, and that it was not until 1933 that all 48 states fulfilled minimum requirements for the registration both of births and of deaths.

The medical discoveries of the later nineteenth century, and the whole series of discoveries which have come in the twentieth, have profoundly influenced the direction and emphasis of practical community effort. Into the community-wide study of "how many," "how often," "where," "whom," and "under what circumstance" people sickened and died, there was incorporated the precise news about "why," which began to flow from the laboratories of medical science. And into these were blended the systematic study and evaluation of "with what result" ensuing community action could be credited. Thus was laid the foundation for the scientific pursuit and classification of knowledge about those characteristics of disease relevant to the development of strategic and effective processe⁻ for protecting the community against their consequences. The year 1872—the year of the first National Conference of the American Public Health Association—is a convenient point from which to date the beginning of this fusion of scientific thought in forming effective community action.

Public health authorities are now somewhat put to it for terminology with which to express this scientific orientation which has been their particular province. Community action against disease had its natural roots in the demand for protection against the great epidemics. "Epidemiology" thus has long stood in popular usage as descrip-

[22] Wilson G. Smilie, *Public Health Administration*, p. 13.

tive of the scientific method appropriate to protective action. But with the traditional killers of epidemic proportions now under control, the word, as one authority protests, is "now loose from its etymological moorings." [23] Indeed, the strategic community-wide processes of which the word is presumed to be descriptive have long been well-anchored off the shore of maternal and infant health, and they may appropriately find shelter in community harbors now congested with cancer, diabetes, heart disease, and others of the more modern fleet of "killers." We might add that the systematic pursuit of epidemiological knowledge seems no less appropriate to the community problems of dependency or of maladjustment disorders, or of recreational liabilities, than to the problems of physical diseases.

For what is essential is a systematic discipline which (1) sees the processes by which diseases or disorders affect the whole community, rather than as they affect single individuals; (2) recognizes the statistical and research techniques appropriate to the analysis of their significant community-wide characteristics; (3) encompasses the practical procedures appropriate to community-wide action to reduce their consequences; (4) and is grounded equally in the sciences which contribute knowledge as to their causation and in familiarity with the diagnostic and treatment practices appropriate to their prevention, alleviation, and cure.[24]

The power of scientific thought in this half century has made an extraordinary contribution to the discipline directed toward the course of community action to protect against certain diseases and conditions. It is a discipline destined, it seems to us, for wider community application in years to come.

COMMUNITY PRIORITIES

Communities generally have a pretty good underlying sense of what is important to them. But about the particularities of their objectives, and the priorities attached to them, there tends to be great confusion. Assistance to community policy by clarifying strategic priorities in matters pertaining to health has been no small contribution of scientific thought during this half century. The systematic collection and analysis of facts about different diseases and the rates of death resulting from them, together with the systematic evaluation of

[23] *Ibid.*, p. 202.   [24] *Ibid.*, summary of, pp. 203-7.

practical procedures designed for their control, have aided in directing first attention to first things.

It was not until 1900 that the sequence of death rates by cause began to portray accurately the role of communicable diseases. In that
year ten of the first twenty causes of death were communicable diseases. Three decades later the scene had changed dramatically, a
tribute to the priority and effectiveness of scientific community attention. The general death rate had dropped from 17.8 to 12.5 per 1,000.
Deaths from the ten communicable diseases, so important as causes
of death in 1900, had been reduced drastically, accounting as a group
for 240 deaths per 100,000 of the population, or slightly less than 20
percent of all deaths. By 1948 they aggregated only 85.4 deaths per
100,000 of the population, accounting for about one out of every
twelve deaths.[25]

In 1900, as we have seen, the hazards of pregnancy, childbirth, and
infancy took a high toll. Reduction of fatalities from these causes
required different methods and procedures from those found effective for the communicable diseases. During the early decades of this
century scientific thought and community interest gave these methods high priority, hard upon those for control of communicable disease, with which indeed the hazards of these conditions were clearly
interwoven. In 1946 infant mortality reached the low figure of 34.6
per 1,000 live births and maternal mortality 1.6. Nearly one out of
every ten deaths is still associated with maternity and infancy, and
relatively little progress has been made in preventing death during
the first month of life, recognized as the most hazardous.

But facts, continuously developed during a full half century,
now point their inexorable finger at new diseases which clamor for
attention—or rather, more accurately, at old diseases which now push
their way to the forefront of public policy by reason of the known volume and fatality. These are the chronic diseases, which for two decades have been increasingly on the community's mind and conscience.
Knowledge about the cause and cure of many of them is still meager.
Community-wide procedures for protecting people against their consequences are yet to be developed and tested, but they hold top
priority for community attention and probably will continue to do so

25 Based on published reports, Office of Vital Statistics, *Deaths and Death Rates for
Selected Causes*, for various years.

for years to come. For two of their number, diseases of the heart and cancer, are now the leading precipitants of mortality, replacing pneumonia and tuberculosis.

COMMUNITY-WIDE PROGRAM ISSUES

The principal systems which protect and promote community health have had their beginnings in different purposes. It was the intent of the public health system to prevent and control communicable diseases and the hazards of maternity, infancy, and childhood on a community-wide basis. The purpose of the community-organized system of medical care was to provide a minimum of medical care and nursing service to the indigent and to the medically indigent. The aim of physicians and dentists in private practice has been to provide the best possible professional care, at fees consistent with the service, and the ability of patients to meet these costs. One would need to search far back in history to find a time when these three systems were not in some measure dependent upon one another. But it is no inconsiderable tribute to the pervasive power of scientific thought that since the turn of the century the measure of their interdependence has been increasing steadily.

The philosophy and concepts of preventive medicine have been steadily incorporated into medical training. With the recognition of preventive medicine and public health together as one of the medical specialties, this concept undoubtedly will be reflected more fully in the private practice of medicine. The foundation of public health procedures are to be found in the disciplines of the medical scientists and the medical profession, and the fullest cooperation of all physicians of the community is essential to a successful program.

Hospital and clinic services, once primarily a charitable device for bringing medical service to the sick poor, early in this century became indispensable for medical education and training. Their facilities have grown steadily more essential to private physicians and to the public health system in connection with the detection and treatment not only of the communicable diseases but also for chronic diseases and conditions.

As this century turns the halfway mark, one may not forget that potential danger from the infectious diseases still is ever present; that the maternal cycle is ever hazardous. Certain chronic diseases clamor for attention. Onset of chronic diseases cannot be prevented by public health measures to control the germs; they are not infectious. The effectiveness of any protective community program requires the cooperation of hospitals and physicians providing facilities for discovery, diagnosis, and treatment.

It is to these old and new issues of community-wide planning that we turn in the succeeding chapters of this section. About the old issues there is much experience, data, and authoritative standard practice to guide the community in improving certain segments of its program. About newer issues, communities have much less to go on, although the directions and trends in respect to many of them are beginning to clarify. But those who wish to give conscious direction to the future course of either general or particular community policy, need to understand:

1. What is now known about the characteristics of the principle groups of diseases which have practical significance to the development of a community-wide program for protection against their consequences

2. The basic service functions which must be provided in order to achieve this purpose

3. The structure through which the three present systems now participate in the administration of these functions and the issues involving their community efficiency and adequacy

4. The opportunities which now seem to emerge for progress toward a more coherent community system and the issues attendant upon its development

Chapter VIII

THE STRATEGIC
CHARACTERISTICS OF
DISEASE

THE STRUGGLE TO CLASSIFY scientific knowledge about the distinguishing characteristics of the different diseases has behind it a long and fruitful history. The work of the English clinician Thomas Sydenham, in the middle of the seventeenth century, began the long process by which medical scientists have identified and classified diseases. Two centuries later, in 1855, the International Statistical Congress adopted the first standard classified list of diseases for use in reporting the causes of death. Five years afterward Florence Nightingale urged a succeeding Congress to adopt a standard list for the purpose of reporting sickness in hospitals. Although it repeatedly revised its classification for reporting deaths, it was not until 1900 that the International Congress approved a list for the reporting of illness. Nearly a half century later (in 1944) Great Britain and the United States adopted their provisional lists for use in morbidity tabulation.[1]

In 1948 the World Health Organization, successor to previous international sponsors of these classificational undertakings, published a single list of diseases for use in reporting both mortality and morbidity. Its 612 categories of diseases and morbid conditions, with supplemental categories for the classification of injuries by their cause and nature, are based primarily on specific disease entities. The degree to which the causes of particular diseases are accurately known has much to do with the precise classification of them as well as with their permanence in a classified list. Hence the list as a whole represents "a series of necessary compromises between classification based on etiology [causation]; anatomical site [the body location of the

[1] World Health Organization, *Manual of the International Statistical Classification of Diseases, Injuries, and Causes of Death, 6th Version,* I, p. xx.

disease]; age, and circumstances of onset; as well as [for practical use] the quality of information available on medical reports." [2]

In the last analysis, classification is determined by the purpose for which it is intended. The sponsors of the international list point out three such special interests: "The anatomist may desire a classification based on the part of the body affected . . . the pathologist is primarily interested in the nature of the disease process . . . the clinician must consider disease from these two angles but needs further knowledge of etiology." [3]

To this they might well have added that the community organizer is interested in classifying diseases by the characteristics which have the greatest significance to establishing community-wide programs of prevention and protection. For such purposes, those associated with the preparation of this volume have chosen a broad fourfold classification: (1) the communicable diseases; (2) the hazards of pregnancy and infancy; (3) the chronic and deficiency diseases; and (4) the chronic physical handicaps. These general classifications are in common usage. Responsibility for programs directed to them, however, is now dispersed among the different systems which serve the community's health, and a comparative consideration of their strategic characteristics is seldom undertaken.

COMMUNICABLE DISEASES

The communicable diseases have receded in importance as causes of illness and death and might well be considered last in this analysis. We choose to discuss them first, primarily because of the successful community-wide attempts to reduce them and the lessons from this experience that may be applied to the reduction of other diseases.

The fact that the epidemic diseases are caused by germs was the great discovery of the late nineteenth and early twentieth century. It was this strategic characteristic, common to all the epidemic diseases, as well as to others which achieved less notoriety, which exerted a profound influence upon the strategy of community action. It gave opportunity to control disease by preventing the transmission of these germs, rather than by reliance on the diagnosis and treatment of the specific individuals affected. The newly organizing public health

[2] *Ibid.*, p. xiii.   [3] *Ibid.*, p. xi.

movement seized this opportunity, and exploited its strategic and tactical potentialities with great success.

GENERIC CHARACTERISTICS

Discovery of the specific organisms causing particular diseases has made it possible to launch effective counterattacks upon many of them. A great deal is known about the manner in which they pursue their deadly purpose, the conditions under which they thrive, and the obstacles which may bar their course. The strategy and the tactics of community action against each have their foundation in this precise knowledge. But for the group of communicable diseases as a whole, certain characteristics have had special significance in determining the underlying patterns of methods for prevention, protection and control.[4]

Acute vs. chronic diseases.—Most communicable diseases are "acute"; that is, they are self-limiting in their duration. A person "catches" one of them, he is sick for a relatively short period (predetermined by the nature of the disease), and at the end of that period he is usually either well or dead.

A few diseases in this group, notably tuberculosis, syphilis, and gonorrhea, do not possess the acute characteristic. They are "chronic"; that is, the disease runs for an undetermined period of time, and people do not fully recover unless aided by specific and continuous treatment. This characteristic, as we shall see in a later chapter, has called for procedures that differ significantly from those that are effective in controlling the acute diseases.

Incubation.—Symptomatic evidence that a person has contracted a communicable disease becomes apparent only after a definite time lapse following the introduction of the infecting agent into the body. It is during this incubation period that the organism produces poisons, or destroys tissues, in sufficient quantity to produce the identifying symptoms. Hence it is part of good public health practice to trace and discover persons who have been exposed to infection and to give specific inoculations, or other known preventive treatment.

Among the comforting characteristics of most of these diseases is

[4] Except as otherwise noted, the material on communicable diseases is based on: American Public Health Association, *The Control of Communicable Diseases*, and Wilson G. Smilie, *Public Health Administration in the United States*.

the fact that when a specified number of "days of grace" have passed following exposure, a person may be reasonably sure that he has weathered that particular danger of infection.

Mode of transmission.—A whole series of specific public health measures have resulted from the fact that specific germs have their own peculiar manner of moving from one person to another. While some travel in a variety of ways, others are so restricted to one method of transport that infection by any other route usually is regarded as highly improbable.

Droplet infection, through coughing, sneezing, or discharge of sputum, is an important method of transmission for the tubercle bacillus. This, indeed, is the usual manner in which most of the infectious respiratory diseases are spread, including the common cold.

Such diseases as typhoid fever, cholera, and dysentery are inducted into the body by way of the alimentary tract through the agency of contaminated milk, water, or food. Certain parasitic infections, of which trichinosis is probably most widely known, are spread through the consumption of improperly cooked food, infected pork in this instance, or through the handling of infected animals, as in the case of tularemia.

The bite of an infected animal or insect, which transfers the germ to the human victim, is a well-demonstrated method of transmission common to a number of diseases which formerly were among the great epidemic killers: plague, carried by fleas infected by the blood of rats; yellow fever and malaria, carried by certain species of mosquitoes; typhus fever, by lice; Rocky Mountain fever, by ticks.

The fact that healthy persons, themselves immune to a disease, may act as chronic carriers has long been typified by the famous case of Typhoid Mary. The discovery that hookworm enters the body through direct contact with the apparently unbroken skin served to explain its prevalence in sections of the country where large numbers of people go about in their bare feet during portions of the year.

Immunity.—A strategic characteristic shared by many communicable diseases is that persons who weather one attack acquire an immunity which usually lasts a lifetime, although second attacks sometimes occur. Important among such diseases are smallpox, yellow fever, whooping cough, and measles. Tuberculosis, gonorrhea, syphilis, and rheumatic fever are examples of diseases in which an attack does not produce immunity. For many others, such as influenza and the common cold, immunity is of such short duration as to be of relatively no help in preventing further attacks.

The public health officer may require that immunity be conferred by artificial means. Since Jenner discovered that smallpox could be prevented by infection with cowpox, a long train of research and experimentation has sought similar means of protecting individuals from other diseases. A variety of vaccines, serums, and antitoxins is now available. Some confer immunity by developing mild forms of the disease in the person inoculated, while others bring about body conditions which are unfavorable to the growth of the specific micro-organism.

As a practical matter, community-wide immunization procedures against smallpox, diphtheria, whooping cough, and tetanus are those in most general use. The effectiveness of vaccinations against small-pox and diphtheria has been demonstrated so thoroughly that health officers consider an unusual number of cases of either disease in the community a reflection upon the administration of their programs. Relatively few people in the general population are ever given the injections which have been developed to provide immunity against such diseases as yellow fever, typhoid fever, and plague; it has been found more effective to control the means of transmission—mosquitoes, water supply, and rodents.

As anyone who has seen military service knows, a person who travels into areas where these diseases are known to be prevalent may be given "shots" for his protection. A typhoid vaccine protects for about two years, a modified living yellow fever virus inoculation for about four years, or a vaccine against plague for only six months—this will require "booster" shots if he remains in dangerous areas for longer periods. Similarly, persons in areas in which cholera is prevalent may be immunized against the disease for periods of six to twelve months through vaccination.

Even at home, if circumstances indicate a special susceptibility to the disease, particular individuals may receive inoculations to protect briefly against such diseases as mumps and measles (especially infants or children under three). People who are bitten or exposed to the saliva of a rabid animal, may be given prophylactic antirabic vaccine to prevent the development of rabies. Furthermore, some who are so inclined, may participate hopefully in current experiments to discover immunizing agents for other diseases, notably the common cold and influenza.

Susceptibility.—In contrast to immunity against specific diseases, either natural or artificially induced, are the circumstances which make persons more prone, or susceptible, to infection. It is well known that children are much more susceptible to many diseases than are adults, and that the chances for fatalities are greater in their early years. Women in childbirth are peculiarly susceptible to infection, and rigid procedures have been developed to assure surgical cleanliness preceding, during, and immediately following delivery. Resistance to diseases may be lowered through deficiencies in diet, exposure to wet and cold, mental fatigue, and alcoholism. Conditions of employment may render persons especially susceptible to such diseases as tuberculosis and respiratory diseases. While it is recognized that infection may occur indirectly, control programs for syphilis and gonorrhea are based on the fact that practically all infection is through sexual contacts.

Treatment.—For most of the communicable diseases, systematic provision of treatment has been of secondary importance to the official health program. Chief reliance for reduction of illness and death from these causes has been placed upon preventing their transmission. Treatment of the individual consisted for the most part of building up general resistance. With a few exceptions, as for diphtheria, medical science had not developed specific therapies for effective treatment of illnesses due to the acute infections.

Since the discovery of the sulfa drugs and the antibiotics, treatment has become of more importance in the official program. Astounding results have been achieved through them in the treatment of syphilis, gonorrhea, meningitis, and scarlet fever and its allied infections. Although its positive therapeutic value has clear limitations, some remarkable results have also been achieved through use of streptomyocin against the tubercule bacillus. On the other hand, drug resistant strains have been found to result from treatment in some cases of gonorrhea and syphilis. Further research and demonstration obviously are required. Without doubt, however, therapies such as these may be expected to become increasingly important in future programs for communicable disease control.

SPECIFIC CHARACTERISTICS

The foregoing basic characteristics have determined the underlying strategy of community action directed toward the communicable diseases as a whole. Each disease, however, has its own peculiar characteristics which govern the specific tactical procedures used in controlling it.

The prevalence of specific diseases, and hence their importance, vary from community to community. This is clearly revealed by the mortality and morbidity rates. Some diseases are earmarked for continued attention even where they are currently negligible as causing illness and death. Public health officials have had ample proof that relaxation of measures for their control brings about conditions under which diseases such as smallpox, diphtheria, and typhoid fever may again reach epidemic proportions. While they may be under control in this country, they are still prevalent in many other parts of the world, readily accessible with modern transportation.

It is beyond the purpose of this volume to reproduce comprehensive guides to the control of all communicable diseases; these are readily available in public health literature. But recapitulation of a few specific characteristics which determine the tactics to be followed in protecting the community against some important groups of infections will illustrate the painstaking attention to detail which is the cornerstone of success.

Childhood diseases.—Public health authorities give high priority to the control of diseases to which infants and children have been found to be especially susceptible. Success in this area of control reaps a double harvest, reduction of communicable diseases in the population as a whole, and reduction in disease, disability, and death among children and young people. Diseases of particular importance in childhood include: scarlet fever, diphtheria, meningococcus meningitis; German measles; whooping cough; mumps; chickenpox; and poliomyelitis. Each of these diseases has specific characteristics which determine community-wide strategy to prevent and control it.

Formerly one of the most devastating of the diseases of childhood, diphtheria now has disappeared in localities in which good control programs are in effect. When 35 to 50 percent of infants and preschool children have been immunized, diphtheria disappears from the community as an epidemic disease.

For the streptococcal infections—scarlet fever, septic sore throat, and tonsillitis—no definite antibacterial immunity has yet been demonstrated. Both sulfonamide and penicillin therapy check the development of the organism, giving the body an opportunity to build up resistance. Use of these drugs may also shorten the period of the illness and are particularly effective in preventing complications.

Probably the most prevalent of all infectious diseases is measles, but one attack usually confers permanent immunity. The concern of the public health program is primarily with preventing measles at the ages, and under conditions, in which the effects are the most disastrous. Formerly considered a variant of regular measles, *German measles* now is known to be a separate and distinct disease. Since a significant proportion of women who acquire this infection during the first three months of pregnancy give birth to a child with some physical defect, community control measures are directed primarily toward its prevention during the period of pregnancy.

Mumps and chickenpox are both mild diseases of childhood, few fatalities occurring from either. One attack of mumps confers permanent immunity; there is as yet no generally applicable method known by which to prevent its occurrence. Chickenpox is one of the most readily communicable of all diseases, and has a low case fatality rate. Its chief interest to health authorities is the fact that its symptoms are similar to those for smallpox and may be confused with it.

Whooping cough has a high case fatality rate among young children and pertussin vaccine is used to prevent its occurrence among children under six years of age. Some well baby clinics routinely use it along with toxoid for diphtheria, and tetanus vaccine. Improved vaccines, and the use of booster doses, give hope that this will be the next disease to be eliminated.

Meningococcus meningitis, under normal conditions, is of relatively little importance to the health officer. Specific treatment has been revolutionized by the discovery of sulfa drugs and penicillin, and there is now much less chance of fatality than formerly.

Poliomyelitis is the outstanding mystery among childhood diseases. Research is being conducted to determine the manner in which the filterable virus which causes it is transmitted, as well as the period during which the disease is communicable. Important aspects of community programs are designed to prevent and correct the crippling effects which still follow in a high proportion of cases.

Tuberculosis and venereal diseases.—For a variety of reasons, tuberculosis and the venereal diseases—syphilis, gonorrhea, chancroid, and lymphogranuloma venereum—are set apart by the community for special consideration. They are highly communicable, but they are also essentially chronic in their nature. They run a progressively serious course if not checked. Recovery does not bring immunity to future attacks, and there are no known measures by which to immunize the population against these diseases.

In almost every sense of the word they are diseases with "social" characteristics. "Consumption" at the turn of the century and the venereal diseases until quite recently were surrounded by tabus stemming from fear and moralistic considerations. Social and economic problems following in their wake have been noteworthy. Syphilis, moreover, has contributed greatly to the incidence of mental disease and defect, as well as to congenital malformations and other physical disabilities.

Resistance to tuberculosis can be increased by special attention to personal hygiene, good food, fresh air and sunshine. Susceptibility to infection may be enhanced, and the course of the disease accelerated, by the contraction of other illnesses, undernourishment, overwork, poor living or occupational conditions.

No generally applicable method of building artificial immunity, or any specific therapy or cure has yet been discovered. While BCG vaccine as well as streptomycin both are promising, their value is yet to be fully tested. Specific protective and therapeutic procedures are directed at the individual patient, in contrast to more general procedures for most communicable diseases.

Syphilis and gonorrhea are the two principal venereal diseases. Their "social" characteristic has greatly complicated their control. Cases are not routinely and completely reported, despite legal requirements, and it is difficult to secure accurate information about their prevalence. Finding and tracing of contacts to find possible sources of infection are hampered by what sometimes seems a general "conspiracy of silence" on the part of the victim, his family, and his physician. Methods of preventing transmission of the venereal infections have been involved with social and moral issues. The main strategy of the community campaign has been, as with the other communicable diseases, to prevent the transmission of the infecting agent. Control of prostitution, prophylaxis immediately after exposure to possible infection, particularly among the armed forces, Wassermann or other serological tests before issuing marriage licenses, and similar tests for expectant mothers, help to reduce the sources of infection.

The advent of the sulfa drugs and penicillin has resulted in greater reliance on treatment as a new strategy for control. Their use has shortened the period required to render the disease noninfectious. Complete cures are effected, also, in a much shorter time than required by the older mercury and arsenical therapies.

Acute respiratory infections.—During the course of a lifetime more people probably suffer more frequently from the acute respiratory infections than from any other group of diseases. Chief offender is the common cold which very few people escape during the course of a year, but which of itself is seldom fatal. Until medical science discovers new preventive or therapeutic measures there is little that the health officer can do to prevent its spread. At present he relies primarily on educating the public in personal hygiene, and urging people to smother the sneeze and the cough.

Pneumonia and influenza together rank as the fifth leading cause of death. Lobar pneumonia is one of the commonest of all the infectious diseases. The pneumococcus, which is responsible for 95 percent of all lobar pneumonia, occurs in more than fifty different types, and treatment formerly was dependent upon the type of pneumococcus determined to be responsible for the particular infection. Through use of the sulfa drugs, this typing became unnecessary, facilitating treatment and materially reducing the former high case fatality rate.

Too little is known about the virus which causes influenza. It appears in epidemic form, is spread by direct contact, and is highly communicable, with an incubation period of not more than three to four days. The sulfonamides and penicillin have no effect upon the influenza virus, but are used to combat secondary infections and to prevent complications. Extensive studies of influenza vaccines have been conducted but none has been found to immunize against all strains. Influenza is reported throughout the country, and health officers keep a careful watch for signs of epidemics.

Potentially fatal epidemic diseases.—Public health authorities, finally, stress the need to be constantly alert to many historically fatal diseases, now largely unknown because of the effectiveness of control measures, but which would return to attack with spirit if these measures were relaxed. Typhoid fever, smallpox, malaria, bubonic plague, typhus, and other enemies lie in wait just outside the gates of modern public health protection.

PREGNANCY AND INFANCY

In the interest of logic one must point out that neither maternity nor infancy, nor in fact any of their transitional stages, is a "disease." Rather, these are normal conditions during which there are special hazards which may adversely affect the health of both the mother and child. The hazardous characteristics of three general periods in this cycle determine the strategy of the community-wide program for protection against fatalities. These periods are the months of pregnancy, childbirth, and the months immediately following, especially the first one.

In past times the period of childbirth itself was the most hazardous. Even today, with all the aids of modern medical and surgical practice, the time honored phrase "woman in labor" is not without meaning. The fact of birth may always be relatively hazardous, but it is much less so than formerly. Puerperal fever, from which many mothers formerly died during childbirth, was induced by infections introduced during the course of delivery. Deaths from puerperal septicemia still occur, but strict asepsis in all things related to obstetrics minimizes the risk. Delivery hazards have been reduced also by the increased medical and surgical capacity to deal not only with normal conditions, but also with hemorrhages, malposition of foetus, injuries, and other complications.

Delivery in a hospital is usually conceded to be the best way to assure proper medical attention at this critical time. Success in bringing about a high proportion of deliveries in hospitals has been a very great factor in reducing the rate of both maternal and infant deaths.

Great emphasis now is laid on good prenatal care to prevent sickness and death from toxemia and other complications. Examination of the pelvic structure during early pregnancy enables the physician to plan in advance for difficult deliveries. Routine blood tests, now required for pregnant women by a majority of the states, enable the physician to institute treatment for syphilis when it is found, not only benefiting the mother but preventing congenital syphilis in the infant. Special attention to nutrition protects the mother by increasing her resistance to disease, and also assures to the foetus the essential food elements required for its proper development. Pregnant women are unusually susceptible to dental cavities, and dental supervision is advised to prevent their occurrence.

For the infant, one of the greatest hazards is premature birth. Actuarially speaking, the most hazardous month of his life is the first one. Of every 1,000 liveborn infants, 34 die in their first year of life, but over two thirds of the deaths occur during the first month, and nearly half of these occur the first day. Neonatal mortality (death during the first month of life) is due primarily to four causes—prematurity, birth injuries, malformations, and syphilis.

Many early infant deaths may be prevented through proper prenatal care of the mother and proper medical attention preceding and during birth. Birth injuries and malformations may be prevented to a considerable degree through good prenatal and obstetrical care. It is felt that eventually most malformations may be prevented as medical science increases its knowledge of the intrauterine development of the foetus. Research into the effects of the Rh factor in bringing about certain malformations in particular is expected to reduce the fatalities from this cause.

But to the present time, the greatest success in reducing infant mortality has been in the later months of infant life. Relatively little reduction has taken place in the early months of infancy. The total infant death rate dropped from 85.8 to 32.2 between 1920 and 1947 for the group of states in the birth registration area. But the drop in this period for neonatal deaths was much less, from 41.5 to 22.8; even less progress is shown for deaths during the first day, the rate for 1947 being 10.7 as compared with 14.7 in 1920.[5]

5 U.S. Bureau of the Census, *Statistical Abstract of the United States: 1949*, p. 77. Tables 84 and 85.

It is difficult to place relative values on the several factors to which reduced infant mortality is due. The better control of the infectious diseases among all ages, but especially the concentration upon the susceptible periods of infancy and childhood, has been a highly important factor. Some consider it of first importance. Improvement in sanitation, particularly of water and of the milk supplies so important to infant and child feeding, have negated a great source of infectious material. As a result, such diseases as dysentery and fatal "summer diarrhea" have almost disappeared from many areas.

Reinforcing and supplementing these community-wide measures has been the development of instructional methods by the profession of public health nursing. It probably is not an exaggeration to say that the procedures through which the mother is given instruction in the proper care of herself and of her infant are the key to the effectiveness of the preventive measures. Instructions encompass not only the generalities, but the specifics against which each case needs protection. Reinforcing the instruction is the assumption of responsibility by the nurse for arranging for proper medical attention when this is necessary.

CHRONIC AND DEFICIENCY DISEASES

Like maternity and infancy, "chronicity" and "deficiency" are terms descriptive of conditions and courses of events, rather than medical classifications rooted in kinship of disease causes. Included are certain of the communicable diseases, diseases of the heart and circulatory system, of the tissues, of the glands, of the bones and organs of movement and so on through a varied list. Irrespective of their causation, they disable their victims for extended periods of time, are not self-limiting as are most communicable diseases, and require extensive treatment or rehabilitative measures.

The detail of any list of chronic diseases will differ according to its authority and purpose. Those associated with the preparation of this volume, as well as many public health authorities, believe that any basic list for community action should include: diseases of the heart and arteries; rheumatic fever; intracranial lesions of vascular origin; cancer, wherever located; arthritis and rheumatism; sciatica, neuralgia, and other diseases of the peripheral nerves; nephritis and other kidney diseases; diabetes; hernia and other intestinal obstructions; asthma, hay fever, and such allergic disorders.

Properly included among important chronic diseases, also, are tuberculosis and a variety of nervous and mental disorders. We have discussed the former among the communicable diseases, and will consider the latter in the section on Maladjustment. We will also consider orthopedic and other handicapping physical disabilities in a special section of this chapter.

GENERIC CHARACTERISTICS

One must admit frankly that medical knowledge about the cause, prevention, and cure of many of the chronic diseases is inadequate, although steadily on the increase. There is relatively little tested experience from which to winnow those strategic characteristics which are significant for the formulation of practical community procedures to protect against their consequences. There are, nevertheless, a number of characteristics which deserve consideration.

Priority.—We have already cited the commanding bid of chronic diseases for community and scientific attention. They are now the principal precipitants of illness and mortality. A small number of chronic diseases now account for nearly two thirds of all deaths in the United States. Among the first twenty causes of death in 1948 seven major chronic diseases were included (in this order): diseases of the heart; cancer; intercranial lesions; nephritis; diabetes mellitus; arteriosclerosis; cirrhosis of the liver; hernia and other intestinal obstructions; and ulcers of the stomach and duodenum.[6] Chronic illness accounts for only 27 percent of the persons disabled by illness of a week or more, but it accounts for two thirds of the days lost during a year on account of illness. For the country as a whole this amounts to nearly one billion days annually.

Noncommunicability.—Chronic diseases are not directly caused by infecting organisms and are not transmitted from person to person. This characteristic is of high strategic importance, for it means that community action directed against the transmission of infectious causative agents is closed as an avenue of approach. Instead, high priority must be given to exploring ways better to exploit what is presently known about recognition of their early stages, retarding

6 National Office of Vital Statistics, *Deaths and Death Rates for Selected Causes, 1948.*

their progress, and effecting rehabilitation of their victims. While recognizing that death may ultimately result, communities need to recognize that fatalities may be delayed and that the victim may live out a normal span of years, provided appropriate measures are taken early enough.

Chronicity.—It may seem redundant to point out that an important strategic characteristic of the chronic diseases is their chronicity. It is well to remember, however, that chronic diseases often disable their victims for extensive periods of time, that there is no immunity from them, and that apparent recovery may be followed by recurrent, prolonged, and more intensive attacks.

An important companion characteristic is that the disease may be mild at onset, the symptoms so vague that the seriousness of the illness is not suspected. Disability may be slight, and the person quite able to continue his usual activities. Yet, medical authorities are agreed, this is the time when treatment should be instituted, because it has the best chance of being effective. Unless a chronic disease is discovered early and effective treatment instituted promptly, it may result in partial or complete disability that may last for years.

This characteristic poses certain considerations that the community has not had to face with most of the communicable diseases. The first of these requires systematic procedures to detect, in apparently well persons, early signs of diseases which are potentially disabling, if not fatal. The second is continuity of treatment, which may well include measures for rehabilitation of the patient as well as alleviation of his illness. Treatment so conceived may embrace a regime of life, involving economic as well as social and health considerations. A third consideration is expense. An acute disease runs its course in a short time, and medical care is needed for that period only, as a rule. A chronic disease may last a lifetime and entail medical as well as other expenses over a long period of years.

Chronology.—The chronic diseases are associated with the degenerative processes of life. Their prevalence increases steadily with age and is especially high for persons over sixty-five. In an "aging population" such as is now found in the United States, these diseases may be expected to continue to increase. The health and medical services which have prevented untimely deaths from health hazards of an earlier generation have resulted in a population peculiarly susceptible to the ravages of chronic diseases. Even so, much may be done to prolong and enrich life, under certain circumstances and conditions, although the chances of ultimate recovery obviously diminish.

Of importance for community-wide strategy, however, is the fact that chronic disease is now being recognized as even more prevalent in the productive than in the degenerative years. According to the National Health Survey, in 1935 fully three fourths of all persons suffering from one or more of the chronic diseases was in the productive ages of fifteen to sixty-four years.[7] One half were below the age of forty-five. Nearly 8 percent of all chronic illness is found among children, and 8.4 percent is among young persons fifteen to twenty-four years of age.[8]

Illness in these early age groups has special community significance. It may affect the whole personal, social, and economic development of the young person. If not arrested, the disease may continue to be a medical problem over a long period of years, requiring continuous medical supervision. Rehabilitative measures for such young persons take on an added importance.

Family orientation.—A characteristic of the chronic diseases not yet fully explored and understood is their vital relationship to family life. Known treatment for many of these diseases requires adherence to a regime made possible only through family support and cooperation. For any family, prolonged illness of any of its members constitutes a drain upon its resources which may seriously undermine its capacity to function normally. When the disabled person is the head of the family, whether breadwinner or homemaker, the situation obviously is even more serious.

Our own view is that the study of the "epidemiology" of the chronic diseases needs to give substantial weight to this characteristic. As the St. Paul project suggested, in a substantial number of chronic disease cases, medical teatment of and by itself is almost bound to be ineffective. Rather, what seems to be required is a coordinated composite of medical care, casework, psychiatric assistance, and other services which would attempt to rehabilitate the entire family situation.

[7] Joint Statement (American Hospital Association, American Medical Association, American Public Health Association, American Public Welfare Association), "Planning for the Chronically Ill," *American Journal of Public Health*, XXXVII, No. 10 (October, 1947), 1257.

[8] Francis Upham, *A Dynamic Approach to Illness*, p. 54.

We may well recall again that nearly one third of all cases of illness known to St. Paul's system of organized medical care, during the month of our study, were cases of chronic illness. And that chronic illness was found among a third of the group of 6,466 very seriously disorganized families whose multiplicity of problems were described in the section on dependency.

SPECIFIC CHARACTERISTICS

Experimentation with systematic community-wide procedures has hitherto been confined principally to cancer, rheumatic fever, and diabetes. Even such experiments are of comparatively recent origin, and the results are still in process of evaluation. It seems clear, however, that control procedures must be based in what is now known, and not known, about the causes of certain diseases, their prognosis, and the present methods of treatment. A brief recapitulation of these factors in relation to some of the more prevalent, and disabling, diseases should serve to illustrate the considerations which community-wide programs need to take into account.

Diseases of the heart and arteries.—In 1948 these constituted the leading cause of death, accounting for nearly one third of the total. Among chronic diseases (exclusive of mental diseases) which produced disabling illness of one week or more in 1935,[9] they stood second in number of cases found, first in number of days lost, and first in number of persons completely invalided.

The diseases which attack the tissues of the heart, particularly those of the heart muscle and the valves, cause a degeneration of the tissues which in turn brings about a disfunction of the organ. There is as yet no known medical treatment which will restore an affected heart to its normal condition. But if the presence of heart disease is discovered at an early stage, social treatment may have constructive results. If a patient can arrange his life so as to avoid overexertion his span of years may be usefully extended. This usually requires that problems be worked out in connection with family life, occupation, and economic status, recreation and social interests, which go well beyond the bounds of medical treatment. For such persons the cir-

[9] Public Health Service, *National Health Survey*, Bulletin 1, Sickness and Medical Care Series, Appendix Table 1.

cumstances of living must be controlled as long as the condition exists, which may be for the remainder of life.

Intracranial lesions of vascular origin.—Closely associated with diseases of the heart, "hardening of the arteries" is most prevalent among the older age groups. The resulting high blood pressure may not be serious if the heart makes sufficient compensation for this condition. If it does not, cerebral hemorrhage or apoplexy may result, and frequently does. With good nursing care, and physical therapy, persons who have a stroke may be made comfortable, and often are able to lead self-sustaining and useful lives.

When death occurs from intracranial lesions, while seemingly "sudden" it is due to a condition which has developed in the circulatory system over a relatively long period of time.

Rheumatic fever.—This is a principal cause of heart fatalities among young people between the ages of five and nineteen, and for that reason special efforts are being made to bring it under better community-wide control. Persons with rheumatic heart disease usually die young, most of them under forty.[10] At present it is not known how this infection occurs, nor in fact what is its precise cause. The disease is not communicable, and an attack does not produce immunity, recurrent attacks being common.

Attacks frequently appear following streptococcal infections of the upper respiratory tract, usually some time after the "strep" infection has subsided, but symptoms are often vague. Recently the administration of sulfonamides in prophylactic dosages, to prevent recurrent attacks of this infection, has been adopted as an important protective measure. Early recognition is important and strict medical supervision imperative.

Cancer.—Next to heart disease, more people die from cancer than from any other cause. Based on the rule-of-thumb estimate of three cases for every death from cancer, it is thought that there are nearly 600,000 cases of cancer in this country at the present time, but there are no complete morbidity data.

Although the resources of chemistry, physics, physiology, and biology have been brought to bear upon it, in a vast amount of laboratory and other research, the cause of cancer still is unknown.

10 Gulli Lindh Muller and Dorothy E. Dawes, *Introduction to Medical Science*, p. 111.

Cancer is more prevalent in the later years, although it may be found in young persons. Contrary to the popular conception that cancer is a disease of women, 47 percent of all persons who die from cancer are men.[11]

Although it is chronic, cancer is essentially a killer, rather than a disabler. Once it takes hold it usually moves with relative swiftness to slay its victim, unless its course can be arrested. For this reason early detection has been the key to experimental effort to exercise community-wide control over the disease.

Surgical removal of the cancerous tissue, and x-ray therapy are the principal methods of treatment. Neither gives complete assurance that the growth may not recur, in the same location or remote from the original site. Both have proved most effective where the growth has been discovered early, and treatment undertaken promptly.

Diabetes.—In 1948 diabetes was the ninth leading cause of death. It stood fifteenth on the list of chronic illnesses in the National Health Survey, fifth in the number of persons completely invalided, and tenth in the total number of days lost. Diabetes probably is the best known of the diseases due to disorders of the ductless glands. Untreated diabetes usually runs a fairly rapid course of acidosis, coma, and death.[12]

The development of commercial insulin (in 1921) extracted from the pancreas of sheep and oxen gave the key to methods for control. The insulin injections do not affect the activity of the pancreas, they merely provide a substitute for the normal pancreatic secretion. Treatment must be continuous and as diabetes usually lasts a lifetime, may well constitute a financial burden to the family of the patient.

Heredity is believed to play an important part in diabetes. As an important control measure, many physicians look for diabetics among the relatives of diabetic patients, and institute early treatment when found.[13]

Nephritis.—Nephritis and other diseases of the kidneys are the fourth leading cause of death in the United States. In the National Health Survey, these diseases were found to be eighth in number of cases of disabling illness, sixth in the number of days lost, and sixth in the number of persons invalided. Very little is known about the

---

[11] *Ibid.*, p. 432.   [12] *Ibid.*, p. 175.
[13] Smilie, *Public Health Administration . . . op. cit.*, p. 376.

causes of the kidney diseases and few therapies are available for their treatment.

Rheumatism.—Rheumatism and related disorders—arthritis, neuralgia, neuritis—do not cause death, but rank ahead of heart disease in the number of cases of disabling illness. This group of diseases ranks first in the number of cases of chronic illness, stands next in rank after the mental diseases in causing loss of working time, and second in the number of persons invalided.

Little is known about the cause or the cure of the rheumatic diseases. Heredity is believed to be a predisposing factor, but exposure and infection have not yet been ruled out completely. Current research, on the other hand, offers real hope of a specific therapy for rheumatism and arthritis, in particular cortisone and ACTH. As this is written their value is still being tested. Certain forms of alleviative treatment continue to be used effectively in the meantime; included among these are short-wave diathermy, infrared rays, paraffin applications and baths, as well as massage and special exercises.

CHRONIC PHYSICAL HANDICAPS

The term "chronic handicap" denotes an impairment of function of limbs, eyes, ears, and speech organs, having the attribute of chronicity. These handicaps do not of themselves cause death, but often the victim requires special medical and rehabilitative services. The common strategic characteristics for guidance in planning community programs lie in these facts: many of them may be prevented; all persons with such disabilities require some medical care and supervision, sometimes continuously; while the physical condition usually is a permanent one, the victim frequently can overcome his handicap to a large extent through appropriate rehabilitative measures.

GENERIC CHARACTERISTICS

Orthopedic, visual, hearing, and speech defects are the principal physical handicaps. While vastly different in specific manifestation, all of these share to some degree certain basic characteristics which are significant to community action.

Prevention by disease control.—Each of these disabling conditions may be caused in some measure by infectious diseases, hazards of the birth cycle, or by chronic diseases. To the extent that this is the case, prevention of the occurrence of the disability depends upon the effectiveness of the community-wide disease control program. It seems pertinent to recapitulate briefly the role of some of the more prominent causes of specific disabling conditions.

About one third of disabling orthopedic defects are due to the effects of disease. Arthritis is by far the most important disease among adults. Poliomyelitis and cerebral palsy (resulting from injuries to the central nervous system during or after birth) accounts for the largest number among children. A relatively small number of children are handicapped by a variety of malformations such as clubfoot, webbed fingers, and so on.[14]

Numerous infectious diseases result in blindness and account for some 23 percent of all children admitted to schools for the blind.[15] Routine injection of silver nitrate in the eyes of all infants at birth, however, has nearly eliminated blindness due to syphilitic or gonococcal infection of the newborn. Use of sulfonamide compounds has drastically reduced blindness caused by trachoma.

The mucous membranes which line the middle ear and the Eustachian tubes are highly susceptible to infection similar to those which affect the nose and throat. Scarlet fever, typhoid fever, diphtheria, whooping cough, influenza, and pneumonia are therefore among the diseases which may impair hearing. Special care must be taken during attacks of these diseases to see that ear, nose and throat drainage is adequate and that infections from the nasal passage are not carried into the middle ear. The auditory nerve seems especially susceptible also to disturbances due to certain of the chronic diseases—diabetes, gout, arteriosclerosis and several of the blood diseases.[16]

Prevention through accident control.—Accidents and injuries are the chief cause of orthopedic defects, accounting for about two thirds of them. At the time of injury, prompt medical service, and especially organized emergency hospital service, is of prime importance as protection against preventable after effects.

It is now recognized that most persons who suffer industrial, traf-

14 Social Security Administration, *Annual Report, 1947,* p. 129.

15 Franklin M. Foote, "Milestones in Sight Conservation," *Yale Journal of Biology and Medicine,* XIX, No. 4 (March, 1947), 595.

16 Waldemar Schwasheimer, "Common Ear Troubles," *Hygeia,* XIX, No. 9 (September, 1941), pp. 690, 691.

fic, and home accidents have some part in their causation.[17] For this reason effective preventive measures must be built around the discovery of persons who are "accident prone" and guarding them from engaging in activities potentially hazardous to themselves and to the public. While there has been considerable research pointing in this direction, so far this significant characteristic of accident incidence has not been reflected in systematic, community-wide programs.

Disability vs. handicap.—The distinction between "disability" and "handicap" is of real and practical significance. Disability is an objective fact, the degree of which can be determined by a physician. Handicap, in contrast, is the "cumulative result of the obstacles which disability interposes between the individual and his maximum functional level."

An ingenious variety of mechanical aids now are available to "interpose" between many of these disabilities and their resulting functional handicaps. The two wars resulted in the development of an extraordinary number of substitutes for loss of limbs and other orthopedic impairments. Glasses compensate for all but the most serious defects of vision. Hearing aids enable many persons with serious hearing impairments to function adequately in a normal setting. These aids are expensive and beyond the means of many; provision of them must therefore be part of any comprehensive plan of rehabilitation.

Also, "interposing" between the "disability" and the resulting "handicap" are the tested potentialities of specialized vocational training. A high proportion of crippled, blind, or deaf persons can be trained for occupations in which their disability constitutes little or no handicap. The demand for manpower during wartime brought out a previously disregarded reservoir of "handicapped" personnel. Their successful adaptation to the demands of industry should not be forgotten.

Family orientation.—Finally, it seems to us that no less than with "chronic" disease does the vital strategic relationship between chronic handicaps and family life need to be much better explored. A permanent handicap in any member of the family constitutes a constant drain upon its resources. The effectiveness of the social, vocational, and perhaps even the medical, treatment required is very likely to

[17] Franz Alexander, "The Accident-prone Individual," *Public Health Reports*, LXIV, No. 12 (March 25, 1949), 357.

depend on the strength with which the family can support a given course of action. It may well be that upon this will be determined to a high degree the depth and breadth of the gap between the "disability" itself and the "handicap" to a normal and successful life.

Indeed, the St. Paul data suggested that the families of seriously handicapped persons now present a range of social and economic problems out of all proportion to their relative numerical distribution. In over 20 percent of the seriously disorganized "multiproblem" families, one or more persons were suffering from a chronic handicap. This was also true of the residual relief load, of the maladjusted families, and of those receiving organized medical care.

SPECIFIC CHARACTERISTICS

There is a considerable difference numerically in the prevalence of the different types of disabilities within the community. Moreover, each disability may arise from factors other than infectious and chronic diseases or the hazards of birth.

Orthopedic defects.—Since these are caused primarily by accidents and disease, the most hopeful prospect is through vigorous prosecution of accident and disease prevention programs. Communities may do much to alleviate the condition and to provide the victims with opportunities for useful and comfortable living. Chief requirements for such a program are the provision of prosthetic devices and rehabilitative training.

Visual defects.—The principal causes of blindness are cataract and glaucoma, diseases of the eye which become prevalent in the middle to the late years.[18] Cataracts, which render the crystalline lens of the eye opaque, are curable by surgery. Persons sixty-five and over are most likely to be subject to cataracts, which account for nearly half the cases of blindness in this age group. Early diagnosis and treatment can halt the progress of glaucoma, but cannot restore tissue already affected.[19]

The person disabled by total blindness is handicapped in almost every aspect of his life. Even more than for some of the other handicaps the program for the protection and rehabilitation of the blind

18 Franklin M. Foote, "Public Responsibility for an Eye Health Program," *The Sight Saving Review*, XVII, No. 4 (Winter, 1947), 232.
19 Foote, "Milestones . . ." *op. cit.,* 599, 600.

must be a composite of specialties, coordinated to deal with the total range of personal and family problems.

Hearing defects.—These are by no means so widespread as visual defects. It is estimated that between 6 and 10 percent of the population suffer some loss of hearing during the course of their lives.

Infectious and chronic diseases may impair hearing, particularly if good medical care was lacking at the time of illness. Otosclerosis, a condition in which the small bones (hammer, anvil, and stirrup) behind the ear drum grow together, is found frequently in older persons. Temporary deafness may develop from obstructions in the outer acoustic duct which interrupt the transmission of sound waves. Accidents, explosions, extreme exposure and a variety of such conditions may injure or completely rupture the ear drum.

Mechanical hearing aids are relatively expensive, and many who could use them with profit are unable to procure them without assistance. For the small, but seriously disadvantaged, group of persons whose loss of hearing occurred before they acquired facility in speech, institutional care and special training are usually available.

Speech defects.—The causes of speech defects may be organic or entirely psychogenic. As far as we know, there are no reliable estimates as to the number who are seriously incapacitated. Diagnosis to determine the cause, and treatment to remove it, require coordinated skills of the otolaryngologist, the psychiatrist, the psychologist, the speech and voice clinicians, and the social worker.

Stuttering, perhaps the most familiar of speech difficulties, is regarded as primarily phychosomatic, emotional factors being highly important. Group psychotherapy is considered the most effective form of treatment. Many persons each year lose the ability to speak through surgical removal of the larynx, injury to the vocal cords, and the like, because of disease or injury. A new technique enables persons who suffer this disability to speak through the esophagus (food tube) instead of the larynx.

THE CRUX OF COMMUNITY CONCERN

Even so cursory a description of the strategic characteristics of certain diseases and conditions shows that there are wide gaps in scientific knowledge about them. For many of the communicable diseases immunity cannot be provided, nor are there specific therapies. The millennium of knowledge about elimination of the hazards of pregnancy, childbirth, infancy, and childhood has not been reached. For most of the chronic diseases and conditions medical science has only reached the threshold of achievement. The marvel of modern medical science, however, is that so much is now known in comparison with what was known even a half century ago.

But the equal marvel is in the systematic manner in which what *is* known about the characteristics of these diseases and hazards has been put together to give form and content to a strategic community-wide attack upon them. The results will bear repeating, lest the significance of this achievement be neglected. In 1900 the general death rate was 17.2 per 1,000 of the population; in 1948, it was 9.9. Ten infectious diseases caused 705.6 deaths per 100,000 in 1900; in 1948 the rate was 85.4. Deaths attributed to maternity and infancy accounted for 88.0 per 100,000 of the population in 1900; in 1948 this rate was 58.1. But nine chronic diseases which caused 435 deaths per 100,000 in 1900 were the cause of even greater fatalities in 1948, the death rate from these diseases having risen to 669.8.[20]

Clearly, the greatest progress in the past has been made in connection with the infectious diseases. Substantial progress has been made in reducing maternal and infant deaths. Control of infection has been an important factor to date in reducing both infant and maternal mortality. But it is generally recognized that further progress will require increased emphasis on medical care and supervision during the months of pregnancy, at delivery, and during the first month of the infant's life.

The chronic diseases and conditions which we have taken to illustrate strategic characteristics for community-wide control include those which rank high as a cause of death. They include also those which rank high as disablers, even when death seldom is attributed to the disease. Undoubtedly advances in medical diagnosis have resulted in precise identification of many cases of chronic disease which formerly would have been included as "senility and ill-defined" causes of death. But communities cannot escape the fact that nine chronic diseases now cause 670 deaths per 100,000 of the population, and that

20 Summarized from reports of the National Office of Vital Statistics, *Deaths and Death Rates for Selected Causes.*

these account for more than two thirds of all deaths.[21] Nor can they ignore the fact that substantial numbers of the population are disabled from chronic diseases and other conditions seldom recorded as a cause of death, but which rank high as causes of family disorganization.

It is well to remember that it is the degree of incapacity which determines the need for community concern for its disabled members. If some accidents did not result in death or serious incapacity, if some visual defects did not result in total blindness, and some hearing and speech defects in the complete loss of means of intercommunication, it is altogether probable that the community would regard these afflictions as the ordinary tribulations of man, about which little needed to be done.

But when the disability does result in serious incapacity, we may say of both chronic diseases and handicaps that the total problem "is not a series of separate problems that can be solved one by one, but rather a complex of interrelated problems which require simultaneous solution." [22] Furthermore, it is apparent that it is "one which is especially important as a family pattern." More than any of the other diseases and conditions which affect community health, both the chronic diseases and the chronic handicaps present the necessity for effective coordination between health, adjustment, and financial assistance services, to strengthen the family's capacity to cope with the "chronic" disadvantages that they impose.

[21] *Ibid.*
[22] Joint Statement, "Planning for the Chronically Ill," p. 1265.

Chapter IX

COMMUNITY-WIDE FUNCTIONS

AS SCIENCE has progressively revealed the causes and strategic characteristics of diseases and disabilities, the three systems which protect and promote the health of the community have increased the variety, and deepened the quality, of their particular services. The services of the public health officer, the public health nurse, the physician and the dentist, pervade all sections of the community. Prenatal examinations, hospital deliveries, pasteurized milk, periodic health examinations, major and minor operations, blood transfusions, oxygen tents, and the persistent admonition to "see your doctor" and "see your dentist" are commonplaces of modern life. All of this is in sharp contrast to the day in which birth was a matter of good luck and early death a matter of course.

These aspects of health protection and promotion are a part of the three major service functions through which a community-wide attack may be made against disease, disability, and untimely death. These three functions, as we see them, are: (1) community-wide disease prevention and control; (2) detection, diagnosis, and treatment; and (3) nursing, including instruction and bedside care. For each of these there have been developed specific principles and procedures as well as qualitative and quantitative standards, and community requirements.

Each of these functions is made up of a constellation of procedures and services. Closely related to them, and supporting them all in a general way, are three important community undertakings: an environmentally safe and clean municipality; a medical profession grounded in the philosophy and practice of preventive medicine; and a popular understanding of matters pertaining to personal hygiene and public health.

A SAFE ENVIRONMENT

Sanitation was once the main activity of the public health move-ment. A "clean-up" was the one thing that seemed to produce measur-able results in the days before the causes of epidemic infections were understood. Garbage disposal, the purification of the water supply system, and the abatement of a variety of public nuisances were the principal responsibilities of the early public health officials. These are now considered part of the ordinary "housekeeping" functions of the community. In many places health officers have been relieved of direct responsibility in these matters, although they may still be required to supervise certain technical details of efficient operation.

Public health laws regulate food, milk, and water supplies, and sewage disposal, as well as many other specific services in the inter-est of public health. It is the duty of the public health officer to see that such laws and regulations are enforced. The control of typhoid fever and of certain other diseases still depends primarily upon the enforcement of the sanitary code. An epidemic of amebic dysentery may well follow in the wake of defective plumbing systems. Mosquito control and control of rats and other vermin, ventilation and illumina-tion of public housing, and hygienic conditions in industry, all have a direct relationship to health, and hence are of primary concern to the public health officer.

Public health departments maintain a corps of sanitarians and engineers to supervise the range of activities now deemed essential. As one health authority puts it, "In a virgin field it may be more im-portant . . . to develop dairying and build manure pits than to study the epidemiology of meningitis, and more important . . . to construct community wells than to install preschool clinics . . . sani-tary inspection may be more important than nursing service." [1]

THE PHILOSOPHY OF PREVENTIVE MEDICINE

In the early years of disease prevention programs, it was primarily the epidemiologists, statisticians, bacteriologists, and sanitarians who gave impetus to finding the means for prevention. With notable ex-ceptions, physicians were preoccupied with clinical measures for the care of persons who were sick. As measures for preventing the onset of

[1] Wilson G. Smilie, *Public Health Administration in the United States*, p. 242.

disease through vaccination, therapy, and health supervision have been demonstrated, physicians have come to play an increasing role in the field of prevention.

Some of the confusion which now exists with respect to the concept of preventive medicine undoubtedly stems from the fact that the earliest and most dramatic successes were with the communicable diseases. In many circles preventive medicine and the public health program for prevention of the communicable diseases are considered as synonymous. Medical scientists, on the other hand, are progressively demonstrating that preventive medicine can be applied to the reduction and control of other diseases and disabilities.

The development of preventive medicine to its greatest usefulness requires reorientation of the physician to his patient. From a concern with restoring his patient to health after illness has occurred, his major concern must be to prevent the occurrence of illness. Up to the present time the greatest progress has been made in this direction by the pediatrician, who is concerned "in large measure with the child and not with the child's diseases—with health promotion and not merely with the prevention of sickness and death." [2]

The private physician and the public health official must place high value on the practical approach of preventive medicine, not only for time-honored communicable diseases, but also for chronic and other diseases and conditions.

HEALTH EDUCATION

The necessity for cleanliness and care of the body nowadays is taken for granted. People generally give special attention to care of the teeth and to providing a varied, balanced, and nutritious diet. The value of good habits of rest and recreation are recognized. It is assumed that the community will see that the water supply is adequate and pure, and that milk is clean and safely pasteurized. Efficient garbage and sewage disposal are taken for granted, and loud protests may be heard if any of the matters of environmental sanitation are improperly administered.

Knowledge about specific diseases and conditions to which people are generally susceptible is widespread. A surprising proportion of the

[2] C.–E. A. Winslow, "Preventive Medicine and Health Promotion—Ideals or Realities?" *Yale Journal of Biology and Medicine*, XIV, No. 5 (May, 1942), 444.

population can list the symptoms and signs by which major disease hazards may be recognized. Newspapers, magazines, and radio programs have increasingly devoted space and time to the more dramatic health hazards and to the scientific advances related to them. Public health authorities and the medical profession have long believed that all persons of a community should possess basic knowledge about health hazards, and have striven to make these available in understandable terms. This knowledge encompasses: (1) the principles of personal hygiene; (2) the principles of environmental sanitation; (3) the prevalence, mode of transmission, methods of prevention and treatment, and other useful information concerning common communicable diseases; (4) the basic facts relating to early recognition of chronic and degenerative diseases. Furthermore, each person who works should understand the basic principles of industrial health, and all potential parents should know something about maternal health and child care. And everyone should know something about the activities and objectives of the public health department and of other community agencies equipped to give information or service related to problems of health.[3]

That ignorance about all these matters still abounds no one can doubt. To the extent that it exists, there is obvious need for continued effort on the part of all concerned, but particularly on the part of the medical profession and of public health officials.

COMMUNITY-WIDE DISEASE CONTROL

At the outset we should make it clear that the term "community-wide disease control" is not to be confused with "community sanitation," although the two are closely related. Disease control procedures are centered upon particular individuals who are ill, or in danger of some specific hazard to their health. Community sanitation procedures are centered on controlling the condition of the environment. Nor should the word "control" be confused with any authoritarian vision of a host of regimented individuals. The term is used impersonally to describe procedures necessary to control the disease or condition, not the person. In an increasing number of instances control can be synonymous with eradication.

[3] Summarized from Smilie, *Public Health Administration* . . . , Chapter XIV, p. 297.

The basic objective of the disease control function is to put to work practically and systematically, on behalf of the community, knowledge about strategic characteristics of particular diseases. Out of the epidemiologic study of these characteristics on the one hand, and experimentation and testing of procedures on the other, the public health functional design has evolved.

Initially its detailed procedures were shaped to control the acute epidemic diseases which had first priority. These had to be modified substantially to control tuberculosis, and to afford systematic protection against the hazards of pregnancy and infancy. The strategic characteristics of noncommunicable chronic diseases and conditions are requiring further modification of procedures. The broad principles upon which disease controls rest are capable of infinite adaptation to fit special characteristics of particular diseases and conditions. Perhaps this is the greatest tribute which can be paid to the creators of this functional design of the epidemiologic approach.

DISCOVERY AND REPORTING

The first step in the administration of the disease control function is the key to all the others. It is concerned with the systematic procedures for the discovery and reporting of individual cases.

Under the public health laws and regulations of every state, physicians—and householders in the absence of a physician—are required to report the onset of a certain number of notifiable diseases. The usual reportable list is apt to include 40 or more diseases, representing actual or potential danger to the community health.[4] The information called for usually includes the patient's name, residence, age, the diagnosis or suspicion of the disease, the date of onset, and the name of the reporting physician or other informant. The list of notifiable diseases varies from state to state. In recent years certain chronic diseases and conditions have been added to the lists in some states.

The primary purpose of disease reporting is to set in motion in each case the chain of actions deemed appropriate to protect the person and the community. Although more systematic facts about the characteristics of chronic diseases would be most valuable, many health authorities doubt the wisdom of mandatory reporting until it is clear that specific action can be instituted with profit to the patient and to the community.

4 *Ibid.,* p. 25.

For some conditions systematic voluntary reporting has proved effective without legal compulsion. Maternity and infancy furnish a good example. The condition of pregnancy is not reportable, but through maternal health services, particularly in the less privileged sections of cities, it has been possible to secure the reporting of a high proportion of the expectant mothers. This has been achieved primarily through strategic location of prenatal clinics, the family contacts of the visiting nurses in the districts, and the voluntary co-operation of physicians, social agencies, and other neighborhood groups.

Certain diseases and conditions develop slowly, and may be well under way before symptoms appear that send the person to a physician. The classic example here is tuberculosis. This disease is treated most easily in its early stages, and it is frequently most infectious to others during this time. For such 'reasons systematic voluntary case-finding procedures were developed. X-ray examinations of hospital and clinic patients, as well as mass x-ray tests of selected industrial populations and other adult groups, have paid dividends in detecting cases of tuberculosis. Much progress has been made in the better discovery of syphilis through routine blood tests in hospitals and clinics, premarital tests and prenatal tests for syphilis, as well as special examinations for industrial groups.

It is obvious that systematic case-finding procedures, both official and voluntary, are important to the development of community-wide programs for the control of chronic diseases. Therapy is most effective in the early stages of many of these diseases, and an early ordering of the patient's activities offers the best known way of halting the diseases' progress. Generally speaking, precise case-finding methods in this area have yet to come into general use. However, official agencies in 53 states and territories are now engaged in some phase of cancer control, in 25 states cancer is now a reportable disease, and 31 states have some cancer detection centers. By 1947 special plans for the discovery of children with rheumatic fever had been established in communities in 29 states.[5]

Reporting from hospitals, on a voluntary basis and with particular reference to chronic diseases and conditions, is urged by some as an

[5] Cancer Control Branch, National Cancer Institute, *Services and Facilities for Cancer Control in the United States, January 1948,* Supplement No. 208 to the *Public Health Reports* (June, 1948), p. 1.

aid to early discovery and appropriate action. The private physicians of Hillsboro, Michigan, have found voluntary registration of cancer cases a great stimulus to early discovery of the disease, and undoubtedly further experimentation and demonstration in the area of the chronic diseases may throw more light on the usefulness of morbidity recording to the development of a comprehensive community-wide program for control.[6]

Experiments with a new case-finding procedure, adapted not only to the discovery of some of the chronic diseases and conditions but also to tuberculosis and syphilis, should be noted. A small number of cities are now experimenting with "multiphasic screening." These procedures are modeled after the mass x-ray examinations for the discovery of tuberculosis. They are founded on the fact that the test or examination given for one disease can be broadened to indicate the presence or absence of others. Such tests indicate the probable presence of the disease or condition. "Suspects" are referred to private physicians, or clinics, for further examination to establish the diagnosis and institute therapy if needed.

CASE HOLDING

Public health authorities use the somewhat undynamic term of "case holding" to describe the second important phase. After the case has been discovered and reported, appropriate action is instituted, and the case is "held" in an active file until the disease has run its course. During the "case holding" period all of the knowledge about the characteristics of the particular disease in question is focused on a practical plan of action to protect the person and the community.

If the case is one of acute communicable disease, action must be immediate. Laboratory tests may be required to verify the diagnosis of the reporting physician. Investigation is instituted to determine the original source of the infection if possible, and steps taken to prevent others who may also be carrying the germ from spreading it further. Milk, food, and water supplies are checked if it is a scarlet fever or typhoid fever case. The patient, his family, and others directly concerned are given specific advice and instruction on how to minimize the danger to themselves and to others. Once the disease has run its

6 Clive Howard, "Every Doctor's Office a Cancer Detection Center," *Readers' Digest* (December, 1950), p. 108.

course, and danger of infection from it ceases, the record is removed from the active file.

Maternity cases are held for a longer period of time and the action taken is quite different. Maternity cases may be "held" by a voluntary nursing association, or some agency other than the health department. In effect a case may be reported by the appearance of the expectant mother at a maternity clinic, or in the office of a physician. Or it may be reported as a result of a visit by the public health nurse, before or after birth. But under whatever auspices, or by whatever method reported, the case is usually held until the newborn infant is at least six weeks old. During this time the agency maintaining the record assumes responsibility for seeing that appropriate plans are made, for medical service, instructional nursing service, delivery, or whatever special attention may be indicated.

MAINTAINING A CASE REGISTER

If chronicity is a characteristic of the cause of illness, the action planned may have to be continuous for a long period of time, and involve a constellation of services by private physicians as well as by a number of public and voluntary community agencies. Experience has demonstrated that these services may best be guided and integrated through establishing a register of cases. The longest, and most fruitful, experience with the use of the case register in connection with case holding has been with cases of tuberculosis. As the disease is both chronic and communicable, control procedures have combined those designed to prevent the spread of infection as well as those designed to benefit the individual patient. Because the use of the case register is potentially applicable to other diseases and disabilities in which chronicity is an attribute, it seems appropriate to recapitulate here the chief purposes which the register has served in promoting tuberculosis control.

The first purpose of the tuberculosis register, of course, was to record all cases in the community as the basis for action to prevent the spread of infection. The second purpose is closely related. As evidence that such action was taken, physicians, clinics, hospitals, and other health agencies providing treatment were asked to send in their reports, including changes in diagnosis and status of the patient. The public health nurse systematically visits all suspected and diagnosed cases of tuberculosis in her district and records pertinent observations made in the course of these visits.

A third purpose in maintaining the register is to help the tuberculous person secure the diagnostic and treatment services most appropriate to his condition. The agency administering the register does not need to provide all the diagnostic and treatment facilities, and indeed seldom does; but it does have a responsibility to determine whether prescribed services are being provided and to make arrangements to secure them if they are not.

A further purpose of the register is to enable the health officer or other competent person in the agency to judge whether or not the type of service seems appropriate to the case. A periodic review of all cases on the register for this and other purposes of systematic evaluation is standard practice in register operation.

A final and extremely important purpose of the register is to provide data on which to evaluate and guide, not merely case by case treatment, but the effectiveness of the total program for protection against tuberculosis. It is this central consolidation of the records about each case, together with administrative responsibility for assuring that treatment is planned and its results systematically reviewed which has provided a foundation for the remarkable success in the community-wide reduction and control of this extraordinarily persistent disease.

The basic principles and procedure of the case register are applicable to other diseases and conditions in which long-term observation and continuous treatment are required for individual patients. Federal appropriations to the states for programs for children crippled by rheumatic heart conditions carry with them the recommendation that registers be maintained.

Most of the cancer control programs represent a pooling of resources and services of "the general practitioner; specialists such as the pathologist, radiologist, surgeon, and internist; medical societies; divisions of the American Cancer Society; medical, dental, and nursing schools; hospitals providing cancer services; research centers; and welfare agencies." [7] With such a variety of participants, it is easy to

[7] Raymond F. Kaiser, "Proposed Elements of a State Cancer Control Program," *Public Health Reports*, LXIV, No. 37 (September 16, 1949), 1171.

see why it is deemed desirable to establish systematic community case registers for cancer control.

CASE FOLLOW-UP

In many chronic diseases and disabilities medical treatment alone is not sufficient to assure complete recovery of the patient; follow-up procedures must be instituted to aid in his rehabilitation. Again, the most extensive experience has been in connection with the fight on tuberculosis. All too frequently patients who had apparently recovered and had returned to former home and work conditions, suffered relapses and became infectious again, thus reinitiating the community control procedures.

It was found that complete recovery of a tuberculous person required bedside as well as instructive nursing, convalescent as well as hospital care. In many instances persons needed special vocational training and assistance in finding new types of employment, as well as assistance in personal and family adjustments. Tuberculosis societies undertook the follow-up of cases on the register to see that all services necessary to ultimate recovery were provided and coordinated into an integrated plan.

Many of these procedures obviously are applicable to the problems of many persons with chronic diseases and physical handicaps whose rehabilitation frequently requires a very broad range of social as well as medical treatment. Certain agencies working with handicapped persons have adopted such procedures. The New York Association for the Blind, for example, maintains a register of all persons who have participated in its broad and comprehensive program. Their status is periodically reviewed with reference to need for medical treatment, educational training, employment assistance, social treatment, and recreational opportunities. This register is not, of course, a complete community register, but for persons on it the Association assumes responsibility for "case follow-up" consistent with their needs.

Registers of varying degrees of completeness are maintained by a number of governmental agencies in connection with certain programs for the handicapped. We have already noted the state registers of the blind and the maintenance of registers for crippled children. State-federal offices of vocational rehabilitation services for civilians maintain registers for persons who apply to them for rehabilitative assistance.

Systematic case follow-up is much less well developed for the other chronic diseases. Communities are beginning to realize that just as early diagnosis is of little avail if treatment does not follow, it is absurd to permit a recovered patient to return to conditions which may aggravate his condition, even to bringing about a recurrence of the illness. Rehabilitative programs for persons with heart conditions, for example, must provide retraining for persons whose former occupations were too strenuous for a cardiac case. The various programs for victims of rheumatic fever, also, recognize a responsibility for ordering the lives of these persons to enable them to avoid unusual stress and strain.

The materials from the St. Paul project underscore the need for experimentation with case finding, case holding, and follow-up procedures for those with chronic diseases and handicaps. Half of all persons receiving medical services from the community health agencies were suffering from one or both of these conditions. Among the small group of seriously disorganized multiproblem families the proportion was slightly higher, reaching nearly 60 percent. Thus chronic disease and chronic handicaps loomed large among families receiving a large share of the total services of the community.

The introduction of systematic procedures should yield valuable data regarding the epidemiology of chronic diseases and chronic physical handicaps in relation to family disorganization. But they should result also in better coordination of the specialized services needed to cure or alleviate these disabilities, rehabilitate the individual, and strengthen the basic family situation. Periodic appraisal of the status of cases should make it possible to evaluate the effectiveness of the community's total program in a manner now impossible.

The essence of community-wide control of disease and disability is to find the case, to keep track of it, and to see that social and medical treatment are given when they will be most effective. This central idea saved many lives during the half century when communicable diseases were the major enemy to health. There is ample reason to believe that it will prove equally effective against the chronic diseases and disabilities.

DIAGNOSIS AND TREATMENT

From the point of view of the sick man, the whole purpose of medicine clearly is to determine the nature of his illness and to eliminate
the condition through appropriate treatment. He expects his physician to arrive at the correct diagnosis without undue delay, and to
prescribe a course of treatment which will cure his ailment.

Because of rapid advances in medical science, the doctor is now
confronted with two perplexing problems. The first arises out of a
multiplying galaxy of expensive diagnostic and treatment facilities.
The second is his frequent need for the assistance of specialists in his
profession, and quite possibly their need of him.

ANCILLARY FACILITIES

For his diagnostic judgments a generation or two ago, the physician
relied mainly on the examination of external, or overt, symptoms.
On the basis of recognized syndromes—that is, certain combinations
of signs and symptoms—he was able to identify most of the diseases
about which there was precise information. These procedures still
are sufficient to enable the general medical practitioner to arrive at
correct judgments about a great many illnesses.

On the other hand, the present-day physician knows that "many
disease processes would remain unsuspected, their nature quite impossible to determine if diagnosis were to depend exclusively on overt
signs and symptoms." [8] During the past few decades an extraordinary
number of mechanical aids and laboratory tests have been developed
which add to the speed and accuracy with which pathological conditions are diagnosed. With these it is possible for the physician to diagnose with certainty diseases formerly unsuspected until their late
stages, when treatment is more difficult and recovery less hopeful.

To the large segment of the population which has by now been included in mass x-ray surveys, the ability to detect early stages of tuberculosis as well as other lesions of the lungs is well known. Less obvious
to the patient, but no less important as diagnostic aids, are the routine
and special laboratory tests made by laboratory technicians. These
tests may involve any of the body fluids or tissues. Many of them have
become essential to the diagnostic art of the physician.

[8] Charles Phillips Emerson and Jane Elizabeth Taylor, *Essentials of Medicine,* p. 17.

Besides these tests, the doctor now has at his disposal many new therapies which have been recently introduced. Drugs usually can be secured easily on prescription or out of stock at the ubiquitous drugstore. But the drugstore cannot supply such things as blood plasma, nor the skills and equipment required for the transfusion.

Treatment of disease by such physical agents as heat and cold, light, x-ray, radium and electricity generally need not only special equipment, but trained technicians for their operation. Minor surgical operations are often performed in the physician's office, but to many of us "surgery" and "hospital" have come to be synonymous. The modern surgical equipment of the average physician's office contrasts sharply with that of the ancient surgeon; yet only the remarkable surgical equipment found almost exclusively in modern hospitals makes some intricate life-saving operations possible.

SPECIALIZATION

Since 1933 the American Medical Association has coordinated the certification of specialists through the American Advisory Board for Medical Specialties. Such certification means that the physician has completed three to five years of hospital residency and other types of training for his specialty in addition to his basic medical education and internship. These officially defined specialties embrace nineteen major fields, among the best known being internal medicine; obstetrics and gynecology; surgery; orthopedic surgery; pediatrics; the special diseases of the eye; and of the ear, nose, and throat. One of the most recent specialties recognized, with a medical specialty board of its own, is preventive medicine and public health.

While it is undoubtedly correct to say that the physician who truly knows his specialty has greater competence than anyone else in its diagnosis and treatment, the reverse is equally true. The very intensity of his specialized training makes him less aware of, less interested in, and hence less competent to recognize symptoms of other conditions and diseases which may be present. The general practitioner in his turn, while trained "to be familiar with the body as a whole, the diseases of all organs, and complications in special organs," [9] may lack the training and experience necessary to recognize early mani-

[9] Carl Eggers, "Education of the General Practitioner," *Trends in Medical Education*, pp. 215, 216.

festations of serious disorders. It is, in other words, humanly impossible for one doctor to encompass all of the knowledge and skill now at the disposal of the different branches of medical practice.

The individual physician is finding it increasingly necessary to associate himself with others in order to assure the patient the full diagnostic and treatment services which his condition may require. One means of doing this, a structure of group practice developing within the medical profession itself, will be described in the next chapter.

THE ROLE OF THE COMMUNITY HOSPITAL

In respect to the diagnostic and treatment function the community hospital is now undertaking an increasingly important role.

The hospital as an adjunct to general medical practice—in effect an extension of the physician's own facilities—is a development of modern times. Early hospitals were designed almost entirely for the domiciliary care of persons toward whom the community's humanitarian or protective impulses were impelled.

Seriously ill persons in all economic groups now expect to go to a hospital, almost as a matter of course. There the patient is assured a regime of quiet, appropriate diet, the regular administration of therapies prescribed by the physician, and continuous nursing care. But the modern hospital goes much further than this. It provides the physician, and his patient, with many of the expensive mechanical and technical resources needed in diagnoses and treatment. It provides the physician, through affiliation with its medical staff, the opportunity for close association with other physicians representing a wide range of specialized practice. For surgery and for childbirth it has long been accepted that the surgical and obstetrical aids of the hospital, including the completely antiseptic conditions, are necessary adjuncts to the physicians' and surgeons' skill.

We have already seen that the hospital has become a center of medical teaching, without which the medical schools could not achieve their present standards of education and training. As we have also seen, a physician may not be certified for specialized practice until he has completed the advance training and service required by the hospital residencies for advanced study. And it is in the hospital that the physicians of the community find an opportunity to continue their medical education and to keep abreast of new developments in medicine.

The quality of the medical care given in a hospital is ultimately the responsibility of the governing board, but it is also related directly to the qualifications of the members of the medical profession who practice there. Among the medical staff there are specialists as well as general practitioners. From their number a physician is able, ordinarily, to secure consultation and assistance in diagnosis and treatment of difficult cases and those requiring the special knowledge and skills of the specialist. The patient in his turn is diagnosed and treated in a setting which makes it easy to bring to bear upon his condition the full battery of technical resources and specialized skills which may be appropriate to it.

NURSING

An objective observer must remark, it seems to us, upon the firm hold which the nursing profession has upon the affection of the American people. There is good reason for it. For whatever may be the scientific nature of our illness, the ministrations of the nurse bring a sense of security and a feeling of comparative comfort.

Nevertheless, it is important to recognize that the primary function of nursing is to aid and implement the procedures of community-wide disease control and of diagnosis and treatment. In a sense, nursing is auxiliary to these functions, but it is an extremely important auxiliary.

Many specific procedures in connection with both the community-wide control of disease and the diagnosis and treatment of the sick patient, are performed wholly by the nurse. In these, as in all others, the nurse directly assists the physician or works under the immediate supervision of the health officer.

But she also occupies a unique position of her own:

The nurse is the interpreter of the findings of medical science. She acts as a "bridge between the sources of knowledge (the physician or the health officer) and the people." Her intimate association with the patient and his family establishes a relationship which affords many opportunities for teaching. There is a direct relationship between the confidence she inspires, the soundness of her preparation, and the effectiveness of her teaching.[10]

[10] Margaret A. Tracy, *Nursing, An Art and a Science*, p. 31.

There is in nursing a power to create in the patient so strong a desire to live that it may become the one factor which decides the issue in the patient's struggle with disease.

Most of the 1,215 state accredited nursing schools are operated by hospitals. Usually they require only high school graduation for admission of students for training, but 90 percent of the schools stipulate that the candidate be in the upper third, or upper half of the class. Standards for education and training of nurses are fixed by states in accrediting the schools of nurses, and nurses are licensed and registered by state boards of nursing examiners.[11] In addition, the National League of Nursing Education, the National Organization for Public Health Nursing, and the Association of Collegiate Schools of Nursing evaluate schools on the "basis of administration, financial support, number and qualifications of faculty, terms of admission, and graduation, curriculum, records, library and classroom and clinical facilities." [12] These standards now are administered by the National Nursing Accrediting Service. To be accredited the nursing school must be connected with a hospital having a daily average of 100 patients, with the necessary affiliation which provides a broad clinical experience.

BEDSIDE NURSING

Many of the duties of the bedside nurse center around the physical care and psychological comfort of her patient. The more helpless the patient, the more skillful must she be in ministering to his bodily necessities.

Her most important skill, however, lies in her ability to carry out the instructions of the doctor and to detect symptoms and signs of changes in the patient's condition which need to be brought to his attention. Her training has included clinical nursing of people with a variety of diseases. She is equipped with a basic understanding of the administration of medicines, and the specific therapies and general regimes appropriate to particular diseases. She not only respects, but generally understands the basis for the doctor's judgments. In all matters relating to the specific treatment of the patient. in home or hospital, her function is to give intelligent aid to the doctor in carrying out the treatment which his judgment dictates.

11 American Nurses' Association, *1949 Facts about Nursing*, pp. 12, 13, 42.
12 Commission on Hospital Care, *Hospital Care in the United States*, p. 131.

PUBLIC HEALTH NURSING

The basic training of the public health nurse, who is a registered nurse, includes skill in bedside nursing. But in addition to this basic training she must complete a full year of postgraduate study in public health nursing, in a school approved by the National Organization for Public Health Nursing. The public health nurse carries heavy responsibilities in connection with the whole function of community-wide disease control.

In the control of communicable diseases, for example, the nurse instructs the family about isolation of the patient, and arranges for immunization of family and other contacts if so instructed by the health officer. She helps secure information about the case, and about home conditions, which may assist the epidemiologist to locate the source of infection. She may arrange for medical attention and supervision if the family has no physician. She may give bedside care, or help arrange for it. She establishes the sickroom procedures, including those for concurrent disinfection, and arranges terminal disinfection where control measures prescribe them. She stresses the importance of measures for convalescent care which will avoid serious after effects of the disease.[13]

Because of its chronic attributes, a great part of the burden of preventing and controlling tuberculosis depends upon the public health nurse. She must visit regularly all tuberculous patients as well as all "suspects" in her district. If a central register is maintained, her reports are of first importance in keeping it up to date. She helps organize the service of tuberculosis clinics, and checks the attendance of cases in her district. She arranges for institutional care when that is necessary. She keeps track of persons who may be in danger of infection and arranges for their examination when that seems necessary. In brief, as one authority put it—"she keeps all tuberculosis cases in her jurisdiction, as well as their families . . . under constant watchful supervision." [14]

So also does the program for the protection of mothers and babies fall heavily upon the shoulders of the public health nurse. The district nurse tries to get in touch with expectant mothers in her juris-

13 Smilie, *Public Health Administration*, pp. 229, 230.
14 *Ibid.*

diction as early as possible in pregnancy. She arranges for medical examination of the pregnant woman, and instructs her in maternity and infant hygiene. She may give bedside nursing care during delivery and visit the mother for several weeks after delivery. The nurse instructs the mother in daily care of her child and in carrying out the doctor's orders for feeding the baby, and in arranging for smallpox and diphtheria immunization. Her attention may continue, if need be, into the later months and years.[15]

It seems inevitable that if community-wide programs are systematically extended to the control of the chronic noncommunicable diseases, the premium placed on the services of the public health nurse will rise proportionately. The maintenance of registers, education and instruction of the family in home care of the chronically ill, assistance in making arrangements for proper medical attention and supervision will be of vital importance.

Today it may seem that to speak of the functions of community-wide disease control, of medical diagnosis and treatment, of nursing, is but to use other language to describe the duties of the health officer with a graduate degree in public health, of the doctor with his M.D., and of the nurse with her R.N. It is well to remember, however, that this was not always so. The officials of the Middle Ages who restricted entrance into their villages of persons from other towns infected by the "plague" were equally undertaking the function of community-wide disease control. The barber or chirurgeon who "let blood" and "purged" his patients, was equally undertaking the function of medical diagnosis and treatment. The ancient crone who listened for the last bedside death rattle was presiding over the nursing function of her day.

The difference in quality, however, is considerable.

[15] National Organization for Public Health Nursing, *Public Health Nursing Program and Functions*, p. 2.

Chapter X

THE PIVOTAL STRUCTURE OF THE THREE SYSTEMS FOR HEALTH AND MEDICAL CARE

THE CHIEF VARIATIONS of disease are in intensity and spread. In every community the same basic service functions are needed to protect the population, and in every community basic facilities are needed to assure control of disease and disability, for medical diagnosis and treatment, and for bedside and public health nursing. The variation is primarily in the extent of facilities required to prevent and control specific diseases and conditions.

The structure, however, of the administrative units through which the basic service functions are discharged in one community is never identical with that of another. Every community needs some complement of physicians, dentists, and nurses, health officers, public health engineers and sanitarians, and a variety of technicians trained in special aspects of health and medical care. Every community needs hospital, clinic, diagnostic, and treatment facilities. The variation is in their extent and completeness, and in the manner in which they are organized for service.

In a community of a quarter million population there are usually twenty-five to forty different tax-supported and voluntary agency units administering different aspects of the health program. There are fewer units in a small community, and many more in a larger one. A few of these agencies are integral parts of state-wide programs, but for the most part they are independent units, under local auspices, deriving most of their support from local sources.

In addition to these community-organized health agencies, physicians and dentists in private practice provide the basic medical services available to the population. Most of this is on a fee for service basis, in home, office, or hospital. For persons who cannot meet these fees, service may be provided without charge by physicians or dentists through the hospitals and clinics with which they are associated. In such matters of common interest and community policy, county medical and dental societies, as well as the hospitals and clinics, participate in determining patterns of service.

But despite differences in the number and variety of community agencies, basic structural patterns recur. In great degree the common features are determined by the manner in which each of the three systems has developed. From the beginning the public health system has endeavored to develop a structure suited to provide a safe environment for everyone, and to prevent the onset of diseases on a community-wide basis. The systems of community-organized medical care and of private practice have been concerned primarily with diagnosis and treatment of specific individuals and much less with the community-wide provision of these services. For each of the three systems, however, circumstances are bringing about adaptations of traditional structural pattern. Taken as a whole, these changes seem to form a basis for greater utility in community-wide measures for the promotion of health.

THE PUBLIC HEALTH SYSTEM

Numerous public and voluntary agencies play highly individualized roles in the control of disease and the promotion of health. Visiting nurses, school nurses, hospitals, clinics, and tuberculosis, cancer and such societies are concerned with special aspects of the public health program. Much thought has been given to welding these different units into a coherent system. Over the years there has been steady progress in establishing the basic principles and procedures required to achieve this goal.

THE LOCAL PUBLIC HEALTH DEPARTMENT

A well-administered health department is generally accepted as the foundation for the whole community public health structure. In this department reside the basic powers to enforce sanitary regulations, the reporting of disease, and other measures required in the interest of community health. These powers place the department in a strategic position to plan an integrated community-wide program so that the services of all administrative units can be coordinated with official activities. Without a coordinated plan, some activities tend to be overemphasized and others neglected. No other single factor is so important to the public health system as the concept that the local health department is responsible for planning in terms of the community-wide realities.

The public health officer.—Authorities agree that the public health officer is the key official in the public health system. The acquisition of a full-time, well-trained administrator is put considerably ahead of any particular scheme of departmental organization and management. The health officer should have a medical degree and be thoroughly conversant with the various disease processes and the procedures of preventive medicine. Graduate education and training of at least one full academic year in the administration of public health activities is considered essential also by the APHA Committee on Professional Education.

A major objective is to increase the number of full-time local health officers with specialized graduate training in public health administration. Criteria for approval of schools of public health have been established by the American Public Health Association. At present there are nine accredited schools which offer postgraduate training in public health. Around 200 physicians receive degrees and certificates annually in public health.

The citizen board.—A citizen Board of Health is considered an essential feature of the local departmental structure. The board selects the health officer, determines the general policies of the department, and approves the budget. It establishes rules and regulations which have the effect of law. In certain matters of health the board also has semijudicial powers. In some communities, however, notably those with the city manager form of government, the health officer is appointed by the chief executive of the city, and is directly responsible to him for the conduct of the department, rather than to a citizen board.[1]

[1] Wilson G. Smilie, *Public Health Administration in the United States,* p. 404.

The staff and budget.—The personnel and the budget of the department should be consistent with the range of activities which must be undertaken. As we have indicated, the basic activities of a health department are: (1) communicable disease control, including tuberculosis and venereal diseases; (2) maternal and child health, including prenatal, natal, preschool and school health; (3) sanitary planning and inspection; (4) laboratory service; (5) vital statistics; and (6) public health education.[2] Some authorities now add a seventh—the control of chronic diseases and disabilities.

For a population of 50,000, health authorities suggest as the minimum full-time staff: a health officer, ten public health nurses, two sanitarians, a health educator, and three or four clerks, one of whom would be responsible for compiling the community vital statistics. A department with such a staff would not attempt to provide laboratory services, but would secure these from a central public health laboratory service. Larger communities would need proportionately more personnel, and could afford also to add personnel to provide laboratory and technical services. As the staff becomes larger, and the program more varied, it is usually desirable to develop, to some degree at least, a specialized departmental structure.[3]

About 71 percent of the population of the United States is served by health departments which, although they may not have met completely these standards of personnel and budget, nevertheless reflect a reasonably effective full-time service. The remainder of the country is served by part-time health officers and through state and district health services.

THE RELATED STRUCTURE

The framework of public health nursing.—Although the public health department provides the cornerstone of the public health system, we may say with truth that the structure of public health nursing provides the operational framework for the system. Progress in improving this structure during the past quarter century has been remarkable.

Voluntary, or district, nursing associations were first organized during the latter part of the nineteenth century to give home care to

[2] Haven Emerson and Martha Luginbuhl, *Local Health Units for the Nation*, p. 2.
[3] *Ibid.*

the sick poor in the country's large urban centers. As the health movement expanded, public health departments added nurses to their staffs to assist in the control of communicable disease. Private nursing agencies expanded their services to include work with tuberculous patients, the conduct of clinics for pregnant mothers, for well babies, and other groups. Insurance companies and industrial groups developed special services for assuring bedside nursing care to certain of their policy holders. Fifteen or twenty years ago, it was not uncommon to find communities in which six or more private and public agencies were engaged in nursing activities.

Leaders in the field have worked steadily toward consolidation of the nursing services in a manner to serve the community best. Now there is general consensus that the total community complement of nurses providing public health and bedside care should be administered through not more than two separate units: [4]

1. A nursing unit in the public health department should be responsible for the nursing services required in the community-wide disease control program, and the maternal and child health program, which should include services to school children. This unit would be directly responsible to the health officer and would be expected to provide any other nursing services required by the department program. Its nurses would perform the services required in connection with school health examinations, including consultation with families and referral to community agencies for health services needed by children if not available through the family physician.

2. A voluntary visiting nursing association should consolidate all private agency nursing service. It should provide service to insurance companies who pay for bedside care on a systematic fee basis for service rendered to their policyholders. Similar arrangements might be undertaken with other industrial corporations. Bedside care should also be provided directly to families on a pay, part-pay, or free basis, depending on the economic circumstances of the family.

By agreement with the health officer, such a private nursing association might appropriately undertake a proportion of the nursing service requisite to the control of communicable diseases, and the promotion of maternal and child health, as well as other public health

[4] National Organization for Public Health Nursing, *et al.,* Joint Statement, *Desirable Organization of Public Health Nursing for Family Service,* p. 2.

programs. The health department may purchase this service on behalf of the community, or the voluntary agency may finance it through contributed income—usually from the community chest. But whatever the arrangement, the public and voluntary services must dovetail to assure community-wide service, without duplication.

Public health nursing authorities recognize that such an administrative division does not assure that all the nursing services needed by a family will at any one time be given by only one nurse. Overlapping activities may still give rise to administrative difficulties, as well as to confusion on the part of the patient and the family. Recognition of these difficulties have given impetus to experimentation with providing all community nursing service through a single, or combined, administrative structure. The pattern through which a complete generalized nursing service can be provided—conserving the values of public as well as of private sponsorship and support—is still in the process of evolution.

Certain basic principles applicable to building a unified nursing structure have begun to emerge: [5]

1. The community nursing program should be carried out with the leadership and full cooperation of a qualified, full-time health officer, regardless of whether he is responsible for its administration.

2. Nursing techniques should be standardized under a nursing director, responsible for the operation of the complete nursing service. The nursing director should have a status in the department of health equal to that of the directors of other divisions of the health program.

3. The nursing program should be financed through a consolidated budget, which pools all income from private contributions, fees for service, and tax funds.

4. A representative board of citizens should be organized, with clearly defined responsibilities to guide the development and operation of a truly generalized, community-wide, nursing service.

The private agencies.—Private agencies account for about one quarter of all monies spent in the United States for activities related to the control of disease and the promotion of health. Many of these agencies concentrate on strengthening the official health services. Well before 1930, and at an accelerated pace in the next two decades, procedures and services under private auspices were absorbed in

[5] Ruth Fisher and Margaret Lovell Plumley, *Development of a Combination Agency*, pp. 1–4.

official public health programs. The course followed by the tuberculosis societies illustrates the point.

Tuberculosis societies early began to experiment with the maintenance of active registers of known cases of tuberculosis in their communities. They employed staff nurses to follow up cases and assisted in arranging or providing needed medical treatment. They established and maintained tuberculosis clinics and sometimes operated a preventorium or a sanatorium. At the time these were new procedures, requiring promotion and demonstration. Now these are recognized as responsibilities of the official agencies. For the most part they have been relinquished by the private societies, which concentrate chiefly on developing more effective procedures for early casefinding, and on measures for the rehabilitation of ex-patients.

Many national and local voluntary agencies are concerned with special aspects of the public health program. Their activities are focused mainly upon the control of specific diseases for which community-wide programs of control are as yet relatively undeveloped. While all of the national agencies raise money through nationwide campaigns, there is considerable variety in the nature of their local activities. Some, such as the National Foundation for Infantile Paralysis, specialize in providing financial assistance for medical expenses for persons who are stricken with poliomyelitis, and in training doctors, nurses, and therapists in care and treatment of cases of infantile paralysis. Some, like the American Heart Association and the American Cancer Society, sponsor the establishment of local detection, and treatment clinics. Some undertake systematic local educational work, while others work only on a national basis.[6]

With all such organizations the public health officer must achieve a working relationship. This becomes increasingly important as communities assume greater responsibility for the control of the "new" problem of chronicity. For under such an extension of services, the public health officer perforce must see to it that his community secures all of the advantages which may accrue from the concerted attack of both public and voluntary agencies. In the interest of coherent development, it is generally agreed, the basic role of the voluntary agency should be one of research, public health education and the development of new and promising procedures. When their ef-

[6] A. L. Van Horn, "Crippled Children," *Social Work Year Book, 1947,* p. 139.

fectiveness has been demonstrated, control procedures should be absorbed into the official system.

INCOHERENCE IN THE SERVICES TO THE HANDICAPPED

Community-wide control of handicapping conditions has usually not been regarded as an integral part of the responsibilities of the public health system. Precautions have been taken to prevent blindness by the use of silver nitrate in the eyes of all newborn infants; to prevent defects due to childbirth; to prevent infections that may affect the hearing, and so on. Even in the case of disabling diseases and conditions, the responsibility has been primarily for protective measures against onset and sequelae. Crippled children are an exception.

Accepted principles which would bring coherence to the present confusion in the community-wide structure of special services for the chronically handicapped are largely lacking. For, in every community, numerous public agencies are chiefly concerned with handicapped persons, and numerous voluntary agencies have a similar concern, all without benefit of any unifying plan or leadership.

State commissions for the blind have been established by almost every state. General practice is to maintain a state-wide register of blind persons, and to arrange for provision of such services as may be necessary for those so registered. Most states have long maintained state schools for blind children where they are given special educational and vocational training.

Since 1940 all states and territories have participated in the federal-state program for crippled children. Federal appropriations are administered by the Children's Bureau. States have tended to place responsibility for administration in the department of health, although in ten states it is in the department of welfare, and in five there is a separate commission.[7] The plans approved by the Children's Bureau include provision for the location and discovery of crippled children, the maintenance of a state-wide register, and case follow up, with the necessary treatment provided by qualified specialists in approved clinics and hospitals, convalescent care, and other services as needed.

All but four states maintain schools for the deaf, and these arrange with neighboring states for special education of their deaf children.

7 *Ibid.*, p. 141.

Twenty-five states also have public day schools, supported by states or communities. These schools constitute the principal public activity for the hard of hearing.

The oldest and most comprehensive public program in the field of rehabilitative services is that of the federal Office of Vocational Rehabilitation. The impetus for this program came originally from "those charged with administering workmen's compensation laws . . . and in 1920 Congress enacted the first legislation establishing grants of federal funds to help states to develop programs for the vocational rehabilitation of the disabled." In 1943 Congress established the Office of Vocational Rehabilitation in the Federal Security Agency. Each of the states and territories now has an agency under the provisions set up by the federal program.[8]

The purpose is to train and place in employment handicapped persons of working age, who have a reasonable chance to become employable. Training is available to civilians with any type of disability. After the handicapped person is "found" the agency meets the expense of medical diagnosis, but he is expected to pay, in so far as he is able, for medical and hospital treatment. All costs of vocational guidance, retraining, and placement, however, are met from the funds of the agency.

Many voluntary agencies concerned with the rehabilitation of the handicapped parallel the activities of the principal public services. It is estimated that altogether some seventeen hundred local and state agencies have crippled children as their special interest. "Lighthouses" and sheltered workshops for the blind have been a common local undertaking. The provision of sheltered workshops for persons handicapped by various disabilities was an early outlet for voluntary enterprise, and it is estimated that there are now some five hundred in operation. A smaller number of agencies have special rehabilitative interest in the deaf, epileptics, diabetics, heart cases, and persons suffering from other special disabilities.[9]

With so many special auspices, it is not surprising that no one of them has taken responsibility for community-wide planning to meet the over-all problem of physical handicap. Such leadership must precede any truly fruitful move toward structural simplification.

8 Michael Shortley, "Vocational Rehabilitation," *Social Work Year Book 1947*, p. 546.
9 *Ibid.*, p. 544.

Great diversity will be found in the structure of the system for organized medical care. Some communities, particularly the larger ones, have a number of hospitals, many of which are general and others specialized. In smaller communities there may be only one hospital. Some hospitals have outpatient departments to provide medical care for the indigent and the medically indigent; others do not. In some communities such services are given through a variety of specialized, independent clinics operated under varied auspices.

THE GENERAL HOSPITAL

Whatever the extent and the diversity of organization of the services, the pivotal unit of the system of organized medical care is the general hospital. Authorities agree that it should provide the basic generalized service to the community. Around this a variety of specialized agencies and services can be developed if needed. A general hospital should be equipped to care for all types of diseases and conditions: acute illness and injuries, maternity cases, chronic diseases, communicable diseases, including cases of tuberculosis, certain types of nervous and mental conditions, and convalescing patients. It should be equipped to care for persons in all economic circumstances.

The concept of this strategic role of the general hospital is essentially a twentieth century growth. It represents a far cry from the days when the hospital was the exclusive prerogative of the poor, and a place to be avoided by anyone able to die in his own bed. Only in recent years have there come into general acceptance, principles of organization and administration governing the manner in which the general hospital can equip itself to occupy such a role.

Community authority.—If the general hospital is to be a truly community institution, ultimate authority for its management and policies must reside in a governing body which represents the community. For voluntary nonprofit hospitals, this should be a citizen board, responsible to the community, "regardless of the special interests which may have brought about the establishment of the hospital." Past practice in establishing the governing authority of public hospitals has pursued a variety of paths. New York has established a Department of Hospitals within the framework of the city government. In some places the public hospitals are operated by the Department of Welfare, in others by the Board of Health. In still others each hospital may be administered by an appointed director or superintendent, responsible only to some higher governmental official. Most authorities now believe that even for public hospitals a "broadened base of authority and responsibility would go far toward awakening public interest and in maintaining standards of service" and that "hospitals operated by state, county, or municipal governmental units should be conducted under the supervision of, or have the advice and council of, boards broadly representative of the public." [10]

The hospital administrator.—There are two broad phases of hospital management. One is a complicated business operation, similar in many respects to the operation of a hotel. The task of maintaining the hospital plant and administering the personnel required to maintain rooms, eating facilities, and similar housekeeping services, is a sizable job in itself. The other phase of hospital management is concerned with the organization and management of technical facilities and professional services required for the care and treatment of sick persons. This involves knowledge beyond that of ordinary business management.

There is as yet, it seems to us, considerable lack of agreement about the basic training and experience needed to qualify the directors of community general hospitals for such a complexity of duties. In fact, they bring to their positions a variety of professional and administrative experiences.

The development of graduate training schools for hospital administrators reflects a similar uncertainty of emphasis. Some of the graduate courses in hospital administration are given in schools of business administration; others in schools for public health. Hospital authorities do agree, however, that there is need for the further development of special training facilities. A broadly qualified and experienced director is considered a first essential for the hospital which undertakes the strategic role in coordinating the community's organized services for medical care.

Organization for medical service.—The manner in which a hospital is organized to assure a high quality of service determines the nature and significance of its status in the community system. Many of the

10 Commission on Hospital Care, *Hospital Care in the United States*, p. 71.

professional and technical problems involved are beyond the scope of this volume. It seems to us, however, that two matters of policy and practice have significant community interest. The first is the provision of facilities and resources needed for proper diagnosis and treatment. The second, and in many respects the most important, is the organization of the hospital medical staff and the policies relating to medical practice within the hospital.

The move to improve and standardize basic hospital facilities began when the American College of Surgeons undertook in 1913 to certify physicians as competent to practice surgery. In the course of their review of medical records of patients, submitted by candidates as "evidence of surgical judgment and technical ability," it became evident that many hospitals lacked services and equipment needed for preoperative study of the patient. In many professional and technical matters there was a general lack of organization and supervision.

The American College of Surgeons stipulates minimum standards for hospitals and since 1918 has maintained a register of hospitals which meet them.[11] These requirements include an x-ray department supervised by a competent roentgenologist, and a laboratory staffed and equipped to conduct urinalyses, blood counts, and specified chemical and bacteriological tests. Larger hospitals are expected to maintain facilities and personnel qualified to provide a full range of chemical, bacteriological, serological, and pathological examinations. Smaller hospitals may be permitted to arrange to secure these, except as noted above, through some approved clinical laboratory.

At all times the hospital plays a dual role in the system of medical care. It serves the physician, putting at his disposal facilities which are essential to the fruitful pursuit of his profession. It serves the people of the community, who built and maintain it. These are not opposing roles, although they are not inevitably synonymous. The medical profession has played a leading part in developing the hospital as a community institution. More than at any other point this dual role is reconciled and implemented through the medical staff and the policies and procedures which regulate their association with the hospital.

[11] For a more complete discussion of standards for hospital facilities and organization of the medical services consult American College of Surgeons, *Manual of Hospital Standardization.*

The medical staff of any hospital consists simply of all physicians who are privileged to work there. The extension of this privilege obviously is the responsibility of the hospital governing board, with implications from which it cannot escape. From the standpoint of the community, the more important of these have to do with the composition of the staff and the methods and criteria applicable to their appointment.

In its general composition the active medical staff is by far the most important group. To the members of this staff are assigned the diagnosis and treatment of all "free" patients. It is extremely important that the active staff include a balanced distribution of specialists in the different branches of medicine, as they form the nucleus of the consulting medical staff, augmented when necessary by arrangements with other physicians.

The active medical staff carries the responsibility by what is in effect a direct delegation from the governing board, for the medical standards of the hospital. It elects a chief of staff, and recommends to the governing board the assignment of physicians to the different departments of specialized practice.

For appointment, physicians must be in good standing and licensed to practice in the state in which the hospital is located. Hospitals may, and often do, establish additional criteria of competence. Autopsies are regarded as important, and both the medical staff and hospital administrator not only encourage this practice, but there is in fact a tendency to view with suspicion any physician who discourages this endeavor to ascertain with certainty why his patient died.

The American College of Surgeons has specified detailed regulations which it regards as essential, and which it considers in certifying hospitals. Following are some of those of general interest:

Except for emergencies, patients should be admitted only on the basis of a provisional diagnosed condition. Authority to admit a patient to the hospital is vested in the hospital administrator. A full record of each patient is maintained. On it is entered not only the identifying information, medical history, and so on, but full data regarding diagnostic examinations, consultation, special treatment, progress made, condition of the patient at discharge, as well as any other pertinent information. The physician in charge of the case is responsible for completing this record, and the manner in which this requirement is fulfilled is systematically reviewed.

The record provides the basis for critical analysis, by the medical staff, of care given in the hospital. Monthly meetings of the medical staff for continuing review of professional performance are mandatory in approved hospitals. The hospital mortality rate is analyzed, with special reference to patients, who, under ordinary circumstances, should not have died. Cases of special interest, by reason of their intricacy, or because of exceptionally good or bad results are selected by the record librarian and the chief of staff for discussion.

It is generally believed that consultation with one or more specialists should be arranged on behalf of from 15 to 20 percent of all hospitalized patients, although there are no fixed criteria by which to determine this. In a well balanced, closely knit medical staff a good deal of informal consultation inevitably takes place, but to be formally recognized the attending physician must request it in writing, and the resultant findings must be incorporated into the medical record. Hospitals may, and often do, require consultation on behalf of patients needing major surgery or any who upon admission are considered as not "good risks," medically speaking.

Outpatient service.—A well organized outpatient department for ambulatory cases is now regarded as an indispensable part of a community general hospital unit. It usually comprises a number of specialized clinics for patients with specific diseases and conditions. Clinics are staffed by members of the active and associate medical staffs, as a part of their regular assignments. Traditionally, outpatient service has been primarily for the indigent, although for a number of years it has been a matter of common practice to charge fees in accordance with the patient's ability to pay.

Theoretically, outpatients receive excellent care. In well-conducted departments this is undoubtedly the case. Patients are assigned to physicians best equipped to treat the particular illness, and consultation is readily available if required. Complete medical records are kept and these are integrated with hospital records for reference if the patient is hospitalized. The full use of laboratory and other diagnostic and treatment services is also available to outpatients.

The outpatient department also serves other extremely useful pur-

poses for the hospital and its medical staff. In the training of interns
and medical specialists its clinics provide a wide range of experience;
they also offer the practicing physician an opportunity to enrich his
own qualifications for practice. For a substantial group of patients, the
facilities for diagnosis and follow-up treatment may simplify the intake and discharge of patients to the hospital itself, a very practical advantage when hospital beds are in demand.

COHERENCE IN THE COMMUNITY-WIDE STRUCTURE

Keeping in mind that the general hospital unit should be its foundation, we will now examine the community-wide structure for organized medical care—the total hospital facilities needed for the area,
the role of specialized hospital facilities, and the policy in respect to
outpatient service.

Community-wide units.—Authorities generally consider as the
urban community standard, 4.5 general hospital beds for every 1,000
of the population. In the larger urban centers these usually are supplied by more than one hospital unit. But there is no general rule by
which to determine precisely the number of different units best
adapted to administer the given number of beds which a community
is presumed to need.

An uneconomical duplication of certain kinds of equipment and
resources was reported by the Commission on Hospital Care. It
pointed out also that necessary diagnostic and therapeutic facilities
frequently were lacking in the smaller hospitals. It recommended the
systematic interchange of service and equipment among hospitals of
the same community. Sharing the costs, it said, "would make available consultation services and part-time service of radiologists and
pathologists in small hospitals which would not be able to finance effective programs of this type on a full-time basis." [12]

Eliminating specialized hospital facilities.—For several decades the
trend to specialization in hospitals paralleled the similar trend in the
practice of medicine. The trend is now being reversed. The general,
all purpose, hospital is considered the most effective as well as the
economical community unit through which to provide the necessary
constellation of specialized personnel and equipment. Special hospitals for the care of the chronic, tuberculous, and mental cases under

[12] *Hospital Care in the United States,* p. 350.

state auspices are now available to many communities. Hospitals specializing in certain diseases and in research and experiments related to them undoubtedly will continue to be built and maintained. But general hospital service, it is now agreed, provides the best foundation structure for the average community.

The St. Paul data suggested also that a sharp division of labor between hospitals which mainly do free work and those which do not may result in an automatic specialization. In that community the public hospitals undertook most of the free work, while voluntary hospitals served pay patients primarily. Since long-term illnesses are most likely to require free care at some time, this resulted in a very real, if somewhat unconscious, specialization in acute diseases by the voluntary hospitals and in chronic diseases by the public hospital. Persons with chronic diseases and chronic handicaps made up 60 percent of the patient load of the public hospital, but accounted for only 20 percent of the total of the private hospitals.

Community-wide outpatient and clinic policy.—Several knotty problems confront the community in developing over-all policies applicable to its outpatient services. As far back as Revolutionary days, dispensaries were established to distribute medicines to the needy. By 1900 there were about one hundred of these throughout the country. In the years following, when the tuberculosis, maternal and infant, and other such specialized health programs were being developed, a great variety of special clinics sprang up under many auspices.[13] In almost every community there are even now some independent clinics, operated by a variety of agencies with special health interests. Many of the early dispensaries and clinics, however, have been amalgamated with hospitals, and there is a tendency on the part of communities to expect general hospitals to provide such services as are required.

Certain underlying issues in connection with outpatient services are badly in need of clarification. While these services were designed primarily to give medical care to the poor, an increasing proportion of the cost is being met by fees. Criteria of ability of a patient to pay all, or a part, of the cost of his care have never been generally accepted and uniformly administered. As community-wide programs are extended to the control of cancer, diabetes, heart and other chronic

[13] *Ibid.*, p. 490.

diseases, it seems very probable that the determination of ability to pay will become even more difficult.

As new detection, diagnostic, and treatment methods have been developed, the length of stay of many hospital patients has been appreciably shorter, and many conditions are now amenable to outpatient as well as to inpatient care. There is a growing trend among hospitals to try to provide some sort of ambulatory service to all hospital patients, regardless of economic status, but there are many difficulties to be faced in working out the details of such a service. As one means of meeting this problem, some hospitals are experimenting with the development of group medical practice units, organized and conducted under hospital auspices. These put at the disposal of the financially able ambulatory patient a coordinated constellation of specialized skills and resources which, in theory at least, has long been available to the needy.

Group practice for ambulatory pay-patients also provides for systematic compensation to the physicians who participate in the service, either by arrangement with the hospital, or under medical care insurance plans.

THE COMMUNITY'S STAKE IN THE STRUCTURE OF PRIVATE MEDICAL PRACTICE

THE INDIVIDUAL PHYSICIAN

The cornerstone of the system of private medical practice, of course, is the individual physician, practicing independently, who makes his living from the fees of his clients. Historically and traditionally, the only responsibility undertaken by the community has been to issue a license to the physician. In certifying the physician's qualifications, state examining boards place upon him an obligation to assist public health authorities by reporting cases of notifiable diseases found in his patients, and by applying certain aspects of preventive medicine in his practice.

The community has an extremely important stake in the manner in which the system of private medical practice is organized. Yet until recently, once the qualifications of a physician were established and a license issued, the community has been disinclined to intervene in the affairs of the medical profession. A very good reason for this is to found in the extraordinarily effective manner in which the medical profession has undertaken to assure the conduct of individual practice of physicians in the best interest of the patient.

Assurance of quality of professional performance.—Medical schools, hospitals, and specialists in the different branches of medicine all are accredited and certified by organized bodies established by the medical profession for this purpose. Standards are high, enforcement rigid, and revision is always upward in the interest of greater competence of practice. In application they reflect the intent of the American Medical Association "to elevate the standards of medical education, to advance medical science and improve medical practice." [14]

At the base of this assumption of responsibility is the code of medical ethics. More than is usually the case with such codes, subscription to it articulates a view which pervades the doctor's way of life. Its emotional roots are in the ancient oath of Hippocrates, dedicating the physician to the service of his patient, and obligating him to pass on his skills to others, as generations of others have to him. This attachment to an ideal is enforced quite realistically through the application of precise rules of conduct, revised and amended over the years to meet what the profession regards as the exigencies of the times.

In conformance to medical ethics, a physician may not procure his patients under any circumstances which might prove to their disadvantage; he may not advertise his wares; he may not split fees with other physicians to whom he may refer patients for special services. There are many other things which he may not do which the medical profession considers inconsistent with the high purpose to which a physician's life is presumed to be dedicated. This century's history of the long campaign of organized medicine against quacks, fakes, patent cures and "medicine men" of all varieties could not have been written as so successful if the profession itself had not labored so assiduously to keep its own house clean.

Organized medicine is now confronted with two problems. It can cope with these only as its traditional policies are adapted to meet the requisite of community cooperation. Communities, on their part, are becoming increasingly insistent that these problems be met. The first has to do with the equitable distribution of medical personnel in relation to the country's needs. The second is concerned with means

[14] *Ibid.*, p. 479.

by which specialized medical knowledge may be integrated into the pattern of community service.

Assurance of equitable distribution of medical personnel.—The medical profession has never taken responsibility for seeing that its members distributed their talents in relation to population needs.

In 1943 there was one physician for every 806 persons in the United States. More than half of the country's physicians were in cities of 50,000 or over, 30 percent in towns and cities from 2,500 to 50,000 and only 15 percent in rural areas. New York had a much higher ratio— one physician for every 480 persons. At the other extreme, Alabama had only one physician for every 1,517 persons.[15]

The problem is considerably more complicated than the undeniable fact that in urban communities there are more people with more money to profit a doctor's practice than in rural areas. The cost of the medical education is high, the period of training long. The doctor may find it difficult to purchase much of the technical equipment which modern practice requires. He is highly dependent upon these facilities, but can put them at his patient's disposal only if he has a hospital connection which makes it possible. It is not unnatural that in setting up in practice a physician tends to gravitate to communities that offer this advantage.

THE MEDICAL SPECIALTIES

A main difficulty for private medical practice seems to be that modern medical knowledge and methods of prevention and treatment, as well as detection of the presence of disease, are altogether too great and too complicated for any one person to encompass. The problem for physician and patient is essentially the same—how to bring the appropriate skill to bear upon a specific disease or condition.

The constellation of specialties.—Nineteen major medical specialties, and a number of important subspecialties of some of these, are currently recognized by the American Medical Association. For each major specialty a board has been established to determine standards of education and experience and to certify physicians who meet these requirements. There is no special board to "certify" the general practitioner, although there has been considerable discussion of the possibility of establishing one.

[15] *Ibid.*, p. 250.

Not every person who is sick from ordinary illnesses needs a full battery of specialized medical services. But so far as we have been able to discover, there are no precise criteria by which to determine how much "pooling" of specialized services there should be.

Presumably, once a diagnosis has been made, it should be a relatively simple matter to see that the patient has an opportunity to be treated by a specialist, if this is indicated. Securing the diagnosis may well be less simple. Not even the most ardent advocates of preventive medicine would argue that the apparently well person should spend an undue amount of time and money proving to himself that he does not have a long list of diseases. Yet it is frequently true that the general practitioner is not equipped by experience and training to rule out certain diseases and disabilities without assistance from one or more specialists.

None knows with greater surety than the members of the medical profession that specialization is in itself forcing physicians to find better ways for pooling their medical knowledge in the interest of the patient.

A balanced distribution of specialized personnel.—While we do not know what the ratio of distribution between general practitioners and specialists should be, we do know that in the interest of certain patients each group needs the resources of the other. Hospitals, to some extent at least, have organized their medical staffs in a manner which facilitates use by the patient of a constellation of medical services. The medical profession invented, and has been developing with some pain, the structure of group practice which brings together the diversified skills of physicians who have specialized in different branches of medicine. The purpose of both of these approaches is the same—to assure to the patient, as he may need them, the combined resources of special medical skills and equipment.

It is not known how many physicians are at present associated in group practice. It is estimated that there are at least 500 such groups in operation, concentrated particularly in the Middle West. Younger medical men especially are entering into group practice of medicine. Groups usually are designed to provide one of three different kinds of service: [16]

[16] Halsey G. Hunt, "Medical Group Practice in the United States," *New England Journal of Medicine*, CCXXXVII, No. 3 (July 17, 1947), 72, 73.

1. *A generalized diagnostic and treatment service.* Such a group expects to furnish a complete medical service to a continuing group of patients. Members include general practitioners as well as specialists and should have at their disposal the basic equipment and technical facilities necessary to provide such a generalized service.

2. *Specialized diagnosis and treatment.* A group organized for this purpose usually sees patients only upon referral from physicians outside their group. Both diagnostic and treatment services are provided, usually in respect to a specific episode of illness, with the understanding that the referring physician is responsible for the continuing care of the patient.

3. *Diagnostic service only.* These groups provide little or no treatment for patients, serving other physicians in diagnosis of diseases and conditions of patients referred. Treatment, as well as continuing care of the patient, remains the responsibility of the referring physician.

Inasmuch as the purposes of group medical practice can be served by a great variety of formal and informal arrangements, data as to who "owns" the groups now in operation, and the manner of their organization, are quite sketchy. Nevertheless most of them are organized under one or the other of three types of sponsors: (1) by physicians; (2) under community sponsorship, connected with some form of prepayment insurance plans; (3) the teaching staffs of medical school hospitals.[17]

The trend toward group practice in the scientific interest of the patient runs counter to the belief that under the system of free competition, the best patient-physician relationship is maintained. A part of the original relationship may be lost if a patient goes to a group of doctors, even though this may be to his diagnostic and treatment advantage.

In the long run the power inherent in scientific collaboration may be expected to outweigh all other considerations in determining trends toward group practice. If the constellation of services which it provides are necessary and economical for only a small proportion of illness at any given time, then it would seem logical to expect that the community general hospitals could organize their services to meet most of the need. On the other hand, if a large proportion of ill people continuously need the advantages of group practice, then one should expect that a substantial number of physicians eventually will work through organized groups, whether under their own or other auspices.

[17] *Ibid.*

FEDERAL-STATE STRUCTURAL REALITIES

The philosophy and traditions of the public health movement and of organized medical care from the first placed basic responsibility on the local community. The medical profession likewise has been a strong believer in the rightness of this view. Now the orientation of these systems seems to be shifting from their traditional base. Approximately 30 percent of the money expended by local and state health departments comes from federal and state funds, and a little over 40 percent of that spent by state departments for administration and direct service comes from federal funds.[18] Since 1946, under the Hill-Burton Act, the federal government has been engaged in spending some $300 million for hospital construction. It would be well to examine two aspects of this trend. The first has to do with the disparate distribution of health services throughout the country. The second is concerned with the principles and methods by which federal funds are now allocated.

DISPARITIES IN NATIONWIDE PROTECTION AND FACILITIES

The public health system.—Disparities in the public health system were systematically revealed in 1942 by a noteworthy, state-by-state study financed by the Commonwealth Fund and directed by Dr. Haven Emerson.[19] In the 48 states are some 38,000 local jurisdictions of civil government—city, county, township or village—which might exercise authority over the public health. In practice 5,519 had appointed public health officials, of whom only 1,202 were engaged full time. There were large sections of the country with no local public health activities. Well-organized municipal health departments frequently operated side by side with poorly staffed county departments which cover rural and village areas.

This realistic examination of public health jurisdictional areas concluded that a total of 1,197 public health units would provide the best and most economical coverage for the United States. About one fourth of the units recommended were county units, twenty-two were city units, the remainder consolidating into one jurisdiction two or more counties. In some instances, it was even envisaged that border

[18] Joseph W. Mountain, *et al.*, *Ten Years of Federal Grants-in-Aid for Public Health*, p. 10, Table 3.
[19] *Local Health Units for the Nation*, pp. 3, 14, Table C.

counties in different states might be joined for public health purposes. The report revealed not only the nationwide maldistribution of public health activities, but, what is less common in nationwide examinations of this kind, the structural inefficiencies in wholly local systems.

Hospital facilities.—Disparities in the distribution of hospital facilities were systematically revealed by the Commission on Hospital Care in 1946. Metropolitan areas had 4.7 general and specialized hospital beds per 1,000 population and their bordering areas, 2.4 beds per 1,000, while at the other extreme were places under 2,500 population with only 0.8 beds, and towns of 2,500 to 4,999 with only 1.4 beds.[20]

Some hospital authorities now recommend a statewide system of hospitals planned in relation to each other. At the base, in metropolitan areas, general hospital units would be fully equipped for detection, diagnosis, and treatment of all diseases and conditions. In smaller communities, hospitals of perhaps 100 beds would provide limited specialized equipment, while in rural areas there would be diagnostic and treatment centers with emergency beds only. Patients thus would "flow" from the smallest to the largest units as their condition demanded, or specialists attached to larger units might provide smaller hospitals and centers with service by arrangement.

FEDERAL APPROPRIATING POLICY

Federal grants to promote public health had quite a history before Congress appropriated federal money to help to build hospitals. Grants-in-aid to states were made in 1918, under the Chamberlain-Kahn Act, for venereal disease control. In 1921 the Shepherd-Towner Act provided grants-in-aid for the development of a nationwide maternal and child health program.[21] The venereal disease program was administered by the Public Health Service, but the Children's Bureau was made responsible for developing and supervising the maternal and child health program.

For public health services.—The Social Security Act of 1935 marked the beginning of what might be called the modern age in federal health financing. Although designed primarily to set up the perma-

---

[20] *Hospital Care in the United States,* p. 149.
[21] Joseph W. Mountain and Clifford H. Greve, *The Role of Grants-in-Aid in Financing Public Health Programs,* pp. 5–7.

nent categorical assistance and social insurance programs, health was not overlooked. The Public Health Service was given $10 million to distribute for public health purposes. The Children's Bureau was given $7.5 million for crippled children and $3.5 million for maternal and child welfare.[22] These agencies together allocated $42 million in grants-in-aid to the states in 1949. Policies governing the allocation of the public health money are somewhat different in the two Bureaus.

The Public Health Service at present allocates funds for promotion of general health as well as special purposes. There is no flat matching formula for allocating funds for public health, as is the case with the categorical assistance grants. Congress stipulated that population and relative disease rates, as well as state financial capacity, should be taken into account, but left it to the Public Health Service to work out detailed criteria to govern allocations. In its turn, the Service took the precaution of working out its policies and criteria in formal consultation with state and territorial health officers.

In order to be considered eligible for an appropriation, a state must submit general information about its over-all organization, program, and budget, and the policies by which it plans to effect improvement and change in public health services. One general stipulation is that all employees must be under a merit system. But the state must also submit specific budgets for each project for which it wishes federal aid. These projects if approved are reviewed annually, both as to their fiscal and their qualitative administration.[23]

Funds of the Children's Bureau for maternal and infant health are allocated through state health departments, as are the funds of the Public Health Service. In 30 states, funds for crippled children are allocated to the health departments; in the remainder they go to other state agencies.[24] For each of the programs administered by the Children's Bureau, half of the money is allocated on the basis of a matching formula, more or less in line with the principles in effect for categorical assistance grants. The other half may be allocated on a discretionary basis, in relation to need, more or less in line with the policies of the Public Health Service. Each state receiving assistance must submit a plan, with a budget for each specific project.

[22] *Public Health Administration in the United States*, pp. 482–89.
[23] Mountain and Greve, *The Role of Grants-in-Aid*, pp. 30–33.
[24] Van Horn, "Crippled Children," p. 141.

Criteria of need take into consideration relative birth rates, the maternal and infant mortality rates, relative number of crippled children needing care, and similar data.

For hospital construction.—The distribution of money for hospitals by the Public Health Service is for two purposes: "To assist the states (1) to inventory and evaluate the existing hospital and health center facilities, to survey their needs for additional facilities; and (2) to construct the needed public or other nonprofit hospitals and health centers in accordance with these programs." [25]

To assist the states in starting their planning surveys the Act provided $3 million to be allocated on a population basis, with a minimum allocation of $10,000. For construction purposes Congress made an initial appropriation of $75 million for the year ending June 30, 1947, and authorized appropriation of a similar amount each year for the succeeding four years. The prescribed formula for allocation of funds takes into consideration both population and per capita income, and was designed to give larger allocation per capita to the low income states. Further consideration to needs of low economic areas was given when the 81st Congress extended the period of the construction program to ten years and prescribed additional appropriations annually; at present this amounts to a continuation for ten years of the annual allocation of $75 million.

The plans divide the state into the three types of area: metropolitan, with provision for general base hospitals; intermediate, with provision for smaller limited purpose hospitals; and rural, with emergency health centers. An upper limit is placed on the bed capacity for the construction of which federal funds may be used in these different areas. In effect this tends to recognize a limit of 4.5 beds per 1,000 of the population, where the population is more than 12 persons per square mile; 5 beds per 1,000 where the population is 6 to 12 persons per square mile; and 5.5 beds where it is 6 persons or less.

A primary intent of the Act, of course, was to build up hospital facilities in the poorer areas of the country, and the great majority of the projects approved have been for areas with less than average income. Certain obstacles, however, have been encountered in inducing these areas to undertake construction of projects, because of their

[25] Vane M. Hoge, "Hospital Survey and Construction Program in the United States," *Public Health Reports,* LXIV, No. 32 (August 12, 1949), 991, 994, 995.

inability to meet the local share of the cost, and to provide the maintenance and operating costs after the hospital is built.[26]

Completion of the construction programs already approved will add around 50,000 hospital beds and 141 health centers to the nation's facilities. General hospital projects account for 85 percent of those approved so far, and are almost equally divided between those under voluntary nonprofit auspices and those under public auspices. A significant item in the federal policy is that the public hospitals must provide service to "pay patients" as do the voluntary hospitals, and not restrict themselves to "charity" patients.

STRUCTURAL POTENTIALITIES

One result of federal grants-in-aid for public health purposes has been an increase in the participation of state health departments in local health department affairs. Substantially larger amounts of state money now are appropriated for local purposes. Fifteen years ago state departments generally undertook the collection of state-wide vital statistics, made sanitary and laboratory services available and exercised their authority over water, milk, and food supplies. By 1940, 38 states were supplying free toxoid for local diphtheria immunization; 34 were supplying smallpox vaccines. By 1946 all but two states were aiding in the development of tuberculosis control programs, and 27 were engaged in cancer control.[27]

Federal money involved in state and local public health programs is for development of community services rather than for direct distribution to the recipient. State and local funds substantially exceed the federal amounts. There are few uniform administrative structural and procedural requirements embodied either in the law or in federal regulations. Nevertheless, the inducement of additional resources always carries with it an influence considerably in excess of whatever the proportional addition may be.

The influence of federal grants-in-aid on the traditional structure of the system of organized medical care is not so clear. Federal money is for hospital and health center construction purposes only, not for continuing maintenance. It was originally for a five-year period

26 John W. Cronin, et al., "Hospital Construction under the Hill-Burton Program," Public Health Reports, LXVI, No. 23 (June 9, 1949), 752, 753.
27 Mountain, et al., Ten Years of Federal Grants-in-Aid, p. 15.

which now has been extended to ten years. If there are continuing appropriations for construction, or for any other related purpose, we may expect a steady build-up of the state authorities under the aegis and influence of the federal program.

Few states before passage of the Hill-Burton Hospital Construction Act had a state hospital authority, other than that concerned with the mentally ill and the defective, or with tuberculosis. Only nine states required that the hospitals be licensed; now most of them have passed licensing legislation. Each state now has designated a hospital authority and each of these now has a state-wide plan. It is presumed to "supervise" the working out of arrangements for integration of the operations of each of the hospitals built with federal money. Inevitably these state authorities must come to exert considerable influence in hospital planning and operation.

Of real significance to future structural developments is the consolidation, at least in over-all administration, of the public health and hospital programs. With the passage of the hospital construction act, public health service at the federal level was joined with that of general hospital service, on a nation-wide basis. Few state health departments then had extensive hospital responsibilities. Now, in a majority of the states the health department has been designated as the state authority to administer the grants-in-aid for hospital survey and construction.[28]

Thus it seems to us fair to say that a local-state-federal structural pattern for the traditional public health services is emerging. The framework for a local-state-federal pattern for an integrated public health and hospital structure has already emerged with considerable clarity. To predict how far that framework may become a reality in the years immediately ahead is beyond our prophetic vision.

FINANCING HOSPITAL AND MEDICAL COSTS

As we indicated earlier, it costs the country about $1.5 billion dollars to finance the system of organized medical care of which hospitals and outpatient departments are the principal units in medical care. It costs about $1.75 billion to maintain the system of private medical practice. Best estimates indicate that from 60 to 75 percent of the cost

[28] Ibid., p. 75.

of hospital care is met by consumers, either directly or by insurance payments. Most of the cost of care through private physicians and dentists is met in this way.

The costs of these medical services have borne down upon both the consumer and the organized community with increasing severity. Hospital costs have more than doubled in the past ten years. In 1939 it cost the average hospital $6.42 to care for one patient for one twenty-four hour day. In 1948 it cost $14.06.[29] It is estimated that families with an annual income of less than $3,000 probably cannot afford to meet the cost of medical care.[30] According to 1950 census income data, nearly 60 percent of all families in the United States fall into this group.[31]

For such reasons as the foregoing, the problem of financing hospital and medical care has assumed mounting proportions, for the community as a whole as well as for persons who need the services. In fact, it is the cause of considerable public and professional hysteria.

PAYMENT FOR INDIGENT CASES

Communities now assume responsibility for meeting the costs of hospital and medical care for the medically indigent, as well as for those who also require assistance in providing the necessities of life. "Medically indigent" is a somewhat elastic term, but in general may be said to include those who cannot afford either to pay the costs of services received, or to insure themselves against these costs through participation in prepayment insurance plans.

Hospital costs.—As we have indicated in earlier sections, it is hardly right to speak of the traditional manner in which most communities pay hospital and medical costs for their indigent and medically indigent families as a plan.

Some public hospitals receive only free cases and all costs are met from tax funds. Others receive both free and pay patients; fees are used to supplement tax funds. A voluntary hospital may pay for all or part of its free work out of: (*a*) profits from its pay business, (*b*) volun-

29 J. R. McGibony and Louis Block, "Better Patient Care through Coordination," Public Health Reports, LXIV, No. 47 (November 25, 1949), 1501.

30 Dean A. Clark and Katharine G. Clark, "Medical Care," *Social Work Year Book, 1947*, p. 303.

31 U.S. Department of Commerce, *1950 Census of Population, Preliminary Reports,* Series PC-7, No. 2 (April 11, 1951), p. 36, Table 9.

tary contributions, and (c) endowments and reserves. A Department of Public Welfare may pay part of the actual hospital cost for (a) families who are on its relief rolls and (b) families able to provide for their basic maintenance costs but who are unable to meet the extra costs of hospital care.

In the section on Dependency we expressed our belief that the full cost of care of medically indigent hospital patients, whether provided in a public, voluntary, or proprietary hospital, should be met by the Department of Public Welfare on an agreed per capita per diem basis. Only in this way can eligibility for free service be determined systematically on a uniform community-wide basis and only in this way can the community know the total which it is in fact spending for this purpose.

Medical costs.—For medically indigent patients who are hospitalized, the cost of the diagnostic and treatment services of the attending physician are borne by the members of the medical staff who donate their services. Free service to ambulatory, nonhospitalized cases is provided principally through outpatient departments and special clinics. For these patients, too, the doctor donates his services.

Thus in effect, almost all of the expense of medical diagnosis and treatment for medically indigent families traditionally has been carried by the medical profession through hospital and clinic connections. But this arrangement, as we have seen, is beginning to break down. Shifts in responsibility are taking place, but in view of deep-seated traditions any change may be expected to be slow, opportunistic, and inevitably experimental.

The extension of voluntary prepayment plans has undoubtedly lessened the burden of free care borne by the community, as well as by private physicians and dentists. It is questionable whether insurance plans could ever eliminate entirely some community responsibility for providing services to the most disadvantaged families. Illness rates among relief families, and among families with marginal incomes of less than $2,000 a year, have been found to be substantially higher than those with larger incomes. Our St. Paul data showed a high proportion of long-time, continuous chronic illness among the most disadvantaged families of that community. Many of these families cannot themselves afford to participate in voluntary insurance plans. It seems to us that even a comprehensive governmental insurance plan, if ever adopted, would still leave to communities a responsibility for some residual group such as this.

VOLUNTARY INSURANCE

When a working person is injured or is taken sick, financial embarrassment may well result. His pay may stop briefly, or for a quite long period. Usually he must incur extra expense for a doctor, and perhaps for a hospital stay as well.

Insurance against these two consequences of illness represent different principles. One is calculated to offset or compensate for the loss of income, the other to offset the additional medical expense. A plan which insures only against loss of income does not include any provision for medical care. Much health and accident insurance, on the other hand, is designed to cover the actual medical costs. Reimbursible items are specified, such as the physicians' bills, medicines and drugs, hospitalization. Benefits are calculated in relation to calculated risks, and coverage provided commensurate with the premiums paid. As a rule the insurance company takes no responsibility for negotiating rates of payment or for assuring that facilities for care are available.

The voluntary nonprofit hospital and medical insurance plans which have spread so rapidly during recent years go further than this.[32] They pay for hospital and medical service, but also stipulate rates, negotiate arrangements, or organize at least some of the conditions under which the service will be rendered. Broadly speaking, these plans not only cover hospital medical costs, but undertake also to assure the availability of the service when needed.

Hospital costs.—In 1929 a group of teachers in Dallas, Texas, entered into an agreement with Baylor University Hospital to supply specific hospital services up to a total of three weeks in return for payment by each teacher of $3 per semester. This experiment is generally credited with "sparking" the Blue Cross hospital insurance plans, although similar arrangements had preceded it in several other communities (Rockford, Ill., in 1912; Grinnell, Iowa, in 1921; Brattleboro, Vt., in 1927). The serious economic straits in which hospitals found themselves in the depression years provided the soil in which these plans were to flourish. The American Hospital Associa-

[32] Except as otherwise noted, discussion of hospital and medical care insurance is based on Franz Goldman, *Voluntary Medical Care Insurance.*

tion went on record in 1933 as approving the principle of hospital insurance, and in 1934 the American College of Surgeons set up precepts to be observed in their development.

While some Blue Cross plans provided for individual membership, policies are sold primarily to blocks of employees from whose wages employers deduct the regular monthly payments. Agreements have been made with the hospitals as to rates and fees to be paid, with the beneficiary choosing his hospital. Special legislation has been passed in a majority of the states to provide for the operation of non-profit hospital service plans. Usually they are regulated and supervised by the insurance department of states, but not subject to the usual insurance laws and regulations.

Up to 1941 most of the subscribers to the Blue Cross plans were from the middle and higher income groups—those who under most circumstances would be ineligible for the traditional charity or free services. Since then, ward service contracts have been offered by an increasing number of plans, and it is presumed that these contracts will reach a marginal income group, some of whom might otherwise be eligible to free service.

The basic services provided under Blue Cross plans include board and room, general nursing care, and some, but not all, of the adjunctive hospital services—operating and delivery room, specified laboratory services and routine medication and dressings. They do not include payment for the services of a physician, and admission solely for diagnosis is excluded by more than half of the plans. Payments are made directly to the hospital and not to the individual beneficiary.

About one third of the plans exclude service for any condition that existed before the effective date of membership. Treatment of communicable and certain other diseases is limited to a specified stay in a number of plans. The general length of stay for which full payment may be made ranges from 21 to 30 days in any one year, although nearly all plans provide for an extension of benefits at half rates if attention is required beyond the usual period.

Beyond question, these insurance plans have greatly helped the financial problems of the voluntary hospital by increasing their pay business from the middle income group. It has been estimated that persons covered by hospital insurance use hospitals about twice as often as those with similar incomes did in 1929. They now use the hospital about as frequently as the families of the $10,000 income group.

According to available data, 66 million persons in the United States were covered by some form of hospital insurance as of December, 1949. Blue Cross plans covered 34,315,000.[33]

Medical costs.—A much smaller number of people are insured against medical costs, that is, payments to their doctor, and for his and other prescribed therapeutic services. In 1949 the American Medical Association estimated the number to be about 9 million, including those covered by commercial policies.[34]

During the past decade the Blue Shield plans, promoted and sponsored by medical societies, have steadily increased. The majority are state-wide plans, operated through a corporate structure on whose board members of the profession are well represented. A characteristic of these and other voluntary plans is their restriction to a specific income bracket. Usually a single insured person has an income running from $1,500 to $2,400; a family income may be $3,000 to $5,000. In this respect Blue Shield plans differ from the Blue Cross, in which subscribers are insured against hospital costs, regardless of their income level.

Any licensed physician may participate in plans sponsored by medical societies. From those who do, the beneficiary makes his choice. Fees are standardized for specific types of service, although physicians are authorized to make extra charges if the patient's income exceeds the amount to which insurance is restricted. The plans do not include hospital costs, but in many instances cooperative arrangements are made with the Blue Cross—in some instances office space and administrative expense are shared jointly.

The Blue Shield plans and others of a similar nature are designed for traditional practice by the individual physician. Others are designed to assure their members the benefits of group medical practice. One of the largest and most comprehensive of these is the Health Insurance Plan of Greater New York, organized in 1944. This plan provides for:

General medical, specialist, surgical and obstetrical care at the home, office, and hospital; diagnostic and laboratory procedures; periodic health ex-

---

[33] American Medical Association, estimates for 1949.
[34] *Ibid.*

aminations; immunizations and other preventive measures; physical therapy, radiotherapy, and other therapeutic services; professional services for
the administration of blood plasma; eye examinations; visiting nurse service at the home; ambulance service from home to hospital; and psychiatric
examination and consultation. It excludes medical service for acute alcoholism, drug addiction, ailments requiring long-term or institutional treatment, treatment by a psychiatrist, purely cosmetic surgery, dental care,
prescribed drugs, appliances, and eyeglasses.[35]

In order to assure that this range of services is provided, the HIP
enters into agreements with groups of physicians, most of whom have
organized for that purpose. Each group must contain in addition to
general practitioners "qualified specialists in at least the following
twelve fields: internal medicine, general surgery, obstetrics-gynecol-
ogy, pediatrics, otolaryngology, opthalmology, urology, orthopedics,
dermatology, neuropsychiatry, roentgenology, and pathology." Physicians are not required to limit their practice to subscribers, but may
serve other private patients as well. The insured person is free to
choose among the participating groups serving the area in which he
lives, and he may choose his own personal physician within this group.

THE FEDERAL PROPOSALS

Proposals for the intervention of the federal government in the
financing of medical costs, as this is written, are in a considerable state
of chaos.[36] The original proposals made by the Roosevelt Administration following the National Health Survey and the National Conference on the Health of the Nation were incorporated in a bill which
covered federal participation in practically every phase of health and
medical activity. The Wagner-Murray-Dingell bill proposed money
for hospitals, for public health services, for teaching, for nurses, and
for laboratory services. It also proposed a system of compulsory insurance for individuals against the costs of medical care. Certain parts
of the original proposals have been incorporated into separate bills,
and for the most part these have met with relatively little opposition.
Notable among these are the hospital program, enacted as the Hill-
Burton Hospital Survey and Construction Act, and the public health
program, embodied in the Local Health Units bill, but which has not
been passed, as this is written.

---

[35] *Voluntary Medical Care Insurance*, p. 179.
[36] Based on analysis of various pending health bills, *Legislative Information Service
Bulletin* (81st Congress).

Major opposition has developed around the proposals for compulsory insurance to help individuals and families meet the costs of medical care. The organized medical profession is vigorously opposing any steps in this direction. As evidence of growing popular demand for better ways than now at hand, however, we may take the fact that leaders of both parties have sponsored bills, although of a contrasting nature, designed to help people meet their medical costs.

The central features of the present Administration (Thomas) bill would:

1. insure approximately 85 percent of the population of the United States against practically all hospital, medical, dental, and nursing costs
2. pay the physician directly from the insurance fund on either
   (*a*) a case by case basis at stipulated fees, or
   (*b*) an annual fee for each patient covering all potential services
   (*c*) a flat salary
3. set up state-local machinery, of lay and professional Committees, to decide in each locality the rate of fees to be paid and permit physicians to select the payment plan under which they would register with the Committee
4. finance the plan through a pay-roll tax of 3 percent, shared equally by employee and employer, and require Congress to review the experience at the end of six years to see whether this had been accomplished

This bill as well as those submitted by minority leaders provide for the distribution of federal subsidies in a good many other directions: for guaranteed incomes to doctors in areas short of physicians; for maintaining and operating health centers and medical group practice units; for research; for teaching and training; and so on. But the heart of the controversy with the medical profession is over the compulsory federal insurance feature.

One may easily see why they do not like it. For a half century organized medicine has struggled with extraordinary effectiveness to develop and guarantee a high standard of competence and a code of professional conduct. These put proper medical service to the individual patient above all else and consider the direct patient-doctor relationship basic to assuring this. Through various self-accrediting devices and the enforcement of rules of professional conduct, the organized medical profession has achieved most creditable results. It is convinced that a system of competitive merit which brooks no interference in the flow of individual patients to the individual doctor is essential to the maintenance of professional alertness and a due regard for professional ethics. It is convinced that only by exercising these controls through their accompanying direct and indirect police powers, under its own auspices, can these purposes be accomplished.

The compulsory insurance proposals undermine these convictions. Rates are set, not by a theoretical process of competitive merit, but on a uniform basis for all physicians in the locality. An inevitable result would be to give almost all doctors a very considerable security of income. Control of the amount, and to some degree in all probability of the manner of payment, would no longer be in professional hands. In a broader and more general way, the consumer would be given an official voice in respect to policies governing the practice of medicine.

The system of private medical practice has not met the problem of potential patients, in many sections of the country, who have difficulty in finding a doctor. Except as it has sponsored insurance plans of its own, it has not met the problem of the person for whom a doctor is an expensive luxury, even if one is to be found. In these respects, the system by which the profession has so ably protected the medical interest of particular individuals has ignored the medical interests of the whole community.

This, it seems to us, is the heart of the present controversy. For our part we should be glad to see the medical profession given time to adjust to these new circumstances and conditions. In the long run it must adjust to them, and a process of slow progression seems to us more likely to eventuate in good results than would a wholesale abandonment of past traditions and established procedures.

Chapter XI

THE ROAD TO
COMMUNITY COHERENCE

THE PUBLIC HEALTH SYSTEM, the system of community-organized medical care, and the system of private medical practice are now interdependent at numerous points. Each has behind it a record of accomplishment in its particular field of endeavor of which it may well be proud. Each has also lent itself to the accomplishment of the purposes of the other in the general community interest. Their increasing reliance upon one another during this half century has been one of slow but pervasive growth.

Nevertheless, the structure of each system has been built to achieve different objectives. The primary objective of the public health system, during most of this half century, has been to develop effective community-wide procedures for the prevention and reduction of communicable diseases and the hazards of pregnancy, infancy, and childhood. The initial objective of the community-organized system of medical care was to provide medical service to those who could not afford a private physician; this concept has expanded steadily so that now it encompasses the provision of the basic facilities necessary for the modern practice of medicine, for all economic groups. The primary objective of the system of private medical practice has been to develop and maintain a high quality of professional performance and ethical conduct among its individual members.

THE DYNAMIC CHANGE

The materials in the preceding chapters have provided ample evidence that events are reshaping the patterns which determine the form and substance of these three systems. In their present state there is a greater fluidity than was apparent as recently as a decade ago.

Essentially it is the dynamic advancement of scientific thought which is producing this fluidity. For scientific thought is making it increasingly clear that the limited objectives of each system restrict the enhancement of the community's total health. Advancement in science is making it equally apparent that none of these systems can continue to pursue its traditional objectives without modifications consistent with community-wide objectives.

THE PUBLIC HEALTH SYSTEM

It would be incorrect to say that the public health system has completely accomplished its earlier objectives. The acute respiratory diseases, including pneumonia and influenza, as well as poliomyelitis and others of serious import, still challenge the best efforts of medical science to isolate their causative factors and to devise means for their eradication. Despite dramatic curtailment, tuberculosis is still a major cause of death. Public health is still struggling to control the venereal diseases. Many fatalities and disabilities occur in the maternal and infant cycle which are considered unnecessary. The formerly fatal epidemic diseases are kept from again assuming a high priority in community concern only by persistent application of tested procedures.

Certain chronic diseases are now moving into the foreground of community concern because of the high proportion of fatalities and disabilities which they entail. Recently the public health system has begun to extend its objectives to their reduction and control.

The pattern of structure and function to which the public health system has become accustomed, and for which its personnel has been trained, is not easily adapted to meet the new objectives. Concentration upon the control of the infecting agents, with only a secondary concern for the concurrent treatment of the sick person, is deeply embedded in the structure of public health.

Nevertheless, partially for maternity and childhood, but especially for tuberculosis, the public health system has demonstrated that its basic patterns can be adapted to community-wide protection against certain hazards through programs directed at promoting the health of specific individuals. In doing so it has required the cooperation of the physicians in private practice as well as the system of organized medical care. Community-wide control of chronic diseases and disabilities also requires the aid of the other two systems in a number of cooperative relationships. These must be on a maximum rather than a minimum scale, not only with private physicians and organized medical care, but with the rehabilitative services as well.

ORGANIZED MEDICAL CARE

The system of organized medical care was "created" initially, as we have seen, to provide free medical service to needy patients. As long as all medical knowledge could be encompassed by the individual doctor, and its necessary appurtenances conveyed in his "little black bag," this charitable purpose defined quite precisely the nature of its structure and function. Hospitals and outpatient departments were all originally places to which poor people came when they were sick, and to which individual doctors came to attend them, without charge.

When the "little black bag" no longer would hold all of the necessary equipment, and the individual physician no longer could encompass all medical knowledge and skills, the breakdown of that simple pattern began. The organization of equipment, and the organization of general and specialized medical skills, became necessities in order to assure that the quality of medical practice kept pace with advances in scientific knowledge.

These were advantages which could not long be restricted to the poor of the community. Today the best general hospitals very nearly approximate a focal community point around which to organize the best constellations of equipment and professional skills available, without reference to the economic level of the patient. Outpatient services still are restricted mainly to the medically indigent, but even here the traditional pattern is beginning to break up.

PRIVATE MEDICAL PRACTICE

The independent practicing physician is still the cornerstone of the system of private medical practice. For our part, we expect that he will continue to be, for many years to come. Association with the organized services of a community hospital has become almost essential to the maintenance of his practice.

As the need for specialized medical knowledge increases, physicians have found the older and more informal methods of securing medical consultation from colleagues inadequate. Many have found their answer to this problem through participation in the group practice of medicine. In a very real sense physicians of today are being driven into such associations by their own desires to achieve the objective to which the medical profession is dedicated—the maintenance of a high quality of medical care in the interest of the patient. To this, many are now adding a newer objective—the advancement and protection of the health and well-being of all members of the families which they serve.

CONVERGING OBJECTIVES

Thus each of these systems is now in the process of dynamic change from the patterns originally molded to fit the pursuit of its own objectives. One result is that the objectives of each are broadening to encompass those of the others.

To illustrate:

A study by the Subcommittee on Medical Care (American Public Health Association) suggests as a nationwide goal: "(1) *Promotion* of positive health; (2) *Prevention* of disease, disability and attendant economic insecurity; (3) *Cure* or mitigation of disease; and (4) *Rehabilitation* of the patient." [1]

"One of the most significant problems of the twentieth century," says the Commission on Hospital Care, "is the remolding of our social patterns so that the discoveries made through scientific research may be utilized." [2]

A directive of the New York Academy of Medicine instructs its Committee on Medicine and the Changing Order to explore means of improving the quality of medical service in "the maintenance of health . . . the prevention of disease, the treatment of disease . . . [and of] making available . . . to the country as a whole the best known practice in preventive and curative medicine." [3]

These are authoritative articulations of a common community-wide objective to promote better health by preventing the onset of disease and by protecting all persons of the community against the consequences of disease.

[1] Subcommittee on Medical Care, American Public Health Association, "The Quality of Medical Care in a National Health Program," *American Journal of Public Health*, XXXIX, No. 7 (July, 1949), 898.

[2] Commission on Hospital Care, *Hospital Care in the United States*, p. 349.

[3] Bernhard J. Stern, *American Medical Practice in the Perspective of a Century*, p. ix.

TOWARD A COHERENT PATTERN

As this fusion of objectives assumes greater practical reality, we may hope and expect that the roads by which each system travels toward it will merge with a greater measure of structural and functional coherence. Route signs pointing to the convergence of these highways have already been put up.

The most important of these signs points to the extension of community-wide control procedures for chronic diseases and conditions. The second points to the maximum development of the resources of the community general hospital as the cornerstone for this extension. The third points to the development of procedures through which private physicians may assist. The fourth points to the achievement of a stable financial underpinning for total medical care expenditures.

EXTENSION OF COMMUNITY-WIDE DISEASE CONTROL

For all practical purposes, extension of control to the chronic diseases and conditions will approximate a program against almost all illness and disability. Especially is this true when control means prevention and ultimate eradication.

This cannot be accomplished overnight, by fiat, legislative enactment, or even solely by the investment of money. On the contrary, it must proceed tested step by tested step.

It seems clear to us that the public health system should provide aggressive leadership. We use "public health system" advisedly, and in a broad sense. Many of the early steps taken in the process of learning to control infectious diseases were taken by voluntary agencies. A similar opportunity is recurrent in this new area. But we would reiterate a primary lesson of that experience. The long-range policies of coherent functional and structural relationship are served only if the voluntary intent is to pave the way for, and strengthen the potentiality of, official action. We also would underscore the fact that the mere provision of clinics, detection centers, and other diagnostic and treatment services does not of and by itself extend the function of community-wide disease control. An agency will take the necessary steps only if it has four purposes: (1) to assemble facts about the community-wide characteristics of the disease; (2) to follow up the detected cases systematically; (3) to maintain a partial or complete register of cases; (4) to evaluate the results of a planned attack upon the disease. It will not assist in the development of the control function if its concern is solely with the diagnosis and treatment of patients if, as, and when they come to it.

There is a tendency to excuse slow progress by pointing to the lack of knowledge on a number of salient points. Leaders within the public health movement, however, know better than any others that the slowly acquired knowledge of the hazards of maternity and childhood and of communicable diseases has steadily increased the efficiency with which these have been controlled. They know better than any others, also, that much of this knowledge was built up during actual efforts at control. It is safe to assume that it probably would not have been acquired otherwise.

A general attack upon the chronic diseases does not presuppose that registers must be established to keep track of everybody with every disease or condition listed as chronic. In developing the procedures to control chronic diseases and disabilities, however, it seems clear that registration must be related to specific strategic characteristics of the diseases.

The best formula is whatever formula works. The public health system has a scientific discipline, and a rich background of experience of what does and does not work in the two areas to which their discipline has been applied. Research and experimentation must be encouraged as the *sine qua non* of progress. There are several strategic points at which it should pay dividends.

Generic characteristics.—First, we need a better understanding and classification of the characteristics of the whole group of diseases and conditions now loosely listed as chronic. The principal data for that purpose come from the 1935 National Health Survey and subsequent studies in particular fields and population groups. Experimentation with actual procedures, and strategical or epidemiological data has so far been limited to a very few specific diseases.

Any fresh contribution to knowledge of the generic problems of chronicity would have high utility. Our St. Paul data point clearly to one manner of making such a contribution. The most disastrous consequences of chronic illness and disability were manifested in the relatively small group of multiproblem families to which we have referred frequently. The specific diseases and conditions found among them covered the whole range of those usually classified as chronic.

A systematic effort to identify this group of the community's families, and the establishment of control procedures aimed to exploit fully their potentialities for rehabilitation, it seems to us, would produce much material that would be useful in directing the strategy of a more comprehensive attack upon the general problems of chronicity. There are, however, other avenues for research designed comprehensively to explore the characteristics of chronicity most significant to a broad attack upon it.

Case-finding tools.—Public health and medical scientists already are at work at another strategic point. Many of the noninfectious chronic diseases are very much more manageable if discovered early; but the condition may have had its inception long before symptoms became readily apparent. Selective and precise methods of detecting the presence of certain diseases are greatly needed.

Mass testing of the population for evidence of tuberculosis is recognized as an effective method of case finding. Mass serological tests for syphilis also have been conducted successfully. Simple as well as economical methods have been devised to determine cases in which there is a high probability of diabetes. The number of persons found with evidence of one of the diseases is, of course, small in proportion to the number examined, but they probably would not have been found in any other way until the disease had reached a more serious stage.

Communities are only beginning to discover the value of the new approach to case finding through multiphasic screening of the population.[4] Proponents are perhaps overenthusiastic and opponents too cautious. Systematic follow-up procedures should be integrated into the community systems for medical care. Used with care and with continuing evaluation of its effectiveness, this new approach may well mark a milestone in public health promotion.

There has been little experimentation with community generalized detection clinics, so far as we know. Well-organized clinics of a hospital outpatient department serve this purpose in part, as do group medical units. Systematic morbidity reporting by hospitals should aid

[4] A. L. Chapman, "The Concept of Multiphasic Screening," *Public Health Reports,* LXIV, No. 42 (October 21, 1949), 1311.

in discovery of conditions which warrant an organized attack upon them. But in the laboratory of community application, the strategic characteristics of chronicity, the improvement and relative utility of the basic methods of case finding, and the effectiveness of specific control procedures clamor for research and experimental attention.

THE COMMUNITY GENERAL HOSPITAL

If the public health system extends its control program to include chronic diseases and conditions, it seems to us that it will have to rely heavily upon the cooperation of the general hospitals in doing so. The reasons are quite obvious: (1) To the extent that detection and diagnostic clinics are relied upon for case finding, the general hospital represents the natural and, under ordinary circumstances, most efficient auspices for their administration. (2) The hospital provides the constellations of equipment and services that may be required, both to diagnose and to treat these different conditions and their complications. (3) Through its inpatient and outpatient services, the hospital offers the final assurance that those discovered with a disease will not lack for treatment because of insufficient money to pay a doctor or to secure the treatment prescribed.

One might add a fourth reason. The fact is, that people with chronic conditions usually spend some time at least in the general hospital when their illness reaches a sufficiently serious stage. Fifty percent of the total volume of business, it is worth repeating, undertaken by the organized medical care agencies of St. Paul, including the voluntary hospitals, was with chronic diseases and disabilities.

In other words, and in simple terms, the extension of the function of control to the areas of chronicity must very largely be the creation of the public health departments and the hospitals. The one must supply the systematic procedures of case finding and reporting, of follow-up and evaluation. The other must supply, in the event and to the extent that they are needed, modern diagnostic and treatment resources. The records of the two must be synchronized so as to be of maximum utility in the epidemiological analysis of the community-wide programs, and in the review of its results.

There is some opinion, as we have seen, that the public administration of the two should be consolidated. There is some precedence for this at state and federal levels. The Surgeon-General of the Public

Health Service administers the federal program for promoting the traditional public health services, and also administers the federal hospital survey and construction program. By far the largest number of states have designated the state health department as the hospital auhority responsible for the administration of the construction program. Furthermore, recent legislation in many states has placed the hospital licensing authority in the state health department.

At the local level we are inclined to view with caution any assumption that consolidation of public health and hospital administration would result in the balanced synchronization of these two functions. Community-wide organization and analysis tends to suffer when combined with responsibility for the administration of a large-scale, direct-service program. Furthermore, the administration of voluntary hospitals, which in most communities provide the bulk of the general hospital service, could not practically be combined with that of the public health department.

But whatever may be the best administrative set-up, development in this cooperative direction means that the public health department and the general hospital should know a good deal about each other's business. Patterns for cooperation must be developed and evaluated by leadership representative of the best experience of both.

EXTENSION WITH THE HELP OF THE MEDICAL PROFESSION

Most cases of acute communicable disease are reported to the health department by private physicians. A laboratory test may be needed to check the diagnosis, the public health nurse will give instruction and may help make certain necessary arrangements, but it is assumed that the attending physician will do whatever can be done to treat the case effectively. A similar assumption is made concerning maternity and child health services by the physician to his own patients. Here again, for some patients a public health nurse may undertake certain supervision and instruction.

In the control of tuberculosis, also, patterns of cooperation have been established between private physicians and the public health department. In the control of tuberculosis the public health department pays much more attention to appropriateness and continuity of treatment than it does in the case of many other diseases. When treatment is given in a hospital or a clinic, cooperation with the health department in keeping the record up to date and in planning for reorientation of treatment is a matter of public policy. If treatment is given in the physician's office or in the home of the patient, cooperation depends largely upon the physician's inclination and experience. The extension of community-wide control to the noncommunicable chronic diseases, it seems to us, will depend to a great extent upon the inclination of the physician in private practice.

Theoretically, his inclination ought to be in that direction. Systematic community-wide procedures for the earlier discovery of the chronic diseases should help the physician to develop his medical practice along the lines of preventive medicine. It seems reasonable to expect physicians to welcome systematic assistance in making arrangements to assure continuation of treatment, either under his or other auspices. Community-wide disease control is an effective method of introducing continuity of treatment.

Extension of control to areas of chronicity other than tuberculosis will mean that the doctor may need to make reports on the progress of the case, undoubtedly a nuisance. Under certain circumstances it may well mean that he must be prepared to discuss the progress or lack of progress of certain of his cases with someone else. Undoubtedly such things represent an intrusion upon his privacy and the autonomy of his judgments.

The development of cooperative procedures in this area has another and equally deep significance to the medical profession. On the one hand, community opinion is developing in support of a control program. On the other hand is the growing belief that medical services should be expanded for the benefit of individuals now unable to avail themselves of them. At first blush this seems a harder objective to achieve, and the path to it harder and longer. Communities will follow it, in our opinion, if given evidence that the system of private medical practice and the public health system are at one in their belief in its utility.

EXTENDING THE ASSURANCE OF SERVICE

The control of health hazards to mothers and children has been established, in no small measure, by directing the control procedures to those who ordinarily would be unable to pay for necessary medical, nursing, and hospital services. Attempts to control any or all of the chronic diseases likewise must include a systematic effort to assure treatment for those who need it. Extension of control procedures to encompass the major disabilities of chronicity should throw very much more light than we now have upon the unavailability of medical service due to economic reasons.

Anyone who buys insurance against any risk must believe that insurance against sickness is a good idea, if actuarially sound, and the parties participating in the risk are able and willing to pay for it. There is at present a tendency to use the principle of insurance as a leverage, either to sustain the traditional organization of medical practice or to reorganize it. Medical societies tend to rely on voluntary medical care plans to insure not only the patient against the costs of medical care, but to maintain the traditional structure of private medical practice. Other private plans which insure against medical expense stipulate the development of group medical practice on behalf of the members. The current federal proposals to insure the individual against all medical expenses involve a strong possibility of disrupting the present structure of medical practice on which responsibility for adequate care inevitably must fall.

The evidence is clear that spread of Blue Cross and other voluntary plans for hospital insurance has greatly increased the use of hospital facilities among the middle income group. They have been a financial boon to sorely pressed hospital administrators and governing boards.

Effective planning for the control of chronic disabilities is the principal link needed to forge the three systems into a coherent pattern for the full protection of the community's health. The principal uncertainty of the system of organized medical care—a clarification of the role of the general hospital in organizing the community medical resources to provide a "constellation" of services—centers in these disabilities. The principal uncertainty of the system of private medical practice—how to adjust its responsibility for a high quality of individual performance to include the essentials of group practice—centers in the diagnostic and treatment requirements of these disabilities. The financial problems, now embarrassing both of the medical care systems, are due primarily to these circumstances of chronicity. The organized and effective extension of the function of community-wide disease control should help to bring about a solution of the problems which each system faces. The resultant harmonious pattern would provide the base for new and greater achievement in the total protection of the community's health.

Unless we misread the signs, community policy about its program for public health is now at the crossroads. One road leads to the community-wide organization of a purposeful program to prevent, control, and reduce disease, and to protect the community as a whole against the principal consequences of ill-health. The other road leads to the expansion of medical services to assure their distribution to individuals who have hitherto been unable to avail themselves of these services.

At first blush, one might assume that travel by either of these two roads would be bound to bring the community to the same destination. Our own experience leads us to the conclusion that this is a very incorrect assumption. For those who follow the second road, preoccupation with the provision of service, as an end in itself, often results in lack of perspective about the priority of the various health hazards and how their prevalence may be reduced. Research into their strategic characteristics takes a minor place, and inevitably more and more treatment is demanded, more and more of which may have to be free to the patient. Such circumstances inflate in importance matters of auspices, administration, and finance. Scientific evaluation of the results achieved is likely to be pushed further and further down in the scale of attention in solving the community-wide problem.

The first road also leads to a better and more adequate distribution of service. But it arrives at this destination with greater flexibility in encompassing its ultimate objective—a demonstrable reduction in disease and protection of the total community against the consequences of ill-health, from any cause. This destination is harder to reach. The road to it is longer and in its beginnings by no means so easily followed. But communities have traveled with distinction and success over part of this route for nearly half a century. Given the opportunity, we have reason to believe that they will follow the leadership of public health and organized medicine for the remainder of the way.

MALADJUSTMENT

Chapter XII

ACCEPTANCE OF
RESPONSIBILITY

THE COMMUNITY, even in the most primitive societies, always has undertaken to protect itself against the behavior of persons unwilling or unable to adjust their conduct to accepted laws and customs. People are seldom as clearly aware of their own social incapacities as they are of their poverty and ill-health.

Recently the term maladjustment has come to describe a composite of behavior disorders and socially unacceptable conduct. Maladjustment, in the sense that we are using it, was defined as precisely as possible in connection with our St. Paul project. In collecting the St. Paul data, we accepted two main types of evidence of the inability of people to adjust successfully to the necessities of social living. The first was evidence of antisocial behavior as reflected by the formal judgments of society, that is, records of crime, delinquency, child neglect, and other types of behavior in respect to which society takes official action. The second was diagnostic evidence. This included mental deficiency as revealed by psychological tests; mental disease, emotional disorders or instability as recorded by psychiatrists; and failure to discharge primary social obligations toward home, school, or work as identified by social workers. During the month of our study the agencies reported the presence of these evidences of maladjustment in approximately 6 percent of the families in the community. In another 4 percent, while there was no evidence of personal incapacity, the family situation was so disorganized that the members could not adjust to it without help.

No similar national data regarding maladjusted persons and families ever have been collected. But there is evidence that a very large number of people throughout the country are failing, in varying degrees, to meet the minimum responsibilities of social living.

Throughout the nation, 600,000 adults each year serve sentences in

jails [1] and another 140,000 in prisons and penitentiaries.[2] About 300,-
000 juveniles spend some time in local detention homes while approximately 30,000 are to be found in training schools for young delinquents.[3]

It is generally agreed that from 1 to 2 percent of the total population is mentally deficient. Over 600,000 mentally ill and 140,000 mentally defective or epileptic persons are so seriously disordered as to
require care in mental institutions.[4] Furthermore, 12 percent of the
16 million men called up during the Second World War were re-
jected for neuropsychiatric reasons.[5]

Each year one family is dissolved in the divorce courts for every
four new families established during the year by marriage. Each year
around 75,000 children are adopted.[6] A study made in 1944 disclosed
that in fifteen states 58 percent of the children concerned in adoption
petitions were born out of wedlock, while more than half of the
others came from families broken by divorce, separation, or desertion.[7]

Most of these evidences of maladjustment have been increasing.
Juvenile delinquency rates went up sharply during the Second World
War, decreased somewhat thereafter, but are still of such proportions
as to cause considerable alarm throughout the nation. Adult crime
rates are increasing. The divorce rate rose 65 percent between 1940
and 1947.[8] It seems to us worthy of note that the increase in these
indices of maladjustment is in contrast to the sharp drop in dependency from its peak of the 30's, as well as to the relatively low death
rates which have been fairly constant for the past two decades.

The total of national expenditures for services to deal with all
these problems is unknown. But on the basis of the available data and
scattered facts about special programs, we have concluded that as a
nation we spend in the neighborhood of three quarters of a billion
dollars annually for adult corrections (excluding jails), juvenile cor-

---

[1] The American Prison Association, *Manual of Suggested Standards for a State Correctional System*, p. 81.

[2] U.S. Bureau of the Census, *Statistical Abstract of the United States: 1948*, p. 191.

[3] Herschel Alt, "Juvenile Behavior Problems," *Social Work Year Book, 1947*, pp. 266,
272.

[4] Thomas A. C. Rennie and Luther E. Woodward, *Mental Health in Modern Society*,
p. 4.

[5] National Institute for Mental Health, *Patients in Mental Institutions, 1947*, pp. 26, 68.

[6] Federal Security Agency, Children's Bureau, *Services for Children*, p. 6.

[7] I. Evelyn Smith, "Adoption," *Social Work Year Book, 1947*, p. 25.

[8] *Manual of Suggested Standards, op. cit.*, p. 15.

rections, mental health, and the social agencies which deal with various evidences of maladjustment.

THREE MAIN SYSTEMS

For our purposes the agencies which give the community some measure of protection against the symptoms and consequences of maladjustment may be grouped under three principal systems: (1) a protective and correctional system; (2) a mental institutional system which represents the beginnings of a mental health system; (3) a social casework system. Only at a few points do these systems have any structural integration. Like the health systems, they are made up mainly of separate agencies, most of them administratively autonomous in the local community. A considerable degree of state authority and operation is to be found in the correctional and mental health systems, but only in the latter are there signs of a trend toward a federal-state structure.

THE PROTECTIVE AND CORRECTIONAL SYSTEM

The protective and correctional system is in reality a constellation of three interdependent subsystems: the police, the judiciary, and the correctional agencies. In combination they protect the community by forcefully restraining people who seek to engage in overt behavior contrary to official laws and customs. In this process the role of the police is to discover and apprehend the offender, the role of the courts is to determine the fact of his misconduct and the penalty he shall pay, while correctional measures aim to mend the error of his ways.

The modern urban police system has many concerns beside the discovery and apprehension of criminal offenders. It regulates traffic, maintains order, suppresses disturbances, and enforces ordinances of all kinds. Somewhat as the public health department promotes a safe physical environment, so an efficient police department promotes an orderly social environment conducive to personal behavior which conforms to the common interests of society.

Our judicial system derives from an effort to protect the individual from arbitrary social authority and at the same time to protect society against infringement of its laws and customs. The system comprises an interdependent structure of administratively autonomous local, state, and federal courts, which differ in their precise make-up in different sections of the country.

After the police department has discovered and apprehended the offender, and the processes of fair trial have determined him to be an offender in fact, the judge must pass sentence, or "dispose" of the case. From 80 to 90 percent of the violations of the criminal law are punishable by fines, and this is the most popular penalty. If the penalty is not a fine, the court may put the offender on probation, sentence him to the local jail or workhouse, or send him to a state prison or reformatory.

The correctional system then takes over. The organization of this system varies from state to state and from community to community. In general, however, it consists of a number of separate, but inevitably interdependent, local and state units. Many authorities are now urging integration of these on a state-wide basis.[9]

The country's jails are strictly local in their auspices and administration, as are the 10,000 or more police lockups where every year several million persons are detained prior to their appearance in court.[10] Detention homes for juveniles also are local agencies. These local institutions deal with by far the largest number of people who fail to behave as society believes they should. Many of the people whom such institutions shelter show other serious and obvious evidences of social instability, social irresponsibility, and physical ill-health.

Prisons or other institutions for more serious adult offenders and their counterparts, the training schools for juveniles, are under state auspices and administration. The commonest pattern is to consolidate the administration of the adult institutions either in a separate state department of correction or in a bureau in some other department. The juvenile institutions are more likely to be administered by the State Department of Welfare.

The final responsibility of the correctional system is to release the prisoner. States have parole procedures by which a prisoner may be returned to his community, but kept under the supervision of a parole officer for a stipulated period. The parole system for adults is usually

9 Alice Scott Nutt, "Juvenile and Domestic Relations Courts," *Social Work Year Book, 1947*, p. 276.
10 Helen D. Pigeon, *Probation and Parole in Theory and Practice*, p. 28.

under a state authority independent of the correctional institutions; at present in less than half the states it is consolidated with the administration of probation. Parole from the juvenile institutions, on the other hand, in most states is not under any central authority but is handled by each institution.

For several decades, leaders in the protective-correctional system have worked for improvement in diagnosis and treatment of the mental, emotional, physical, and social maladies which apparently lie behind the antisocial behavior of those who come into their custody. The responsibility falls principally upon the correctional segment of the system, and this will be our primary concern. But at certain points the processes and policies followed by the police in apprehending a suspect, and by the courts in disposing of a case, have a vital bearing upon the diagnostic and treatment processes which the correctional system may wish to initiate later.

THE MENTAL HEALTH SYSTEM

Traditionally, the state government has carried the principal responsibility for the institutional care of both the mentally ill and the mentally defective. This responsibility, like that of the protective and correctional system, grew out of the compelling necessity to accept responsibility for those whose overt behavior made them unfit for life in the general community. The great majority of the 130,000 persons who each year enter the state hospitals for the mentally ill [11] are still admitted by order or "commitment" from the local court. All states provide for this type of official commitment. In 34 states, however, it is possible for a person to be admitted voluntarily, and 18 states permit emergency admissions on certification by one or two physicians.[12]

At its best the state mental hospital is now coming to be regarded as a "treatment" rather than merely as a custodial institution. Everywhere today mental health authorities are striving to equip these institutions to diagnose, treat, cure, or improve the condition of the patients so that they may be returned to their own communities.

Although practice here, as in the correctional system, falls far short of its goal, these state institutions constitute the country's principal

[11] *Patients in Mental Institutions, 1947,* p. 28, Table 1.
[12] George A. Kempf, *Laws Pertaining to the Admittance of Patients to Mental Hospitals,* pp. 4–12.

resource for the care of persons with serious mental illness or severe mental defect. Private payment hospitals for mental illness, available to those who can afford them, offer care to relatively few patients— particularly on a long-time basis.

Only six states have a separate department of mental health administering these state institutions. They are administered by the state welfare department in 10 states, by a general department of institutions in 14, a central board of hospital control in 5, by the state health or combined health and welfare department in 3, and function as independent units in the others.[13]

In the local community a clinic or hospital outpatient department is the most common type of agency for dealing with less serious cases of mental illness or emotional instability. Every such clinic is served by a psychiatrist and most of them are also staffed by psychologists and caseworkers.

At last report there were approximately 1,200 psychiatric clinics in the United States—a phenomenal increase since 1947 when some 700 were reported. Some 250 are for adults only, including those restricted to veterans.[14] In large urban communities some public and private general hospitals maintain psychiatric services for the observation, diagnosis, and short-time care of borderline cases of mental illness. While many such hospitals formerly refused to admit psychiatric cases, an increasing number of general hospitals are today providing psychiatric care.

Finally, a small number of large urban centers maintain city or county hospitals for the long-time care of patients with serious mental illness. Sometimes these institutions are limited to a special class of patients, such as the senile or alcoholic, but in other instances they represent the city's general effort to care for its own when the state institutions are overcrowded and inadequate.

Practically everywhere the only local community service for mentally defective persons is the school system's provision of special classes for children whose intelligence quotients generally fall in the range of 50–75, and who are considered educable on the basis of psychological tests. While this program enables them to receive the maximum edu-

[13] National Institute for Mental Health, personal communication.
[14] *Ibid.*

cation possible, the school system does not assume continuing responsibility for their later adjustment to community life.

In the past there has been little connection or interdependence between the state institutions and the local agencies concerned with the promotion of mental health. The passage of the National Mental Health Act in 1946 may mark the beginning of a more integrated system. Certainly it constitutes tangible assistance to preventive efforts in a badly neglected area. Under its provisions, federal funds are available for grants-in-aid to the states for local clinics as well as for training, research, and other purposes. But at present, in 32 states the federal money is disbursed through the state health department, acting as the state mental health authority,[15] rather than through the unit responsible for the state mental institutions.

THE SOCIAL CASEWORK SYSTEM

Private agencies constitute the core of the social casework system although even less than in the systems of correction and mental health do they have any organic, structural, or administrative unity. They are found almost exclusively in middle-sized and larger communities. Practically without exception, private casework agencies are separate, autonomous, locally financed and locally administered units. Nevertheless, during most of the present century the philosophy and methods of professional casework have had a profound influence on their objectives and policies. It is in this sense that private agencies which deal with the various evidences of maladjustment constitute a system with a common orientation.

At the center of this system is the family casework agency which grew out of the charity organization societies of the late nineteenth and early twentieth centuries. The original intent of these societies was to organize community resources in the best way to meet the particular relief needs of each family who came to them for help. Out of this experience in "individualizing" the needs of each family and in "organizing" the resources required to meet them there evolved the modern professional skill of social casework.

Children's agencies outnumber all others included in this general system. Until the beginning of the present century children without

15 *Ibid.*

families, or with families unable or unwilling to provide for them, were cared for mainly in institutions known as "orphan asylums"— although the number of "whole orphans" in them was often quite small. Then, early in the century there developed a growing realization that children brought up in an institutional setting were missing the important social and affectional influences of family life. At the same time the emergence of "individualized" casework methods began to have a profound influence upon the program. The result was the development of foster homes where children could live in a normal family environment, while the supervising skill of the caseworker was utilized to help both the child and the foster parents make the necessary adjustments to the new relationship. Today, authorities in children's work believe that there should be a balanced provision of both institutional and foster home care. They also believe that children in institutions, no less than children in foster homes, should have the benefit of skilled casework service, especially in connection with admission and discharge.

Exactly what proportion of the nation's agencies are private, and what proportion are public we do not know, but we do know that the majority of all children under agency care are reported by private agencies.

A substantial proportion of the private children's institutions and foster home agencies are under Catholic, Jewish, or Protestant denominational auspices. Private nonsectarian foster home agencies, somewhat like family casework agencies, are limited primarily to the larger and middle-sized urban communities, although in some instances state-wide organizations service the entire state.

It is also in the urban community, under private auspices, that we find the most pronounced trend toward categorizing casework service around various evidences of children's adjustment difficulties.

In a few places one finds "study homes," that is, small institutions which seek to provide an opportunity for intensive observation and treatment of children with special personality difficulties. Some cities have separate agencies which give casework help to unmarried mothers and their babies, while maternity homes or hospitals which care for the same group during the prenatal and postnatal period also may provide casework assistance in connection with this difficult adjustment. Occasionally an agency limits itself to the adjustment of adolescent "problem" girls, while the humane societies and societies for the prevention of cruelty to children still have as their main concern "child neglect" and nonsupport. Although public day nurseries for the care of children of working mothers were expanded greatly during the war, those now in operation are more likely to be under private auspices. The provision of "homemaker" service has increased rapidly in recent years.

The categorical approach in private casework service, however, has not been limited to children. The Red Cross provides casework assistance to veterans in every community of any size. Most urban communities have a Travelers Aid Society which uses a casework staff to help transients or nonresidents meet emergency adjustments. Some hospitals with large outpatient departments have a staff of medical social workers who assist patients to carry out the treatment prescribed and in making the adjustments necessitated by their illness. The demand for this type of service is increasing.

Public agencies in most communities use personnel with some casework training or orientation. We have seen that in varying degrees public welfare departments provide casework help to families receiving relief. When the welfare department administers foster home or other special programs for children, personnel with casework training are regarded as essential. Juvenile courts offering probation service and school systems which employ visiting teachers or school social workers, also desire staff who know how to use casework methods.

The public welfare unit is an integral part of the assistance system; the probation unit is a part of the correctional system; and the school social work unit an adjunct of the school system. The community outlook of each agency is influenced by many factors unrelated to the philosophy of professional casework. For these reasons it has seemed to us better to characterize such public agencies in their natural framework, rather than as part of a "social casework system." A general exception may be noted in the field of public child welfare. Influenced especially by federal grants through the Children's Bureau, caseworkers providing public child welfare services in the states have steadily increased in numbers. Their orientation, in philosophy, training, and professional practice, has a close kinship with the casework of the private system.

We do not know how many persons or families in the country are served by the many local agencies which make up this casework system, nor do we have data to show the approximate amount of money spent by them.

In St. Paul, the private agencies system spent approximately $900,-000 a year, or a little more than one third of the total expenditures for all adjustment services exclusive of adult corrections. Similar data from 29 urban communities in which over 13 percent of the country's population live, show expenditures of over $37 million, or $1.94 per capita.[16] Inasmuch as this private agency system is limited mainly to urban centers and the agencies comprising it are found only occasionally in small towns and rural areas, we think a reasonable estimate would put its nationwide expenditures at over $100 million.

THE TANGLED ROOTS OF PUBLIC POLICY

During much of their history, the three systems which reflect the community's attempt to protect itself against the consequences of maladjustment have tended to regard crime, delinquency, child neglect, illegitimacy, mental disorder, and a host of other particular symptoms as separate and more or less unrelated entities. Without unduly pressing the analogy, one might say that public policy has had its roots in concepts not unlike the public attitude toward consumption before the discovery of the tubercle bacillus, when each type of disorder produced by this germ was regarded as a distinct and separate disease.

Nevertheless, in the past no less than now, each of the three systems has been concerned with the problem of human behavior. Or it might be more accurate to say that each has been concerned with the problem of socially unsatisfactory or unsuccessful behavior. Since knowledge about the cause and cure of such conditions has been extremely meager, public policy has had its roots in a confusion of beliefs about what action should be taken in regard to human conduct inimical or detrimental to the general community welfare. This confusion in thinking is compounded, it seems to us, out of (1) the elusiveness of social judgment, (2) the simplicity of traditional concepts about cause

16 Community Chests and Councils, Inc., *Expenditures for Community Health and Welfare, 31 Urban Areas 1948*, p. 39.

and cure, (3) the impact of the humanitarian impulse upon these concepts, and (4) the increasing intrusion of scientific thought.

THE ELUSIVENESS OF SOCIAL JUDGMENT

In the last analysis what constitutes an unsatisfactory or an unsuccessful adjustment very often depends upon social judgments. As one authority puts it: "All we can do is to fix a very broad average of social conduct, and if anyone departs too far from what we feel to be the limits of this average, we are constrained to put him in jail or in a hospital for the insane, or to call him 'peculiar.' " [17]

It is scarcely necessary to remind ourselves that social judgment about the kind of behavior regarded as unsatisfactory is changing constantly. Many actions offensive to one generation either have become common practice in another or have disappeared entirely from social custom. In the early years of American history, public judgment called for protection against witchcraft, failure to observe the Sabbath, disobedience on the part of slaves. But in those days society did not demand protection against the hazards of motor vehicle traffic. At any given time and place, some people will feel that public requirements for protection against particular acts or types of behavior have become outmoded, and there is an incessant struggle to register in official policy the inevitable and dynamic change in public attitudes. Hence, any attempt to anchor public policy in respect to the program for maladjustment exclusively in the shifting currents of social judgment is bound to produce considerable confusion.

THE SIMPLICITY OF TRADITIONAL CONCEPTS

During the Middle Ages, and indeed until much later, the cause of knavery, vagabondage, and other attributes of misconduct was considered a simple matter. Man was believed to be a free moral agent directly responsible for all his acts.

Not only were savage punishments considered the just reward of those who had set themselves against the company of honest men, but gibbets and stocks also served as an object lesson to potential wrongdoers. Only those manifesting obvious and extreme mental deviations were not held wholly accountable for their actions, and such

[17] George K. Pratt, *Your Mind and You*, p. 57.

people commonly were thought to be possessed of the devil, who had to be exorcised by religious rites. It was left for the political philosophers of the eighteenth century to conceive that the purpose of "punishment" was not social revenge, but rather to deter the individual from committing and continuing to commit illegal and antisocial acts. They proposed that "the penalty for each crime be so fixed that the pain imposed would be sufficiently in excess of the pleasure derived from its commission to deter men from committing crime." [18] This philosophy, as embodied in the reforms of the early nineteenth century, still exerts a powerful influence on our juridical system.

"Spare the rod and spoil the child" thus is no glib slogan of parental irritation. Nor are the fortress-like appearance, the unscalable walls and dreary cell blocks of most of our prisons and penitentiaries solely the consequence of the necessity for security. Neither is the traditional "30 days for drunkenness and disorderly conduct" merely a means of keeping the town drunkards away from their cups. All use "punishment" as the principal method of "treating" the individual so as to improve his adjustment to society. The powerful appeal of this concept lies in its simplicity. So long as we believe that people do what they do willfully, with perfect and equal freedom, it is not illogical to blame them and to use punishment as the principal method for improving the quality of their relationship to society. Moreover, society inevitably will continue to rely upon this method of curing misconduct and protecting itself until some better method has been demonstrated successfully.

THE IMPACT OF THE HUMANITARIAN IMPULSE

Man's capacity to abuse his authority to punish his fellowmen needs no elaboration. But fortunately for us, humanitarian concepts, rooted in our Judeo-Christian philosophy and in a belief that the individual personality has intrinsic value, now exert a powerful counteracting force. Gradually they have changed the system whereby everyone who offended against society was decapitated, hanged, flogged, mutilated, or chained in darkened dungeons, until today capital and corporal punishment have been eliminated almost completely. Gradually, also, these concepts have done away with the use of chains and handcuffs,

18 Harry E. Barnes, "Criminology," *The Encyclopedia of the Social Sciences*, IV, 585.

prevalent in the early nineteenth century, whereby lunatics and idiots were forcibly restrained from presumptive violence.

Out of this humanitarian wellspring came the great reform waves of the nineteenth century against the indecencies, perversions and brutalities which characterized the administration of the correctional and mental disease activities in those days. The same humanitarian ideal is the inspiration for present-day public protests over abuses in the administration of our prisons and mental institutions. The community's casework services, the core of the social work movement in this country, can be traced directly to the humanitarian impulse to help man improve his lot.

Of and by itself, however, the humanitarian motive does not lead us to discover the cause of socially unsuccessful behavior, or how it can best be cured, or how to prevent it. It makes us revolt against man's inhumanity to man; it causes us to regard as precious every individual personality, no matter how damaged. But this powerful urge does not contain within itself the knowledge of how best to achieve the goals it sets up.

THE INTRUSION OF SCIENTIFIC THOUGHT

Into an area formerly dominated by elusive social judgments, simple confidence in the rightness of blame and punishment, and an emotional conviction of human worth, there has intruded with increasing force during the past half century a new element—scientific thought and inquiry into the causation of unsuccessful behavior.

Criminology and psychiatry had quite different beginnings. Modern criminology, dating from the mid-nineteenth century, began by an effort to identify the criminal as an abnormal hereditary type, with definite characteristics—anatomical, physiological, and psychological. Though we know now that the explanation for crime is not so simple, the work of those early scientists marked the first attempt to study the individual criminal offender: not merely *what* he had done, but *why* he had done it. Psychiatry began with the small group of medical men who were practicing their profession in institutions for the insane. They too began to inquire *why* these afflicted people behaved as they did.

In the attempt to explain criminal behavior, criminology has drawn upon the findings of anthropology, sociology, psychiatry, psychology, which have done so much during the present century to advance our knowledge of the causes and patterns of human behavior.

We know now that the causes of man's failure to make successful social adjustments are infinitely complex, lying for the most part in a dynamic relationship between the inner person and the outward circumstances under which he lives. But this intrusion of scientific thought is still in the process of working its way to the foundation of public policy. In so doing it is creating a transition in the purposes and methods of our organized programs to deal with maladjustment.

COMMUNITY-WIDE PROGRAM ISSUES

By its very nature, the protective and correctional system always has had a community-wide purpose. Necessarily its concern has been the protection of the whole community against the total volume of unsocial behavior. The same approach has not characterized the mental health and casework systems, whose concern has been primarily to give care or service to the people who came to their attention.

Moreover, except at specific points the three systems have not been greatly dependent on one another. From the protective and correctional systems, the courts still commit cases to the mental hospital system. They also commit children to casework agencies, and casework agencies are likely to be involved in legal processes in certain other ways. There are also referrals back and forth between the various agencies in the various systems. But except at the point of commitment it is difficult to identify patterns of interdependence.

Each of the three systems, however, has been for some time in a process of fermenting change. The desire to "punish" where it is merited and the urge merely to "help" people are giving way to an intention to "diagnose and treat." In all three systems the traditional intent to protect the community by force and restraint against the antisocial evidences of maladjustment is being matched by a growing intent to prevent other evidences of unsatisfactory behavior and protect the whole community against them.

In the materials and processes now in the making, one may hope to find the ingredients for a community-wide program to prevent maladjustment and to provide protection against its consequences.

As in the other principal fields with which this book is concerned, those ingredients are to be found in:

1. Knowledge about the characteristics of the problem which have practical significance to the organization of a community-wide attack upon it
2. The functions which are indispensable to any community-wide plan for prevention and protection
3. The significant characteristics of the community-wide structure through which the agency systems administer these functions
4. The pathways which should lead to a more coherent and better integrated community-wide system

Chapter XIII

SOME STRATEGIC CHARACTERISTICS OF MALADJUSTMENT

THE FORCES which impel people to do the things they ought not to do, and to leave undone the things they ought to do, baffle the learned as well as the common man. Instead of giving us a final answer, scientific thought, in an area formerly dominated by social judgments, humanitarian ideals, and faith in the efficacy of punishment, has opened up opportunities for still further penetration into the unknown.

So far, in spite of scientific progress, there has been little systematic effort to develop and assemble data which have, or should have, strategic significance to a community-wide attack upon pathological behavior. The various parts of the community's correctional and casework systems have been organized mainly around the particular symptoms of maladjustment—a *crime,* an act of *delinquency,* a *neglected or dependent child,* a *broken family,* a *relief family,* or a stranded *transient* family. Psychiatry, up to the present, has concerned itself largely with perfecting its capacity to diagnose the individual case, rather than in dealing with the manifestations of mental disorder on a community-wide basis.

As a means of furthering their objectives, both the mental health system and the correctional system are schooled in the use of classification procedures, those prerequisites in the advancement of scientific knowledge. The former system classifies its materials primarily in order to further the diagnostic and treatment process. The latter uses classification primarily to organize its work processes. During the past quarter century the casework system on the whole has resisted the application of classification procedures to its materials and processes.

The systems in this field have not been greatly interested in developing and classifying data primarily for use in conducting a community-wide attack either upon the overall problem of maladjustment, or upon any of its segments. In contrast to ill-health, where much has been accomplished in this direction, for maladjustment these authors have had to rely mainly on their own experience and research in organizing the materials which follow.

For the purpose of summarizing what is known about the characteristics of maladjustment which may be most useful to the development of community-wide plans for prevention and protection, we have chosen to break the materials down into two main areas: (1) behavior disorders, including mental defect, mental disease, and antisocial behavior; and (2) disorganized situations. The mental health system is concerned primarily with mental defect and disease; the correctional system with antisocial behavior, and the casework system with the interaction of personality and situation.

The agencies of each system are responsible for the diagnosis and treatment of many cases whose symptoms have been the principal preoccupation of one of the others. But until recently there has been little or no common foundation for the community-wide planning implication of these composite evidences of pathological, antisocial, socially unsuccessful, or socially inadequate behavior. Sporadic efforts to plan a community-wide strategy to prevent delinquency, or child neglect, or mental disorder, have tended to take on the attributes of impulsive attacks upon the "little man who wasn't there."

The point of greatest strategical significance in our treatment of these materials is the fact that we have attributed generic characteristics to the specific evidences and symptoms which are dealt with by the three systems.

Increasingly in the last decade the term maladjustment has come into popular usage to characterize the general area of personality difficulties and situational trouble. Leaders in each of the three systems, as we shall see, now wish to have essentially the same basic professional resources at their disposal in order to diagnose and treat the various symptoms with which each system must cope.

Our assumption that the different symptoms reflect a common area of strategical significance to community planning and community action grew out of our experiences with a series of local community surveys. Materials from these surveys began to indicate that different evidences of social trouble, regarded in practice as unrelated entities, tended to appear in the same person, and especially in the same family. We also found that in a high proportion of cases the work of the separate agencies concerned with these different symptoms converged upon the same families.

We devised a practical reporting tool for obtaining evidence on a family basis regarding the extent and spread of at least a portion of the signs and symptoms which indicate behavior and adjustment difficulties. As part of an experiment in Stamford, Connecticut, procedures were perfected for the continuous and uniform reporting of official cases in six categories of social breakdown: crime, delinquency, child neglect, divorce, mental disease, and mental defect.

In 1937, the year the project was undertaken, 560 Stamford families were involved in one or more of the six official categories. At that time we traced the records of these families for similar incidents back to 1927. Stamford has continued the records, so that with information for the 560 families reported in 1937, we can present a complete and accurate picture of their involvement in the six types of behavior over a twenty-year period.

TWENTY-YEAR HISTORY OF 560 FAMILIES WITH SOCIAL BREAKDOWN IN 1937 [a]

	Number of Families	Percent in Other Categories	NUMBER OF FAMILIES FOUND WITH					
			Mental Disease	Mental Deficiency	Divorce	Crime	Delinquency	Child Neglect
Mental Disease	117	54.7	..	5	11	55	24	6
Mental Deficiency	32	90.6	5	..	2	22	21	11
Divorce	90	46.7	11	2	..	31	14	8
Crime	303	67.3	55	22	31	..	143	29
Delinquency	284	58.1	24	21	14	143	..	31
Child Neglect	49	89.8	6	11	8	29	31	..
Unduplicated total	560	nr.[b]						

[a] Unpublished material collected during a study made in 1946 by Community Research Associates, Inc., for the Connecticut Public Welfare Council.
[b] Not reported.

In the span of less than a generation, constellations of these different symptoms of maladjustment appeared in the same families with extraordinary frequency and variety. The reporting of mental defect and mental disease included only those persons officially committed to the state institutions. If other diagnostic evidence of these conditions could have been included, there probably would have been even more evidence of intermixture with the other symptoms.

THE UNDERLYING CHARACTERISTIC

Just as the presence of some impairment to one's financial ability to obtain food, clothes, and shelter is the underlying characteristic of dependency, and the presence of impairment to the physical processes of the body is the underlying characteristic of ill-health, so the presence of some impairment to the process of adjustment is the underlying characteristic of maladjustment. For an attempt to understand the nature of the adjustment process itself, we turn to the findings of psychiatry.

Psychiatry's interest has only recently shifted from patients in institutions to the functioning individuals in the community. Stimulated largely by Freud's epoch-making concepts of personality development, there is today a widespread popular curiosity, as well as a deeper professional interest, in the underlying factors of human behavior. As would be expected, several schools of thought have evolved out of the varying connotations and emphases accorded to the generic factors involved. Common to all, however, is the concept that human personality in its developmental stages is malleable, the individual's basic inheritances and drives being constantly shaped by the conditioning effects of life experiences.

According to orthodox Freudian interpretations, we are impelled throughout life by a primitive instinctual stream of energy pushing us to accomplish certain ends. Its two most elemental manifestations are the so-called instinctive urges to preserve one's self and to preserve the race. Under social pressure these basic drives—self-preservation and race preservation—may become masked and modified, but never completely tamed. The essence of balanced and satisfactory living resides in the finding of socially approved outlets for these energizing drives. Successful accomplishment of this balance constitutes *adjustment* in the sense of our present thesis. Failure to achieve it constitutes *maladjustment*, which may manifest itself in terms either of antisocial behavior, emotional disturbances, physical or mental illness, or in various combinations of these.

It is to be noted in passing that the interests of modern psychiatry are becoming ever more closely integrated with those of modern medicine. One of the consequences of this is that it is moving away from what has been described as predominantly a "manipulation of abstractions." At the expense of relinquishing some of its more cherished assumptions, psychiatry today is hopefully seeking the answers to some of its most baffling problems in the widening implications of the current scientific approach to disease processes in general. At the moment, for example, considerable attention is given psychiatric as well as other medical aspects of the "general-adaptation-syndrome," which represents the recently differentiated basic physiological response to the extremely variable factors of stress. This advance in our knowledge concerning the behavior of the total personality in relation to stress is an important step toward reducing the mysterious and hitherto altogether elusive quality of certain types of behavior. In the light of advancing knowledge we can detect tangible evidence of the coming possibility of screening and measuring the different degrees of tolerance to stress.

In this connection, Lemkau's formulation of personality developments is particularly pertinent.[1] Briefly the central concept is that:

the stresses and struggles experienced by the developing personality can in some way produce such warping of the personality that it can no longer cope successfully with the stresses directly. . . . Since all persons do not get sick when they are faced with situations involving stress, two factors in causation are postulated. These factors, environmental stress and inherent strength of personality, are directly related; the greater the stress, the greater the inherent strength must be to protect from actual disease. . . . The inherent strength of personality is not static, although it is generally agreed that it has a large genetic element that is not subject to change . . . each experience of the individual is assimilated to some degree and is built into the emotional and behavioral pattern of the personality. . . . Thus the strength of the personality at any time depends not only upon the inborn element, but upon past experience and reaction to past experience as well.

Lemkau appropriately uses the term "mental hygiene" to express the idea that we can assist in the process of building better mental health:

the personality is the product of accumulated experience and attitudes acting together with a unique constitution to give rise to a more or less

[1] Paul V. Lemkau, *Mental Hygiene in Public Health*, p. 4.

integrated personality structure. Depending on how well experience is integrated in this structure and on the inherent strength of the constitution, it is strong and can withstand stress, or weak and succumbs easily, the person slipping into maladjustment or mental illness.

It is obvious that the concept of personality development just described is complementary to, rather than inconsistent with, the psychoanalytic concept cited earlier. As we grow older, the two elemental drives for self-preservation and social preservation diffuse into a complex pattern of human urges, drives, desires, motives, attitudes and habits. The process through which each personality adjusts and accommodates his peculiar pattern of behavior to the peculiar realities of his environment ends only with life itself.

We have for a long time recognized two types of impairment which hinder adjustment and make success difficult if not impossible; namely, intellectual impairment and emotional impairment. We are now coming to recognize a third, or situational, factor not infrequently handicapping the adjustment process.

Impairments of the first sort are those of our intellectual processes, that is, the processes through which a person achieves and maintains conscious awareness of the external world of events and is able to exercise some measure of control over his response and adaptation to them. The intellectual processes are functionally related to the activities of the cortex of the brain. It is here that memories of past experiences are stored; new sensations and perceptions compared with previous experiences; and sometimes both reformed and regrouped to form new ideas. Psychologists have found it desirable to identify three types of intelligence—social, mechanical, and abstract.

Some individuals are born with structural defects in the formation of the brain substance, which partially or almost wholly impair the functioning of the intellectual processes necessary for adjustment and adaptation. Such individuals, and others who acquire similar deficiencies early in life, are called "mental defectives." The brain also is affected by disease later in life; and changes in tissue, degeneration of nerve cells, growths and tumors account for many forms of mental impairment.

Emotional impairments constitute a second type of serious handicap to the adjustment process. We cannot be as precise about the bodily location of the emotional processes. But modern psychiatry's interpretations of the powerful influence of the emotions on human behavior are making a new and signal contribution to our understanding of the degree to which emotional defects impair the personality's capacity for adjustment. The chief emotions influencing directly or indirectly the adjustment processes are those of anxiety or apprehension, tension unconsciously or consciously experienced, and resentment. In any of these, the overt avenue of expression may be through the symptoms of physical illness. The person suffering from such impairment may indeed be unaware of either the emotion itself or its cause, the latter not infrequently being buried in the subconscious area of the person's mind.

Unusual obstacles in the situations to which certain persons are forced to adjust seem to us to constitute a third type of impairment to the adjustment process. Impairments of this type, however, have received much less scientific attention than the others. Traditionally, psychiatry has not considered this area to be within its scope. But in recent years, especially as a result of experience in the war, psychiatry has become increasingly aware of the significance of the situational component in mental disorder. In military service even normally stable men became emotionally upset. Many who apparently were well adjusted in terms of their home environment could not adjust readily to new situations. Army and Navy psychiatrists during the Second World War found that the character of ties with the military unit and with home and family, past employment and community experience, were related directly to the capacity for personal adjustment and sustained morale.[2]

Both the casework system and the correctional system have had more practical concern than psychiatry with such situational maladjustments. As yet, however, there has been little attempt to classify materials in such a way as to throw light upon the precise significance of specific situations in relation to the adjustment process. Thus Dr. Karl Menninger's comment holds generally true for our present knowledge about this impairment: "Our ability to speak of the environment in scientific terms, to describe social forces systematically, has been of such recent development that psychiatrists have as yet no adequate technique or terminology with which to record it."[3]

[2] Thomas A. C. Rennie and Luther E. Woodward, *Mental Health in Modern Society*, p. ix.
[3] Karl A. Menninger, *The Human Mind*, p. 369.

BEHAVIOR DISORDERS

There were persons with behavior disorders in nearly two thirds of the families with adjustment difficulties reported in the St. Paul project. In each such family there was either an official record of antisocial behavior, a diagnosis of mental defect or mental illness by a psychologist or psychiatrist, diagnostic evidence of social irresponsibility reported by a social caseworker, or, as it turned out in a high proportion of cases, a combination of these evidences. In the bulk of the remaining third of the cases, there was evidence of a "situational" problem—an emergency with which the family was unable to cope without help—but no evidence of a personality deviation. While a firsthand clinical examination of the families in which the maladjustment was reported as "situational only" probably would have revealed the presence of mental or emotional disturbances in some of them, it is impossible to estimate in what proportion.

As far as we know, the St. Paul project represents the first attempt to obtain material about the relative community-wide distribution of the three types of impairments to the adjustment process. If, as our experience suggests, behavior disorders are to be found in such a high proportion of the families who come to the agencies of the three systems, the development of systematic data about the strategic characteristics of these disorders is of great importance in creating a plan for community-wide attack upon them.

GENERIC CHARACTERISTICS

The nature of the adjustment process and the basic types of obstruction to its success point to two generic characteristics of maladjustment: chronicity, and family functional capacity.

The implications of chronicity.—Among public health statisticians, it is frequent practice to classify mental illness among the "chronic" diseases. One sees readily why this is so. Emotional impairments usually develop slowly. Their roots are deeply embedded in a long sequence of suppressed and repressed desires before they break out in failures which command social and community attention. Many of the organic diseases which may affect the perceptual, intellectual, or emotional processes also develop slowly. Mental defect from hereditary or congenital impairments becomes evident at an early age, but the resultant chronic inability to adjust to social situations may develop no less gradually than a comparable inability resulting from faulty emotional responses, injury, or disease. In general, and often no doubt for the same reason, antisocial behavior develops by progression. The juvenile delinquent of today becomes the adult criminal of tomorrow, and lesser crimes pave the way for those of a more serious nature.

The characteristic of chronicity in maladjustment, no less than in physical disease, has special implications for community strategy.

Early discovery is highly important. All authorities agree that treatment in the early stages of any mental or emotional disability shows by far the best results. Except in respect to mental defect, however, there has been very little community-wide experimentation with procedures for early discovery. Routine psychological tests to establish levels of intelligence capacity through the public school system serve amongst other things, as an excellent device for the identification of mentally defective children when they reach school age. Research and experimentation are needed to perfect practical tools for the earlier identification of other symptoms of behavior disorders.

One clue to the development of such procedures is the growing evidence of a predisposing tendency toward behavior disorders in families with a history of mental, emotional, or antisocial difficulty. The mass of data about psychoneurotic disability accumulated during the war demonstrated that many men who broke down in the face of military life came from broken families or from families with a history of nervous, emotional, or mental illness. Facts from certain cities that have kept the social breakdown index for a number of years indicate that from 40 percent to 50 percent of those who each year give official evidence of behavior disorders come from families with a previous record. This suggests the possibility of developing procedures for identifying families whose background indicates a predisposition toward disordered behavior, and for maintaining an alertness toward the successive recurrence of new symptoms.

The strategic importance of such procedures is illustrated by the St. Paul data. In over half of the families with adjustment difficulties to which the total group of agencies was attempting to give treatment, the disorder had reached the serious stage evidenced by commitment to a state mental or correctional institution, or by recourse to the department of public welfare for assistance.

The importance of continuity in treatment is also implicit in the attribute of chronicity. There are few specific therapies for the treatment of personality defects. Surgery is sometimes used successfully for brain tumors, but in many cases even the modern "shock treatments" and special surgery are merely a part of a regime which aims gradually to renew the patient's effective contact with reality. Treatment must be given in relation to the continuous process of adjustment. Its effectiveness is measured by the gradual, step-by-step modification of defective motivations.

The mental hospital or institution naturally assures continuity in such treatment as it may give, for as long as the patient is under its care. In like manner the correctional system may be said to have continuing responsibility as long as a person remains in its custody.

On the other hand, in many communities and in many cases, the service rendered by noninstitutional agencies is episodic and unrelated. It is human nature to seek help primarily at the time when some specific crisis or emergency arises. The result is that people are given help mainly in getting over, or in finding their way through or around, a particular circumstance. But after that situation has been cleared up, the case is closed. When the same people are again confronted with a new situation beyond their mental or emotional capacity, another agency is very likely to get the case.

As we have seen, the service systems concerned with physical illness, confronted by much the same problem, have endeavored to meet it in two ways. The first is through the importance attached to the continuing use of a "personal" or "family" physician. The second is through community-wide disease control procedures which assure systematic contact with the patient during the entire course of a disease like tuberculosis. In our opinion, the essentially chronic characteristics of behavior disorders point to the strategic importance of developing comparable and equally effective procedures for assuring continuity of treatment.

The implication of family functional capacity.—A successfully functioning family seems to us to be even more important to the supportive treatment of behavior disorders than it is to the treatment of chronic disease. In the absence of specific therapy, a comprehensive treatment regime usually has to be set up for the person with the disorder, and the support and cooperation of the family in carrying it

out are almost always indispensable. The quality and character of
that support obviously depend upon the integral strength of the family
unit and its capacity to function successfully in the face of the disability of one of its members.

But in contrast to the family role in physical disease, as we now
understand it, the psychiatric interpretation of the adjustment processes makes clear that family functional incapacity may be a cause of
behavior disorder, as well as a detriment to effective treatment. During the years of infancy and early childhood, the family is *the* "situation" to which a child must "adjust." Psychiatrists say that the first
few years of life outweigh all others in molding and fashioning the
emotional characteristics of personality. But even afterward, in childhood, adolescence, and later life, the circumstances of the family
determine in large part the characteristic situations to which its personalities must make a continual adjustment.

These intrinsic attributes of behavior disorders lead us to question
whether the basic nature of these personal disorders is not so closely
related to family life that treatment should be given only against the
background of a family diagnosis. Even a partially affirmative answer
would require a substantial reorientation of the present focus of the
three systems concerned with maladjustment. Obviously, therefore,
this generic characteristic of behavior disorder is of the highest strategic importance.

SPECIFIC CHARACTERISTICS

Among the specific types of behavior disorder, mental defect denotes a condition; mental illness the presence of disease; and antisocial behavior the commission of specified kinds of overt acts. From
what is known about each disorder, it has seemed to us possible to
summarize certain distinctive characteristics of strategic significance
to any community-wide program.

Mental defect.—Intelligence tests were invented almost fifty years
ago and were tried out on thousands of children in order to establish
norms of performance for each age level. It was found that children's
scores in such tests increased with age up to fifteen years, which therefore was taken as the basic level of intelligence for adults. In the standard scoring devices, idiots, the lowest grade of defective, will never
rate above about 20, which represents an average intellectual level

or mental age of less than three years. The next higher grade, imbeciles, usually do not rate above 50, reflecting an average capacity of from three to seven years. Morons, the grade most nearly approaching normal mentality, score below 70, reflecting an average intellectual age of from 8 to 11 years inclusive.[4] The average score of normal adults is between 90 and 110, and persons scoring over 70 but less than 90 usually manifest some degree of mental dullness, at least as far as capacity for ordinary schooling is concerned.[5]

The characteristics of mental defect which have special significance for a community-wide program seem to us to lie in the following facts. Direct treatment of the condition can yield results only in limited and special circumstances. While most of the morons and some of the imbeciles are able to function fairly satisfactorily under the circumstances of ordinary community life, their intellectual handicap makes them very likely to manifest other symptoms of maladjustment. Continuity in the social treatment of this group is, therefore, especially important.

The St. Paul data illustrate the extensive failures to which the large group of defectives who remain in the community are subject unless they are provided with supportive service and supervision. In the total group of families with maladjustment, 9,794 persons were reported as showing symptoms of behavior disorder and of these almost 25 percent were mentally defective. If the national estimates concerning the population of defectives in the population are correct, this number may represent almost all the mental defectives in St. Paul. Only 457 of those reported were in the state institutions. The remainder (some 1,900) were making such adjustments as they could out in the community. Neither they nor their families, however, were having much success in this attempt. Over half of all the defectives were members of that small group of seriously disorganized multi-problem families which accounted for such a high proportion of the total relief, health, and adjustment services rendered by community agencies during the month of the study. Another third were members of some 2,500 families which were the exclusive concern of the community's adjustment agencies.

These data are for one month only. The data from Stamford, Con-

[4] National Institute for Mental Health, *Patients in Mental Institutions, 1947,* p. 22.
[5] D. K. Henderson and R. D. Gillespie, *A Text-Book of Psychiatry,* p. 567.

necticut, mentioned earlier, indicate the extent to which families with mentally defective members may continue to pile up symptoms of social failure, and therefore require systematic and continuous service and supervision.

Recognition that mentally deficient people require a continuity of social treatment led the White House Conference (1940) to point out the desirability of a well-coordinated program of identification, registration, education, and training for mentally retarded individuals in the community. So far, however, communities throughout the country have taken few steps in this direction.

Mental disease.—The broad distinction among mental diseases which seems to us to have the greatest strategic significance to community-wide planning is the distinction between the psychoses and all the other forms of mental illness, that is, the psychoneuroses and various types of emotional instability. Psychosis covers most of the mental aberrations included under the traditional term insanity. The psychotic is indeed a very sick person. His whole personality undergoes a change and his illness often involves incoherence in verbal expression and regression toward an infantile level of behavior. Although some people with psychoneurotic symptoms may also be very sick, the term psychoneurosis covers many symptoms of emotional disorder of a much less serious nature. In a psychoneurotic, in contrast to a psychotic, only part of the personality tends to withdraw or function at variance with outward reality. It seems to us that there is considerable strategic significance also in the fact that psychoneurotic and emotional states usually are not transitional steps toward the psychotic states, but instead apparently represent a distinctive area of illness.[6]

Among the group of maladjusted families in the St. Paul project, 1,822 persons were reported with diagnosed mental illness or emotional disturbances. Approximately two thirds of this group were psychotic, most of them in the state mental institutions. The remainder were diagnosed as showing psychoneurotic symptoms or other symptoms of emotional disorder.

The psychoses thus not only represent the most seriously disabling types of mental and emotional illness, but require more of the most expensive type of institutional care. A large number of patients admitted to state hospitals are older people suffering from disease or

[6] *Ibid.*, pp. 20–23, 144.

from deterioration of the brain or central nervous system—especially from conditions of senility and cerebral arteriosclerosis. The prognosis is poor for both these groups.

The two most common types of psychoses for which there is as yet no organic explanation—the schizophrenic and manic-depressive states—together account for over one fourth of all first admissions to hospitals, whether state or private. These diseases occur in the productive years: schizophrenia usually starts in adolescence and seldom develops after 40; the manic-depressive states occur later in life, with a median age of 40 at the time of first admission to a state hospital.[7] The known characteristics of these conditions give several clues as to strategy in a community attack upon them.

Schizophrenia is the more serious, both in the nature of its symptoms and in the proportion of those for whom hospitalization is required. Its many different symptoms center around progressive introversion, a withdrawal from communication with one's fellows to an inner world in which the real environment has no meaning. The schizophrenic personality may express "without any show of emotion, ideas which in the ordinary person would produce remorse, or pity, or profound depression." [8] A schizophrenic may be dangerously antisocial. Some of the most sensational front-page homicide cases have involved schizophrenic personalities. The chief hope of recovery lies in early recognition of the disease and in its early treatment. At present, however, many schizophrenic patients enter the hospital early in life but late in the course of their illness. Therefore they are likely to make up a substantial proportion of the long-time institutional load.

In the manic-depressive states, as the term implies, the condition centers around symptoms of pathological elation and depression. Younger patients usually recover from their first illness, but it has a tendency to recur and the later attacks are likely to be increasingly serious. Women are more prone to manic-depressive psychoses than men, accounting for about two thirds of those admitted to state hospitals. When the disease appears first after the age of 40, the prognosis is not good.[9]

[7] *Patients in Mental Institutions, 1947,* pp. 41, 44, 59.

[8] *A Text-Book of Psychiatry,* p. 299.

[9] *Patients in Mental Institutions, 1947,* pp. 42–43.

Thus, early discovery is the key to protection against the most serious consequences to the individual and the community in both these psychoses. Even if discovered early, however, the patients require a maximum of psychiatric and medical resources for constructive treatment. Both these illnesses are extremely serious, and there is no substitute for the best scientific knowledge about their cause and cure.

Psychoneurotic and other emotional states.—Psychoneurotic conditions can be very serious. Patients with this diagnosis accounted for almost 5½ percent of all first admissions to mental hospitals in 1947.[10] Many psychoneurotic symptoms center around anxiety and around all sorts of malfunctioning for which there is no obvious physical cause. Many common symptoms such as the inability to concentrate, mental and physical fatigue, or poor sleep, if persistent and extensive, also may be indicative of an emotional disturbance arising from the unconscious. One of the psychiatrist's skills is his capacity to sift out these symptoms and determine their meaning.

The St. Paul data suggest one strategic characteristic of these cases. Like mental defect they tend to come to community attention through some overt manifestation of failure in the adjustment process. In St. Paul over 70 percent of the six hundred or more persons who, though not psychotic, were diagnosed as suffering from mental illness, were from that group of seriously disorganized families to whom the public welfare and adjustment agencies were giving so much service.

Another point of strategic importance is found in the considerable evidence that proper treatment of these cases shows good results. The army experimented during the war with separate battalions for retraining psychoneurotics under the direction of picked officers, psychiatrists, psychologists, and psychiatric social workers. At the end of three months "70 percent of the entire group were returned to duty, and of that number at least 75 percent were still on duty six months later." [11] Similar results also have been achieved by community agencies. The Family Service of St. Paul, which combines casework service with psychiatric consultation, reports improvement in capacity to deal with situations of various kinds in over 70 percent of the cases which the agency treats.

The final significant characteristic of these emotional conditions is

10 *Ibid.,* pp. 41, 44.
11 *Mental Health in Modern Society,* p. 26.

that psychiatric and medical treatment is not the only key to successful treatment. Interplay between intrapsychic and situational factors in maladjustment creates a series of confusing issues which relate to agency function and structure. How these issues are settled will affect the future course of all three of our service systems.

Antisocial behavior.—Under this heading we are referring to behavior which is antisocial by some type of official definition. For its own protection society must establish rules for proper conduct, and it must do something about the people who do not obey them. In the past what it has done has been to resort to restraint and punishment as a deterrent to further misbehavior. How much it will continue to rely on these methods in the years ahead will depend upon our capacity to reduce and prevent basic failures in the adjustment process in some other way. In the first half of the twentieth century, in fact, considerable headway has been made toward emphasizing treatment instead of punishment.

To our mind, therefore, the principal point of strategic importance in respect to this type of disorder lies in the reasonably convincing evidence that society's official procedures do identify people whose failures in the adjustment process are symptomatic of underlying behavior disorders which require treatment. In the St. Paul project and in the prior development of the social breakdown index, as we have indicated, the official evidences of crime, juvenile delinquency, child neglect, illegitimacy, and divorce show a high degree of interlocking in the same families. In other words, it is as if an underlying disorder were breaking out in a variety of symptoms. Just as other studies have shown the high rate of recidivism in crime alone, our data have indicated repeated involvements in various disorders on the part of the same persons and families.

Even if we eliminate those who violate traffic and other similar regulations, the largest group among the lawbreakers are persons whose behavior is antisocial. The great majority go free after paying a fine. But of those kept under continuing supervision, by far the largest number are sentenced to the local jail. The inmates of these institutions are the sick and the senile, as well as hardened and experienced criminals. The charges for which the great majority are incarcerated—vagrancy, disorderly conduct, and drunkenness—suggest personality defects rather than professional criminality.

The considerable proportion of more serious offenders who are mentally defective, mentally ill, or emotionally unstable, and affected by a disorganized family background has been revealed in numerous studies. The Gluecks, for example, in their study of "500 Criminal Careers," found that one fifth of the men were feeble-minded, and one fifth were psychopathic personalities (3 percent with definite psychoses). In addition, a high proportion were suffering from temperamental and emotional handicaps. Sixty percent came from homes broken by the prolonged or complete absence of one or both parents. Over half of the families from which they came had a record of criminal arrest or commitment, some 30 percent more contained delinquent or criminal members who had escaped arrest, and in 17 percent a condition of mental disease or mental defect was noted.[12] A more recent study of 10,000 inmates in Sing Sing Prison found that only 31 percent were mentally and emotionally normal. One percent were psychotic, 35 percent psychopathic, 20 percent psychoneurotic or alcoholic, and 13 percent mentally defective.[13]

A state-wide study of juvenile delinquency and child neglect, made under our auspices in Connecticut in 1946, showed that 80 percent of the juvenile offenders on whom there was information came from families with real adjustment difficulties—mental deficiency, emotional instability, or disrupted or disorganized family life. All but five of the 57 cases of child neglect reflected a composite of other difficulties, and they averaged nine breakdowns per case. Divorce is a frequent solution for marital difficulties. But society's belief in the importance of preserving the family structure is evidenced by the fact that official procedures are necessary to dissolve it. Children from families broken by marital discord swell the ranks of those who must be cared for in foster homes and institutions. In some 400 child neglect cases in Connecticut, 31 percent of the fathers and 20 percent of the mothers were divorced or separated or were absent because of desertion.[14] Similarly a study of aid to dependent children found that in 36 percent of the cases the father was estranged from the family

[12] Sheldon and Eleanor Glueck, *Later Criminal Careers*, pp. 3–4.

[13] Thomas C. Desmond, "Let Science In," *Survey Midmonthly*, Vol. LXXXII, No. 10 (October, 1946), 254.

[14] The Public Welfare Council, *Needs of Neglected and Delinquent Children* (a report to the 1947 Connecticut General Assembly), pp. 19, 23.

because of divorce, desertion or separation, or because no marriage ever had taken place.[15]

From such evidence it seems fair to conclude that the machinery which expresses the official judgments of society does provide a *mechanism for the systematic identification* of persons whose behavior is symptomatic of mental, emotional, or social instability. But as a rule, this identification is made only after the pattern of disordered behavior is well advanced.

The fact of strategic importance is that the official discovery and determination of antisocial behavior sets in motion a chain of action. But only infrequently does that action involve the diagnostic and treatment services of the mental health and casework systems. When these agencies do become involved it is usually by happenstance rather than in accordance with a systematic plan. One cannot but wonder what the result would be if their services were focused deliberately on the considerable volume of disordered behavior which the official machinery of society systematically discovers and reports.

DISORGANIZED SITUATIONS

As we have noted, approximately one third of the maladjusted families reported in the St. Paul project were confronted only with situational problems. So far as the reporting agencies knew, no persons in these families showed evidence of personality defects or deviation. The failure to adjust was the result of situations and circumstances too difficult for what might be construed as the family's normal capacity for self-management. The largest group of these situations centered around health problems—a death in the family, an accident, acute or chronic illness. Another large group centered around income —loss of employment, or loss of support from relative or other sources. A small number of families was in legal difficulties, still others were in trouble with their landlords or had other housing problems. The service required by these people was primarily "help" in surmounting a specific difficulty.

Data accumulated for various purposes show, in general, that the

15 Federal Security Agency, Social Security Board, Bureau of Public Assistance, *Families Receiving Aid to Dependent Children, October 1942, Part I,* pp. 25–27.

impairments in family structure which result in broken homes create serious obstacles to successful adjustment. In our St. Paul project, broken homes were found four times as often among the group of families with the most complicated problems as among those with the the least complicated problems.

At its best, the profession of social casework is concerned not only with helping people to meet an immediate crisis, but also with the dynamic interplay between personality and situation. Beyond question, the best-trained members of the casework profession bring to their daily pursuits a greater knowledge about the nature of situations which impede the adjustment process, and a greater understanding of the relationship of personality to them, than are possessed by any other professional group at the present time.

Nevertheless, the combined materials from all these sources, systematically organized and classified, do not give us much information about the dynamic relationship between typical disorganized situations and typical behavior disorders, or about the resulting successes or failures in the adjustment process. Sociologists, economists, and others have been interested primarily in analyzing conditions. The professional preoccupation of social casework has been with processes, methods, and skills, and not with the scientific systematization of the problems with which it deals. It has leaned heavily upon psychiatry to enhance its understanding of personality, but it has tended to resist making case definitions and even more to classifying the materials which are peculiarly its own.[16]

This inability to speak from any systematic body of knowledge about the situational characteristics of maladjustment handicaps community-wide strategy at two important points. In the first instance, it leaves to the realm of speculation how much maladjustment, sufficiently serious and emergent to require community attention, involves no evidence of behavior disorder. Communities apparently have had the general impression that a substantial proportion of the total problem was of this character. But, as far as we know, the St. Paul project was the first serious attempt to separate out the maladjustment problems which are restricted to environmental characteristics. The result certainly suggests that problems of this type are not relatively as important as has been assumed. Services equipped to deal exclusively

[16] Gordon Hamilton, *Theory and Practice of Social Case Work,* p. 147.

with them, therefore, may be required in a lesser proportion than usually is assumed to be necessary.

In the second instance, the present lack of knowledge about the situational characteristics of maladjustment also handicaps analysis of the interplay between psychiatry and casework in the diagnosis and treatment of behavior disorder, and it leaves to speculation the principles which should guide a community in planning for a proper balance between the two services.

NEEDED: A SCIENTIFIC DISCIPLINE

We trust this review of the significant characteristics of maladjustment will attest the need for a more scientific professional discipline of community-wide analysis. One handicap to the development of such a discipline has been the lack of "vital statistics" about maladjustment comparable to those which have proved such an effective spur to, and resource for, the systematic analysis of the community-wide problems of ill-health. We ourselves have experimented with two procedures designed to help fill this serious gap.

The first is the social breakdown index to which we referred earlier. The second is the classification of maladjustment in the Family Unit Report System used in the St. Paul project. In both, the *family* is the basic unit for reporting the different evidences of maladjustment. We are convinced that this is fundamental in any system for collecting "vital statistics" on the total problem. Family reporting puts in proper perspective the social unit which is a key factor both in the adjustment process and in any plans for the community-wide provision of diagnostic and treatment services. Moreover, use of the family unit also provides what has heretofore been lacking—a scientific basis for consolidating statistics on the many separate evidences of adjustment failure.

The social breakdown index analyzes only those families whose manifestations of maladjustment are recorded by the community's official agencies. Some twenty-five cities have used this procedure at different times and for different periods. Because the exact methods employed in compiling these data have varied somewhat from place to place, the resulting annual social breakdown rates, that is, the proportion of families with one or more types of breakdown, are not strictly comparable. However, such rates running from 29.4 per 1,000 families in Ann Arbor, to 204.1 per 1,000 in Galveston, give some basis for rough comparisons of the relative incidence of this type of behavior. In half the cities the rate was above 67 per 1,000. Southern cities uniformly have higher rates than Northern and Eastern cities, just as they show higher rates in practically all indices relating to health. The range in Northern and Eastern cities is between 29.4 and 78.3 per 1,000.[17]

The St. Paul rate of 102 maladjusted families out of every 1,000 in the community, established for the month of our study, was based on evidence regarding maladjustment collected from all the organized agencies in the community. Thus it included data from the official categories of the social breakdown index. Our own view is that this rate is reasonably complete for adjustment failures from situational difficulties only; that it probably includes most of the cases of serious psychoses and of severe mental defect. It seems altogether unlikely that it includes more than a small proportion of the psychoneurotic and emotionally unstable personalities in the community.

Even so, the rates revealed by these devices reflect a community-wide problem of substantial proportions. With national indices of several of the separate evidences of maladjustment going up, the desirability of perfecting devices for collecting community-wide statistics to reflect trends seems obvious.

But the underlying need is for a foundation on which to build a scientific discipline—a discipline competent to pursue and interpret data about the strategic characteristics of the total problem of maladjustment, for use in developing community-wide plans for prevention and protection. "Vital statistics" serve little useful purpose except as they are given meaning through the competence of such a discipline.

[17] Data furnished by Community Chests and Councils, Inc., June 23, 1950.

Chapter XIV

THE EMERGENCE OF COMMUNITY-WIDE FUNCTIONS

ONLY WITHIN RECENT YEARS has it become possible to speak about a community-wide program for prevention of maladjustment and for protection against its consequences. Until recently the various systems were preoccupied with the particular symptoms of disorder for which tradition gave them special responsibility. Each system had its own terminology to describe the processes by which it dealt with them. The differences rather than the similarities in these processes usually were regarded as of first importance. But the great barrier to common thought was the general assumption that the problems with which the three systems were concerned had little in common.

Now that this barrier is breaking down, we are better able to consider the potentialities of a program, community-wide in scope, for attacking the generic problem. Out of greater knowledge about the characteristics of maladjustment, and the increasing awareness of common processes among the different types of agencies concerned with it, we may note the emergence of basic functions which are strategically indispensable to such a community-wide approach.

We believe these functions to be (1) the diagnosis and treatment of behavior disorders, (2) the diagnosis and treatment of disorganized situations, and (3) the community-wide prevention and control of behavior disorder. Concern with these functions, from the point of view of community-wide planning, has been in this descending order, and there are many issues in respect to all of them on which little thought, experience, or material is available.

Preventive practice in regard to maladjustment has not developed as a disciplined movement comparable to that in the field of public health. Nevertheless the goal of prevention is one which the leaders of all three systems heartily endorse.

Today socially minded psychiatrists and public mental health workers are putting faith in education, and are expending considerable energy on developing methods to inform the public at large, or at least certain key groups in the population, about the nature and consequences of emotional insecurities and instabilities. Leaders of the casework system have been slower to develop similar practical educational procedures, mainly, it seems to us, because the materials from professional casework experience have not been classified and interpreted so as to facilitate their use for this purpose. Leaders in the correctional system are making slow but steady headway in their struggle to correct by education the traditional misconceptions about the criminal offender which handicap progressive thought and practice in their areas.

Unquestionably these educational endeavors should be regarded as essential underpinnings for the provision of more precise community-wide functions such as the diagnosis and treatment of behavior disorders, the treatment of disorganized situations, and the direction of processes for discovering and channeling cases through successive courses of treatment. It should be obvious, however, that to rely on a strategy consisting exclusively of educational measures, or other "preventive" procedures, would be somewhat like placing primary reliance upon the "Voice of America" to win the cold war, if we may use an analogy from the state of international affairs during which this is written.

THE DIAGNOSIS AND TREATMENT OF BEHAVIOR DISORDERS

For most of this century it has been possible to say with great simplicity that medical diagnosis and treatment is the function of a doctor. No such easy statement can be made about the diagnosis and treatment of behavior disorders. Nevertheless, there is now substantial agreement about basic attributes of this function. There are available also certain authoritative materials which furnish criteria as to what agencies possess the competence of personnel and the kind of operating policies necessary to perform it. These criteria, however, are sponsored by separate national bodies and are seldom viewed in relation to each other.

THE PREREQUISITE CONSTELLATION OF SPECIALTIES

Each of the systems must have at its disposal some combination of specialized psychiatric, psychological, casework, and other personnel in order to diagnose and treat behavior disorders and to carry on preventive activity. This fact is one measure of the present agreement regarding the attributes necessary for performing this function.

It is the custom of many national agencies or authorities to devise standards for agencies which follow the pattern of their leadership. The American Psychiatric Association and the National Association for Mental Health are developing and improving standards for mental hospitals, outpatient services and clinics. The American Prison Association has issued standards for all parts of the adult correctional system; the National Probation and Parole Association has standards for probation and parole and for juvenile courts and detention homes; and the United States Children's Bureau has listed the essential elements for various parts of the juvenile courts and the juvenile correctional system as well as for other types of children's work. Likewise the national agencies in the casework system—such as the Family Service Association of America and the Child Welfare League of America—have standards for the operating agencies which are their members.

All these standards, as well as authoritative opinion in fields not covered by them, refer to the necessity for psychiatric, psychological, and casework service. They also recognize the role which physical health plays in behavior, by the explicit or implicit inclusion of medical service to the required galaxy of "adjustment" talent.

The types of training and experience believed necessary have been expressed quite precisely by appropriate professional authorities. Measured in academic terms, the qualifications for the psychiatrist are most rigorous. He must have his medical degree, with its four years of graduate work in a College of Medicine and its year of internship in a general hospital. The tendency is to upgrade the requirement for two or three additional years of specialized psychiatric training, with different degrees of hospital and clinical experience appropriate to the type of practice intended. So also is the tendency on the part of the psychological profession, to upgrade the requirements for the clinical psychologists. A doctor's degree in psychology or its equivalent, together with supervised clinical experience, is now believed to be desirable.[1]

A thoroughly trained caseworker is expected to be a graduate of a school of social work, that is, to have completed six academic quarters or four academic semesters, which always include supervised field work experience. In practice, however, it is sometimes permissible to substitute experience under qualified supervision for some part of the formal training.

Standards are constantly changing in detail but at last report the following combinations of psychiatric, psychological, and casework skills were believed to be necessary for various segments of the three systems:

Mental disease hospitals.—Different ratios are applicable to hospital wards treating different types of patients, but the general requirements are: [2] one psychiatrist for every 150 patients; psychologists as needed; one caseworker for every 100 annual admissions.

Institutions for the mentally defective.—We have discovered no pronouncement of official standards, but two California authorities recommend: [3] one psychiatrist for approximately every 300 patients; one psychologist for every 300 patients; one caseworker for every 400 patients.

Correctional institutions: adult.—For prisons housing 1,000 to 1,200 men, the American Prison Association recommends: [4] one psychiatrist; one psychologist; caseworkers, as needed.

Adult probation.—Standards relating to adult probation recognize that while it is impractical to require all probation officers everywhere to have graduate degrees in casework, "professional training and experience are essential and any list of qualifications should require them on as high a level as the salary scale and the supply of available candidates permit." [5] In any event, there should be a trained casework

1 Mental Hygiene Committee, "Conclusions Concerning Psychiatric Training and Clinics," reprint from *Public Health Reports,* LXI, No. 26 (June 28, 1946), p. 14.

2 *Ibid.,* pp. 5–6; and Dallas Pratt, *Mental Health Statistics,* p. 6.

3 Robert E. Wyers and George Tarjan, "Administrative Practices to Provide Better Psychiatric Care of Mental Defectives," *American Journal of Mental Deficiency,* LIV, No. 1 (July, 1949), 34.

4 The American Prison Association, *Manual of Suggested Standards for a State Correctional System,* Chapter 7, p. 25, and Chapter 5, p. 20.

5 *Ibid.,* Chapter 3, p. 14.

supervisor, at least in the larger departments, and psychiatric and psychological service, as needed.

Correctional institutions: juvenile.—We have found no definite staff standards for a juvenile institution, but authorities seem to agree that there should be: either a resident or a consulting psychiatrist; either a resident or consulting psychologist; caseworkers, as needed, both to work with children in the institution and to make the necessary preparations for their return home.

Juvenile court and probation service.—Authorities similarly agree that juvenile courts and juvenile probation departments should have the benefit of: psychiatric service, as needed; psychological service, as needed; casework training for the probation staff.

Community mental health clinics.—An all-purpose community clinic should have: [6] psychiatrists, in the ratio of one full-time practitioner for every 20 treatment cases; one psychologist for each one or two full-time psychiatrists; two or three caseworkers for each full-time psychiatrist.

Casework agencies.—National organizations representing the various specialized casework agencies have suggested standards for various aspects of their agencies' organization and administration but, to the best of our knowledge, such standards are never specific as to the use of psychiatry in connection with agency functions. However, the following is a summary of the practice that has become common in the better family casework agencies throughout the country: psychiatric consultation as needed in connection with the casework diagnosis and treatment of particular cases or staff development, and referral of individuals for psychiatric treatment, as needed; psychological examinations, as needed; casework supervisors, qualified by a graduate degree in social work and additional practical experience, who are responsible for not more than five or six workers; a casework staff of graduate level, and some provision of equivalent training opportunities for those workers who do not yet meet this qualification; an active case load of not more than 25–35 cases per worker.

In present practice this fundamental recognition of the identity of the problem which each system or individual agency desires to treat, and of the professional skills which it must possess to do so, is causing considerable ferment. Agency executives are busily, sometimes fran-

[6] "Conclusions Concerning Psychiatric Training and Clinics," pp. 13–14.

tically, trying to recruit psychiatrists, psychologists, caseworkers and, often, doctors to fill required staff complements. Agencies not actively recruiting these specialists are very likely to be looking for money to enable them to do so.

The reason behind the need for this constellation of specialties is relatively simple. Psychiatry, as a branch of the medical profession, with its roots in institutional responsibility for the insane, has been concerned primarily with what are sometimes called the "intrapsychic" factors of personality, that is, mental and emotional processes with inherent defects which impair their functioning. Psychology, the science of mental phenomena, in its effort to establish the norms of human behavior, has devised tests of intelligence, aptitudes, and interests which are of great diagnostic value in measuring deviations, and has developed educational procedures adapted to various levels of capacity. Casework, with its roots in the practical problems of disadvantaged family life, has of necessity kept its focus on "situational" reality.

The three professions gradually have become more and more aware of the contribution which each has to make to the other. Both psychiatry and casework have long used psychology's special measuring skills in dealing with their cases. At present psychiatry is attaching increasing importance to the social factors in mental illness. On the other hand as Gordon Hamilton puts it, "Casework . . . was one of the first fields in which were recognized the implications of psychiatry for the understanding of every-day social behavior problems." [7] Indeed the principal difference of opinion among present-day caseworkers is based on differences in the schools of psychiatric thought which they follow.

THE PROCESSES OF DIAGNOSIS

Both psychiatry and casework have a more or less systematic pattern which they follow in assembling information for use in diagnosis. Dr. Menninger mentions several points to be covered in the pattern of information needed by the psychiatrist: (1) Background of the personality, including family history, developmental history, vocational history, medical history, and social history; (2) physical, neurological,

[7] Gordon Hamilton, *Theory and Practice of Social Case Work,* p. 347.

and chemical examinations; (3) psychological examinations; and (4) psychiatric examination as to the exact nature and implications of the present difficulty.[8]

The psychiatrist's training gives him a special discipline in identifying and diagnosing defects of personality. His is the task of determining whether the patient's symptoms represent a type of behavior indicative of mental or emotional disturbance requiring psychiatric study and treatment.

The caseworker's training develops a special facility in investigating and identifying the relevant situational factors. The extent to which it also develops competence in diagnosing personality and emotional disorders is the subject of much intraprofessional debate. The caseworker does not have the more precise classification aids used by the psychiatrist, and as a result finds it much more difficult to record conclusions about the case. In practice the summary in most case records has been essentially descriptive.

Neither psychiatry nor casework has any classifications for diagnosing the interplay between the personality and the situation, and the precise relation of the one to the other. Casework, at its best, however, is greatly concerned with this relationship, and the ability to deal with it is the essence of the casework treatment process. A caseworker's diagnostic knowledge and skill must "include familiarity with the interaction of inner and outer experience" and if possible, the ability to identify causal relationships between the two.[9] In working together, the caseworker and the psychiatrist find that their principal method of communication must be "talking it over" so that each may arrive at an understanding of what the other thinks.

The psychologist, likewise, plays an important role in diagnosis. As Rennie and Woodward point out, "The finding from tests used in measuring verbal and non-verbal intelligence, educational achievements, aptitudes, interests and personality factors, and the psychologist's description of the patient's behavior during the test situation . . . yield much that is of diagnostic value in understanding the patient and his problems."[10]

[8] Karl A. Menninger, *The Human Mind*, pp. 369, 371.

[9] Hamilton, *Theory and Practice of Social Case Work*, p. 142.

[10] Thomas A. C. Rennie and Luther E. Woodward, *Mental Health in Modern Society*, p. 233.

THE PROCESSES OF TREATMENT

For the psychiatrist, his diagnosis of personality defects furnishes a directive as to the type of treatment. The same direct relationship between diagnosis of defects and treatment prevails when the psychiatrist, the psychologist, and the caseworker cooperate on a case. When the caseworker acts alone, however, it is usually in relation to an urgent situation which has brought the individual or family to seek help. If no obvious pathological factors are present, the casework diagnosis may consist largely in determining what can be done to remedy the immediate and apparent difficulty.

The caseworker's awareness of pathological behavior grows with the attempt to deal with the situation. The distinction between the processes of diagnosis and treatment in casework practice has not been so sharp as in psychiatric practice. But both casework and psychiatric treatment are conditioned by the professional practitioner's grasp of the underlying causes of the difficulty.

Although the brunt of the responsibility for treatment falls primarily upon the psychiatrist and the caseworker, yet psychologists carry the major responsibility for treatment in special instances. They often undertake the corrective work with children who have educational problems, and in some clinics engage in group therapy with children, with adults, or both.

Broadly speaking, there are three tools which the psychiatrist, psychologist, and caseworker utilize, in varying combinations, with varying degrees of emphasis, as they deal with disordered behavior. The first is a prompt recourse to the necessary medical skills; the second is the supportive influence of a direct relationship with the client; the third, the manipulation of the client's environmental situation.

Health, in all its various aspects, is one of the important general factors in the total personality. The maintenance of good physical health, through medical examination and treatment, should be regarded as the first essential by both the caseworker and the psychiatrist. This basic requirement, which involves access to appropriate medical services, is too often disregarded.

With respect to the factors of mental health, each member of the team enters into the therapeutic situation to "effect a change," "overcome resistance," and otherwise "transform the patient's energy from harmful to useful forms." The use of this relationship has been the psychiatrist's principal reliance in dealing with emotional difficulties. Chiefly by means of interviews, a personal relationship is established with the patient that is designed to help the latter understand the unconscious motivations which lie behind his own behavior.

In casework the "worker-client relationship" is used as a means of giving the client a better understanding of his problems and thereby enabling him to modify unhealthy attitudes and behavior patterns. Hence the caseworker tries to understand "what a person feels about his situation and what he wants to do to correct it, what he wants to become." [11] What the caseworker does is to try to bring about a modification of the client's attitude and behavior so that he may be able to adjust to the realities of his situation and gain an opportunity for growth and development.

Psychiatrists and caseworkers also "manipulate" the situation or environment as a means of influencing the personality. The psychiatrist can do this most efficiently in an institutional setting, where it is possible to exercise a high measure of control over the patient's daily life, prescribing the diet, medical treatment, social contacts, occupational therapy, and recreation activities believed to be best suited to recovery. Although attaching increasing importance to situational factors in adjustment, the psychiatrist finds it impractical to maintain as firm control over the environment of his noninstitutional patients.

The caseworker, on the other hand, purposefully takes on the job of removing environmental obstacles and irritants, helping the client to make the most of his resources and organizing help for him from other resources in the community. In other words, an attempt is made to remedy defects in his situation in a manner that will contribute to the amelioration of his personality defects.

Understanding the respective methods and skills of the three professional disciplines gives us the background against which decisions are made concerning the relative proportions of each type of service needed. However, as we have seen, the standard recipes for mixing the three service ingredients have been written independently—and with varying degrees of precision—by the several authoritative bodies.

What is needed from the standpoint of social planning is a com-

11 Hamilton, *Theory and Practice of Case Work*, p. 140.

prehensive classification of the principal types of disorders which the total community program must combat, and the typical constellation of services most appropriate to their treatment.

CURRENT DIAGNOSTIC AND TREATMENT REALITIES

In giving this summary of current thought regarding the skills and tools necessary for diagnosing and treating behavior disorder, we ourselves might seem to be suffering from a serious mental aberration if we failed to face the realities of current professional resources for diagnosis and treatment.

According to an estimate made in 1947 there are about 4,000 psychiatrists in this country.[12] This is considerably less than half the number necessary to staff adequately even the existing institutions and clinic facilities. A recent estimate puts the number of practicing clinical psychologists in the country at about 1,000, of whom over 80 percent have either an M.A. or a Ph.D. degree.

It is estimated that there are now in active practice not more than 15,000 caseworkers who have completed a full two-year course in a professional school of social work.[13] Personnel in casework far outnumbers the other two fields. Casework has been primarily a feminine profession; staff turnover, a common phenomenon in many fields where demand exceeds supply, has been accentuated by the circumstance of marriage, pregnancy, and other family responsibilities.

Under the National Mental Health Act, money is available for greatly needed expansion of training facilities for scholarships, and for expanding recruitment in all these professional fields. Nevertheless, in discussing this program, or any other effort to increase the numbers of available personnel, one should bear in mind always that education for the three professions is a time-consuming process.

It is a gross understatement, therefore, to say that the personnel required to perform the function of diagnosis and treatment is at present in short supply—and is likely to continue in short supply for some time to come. How great the shortage is, no one knows. But one does not have to speculate concerning the meager resources at hand to

12 Pratt, *Mental Health Statistics*, p. 6.
13 Sue Spencer, "Great Success in Professional Education," *Survey Midmonthly*, LXXXIII, No. 6 (June, 1947), 167.

diagnose and treat the large group of people about whose serious behavior disorders we do have fairly precise data—those under the care of our mental institutions and our correctional agencies. In state hospitals for mental diseases the country-wide average number of patients for each staff physician in 1947 was 276.[14] At last report there was only one graduate nurse per 138 resident patients. Attendants seldom have adequate training in the proper care of mentally ill patients, and scandals involving brutal, abusive, and neglectful treatment still occur.[15] Overcrowding is common, expenditures per patient average around $1.50 per day, and in the words of two national authorities, "on the whole, service has tended to sink to the level of minimal requirements for chronic incurables." [16]

By way of contrast are the mental hospitals of the Veterans Administration where the average per patient expenditure of $5.74 per day covers the cost of professional teams of psychiatrists and other physicians, nurses, clinical psychologists, caseworkers, and therapists. Their combined efforts, it is authoritatively stated, have "enhanced the completeness of recovery and rehabilitation." [17]

The situation in institutions for mental defectives is even worse than that in the state hospitals for mental diseases. Moreover, the custom in many states is to put the defectives on waiting lists when the state institutions are crowded to capacity—as they usually are. In many states the number of defectives who are waiting to be admitted to a state school equals or exceeds the number of those actually in institutions. The futility of making application for admission frequently discourages the attempt to get on a waiting list. Instead, many defectives find their way into county almshouses, prisons, and other institutions, including the state hospitals for the mentally ill.[18]

When we turn to the correction system and consider the local jails, use of the phrase "diagnosis and treatment" sounds like something out of *Alice in Wonderland*. The turnover is enormous, and a high proportion, particularly the drunk and disorderly, are repeaters. Conditions in most of these local institutions defy description. Of

[14] National Institute for Mental Health, *Patients in Mental Institutions*, pp. 12–13, 66.
[15] George Thorman, *Toward Mental Health*, p. 25.
[16] Rennie and Woodward, *Mental Health in Modern Society*, p. 155.
[17] *Administrator of Veterans Affairs, Annual Report 1948*, pp. 10, 17, 22.
[18] Samuel Hamilton, "Public Institutions for Mental Defectives, Their Organization and Equipment," *American Journal of Mental Deficiency*, L, No. 3 (January, 1946), 452.

3,154 local jails inspected by the Federal Bureau of Prisons, only 82 met as high as 60 percent of the standard requirements for decent care, and well over 2,000 were rated as unfit for use.[19] Many jails are operated on a fee system whereby the sheriff contracts to run the institution for so much a day—with attendant evils reminiscent of the English contract workhouse system in the eighteenth century.

State prisons are somewhat better off, but a study made before the war by the Attorney General's office reported that 29 percent of the male prisoners were "living under conditions harmful to their moral and physical well being," 41 percent were idle, 74 percent were without educational opportunities of any type, and the majority of the institutions lacked an adequate classification service.[20]

The correctional system has put great faith in probation as a means of treating both the adult and juvenile offender, and at last report there were between five and six thousand probation officers employed throughout the country.[21] Standards for probation personnel, written in 1923, set minimum requirements of college graduation plus one year of supervised casework experience. But unfortunately, as a national authority has pointed out, "in the vast majority of courts not even a minimum level of 1923 standard has ever been attained." [22]

In the face of existing conditions, it seems to us unrealistic to hope that in any near future there will be qualified personnel in adequate numbers to meet the community's full need for diagnostic and treatment service. Obviously this fact puts great premium on careful planning to make the best and most economical use of the personnel that is available.

THE TREATMENT OF DISORGANIZED SITUATIONS

As we noted earlier, in about one third of the St. Paul families who were reported to have problems of maladjustment no member was known to be manifesting symptoms of behavior disorder or personality defect. It seems to us that the service required by such families constitutes a second distinct function in any program for community protection against the over-all problem of maladjustment.

19 *Manual of Suggested Standards for a State Correctional System*, Chapter 15, pp. 81–82.
20 Helen D. Pigeon, *Probation and Parole*, p. 166.
21 National Probation Association, *Directory of Probation and Parole Officers*, p. 273.
22 Pigeon, *Probation and Parole*, p. 95.

These families were confronted by a great variety of external situations with which they were unable to cope. Every caseworker is familiar with the catalog of these difficulties, as well as with the kind of help which may be given to meet them. This type of aid is often referred to as "environmental casework." We use the phrase "situational treatment" rather than "environmental casework" as more compatible with our general terminology. The methods to which both terms refer date back to casework's professional beginnings, when workers in charity organization societies first substituted systematic helpfulness for unorganized and sporadic acts of charity and neighborly goodwill. This type of helpfulness requires a thorough knowledge of community resources, an understanding of the variety of troubles which beset disadvantaged families, and a capacity to cooperate successfully with people in different situations. Inevitably, the process involves a "diagnosis," since an understanding of the situation is necessary in order to decide what to do about it. But the emphasis is on action. So far no great stress has been laid on the intellectual process involved in making a formal diagnosis.

As we have indicated, the failure to develop scientific data about the role which typical situational defects play in the adjustment process presents a practical obstacle to sound planning to meet the need for caseworkers equipped only to do "environmental casework" where there is no evidence of personality disorders. Better analysis of the situational component also is needed to help measure the importance of casework in the combined psychiatric-psychological-casework diagnosis and treatment of behavior disorders.

For although there has been tacit acknowledgment that there are two kinds of casework, there has not been a correspondingly realistic acknowledgment that there may be two kinds of problems. Instead, the tendency has been to assume that all the people in social agencies who are classified as caseworkers should be upgraded to meet the training standard required for the treatment of personality defects.

This assumption in turn has led to the invidious tendency to classify as "good" those caseworkers who possess sufficient professional training to deal constructively with the dynamics of the relationship between personality and situation, and as "poor" those who are equipped to deal only with the situational component.

Confusion is further confounded because we have no authoritative criteria by which to determine what kind of caseworkers, under what circumstances, can be truly helpful in the treatment of situational defects. A caseworker who has had two years of graduate training is presumed to possess the capacity to deal effectively with the intricate relationships between personality and situation. There are no national standards by which to distinguish between a caseworker able to treat situational defects and an ordinary citizen with common sense who desires to be helpful. Each agency simply uses its own best judgment as to the qualifications required of its staff.

In making this distinction in the St. Paul project, we used as a realistic index of necessary training the standards formulated by the New York State Department of Social Welfare, which has a relatively high standard for its assistance personnel. Requirements include graduation from a high school, plus college training and experience in varying combinations. In general, the more experience one has had, the less training is required, and vice versa. Junior caseworkers are expected to be college graduates or to have had two years of college and some experience. Requirements for senior caseworkers in public assistance are college graduation and four years experience, although less experience is demanded of those who have had some graduate training. Supervisors and senior workers in child welfare, in addition to considerable experience, should have completed one year of training in a graduate school of social work.[23]

Case and work loads can be higher, of course, in agencies where service is focused primarily on situational defects. Approved public welfare practice in New York State would permit 10 to 12 workers per supervisor; active case loads of 100 per worker in public assistance and of 50 to 75 in child welfare. Similarly a recent study of medical social work in New York City suggested an active load of 60 cases per worker; standards relating to probation and parole usually stipulate case loads of 50 to 75.[24]

THE COMMUNITY-WIDE CONTROL FUNCTION

In thought and practice respecting community-wide procedures for prevention and control one should recognize a subtle distinction in

[23] These requirements are based on those set by state welfare departments.

[24] Information furnished by Harry O. Page, Deputy Commissioner of Social Welfare, New York State.

the object of concern: is it control of a *person,* a *process,* or a *disorder?* Although these three concerns are not mutually exclusive, the distinction is important.

All three systems concerned with maladjustment now exercise certain official or unofficial controls over at least a portion of the *persons* whom they serve. The correctional system has legal control over all of its cases. The mental health system has a great measure of official or unofficial control over those committed or admitted to its institutions. The casework system has official or unofficial authority over children who are committed or admitted for institutional or foster home care. Control of this sort, however, is not necessary to insure that each case of disorderly behavior will receive a competent diagnosis and will proceed through an appropriate course of treatment. In fact, regulations requiring official or semiofficial control over the person may obstruct, rather than facilitate, such action.

Each system also has made efforts to control the *processes* by which cases come to its agencies, and the flow from one agency to another in the course of service or therapy. In certain instances great stress is laid on these procedures per se, often resulting in a confusion of thought and a distortion of values. For the true purpose should be to control the *disorders* which afflict the individual and menace the welfare of the community, with control of the *person* and the *processes* used only as they are demonstrably effective in realizing this larger end.

THE TRADITIONAL CONTROL OF PROCESSES

Numerous devices have been developed to direct and control the processes by which cases come into and flow through the agencies of the three systems. Under certain circumstances these devices may be extremely useful, and a brief analysis of them is therefore necessary. For out of the background of the thought and experience which produced them must come any serious attempt to develop the principles and procedures focused upon the community-wide prevention and control of behavior disorders.

In the correctional system.—When a person commits an illegal act, the course which his case must take is quite clear. Inasmuch as those who engage in such activities seldom apply for "correction" to the institutions which ultimately receive them, the offender first must be discovered and apprehended by the police, who are responsible for his safekeeping prior to an official disposition of the case. When a misdemeanor—an offense of a minor nature—occurs, the period of detention seldom exceeds 24 hours or a weekend at most. At the expiration of that time a lower court either dismisses the case or disposes of it summarily, usually by the imposition of a fine.

If the offense is of a serious nature, the case receives only a preliminary hearing in the lower court, and the accused person is bound over to the superior court. Depending on the circumstances, he may be released on bail or transferred to the county jail for further detention. Then if he is adjudged guilty, he becomes the responsibility of a correctional agency—either a probation unit, or a state institution. In the latter case, after serving some portion of his sentence, he may be released to a parole authority and allowed to return to his community under supervision. The final step, of course, is his unconditional discharge from custody or supervision.

Because of the formal, legal characteristics of the protective and correctional system, all cases flow through these same general processes. The sequence is basically the same. Each step may be taken under a separate and independent administrative unit—the police, the courts, the correctional agency, the parole authority—but law and regulations dictate their basic relationship. Traditional practices of these agencies, however, stem from the days when the sole purpose of this system was to effect punishment appropriate to the crime. In many cases, this raised almost insuperable obstacles to any effective application of the newer philosophy of treatment. Thus for more than half a century the correctional system has been struggling to change these traditional processes so that the best interests of treatment may be served.

To this end it has "invented" a series of new procedural devices at the points of apprehension, disposition, correction, and discharge. These include the juvenile crime prevention bureau, the juvenile court, the domestic relations court, nonjudicial disposition, probation, and parole.

Change in the processes for apprehending juvenile offenders is the purpose of one of the more recent of these inventions—the crime prevention or juvenile aid bureau in the police department. Juveniles who get into trouble come first to the attention of the neighborhood patrolman, "the corner cop." Formerly they were taken to the police station, "booked" on the appropriate charges, and sometimes detained overnight or longer in jail or in a detention home. But by 1947 there were 70 cities of 100,000 or more, with specialized juvenile bureaus in their police departments.[25] In these cities any youngster picked up by the police is taken directly to the juvenile bureau, which decides whether his trouble is of a minor nature requiring no official action, or whether it is serious enough to be referred to the juvenile court.

This procedure is believed to improve the chances of treatment in two ways. The neighborhood patrolman, burdened with many other duties, cannot be expected to have special skill in handling children or in evaluating the seriousness of their offenses. The patrolmen of the crime prevention bureau are presumed to be specialists, better able to do so. Moreover, authorities are agreed that it is harmful to the young offender to expose him to any contact with older lawbreakers or with the machinery for handling them. The new method of apprehension keeps the juvenile away from these unsavory influences.

It is our experience that the juvenile bureau serves quite well to accomplish these purposes relating to apprehension. But the confusion which results from placing value upon a process apart from the disorder it is designed to help control is illustrated by the fact that the bureau has fallen heir to a community-wide role for which it is likely to be ill-equipped. In many instances it has become a potential clearing point for the early discovery of symptomatic behavior, much of which appropriately might have been referred to the noncorrectional diagnostic and treatment agencies of the community. The discriminating identification of symptomatic evidence, however, requires a professional skill which the juvenile bureaus we have known have not possessed. What they are most likely to do, therefore, is to route many cases unnecessarily to the juvenile court, to deal by admonition and encouragement with other children who should receive skilled diagnosis and treatment, and to take on additional functions, especially recreation activities, which are thought to have preventive value.

Change in the traditional processes for the disposition and correction of the juvenile offender was the purpose of the juvenile court, one of the first inventions to achieve better treatment. Designed to re-

---

25 Lawrence D. Morrison, "The Police and the Delinquent Child," *Redirecting the Delinquent Child, 1947 Year Book, National Probation and Parole Association*, p. 124.

move the juvenile from the influences of adult criminal justice, this court has placed great stress on unofficial informality and flexibility. After a child has been apprehended, the probation officer attached to the court is expected to make a careful analysis of his personal capacities and problems, his family background, his school record and social history, so that the judge may study all this material before he hears the case and makes a disposition. In preparing such analyses a few courts now have available a complete range of psychiatric, psychological, and casework diagnostic services. Moreover the judicial authority over disposition may be exercised with great flexibility, to suit the treatment of needs in each case. One of the prime purposes of the court always has been to put juveniles on probation so that they may avoid the deleterious effects of institutional life. And now many cases are carried "unofficially" by the probation officers, without benefit of judicial pronouncement.

But the confusion of processes with the purposeful control of disorders is again illustrated by the fact that in their earlier years juvenile courts fell heir to community-wide functions for which they were— and in our experience, generally still are—ill-prepared. Prior to the development of the modern public welfare department, the court was often the only official agency in the community concerned with the problems of children. For this reason it frequently was saddled with many other activities, such as the administration of the mother's pension laws, foster home care for dependent and neglected children, and so on. The almost inevitable confusion of judicial and administrative responsibilities often resulted in an inefficient discharge of both.

The development of the modern public welfare departments, with a child welfare division, has brought about a wholesome trend toward returning the court to its primary role—that of guiding the processes of disposition and correction in a manner which makes it possible to give juvenile offenders constructive treatment.

A change in the processes of disposition in cases of divorce, desertion, separation, nonsupport, illegitimacy, and other family matters, has been the purpose of domestic relations courts. The general theory has been that these courts seek to apply to all of their cases the same types of investigatory, clinic, and probation services as those of the juvenile courts, with which they are often combined. Practice, how-

ever, has been considerably short of this theory and presents even
clearer evidence of the shortcomings of "process" alone as a program
solvent for community-wide disorder. In only a few instances is there
a marriage counseling service through which attempts are made to
prevent divorce and deal with other marital problems. In fact, although the first domestic relations court was organized in 1910, such
courts are found today in less than half the states, usually only in
the larger cities.[26]

The indeterminate sentence, in which the court sets an indefinite
period of imprisonment within the minimum and maximum fixed
by statute, constitutes a change in the processes for disposition of adult
cases. In traditional practice, the court set a definite period of time
which the offender was to serve in full. This practice, as we indicated
earlier, had its roots in the attempt to define the degree of punishment
most likely to prevent a particular offense. Where indeterminate sentences are authorized, the correctional authority has the discretional
power to base the date of the prisoner's release upon the progress or
response which he shows to treatment. The laws of three fourths of
the states now provide for an indeterminate sentence, and nearly 60
percent of the sentences to state prisons each year are of this character.[27] But here again, the test of the device lies in the treatment
skill by means of which the length of the sentence is fixed.

Complementary to this scheme and serving much the same purpose are two practices which the correctional agencies themselves use
to make sentences more flexible—parole and time off for good behavior. Under parole the prisoner's record both prior to and during
imprisonment is studied carefully by a parole authority, which in
effect "diagnoses" his capacity for return to community life. When
it is believed that his return will be beneficial for him, and at the
same time will present no menace to the community, he is released
under the supervision of a parole officer. Prisoners may also shorten
their sentences by earning credits for good behavior during imprisonment. The "good time laws" which govern this practice are of two
types—those that reduce the time which must elapse before the pris-

[26] Alice Scott Nutt, "Juvenile and Domestic Relations Courts," *Social Work Year Book,
1947*, p. 273.
[27] Bureau of the Census, *Prisoners in State and Federal Prisons and Reformatories*,
p. 14, Table 8.

oner can win absolute release, and those that hasten his eligibility for parole.[28]

A change in the processes of disposition is the purpose of still another innovation—the nonjudicial sentence. California, which authorities agree has developed one of the best correctional systems in the country, is the leading exponent of this procedure, and several other states with Youth Authorities have adopted it for offenders under 21.

Under this scheme the judge himself does not decide the institution in which the sentence should be served. Instead the prisoner is turned over to a state authority which brings to bear upon the study of the case a whole battery of psychiatric, psychological, casework, medical, and other specialists. The offender is then recommended (by classification) for commitment to the institution best equipped to deal with his particular problems. Some states achieve the same end by the use of "diagnostic centers." This procedure carries to a logical conclusion the individualization which progressive correctional authorities insist is the key to successful treatment. At present in most states, however, classification procedures are used only within the institution to which the prisoner has been committed.

A change in the processes of correction was the original purpose of probation. Like the juvenile court, probation came into prominence before the turn of the century as part of the agitation for "reform" in the severe and rigid criminal code. At present, probation rather than institutional commitment is the usual procedure in the vast majority of juvenile cases, but the situation in respect to adults is quite different. Although all but five states now make some provision for adult probation, its use often is restricted to certain types of offenders, and in only a few states is any substantial volume of cases handled in this way.[29]

Thus over a period of more than a half century, all these inventions —the crime prevention bureau, the juvenile court, the domestic relations court, the indeterminate sentences, the nonjudicial sentencing authority, probation and parole—have laid the foundation for a fundamental redirection of the processes that begin with "apprehension" and end with "discharge." Each procedure helps to assure that the

28 Pigeon, *Probation and Parole*, pp. 162.
29 *Ibid.*, pp. 100, 101.

offender will be dealt with as an individual in a more intelligent and humane manner.

But we believe it important to understand that these processes do not automatically guarantee a systematic effort to control and prevent the occurrence of the disorder which lies behind the offender's anti-social activity. They remove many traditional obstacles. But the essence of prevention and control within the correctional system should, in so far as possible, guarantee:

Competent diagnosis before disposition and commitment

Disposition for treatment appropriate to the diagnosis

Flexibility of treatment by the correctional authority to conform with the diagnostic understanding of the psychological and social factors in the case

Release as part of continuing treatment during what might be termed a "convalescent" period

Discharge in relation to the probable effectiveness of the cure

Evaluation of the entire process in the light of recidivist behavior

In the mental health system.—At only a few points has there been any invention, or experimentation with procedures for improving the process by which cases are discovered and flow for treatment from one mental health agency to another. In connection with the admission of patients to state mental hospitals we have noted a fundamental change in the traditional process of court commitment. Experimentation with two more direct devices for controlling the processes of admission to these state institutions deserves special attention.

Eleven states have set up special hospitals to which people with mental illness are sent for observation, diagnosis, and short-time therapy, before commitment or admission to institutions for long-time care. The purpose is to secure a more thorough diagnosis and to exclude those whose condition does not require prolonged institutional care. Authorities believe that this is the strategic point at which to concentrate the best psychiatric, psychological, casework, and other specialized services available. This is, in fact, the crux of the utility of this procedure as a means of better control of the disorders with which state institutions deal. Ohio, which is making systematic use of this procedure, handles admissions to all the state institutions for permanent care through six receiving hospitals. In its first three months of operation, the Youngstown Receiving Hospital discharged all but 18 of its 89 patients, who otherwise might have become at least a temporary burden on the state's regular institutional facilities.[30]

For some years Massachusetts has had a plan for controlling the course of treatment for mental defectives which corresponds to California's nonjudicial sentencing and classificational procedure in the correctional system. The court, instead of committing the case directly to a mental institution, assigns it to the State Department of Mental Health. Social workers from the department investigate, decide whether or not the patient can be cared for under community supervision, and if institutionalization is considered necessary, select the institution to which he should go. The department itself supervizes noninstitutionalized cases.[31] New Jersey accomplishes something of the same purpose by providing supervision and home training to cases on the waiting list for admission to its institutions—a procedure which enables the state training schools to give priority to the children who are most urgently in need of their care.[32] Such programs of home supervision also make possible the earlier discharge of patients from the institutions. Another device used successfully by New York and other states is supervised foster homes or "family" care of patients of low mentality who have had a preliminary period of institutional training.[33]

Thus in the mental health system better procedures for discovering cases and controlling the course of treatment have been designed primarily to redirect the flow of cases into and out of the state institutions. In most instances these procedures have been initiated by the state and have come down to the local community as state procedures, administered by state authorities. Unfortunately, even the use of these control processes is not widespread.

In the casework system.—Like the mental health system, the case work system throughout its history has afforded few illustrations of procedures designed to give better direction to the processes by which cases flow into and through it. Two principal exceptions may be noted, however.

[30] Henry H. Kessler, *Rehabilitation of the Physically Handicapped*, p. 162.
[31] Stanley P. Davies, *Social Control of the Mentally Deficient*, p. 329.
[32] Vincentz Cianci, "Home Supervision of Mental Deficients in New Jersey," *American Journal of Mental Deficiency*, XLI, No. 3 (January, 1947), 519.
[33] Hester B. Crutcher, "Family Care of Mental Defectives," *American Journal of Mental Deficiency*, LIII, No. 2 (October, 1948), 345.

The first is in respect to the processes by which children are separated from their own homes and placed under the care of a foster home or institution. One of the commonest devices for controlling these processes is used successfully by Catholic and Jewish agency federations in urban areas, as well as by some Protestant groups that maintain a combination of foster homes and institutional resources under separate and independent agencies. According to the Catholic pattern, when a child is to be removed from his home the case is investigated by a central diocesan bureau, and not by the individual agency or institution. Then, after study and diagnosis, the child is assigned to the foster home program or to the institution best equipped to care for him. The Jewish pattern is similar, although in most communities fewer agencies and institutions are involved. The procedure corresponds in principle to California's "nonjudicial sentence," for it makes diagnosis possible before disposition and permits assignment to the most appropriate agency. Such procedures, however, are not community-wide. They apply only to children of the faith of the sponsoring agency. Efforts to apply similar procedures among nonsectarian agencies have met with comparatively little success. And once again it must be stressed that the utility of the process depends upon the degree of skill with which judgments are made and the disordered circumstances effectively treated.

Of greater community-wide significance is the fact that a substantial proportion of the children dealt with by private agencies, both the sectarian and nonsectarian, are neglected or dependent children removed from their own homes through commitment. Frequently this carries with it a subsidy from public funds to the private agency for the care of the child. While some requests for commitment are made by the child's family directly to the court, usually they are made by the agency which plans to undertake the care and supervision of the child.

Prior to considering such cases, the courts usually require a case study, similar to that made by probation officers in delinquency cases, to guide the judge in making his official disposition. Too often, in practice, the decision of the agency and the parents that the child is to be removed from the home has already been taken by the time this study is made, and it serves chiefly to facilitate the action.

Removal of a child from its own home should be considered a drastic step and as a last resort. Our experience leads us to believe that the best time to prevent the breakup of the home is before, not after, the agency and the parents have agreed upon removal of the children. In fact, a few communities actually have experimented with voluntary procedures directed to diagnosis at this earlier stage. We are most familiar with those followed at St. Paul. In that city when an agency first considers removing the child from his home, the case is brought before a continuing community-wide committee, which includes representatives of family agencies, protective and child caring services (public and private), and the juvenile court. Each case is reviewed and the advisability of separation considered carefully. If removal from the home is deemed necessary, a recommendation is made regarding the best method of care and treatment, and the agency best equipped to undertake it. Testimony to the value of this procedure, when accompanied by skillful, diagnostic judgment, is found in the fact that, where it has been adopted, the number of children placed under care away from home has shown a marked decline.

The social service exchange is the second contribution made by the casework system in this direction. This device was invented and administered by the early charity organization societies as a means of systematizing relief procedures in the community. The early exchange was actually a central depository of case records, and all the record-giving agencies were expected to submit a full history of every family to whom they gave help. Ultimately the information was limited to the family's name, address, and other identifying data. Any agency which registered with the C.O.S. exchange could check against this file any family applying for relief and find out whether some other agency was currently active in the case.

By the end of the first quarter of this century, however, relief had become too large a problem for any single private agency to handle. Charity organization societies were being transformed into family service agencies, with a primary interest in providing casework service to the families who sought their help, rather than in organizing community relief resources. Moreover, the number of agencies registering in the exchange had increased greatly. Family societies began to feel that operation of the exchange was inappropriate to their new role, and the trend everywhere was to transfer administration of the exchange to the community chests and councils of social agencies which were organized in most urban communities during the 1920s. In this transitional sequence, however, the exchange has become dissociated from the community-wide direction, or control, of relief giving. Its records are usually simply a central file maintained for others who wish to use it. With the current trend toward consolidating relief administration in a single public welfare department, use of the exchange to coordinate community relief resources obviously has become increasingly unnecessary. The amount of relief now given by agencies other than the public department is so small as hardly to justify the maintenance of a complicated community-wide exchange to keep track of it.

Gradually it came to be assumed that the exchange should serve all agencies as a central source of information, useful in the coordination of the medical, nursing, casework, probation, institutional, and other specialized services rendered to the same family. For several reasons, however, the procedures which once were used to bring about better organization of relief are not effective in control of a complexity of health and adjustment problems. The exchange of information about relief is relatively simple: it has to do with how much money is being given to a family, and under what circumstances. Not only is exchange of information about health and adjustment services more complicated, but most agencies feel that their own particular service is distinctive, and one from which the family in question should be allowed to profit, even when other services are provided simultaneously by other agencies.

Of even more significance is the fact that in the early days the Charity Organization Society took administrative responsibility for follow-up of plans for the cases registered with it. The general purpose of the societies was to organize the relief resources of the community so that they would be put to the best use in each case, and the exchange was considered as a tool to that end. As the largest relief agency in the community, many families reported by other voluntary groups were already under its care. The present-day Council of Social Agencies has no such community-wide administrative role. The service of its exchange is confined to registering the daily reports received from agencies, notifying them of new registrations of cases already known to them, and clearing through the files any cases for which agencies may request such service. The Council takes no responsibility for guiding or evaluating the processes by which use is made of this information. In fact, to undertake such a responsibility would be contrary to its generally accepted philosophy.

REDIRECTION OF FUNCTIONAL STRATEGY

The fact that for some time the leaders of the three systems have been moving toward a common basis of professional skills signifies the usefulness and indispensability of diagnosis and treatment as a function of a community-wide program of prevention and protection—and the requisites for performing it. The corresponding usefulness of situational treatment and the requisites for it are more obscure, but a first step toward clarification is the recognition that this is a separate and distinct function.

Each system has had experience in controlling the processes by which cases flow from one agency to another. But there has been no development of functional principles applicable to the community-wide prevention and control of behavior disorders. The tendency to focus upon the control of processes apart from disorders—rooted as that is in meager knowledge about the community-wide characteristics of the generic problem of maladjustment—has resulted in three interrelated weaknesses whose remedy calls for a strategic redirection of thought and practice. As we see them, these weaknesses are (1) functional imbalance, (2) "symptomatic" referral (referral based on symptoms), and (3) episodic treatment.

Functional imbalance.—As far as we know, the St. Paul project represented the first systematic attempt to make community-wide comparisons between the families with behavior disorders known to community agencies, and the families in which a disorganized situation was the only apparent trouble. To our knowledge, the project was also the first systematic attempt to compare the total community service available for the "diagnosis and treatment" of the former group of cases, with the services available for the "situational treatment" of the latter group. In over two thirds of the cases comprising the total known community problem of maladjustment, mental defect, mental illness, emotional defect, and disordered behavior were interwoven with each other in relation to very disorganized situations. Obviously such conditions demand the maximum of diagnostic and treatment skill. In less than one third of the cases was a situational problem the sole factor of the family's trouble. The functional service available in the community, however, was in inverse ratio to this proportion. Only 13.3 percent of the service provided to these families during the month of the project was by agencies equipped for diagnosis and treatment; 73.2 percent was by agencies equipped to give situational treatment; and 13.5 percent was custodial care only.

None of the state mental or correctional institutions was adequately equipped for a therapeutic program, and only about 15 percent of the casework agencies had the personnel required for treating cases in which "personality" and "situational" defects are in serious combination. The other 85 percent were equipped to give no more than situational treatment, although this apparently was required by only 29 percent of the total group of families.

These proportions undoubtedly would differ in other communities, but our experience indicates that the relative division between the two types of service is usually basically the same. Communities at present are making a very substantial investment in service adapted to meet the lesser of the two needs represented in their total problem.

Symptomatic referral.—Even a casual look at any handful of family cards from a social service exchange will give ample evidence of what looks like a mass movement of cases back and forth among various agencies of the three systems. Among the families in St. Paul in which maladjustment was the only known problem, 27 percent were being served concurrently by two or more adjustment agencies during the month of our study. How much of this concurrent service was the result of referral from one agency to another, and how much was on the family's own initiative we do not know. But we do know that in St. Paul, and elsewhere throughout the country, a considerable volume of cases move by referral from agency to agency.

Our own firsthand knowledge and the data from our local surveys indicate clearly that the great majority of these referrals are made in order to procure some immediate help in dealing with a particular symptom of trouble, and not as part of a plan for thorough diagnosis or basic treatment of the underlying difficulty. Indeed, a three months study of intake and referral among all the agencies in Memphis, Tennessee, showed that about one third of the completed referrals were what might be called "traffic" referrals. They were made simply because the person who applied for a particular kind of aid happened to come first to an agency which did not provide the service he was seeking. Perhaps, too, it was in part because most of these referrals were made on the basis of symptoms that about 50 percent of the persons referred to some other agency never turned up there.[34] It may be that in the meantime the symptoms either disappeared or came to seem less serious to the applicant himself.

The current preoccupation with help in dealing with symptoms is quite understandable, since many agencies are not equipped to recognize the underlying troubles of which the situations may be symptomatic. It seems to us, therefore, that the development of classification aids and special procedures to improve agency capacity in this respect must become an important part of future strategy.

Episodic treatment.—As we have seen, chronicity is one of the underlying attributes of serious maladjustment. Much of the service now rendered, however, is on the assumption that the problem is an "acute" condition.

The St. Paul data covered only a one-month period and, therefore, threw little light on the responsibility which the agencies in the three systems took to insure continuing treatment. It is obvious that the state mental and correctional institutions do assure continuity of treatment during the period in which an individual is in their custody. But even in the correctional system, the great majority of juvenile and adult cases are under short-time custody. No legal rules govern the practice of other mental health agencies or of the casework agencies, except when the children are committed to the latter's custody for indeterminate care.

Materials furnished by many local surveys leave no doubt that the bulk of service rendered by the local community agencies of all three systems is episodic in character. In every community we know, there are records of families who have received service from agencies of one kind or another periodically over a lifetime, with no one agency responsible for a continuing plan of treatment. These families get into trouble again and again and apply first to one and then to another agency to help them out. The current "acute" situation is often patched up, only to have the trouble break out again in some other area requiring a different kind of patch.

With the bulk of the community's adjustment services primarily

34 Unpublished material from the Community Council, Memphis, Tenn.

geared to recognize and deal with situations, the episodic character of present service is not surprising. For situations are presumed to be urgent, emergent, and acute. Once the immediate obstacle is overcome, both the applicant and the agency are likely to feel that all will be well. It is an unfortunate illusion which has cost communities throughout this country an untold expenditure of energy and money.

CREATING THE MISSING FUNCTION

We would be doing our readers a disservice if we led them to think that any simple device can be used to remedy these major imperfections in our present programs. They arise out of deep-seated misapprehension and confusion about the nature of the problem and what the community should do about it. Indubitably the necessary redirection of thought and practice will come painfully and slowly.

It is our view, however, that the serious and painstaking focus upon creation of the principles and procedures necessary to the now missing function of community-wide prevention and control should provide the key to this reorientation.

Control of a disordered or pathological condition entails some measure of community-wide responsibility for assuring competent diagnosis and the sequence of treatment indicated. Moreover, responsibility continues as long as the condition persists. It involves a record of progress or retrogression, and, finally, an evaluation of the whole community program concerned with the condition. These are the basic principles which have proved so successful in the community-wide control of disease as carried on by the public health system. Indeed some of the procedures which would be involved are not too different from certain of the early principles which charity organization societies developed in the community-wide organization of relief.

From a practical standpoint the application of these procedures would be especially fruitful with at least two groups of cases, which are by no means mutually exclusive. The first is the group of multi-problem families whose pathological condition absorbs so much of the community's adjustment services, as well as a large proportion of its health and dependency services. The second is the group of families in which there are mental defectives. The families with mental defect reported under care in St. Paul were in many different kinds of social trouble, and accounted for an undue proportion of the total maladjustment problem with which the community agencies were concerned.

Procedures which would prevent and reduce the amount of community trouble emanating from either of these two groups would have great significance for planning and practice in the future. In the final chapter of this section we suggest some of the ingredients necessary to experimentation in this direction. In the development of such control procedures there must be provision for a competent diagnosis and prognosis of the course of the disorder in terms of the family capacity or incapacity to deal with it. Once the case is identified, discovered, or reported, securing such a prognosis inevitably becomes the first step toward control and treatment. Strategically, it is a step which may well prove of sufficient importance to justify the community in concentrating upon it a considerable portion of all the diagnostic and treatment resources that are available.

Chapter XV

COMMUNITY-WIDE STRUCTURE WITHIN THE THREE SYSTEMS

IN AN URBAN COMMUNITY one customarily finds that the various agencies administering adjustment services considerably outnumber those occupied with problems of dependency, ill-health, or insufficient recreation. This relative numerical superiority in administrative units is not an unmixed blessing to the program responsible for adjustment services. Rather it gives evidence of a complex administrative pattern which at many points may lack accepted principles for achieving community-wide structural efficiency.

As in other fields with which this book is concerned, basic patterns are recurrent, despite great community differences. Every urban community is served by various local and state correctional agencies providing probation, institutional custody, and parole; by a group of local and state agencies providing clinical and institutional services in the field of mental health; and by a group of private casework agencies which are organized around the problem of families, children, veterans, travelers and perhaps other special groups. These private casework agencies are usually complemented by public welfare and health agencies employing caseworkers.

Since the protective and correctional system has an obligation to protect the whole community against nuisances and menaces of overt antisocial behavior, the structure of the system must serve a community-wide objective. The thoughtful leaders of the system, aware of this responsibility, have reached sound and authoritative conclusions about how to simplify and integrate their various administrative units so that they may accomplish this purpose more effectively and economically.

On the whole, the mental health and the casework systems have limited their objectives to serving the people who happen to apply to their agencies. Nevertheless, in both systems one finds evidence, in past experience and current trends, which suggests the evolution of a more efficient structure to serve a community-wide purpose.

THE CORRECTIONAL STRUCTURE

In the preceding chapter we summed up the results of more than half a century of effort to change the processes for apprehending offenders and disposing of their cases. Through the crime prevention bureau, the juvenile court, the domestic relations court, the indeterminate sentence, probation and parole, there have been progressive efforts to administer the essential processes of the correctional system in a way that would contribute to the better treatment of the individual offender. Throughout, qualitative results depend upon the professional competence of diagnostic and treatment personnel, and the manner in which their service is coordinated during the different steps in the process. At many points administrative characteristics of the separate units are of secondary importance.

However, internal structure of the two main types of correctional institutions—for adults and juveniles—very directly affects their potentialities for constructive treatment use. In each case, both the plant and the administrative organization must be designed to bring to bear upon different types of cases the best possible combination of institutional regimen and specialized professional personnel.

Authorities agree that there should be three general types of correctional institutions for adult prisoners: (1) maximum security institutions with walled enclosures, where the majority of prisoners are housed in cell blocks and where shops, recreation grounds, and all other facilities are located within the enclosure so as to reduce the danger of escape; (2) medium security institutions, where there is no wall but perhaps a wire fence of the industrial type, where housing is mainly in outside cells or dormitories, and where prisoners are employed outside the institution as well as inside; (3) minimum security, usually of the farm-camp type, where the men live in unlocked and unfenced buildings and work outdoors, supervised by overseers instead of the usual prison guards. Besides classifying offenders by the type of security risk they represent, a modern prison system also endeavors to provide diversified institutions or facilities on the basis of age, sex, and amenability to treatment. There should be separate institutions for men and women, and separate facilities for such groups as defective delinquents, alcoholics, and those needing intensive or prolonged medical care.[1]

The organization of each institution should provide for a program appropriate to the type of care, of employment, vocational training and education, with provision for recreation, library service, and religious activities. In addition there needs to be a diagnostic and receiving unit, a psychiatric clinic, a psychological department, complete medical, laboratory and hospital facilities, and a social service department.[2]

Similarly, authorities agree that in order to furnish the best setting for treatment, correctional institutions for juveniles should follow the cottage plan. Besides the cottages in which the children live, the physical plant should include a school, shops for vocational training, space and equipment for entertainment and recreation, a chapel, and a medical unit with hospital and clinic facilities. If the institution intends to provide a full treatment program, it should have the following departments: education; home life, or supervision and cottage service; and clinical study, which includes "medical examinations, psychiatric examinations, psychological examinations, and appropriate treatment in these fields." [3]

CONSOLIDATING THE SEPARATE ADULT UNITS

In the sense that each agency has specific duties, related by law and custom to a comprehensive series of duties, there has always been "coherence" within the correctional system. However, except in a very few states, there is no pivotal agency with accepted responsibility for seeing to it that the various units in the system work together smoothly to accomplish a common treatment purpose. Leaders in the field of adult correction apparently now believe that this pivotal agency should be a consolidated state department of corrections, with administrative as well as planning and coordinating authority over the en-

---

[1] The American Prison Association, *Manual of Suggested Standards for a State Correctional System*, Chapter 4.

[2] *Ibid.*, Chapter 6, 7.

[3] Federal Security Agency, Office of Education, *Education in Training Schools for Delinquent Youth*, pp. 13–21.

tire system. Their belief is backed by long experience, penetrating thought, and leadership of a high order in what is undoubtedly the most difficult of all fields of public service with which we are concerned. There is, in fact, a slow trend toward consolidation.

Their reason for this belief becomes clear when we review the duties now prescribed for California's three-member Adult Authority, a key segment of what is to date one of the most consolidated state structures of its kind in the country. The duties, in effect, place upon the Adult Authority responsibility for seeing to it that each state prisoner receives a competent diagnosis and that his treatment up to and after discharge is conducted in accordance with a systematic plan. The Authority has the following responsibilities:

1. Supervision and control of the Diagnostic Clinic (reception center)
2. Determining and redetermining terms of imprisonment
3. Classifying prisoners to determine where they are to serve their sentences; supervising a classification and treatment program within each institution
4. Transferring prisoners between institutions
5. Prescribing punishment for infractions of prison discipline, and awarding or forfeiting credits
6. Restoring civil rights
7. Granting or revocation of parole
8. Directing the operations of the Bureau of Parole
9. Making investigations, at the request of the Governor, on applications for executive clemency and providing him with reports and recommendations [4]

Members of the Adult Authority also serve as members of the Board of Corrections, the governing board of the Department of Corrections, which is responsible for administering the state institutions.

In line with the general plan in effect in California, most authorities now agree (although some points are in professional dispute) that the entire adult correctional program, including the necessary classification units, prisons and jails, as well as probation and parole, should be administered by a single state agency, with appropriate administrative subdivisions. There is debate as to whether there should be a separate

[4] State of California, *Partial Report of Assembly Interim Committee on Crime and Corrections*, pp. 30–31.

Department of Corrections or a Division of Corrections in the State Department of Welfare, with opinion favoring the former for the more populous states, and the latter for states in which the volume of correctional work is not large.[5] Certainly there has been a definite trend toward more state authority over the separate segments of the adult correctional structure during the past fifteen years.

The classification program or system, all authorities agree, must be a key part of any unified state structure. In brief, this means that the system should be able to classify every person committed to it in terms of a competent diagnosis, and should be equipped with specialized medical, psychiatric, psychological, casework, educational, and vocational personnel necessary to provide that diagnosis, and to follow it up with appropriate treatment. For the larger states many authorities favor the type of classificational system now found in California and New York. All offenders sentenced to prison in these states are sent to a reception (or diagnostic) center for a period of study and observation.[6] Then on the recommendation of the center, the prisoner is sent to the institution which seems to offer the best chance of constructive treatment. These institutions in turn have their own classification programs for planning the specific course of action, for observing the inmate's progress, and for making such changes in his treatment as may be required. The administration of the reception center and of classification activities in the several institutions are closely linked and coordinated through the office of the director of classification in the state department.

Although some of the other large states are considering this type of reception center, the location of a separate classification unit in each of the several institutions is now the more common practice. But even when each institution provides its own reception procedures, authorities insist that there should be a state director or supervisor of classification to standardize practices and facilitate transfers from one institution to another.[7] Authorities also insist that these institutional units should be staffed by the proper quota of psychiatrists, psychologists, caseworkers, and other specialists, to give effective diagnostic and treatment service.

[5] *Manual of Suggested Standards for a State Correctional System,* Chapter 2, p. 9.
[6] The American Prison Association, Committee on Classification and Casework, *Handbook on Classification in Correctional Institutions,* p. 22.
[7] *Ibid.,* pp. 14–15.

When institutional reception units operate purely as diagnostic clinics, as some of them do, there is danger that they will stand apart from the ongoing life of the institution and will have little bearing on the subsequent experience of the offender during his imprisonment. Experience shows that the best way to meet this danger is through an active classification committee representing both the administrative personnel of the institution and the professional personnel responsible for diagnosis.[8]

In fact, correctional leaders stress the importance of the institution's classification committee, whatever the procedures for reception or quarantine may be. Not only does this committee study each "admission summary" and set up a practical program for each individual, but it periodically reviews his case and checks his progress. In this way treatment becomes the responsibility of the entire institutional staff.

Probation traditionally has been a local, rather than a state function, but today authorities agree on the desirability of state supervision. Many would like to see this service administered entirely by the state, preferably by a consolidated department of corrections.[9] At last report, nearly half of the states were administering probation on a statewide basis, although in some of these the larger cities and counties were excluded from the state board's jurisdiction. So far, however, the move to consolidate the present state probation services in a state department or bureau responsible for corrections has not made much headway.

The local jail presents so many administrative problems that some authorities boldly suggest that the best way to improve it is to abolish it entirely. In its place, they would establish regional institutions, administered by the state department of corrections, to care for sentenced prisoners. Detention for those awaiting trial might be provided in a separate action of the new institution if it was conveniently located for this purpose; otherwise facilities for detention would be arranged near the courthouse.[10]

In general the design for the regional institutions should follow the lines essential for any correctional institution which has a thera-

---

[8] *Ibid.,* pp. 20–21.
[9] *Manual of Suggested Standards for a State Correctional System,* Chapter 3, p. 15.
[10] *Ibid.,* Chapter 15, p. 82.

peutic purpose, with special departments for medical service, the treatment of alcoholics, and casework service. All offenders destined for the new institution would be committed to the custody of the state correctional department under an indeterminate sentence, and each institution would have a reception unit to provide proper diagnosis and classification.[11]

Such a plan, in our opinion, would help to focus diagnostic and treatment resources on a group which deserves but never has received priority in community attention. Prisoners who need medical attention usually are found in even larger proportions in short-term institutions than in long-term institutions. Alcoholics always make up a large part of the jail population, and some authorities believe it likely that jail inmates, as a class, are even more in need of intensive social and psychiatric treatment than are prison inmates.[12]

Correctional leaders who are realists have no illusions about the obstacles they face in substituting a program of state-administered regional institutions for the traditional county jails and workhouses. Therefore, as an interim program they advocate legislation "to make all jails and other places of detention, whether for sentenced prisoners or those awaiting action, subject to inspection by the state, with power to close those not meeting minimum standards." At present, less than half of the states have made any legal provision for inspection or other limited supervision, and no state as yet has full administrative authority over its local institutions.[13]

The state prisons, of course, should be administered by the central department of corrections. At present, the degree of centralized administrative control which the state excercises over these institutions varies greatly. In some states the institutions are under the control and supervision of a strong state department of corrections; in others the central office has little authority, and sometimes there is no central administration at all.[14]

Parole generally is administered by a state authority, rather than by the separate institutions. But there is considerable resistance to the idea that administration should be consolidated under an over-all correctional authority. This resistance is due in large measure to the

11 *Ibid.*, pp. 82–87.
12 Helen D. Pigeon, *Probation and Parole*, p. 144.
13 *Manual of Suggested Standards for a State Correctional System*, pp. 81, 82.
14 *Handbook on Classification in Correctional Institutions*, p. 11.

fact that parole involves two steps: the semijudicial function of determining when a prisoner is to be paroled, and the administrative function of supervising the parole. Authorities agree that the independence of the judicial function must be guarded. Consequently, some hold that this part of the correctional system should not be integrated administratively with a state department of corrections. For the same reason, there is objection also to the practice of combining probation and parole under an independent state board as it now is in 19 states. The truth, as we see it, is that the humane procedures of probation and parole, like so many other segments of welfare service, came to be accepted only after their advocates had waged a long hard battle against traditional practice and public apathy. The strategy in such struggles almost always focuses on some separate structure as a practical device for getting the new program established. Once the battle has been won, however, a struggle of almost equal proportions is necessary in order to integrate the new service with kindred services in a manner which makes for effective use and efficient administration.

ISSUES REGARDING THE JUVENILE STRUCTURE

There is some trend toward state administration and consolidation of the several units which deal with juvenile offenders. But there is not such general agreement here as is the case in adult correction circles. Indeed, both correctional and welfare authorities tend to take different views about the structure most appropriate for the administration of the separate units of this system.

Juvenile correction institutions first functioned as independent state units, each under its own board of trustees; today they are usually under the bureau of child welfare in a state department of public welfare. Since juvenile institutions almost everywhere administer their own parole cases, the quality and degree of the state's program of institutional supervision determines the amount of state control over this service also.

Four states have carried integration a step further by setting up a Youth Authority, which not only exercises the nonjudicial sentencing power, and handles classification, parole, and discharge, but may even operate the juvenile institutions. The 81st Congress also established a Youth Corrections Division of the Department of Justice, patterned along these lines, for youths who have committed federal offenses.

Where there is a Youth Authority, courts commit delinquents under 21 years of age to it, rather than to a specific institution. The Authority is then responsible for making a diagnosis of each offender and for providing the treatment indicated. It may make use of all existing institutions and facilities, both public and private, and may also establish new types of treatment and training units if so required, and funds permit. The Authority is under compulsion to return the offender to his community under supervision (parole) as soon as possible, and generally cannot hold him beyond a clearly defined maximum period.[15]

A number of states which have not adopted the Youth Authority plan have accomplished somewhat the same purpose by establishing a diagnostic and classification center in the social welfare or correction department. The center "receives" the child after sentence and recommends the correctional institution best suited to meet his problems, the type of program to be followed, and the approximate length of the treatment.[16] In the remaining states, diagnostic study, if any, is made in the reception cottage or wing of the institution to which the child is sent by the court. The quality of the diagnostic and treatment resources available to these institutions varies widely.

Local detention facilities for children are as much of a problem to juvenile correctional leaders as the local jail is to leaders in the adult field. It is estimated that the number of children detained in them for varying lengths of time may run as high as 300,000 a year. In a recent study of the 68 programs which were believed to represent the best in detention care, the National Probation and Parole Association failed to find a single one that was completely satisfactory.[17] To remedy this situation the study advocated restriction of the use of detention to a minimum, and community insistence on high standards of physical facilities, personnel, and program. Welfare authorities, while agreeing with these principles, believe that detention homes should be under the auspices of the public welfare department.[18]

15 John R. Ellingston, *Protecting Our Children from Criminal Careers*, pp. 55–56.
16 Herschel Alt, "Juvenile Behavior Problems," *Social Work Year Book, 1947*, p. 269.
17 Sherwood and Helen Norman, *Detention for the Juvenile Court: a Discussion of Principles and Practices*, Introduction.
18 Alice Scott Nutt, "The Responsibility of the Juvenile Court and the Public Welfare Agency in the Child Welfare Program," *Redirecting the Delinquent*, p. 218.

Parole or "placement," in both the judicial and administrative sense, almost always is the responsibility of the institution to which the juvenile has been assigned. Exceptions to this rule are found in states where a Youth Authority is responsible for deciding when to release and discharge the offender, and in a few other states where the parole supervision is carried by a central state agency and decision to release remains in the hands of the institution as answer to the administrative problem. Some authorities advocate better supervision from the state welfare agency charged with oversight of the institution, rather than the establishment of a central parole system. The supervisory agency should have the power to establish and enforce adequate standards of service and personnel, and should be able to give technical advice and assistance.[19]

The pivotal units in the juvenile structure during most of the current century, however, have been the local juvenile court and its probation service. Thus methods followed in dealing with juveniles are in sharp contrast to those prevailing in the adult courts, which never have used probation for any substantial proportion of their cases.

At present three states, Connecticut, Rhode Island, and Utah, have state-wide juvenile courts, and in several other states the probation service is administered by a state-wide agency, although the courts are local.[20] In most states, however, both the court and probation are administered locally, and usually the court itself is responsible for administering probation.

In regard to the most appropriate structure for the administration of these pivotal units in the juvenile system, there is considerable difference of opinion. It seems to us that underlying these differences is the confusion of opinion about what the court should do. Only as that is clarified can issues of structure and administration be seen in proper perspective.

In the course of its development the juvenile court tended to become a generalized child welfare agency responsible for all manner of children's problems, as well as a correctional agency, responsible for the adjudication and authoritative supervision of children whose behavior is a serious community nuisance or menace.

19 Pigeon, *Probation and Parole*, p. 176.
20 Alice Scott Nutt, "Juvenile and Domestic Relations Courts," *Social Work Year Book, 1947*, p. 276.

Organizationally, however, the situation has changed markedly since 1935. The Social Security Act, under Title V, authorized federal financial aid to assist state public welfare agencies "in establishing, extending, and strengthening, especially in predominantly rural areas, public welfare services for the protection and care of homeless, dependent, and neglected children, and children in danger of becoming delinquent." [21] To take advantage of federal funds, a state must formulate a plan acceptable to the Children's Bureau and agree to assume some part of the cost of child welfare services in its own rural areas.

This legislation is credited with stimulating a tremendous expansion in state and local public child welfare services throughout the country, in urban as well as rural areas. Every state department of welfare now includes a child welfare division, and in 1948 there were 2,753 public child welfare workers providing service to children in local communities, the bulk of it financed by state and local funds. These workers undertake a great range of activities. In some states they are responsible for both foster care and protective services to delinquent or neglected children. In other states the program is confined almost entirely to foster care, and in still others most of the service is to children in their own homes where there are various types of family troubles. But by 1950 these activities were reaching 231,000 children.[22] In most cases the local administrative unit for the program is either a county department of public welfare or a district office of a state child welfare division.[23]

It is now generally agreed that the public welfare department rather than the juvenile court should administer the foster home programs for dependent and neglected children. There is no such general agreement regarding the handling of cases involving behavior disorders. From the traditional and still generally current practice whereby all degrees of juvenile misbehavior are handled by the juvenile court and its probation staff, some would swing the pendulum to the other extreme. Except for adjudication, they would give the public welfare department the responsibility for handling delinquencies evidencing serious behavior traits as well as those of a minor nature.

[21] Federal Security Agency, Social Security Administration, *Compilation of the Social Security Laws*, p. 40.
[22] Federal Security Agency, U.S. Children's Bureau, *Services for Children*, p. 6.
[23] Mildred Arnold, "Children's Services in the Public Welfare Agency," *Child Welfare Reports*, No. 3 (May, 1947), p. 2.

Many organizational interests are in conflict over these issues. The availability of competent public welfare services to take over either a portion or all of this responsibility varies greatly in different sections of the country. Our own experience is that there comes a point in symptomatic misbehavior when both the protection of the community and the treatment of the individual require the exercise of a type of authority which should be dissociated from the treatment and supportive supervision of cases of less serious maladjustment. For a court and probation service so focused, the advantages of a state-wide administration, integrated with that of the correctional institutions, seems to us to be more apparent.

The truth is, however, that there has been little thought, research, or experimentation systematically directed toward determining the characteristics of this behavior point, or setting up classificational procedures that could be used to indicate which of the two kinds of treatment was needed in a given case, or creating devices to direct the flow of cases to the appropriate kind of treatment. Such thought and research are badly needed to provide a workable and sound solution to the structural issues in this field.

THE MENTAL HEALTH SYSTEM

State institutions for the insane go back to colonial days, and special institutions for the mentally defective date from the middle of the nineteenth century. Our own century, particularly the past 25 years, has seen the development of the various types of community clinics and other outpatient services for mentally ill and emotionally disturbed persons. But until quite recently the principal justification for characterizing these different agencies as a system was the fact that they were dealing with similar or related problems. Little thought has yet been given to the principles of relationship that should apply among the various units administering mental health services. Increasingly, however, leaders in the field are coming to recognize these issues.

The plant and administrative structure of the mental institutions has much to do with their potential use as treatment centers. Much thought has been given to establishing standards for them. Authorities agree that institutions for the mentally ill should be so constructed that the physical plant will provide two essentials.[24] First, there should be a small, well-staffed receiving unit where new patients may be observed for a brief period so that they may be classified and housed according to their condition. Second, the hospital should provide special units or departments (each with appropriate staff and facilities) for various groups of patients classified by the nature of their illness, their age, and the kind of treatment which is indicated. These groups include the acutely ill receiving intensive therapy, convalescents, those with a favorable prognosis requiring prolonged treatment, those requiring long-time care, senile and arteriosclerotic cases, those who are physically ill and require medical or surgical treatment, children under sixteen, alcoholics and drug addicts, and tuberculous patients.

The institution also should be equipped with facilities similar to those found in any modern hospital, for example, clinical and pathological laboratories, a roentgenological department and a medical library. It should provide for a staff of psychiatric, psychological, and casework and nursing personnel.

Institutions for the mentally defective should be of the "cottage plan" type. In addition to the usual cottages for resident patients, who are separated into groups on the basis of ability or accomplishment or both,[25] there should be a temporary receiving unit and the following special facilities: a ward for the acutely disturbed patients with severe behavior problems, a medical and surgical unit, a ward for tuberculous patients, a nursery for infants under one year of age, a separate cottage or facility for children of low mentality under six years of age, and an infirmary for those with severe physical handicaps. It is recommended that school facilities be provided for an estimated 10 percent of the institution's population and occupational therapy for 20 percent.[26] In this field also, if an institution is to move in the direction of becoming a treatment agency, it must provide competent personnel in adequate numbers in all the following departments: psychiatry, psy-

24 Mental Hygiene Committee, "Conclusions Concerning Psychiatric Training and Clinics," *U.S. Public Health Reports*, LXI, No. 26 (June 28, 1946).

25 Samuel Hamilton, "Public Institutions for Mental Defectives, Their Organization and Equipment," *American Journal of Mental Deficiency*, L, No. 3 (January, 1946), 452.

26 Robert E. Wyers and George Tarjan, "Administrative Practices to Provide Better Psychiatric Care," *American Journal of Mental Deficiency*, LIV, No. 1 (July, 1949), 34.

chology, social service, general medicine and surgery, nursing, and education which includes recreational, occupational, and musical therapy.

STATE AUTHORITY

By far the largest number of mentally ill and mentally defective persons receiving attention from organized agencies are those cared for in the state institutions. These institutions also represent the community's largest financial investment in protection against mental disorders. At present there are hospitals for mental disease in all states, while all but three states have one or more institutions for defectives.

Usually both types of institutions are administered by the same agency of the state government. But a separate mental hygiene department, with authority to administer both types of institutions and integrate them with related mental health activities, exists today in only six states.[27] Twelve states place supervision of mental institutions in a division or bureau of the department of public welfare. In 13 states supervision of mental institutions is under a general department of institutions, handling all mental, correctional, and other institutional facilities for which the state is responsible. For the most part these departments reflect a structure devised when the routines of management and care outweighed concern for program issues. In eight states there is a unified board of control for mental institutions and the rest of the institutions function as separate and independent units.

DIAGNOSTIC AND SCREENING CLASSIFICATION

Mention has been made of psychopathic hospitals. In many instances these are designed to provide temporary care. In some states patients may be assigned for temporary care prior to admission to institutions for prolonged care; in some instances, these temporary care hospitals are operated by the same agency which operates the regular institutions.

At least three states have a central structure responsible for the diagnosis and classification of mental defectives *before* they are assigned to institutional care. Massachusetts, New York, and Pennsylvania clear all cases through state-operated clinics before admittance

[27] *Directory of Psychiatric Clinics in the United States and Other Resources.*

to the state institution.[28] As in the correctional field, these precommitment services are designed to provide the basis for more discriminatory treatment, as well as to cut down the load of the institutions which provide long-term care. But, as in the correctional field, these central classificational units or procedures are not presumed to take the place of adequate diagnostic and treatment units within the separate institutions.

In most states, therefore, the standard plan for classification of both the mentally diseased and the mentally defective calls for a receiving unit in each institution for observation, diagnosis, and prognosis. The resulting assignment to different departments or units naturally will depend on the degree to which the internal structure and the available facilities of the particular institution meet the standards cited earlier.

Institutional care has been diminishing for one class of mental defectives on which earlier programs laid great stress—the patient of relatively high mentality. Formerly a number of states established, under the parent institution, "colonies" of such persons, training them for industrial, agricultural and, in some instances, domestic labor. Most defectives with these potential capacities are now trained in the ungraded classes of the public schools. Hence, today institutions receive a much larger proportion of the lower-grade defectives who are unfitted for community life. Many of the latter, however, can be placed in foster homes under family care after the institution has given them all the training they can absorb.

PAROLE OR RELEASE

Today modern hospital practice is discontinuing the use of the term parole in favor of "trial visit" or "home visit" to designate the status of a patient carried for a long time under extramural supervision. All state hospitals now make use of this procedure for some cases, that is, they have an arrangement whereby the patient may be continued under care at home for some time before his formal discharge. Most training schools for defectives have a similar arrangement for patients returned home or placed in jobs outside the institution.

[28] Arthur W. Pense, "Trends in the Institutional Care for the Mentally Defective," *American Journal of Mental Deficiency*, L, No. 3 (January, 1946), 453; Hilding Bengs, "Department of Public Welfare's Approach to Mental Deficiency," p. 644; and Stanley P. Davies, *Social Control of the Mentally Deficient*, p. 329.

In most states such procedures, together with release, are a responsibility of the individual institution and not of the state department
which supervises them. But in the states with a separate mental hygiene department more attention is being given to state-wide procedures for extramural supervision. California, for example, has a consolidated Bureau of Social Work which handles extramural cases for
all state mental institutions.[29] A demonstration in the case of dementia
praecox patients cared for extramurally, according to the New York
Department of Mental Hygiene, showed improvement among 70 percent of those who received intensive psychiatric casework as compared
with 51 percent of those who received the regular state hospital supervision (which in New York is relatively good).[30] New York and other
states also are developing outpatient clinic sessions in order to make
institutional psychiatric staff and social workers available for consultation with released and convalescent patients, their families or
relatives, and with community agencies which may be giving them
service.[31]

THE COMMUNITY CLINIC

There are now about 1,200 mental hygiene clinics or psychiatric
outpatient units in local communities throughout the country.[32] In
1947 it was estimated that the country as a whole had only about one
fifth of the clinic services it needed, and present facilities are being
concentrated almost entirely in large population centers.[33] Even the
remarkable addition of 450 clinics since that time still leaves the country far short of its estimated needs. The greatest need today is for the
all-purpose clinic, with services unrestricted as to sex or type of mental or emotional difficulties. These are destined to play a strategic role
in the development of community mental hygiene services, although
it is not yet clear how they can best be related to the other parts of the
mental health structure.

A substantial number of the existing clinics, including many of
those restricting their service to children, are under independent
local private auspices. Some clinics are operated as outpatient serv-

---

[29] U.S. Public Health Service, *Summary, Surveys of California's Mental Institutions
and Mental Hygiene Clinics*, p. 8.
[30] *Mental Health in Modern Society*, pp. 201–2.
[31] State of New York, Department of Mental Hygiene, *57th Annual Report*, pp. 99, 122.
[32] National Institute of Mental Health, personal communication.
[33] Robert H. Felix, "The Relation of the National Mental Health Act to State Health
Authorities," *Public Health Reports*, LXII, No. 2 (January 10, 1947), 6.

ices of local private or public hospitals. One finds also a variety of other public auspices, such as the schools, the courts, and the Veterans Administration, and in at least one third of the states there are some local clinics under the same auspices as the state institutions.

Our own experience is that the operational policy of community clinics may be pointed in one of two general directions. These directions may not be mutually exclusive, but we have found that the distinction between them helps to clarify structural issues about which there is now considerable uncertainty.

The first direction is toward the psychoses, the more serious psychoneuroses, and the more serious cases of defect. Clinics with this orientation must have psychiatric and supporting staff adequate not only to diagnose but also to give intensive treatment to cases which lend themselves to noninstitutional therapy. Such an orientation clearly suggests a structure and policy closely integrated with the state institutions to which many such cases ultimately find their way for care. Logic, at least, points to the use of these clinics for assistance in diagnostic screening and classification before commitment or assignment for institutional care. Logic also suggests the possibility of using such clinics for outpatient treatment and consultation service to patients on leave or released from the institutions, even though responsibility for follow-up supervision may rest in a central state-wide staff.

The second possible direction for clinic policy is toward those psychoneurotic and emotional disturbances which accompany the larger volume of symptomatic disorder and maladjustment with which every community must deal. This is a direction which leads us logically to the structural and operational integration of the clinic with agencies whose chief concern is with the *situations* in which such emotional disturbances so often manifest themselves. The premium in these cases is upon competent diagnosis and the maximum use of casework in treatment, rather than upon intensive psychotherapy. This indeed has been the focus of many child guidance clinics and of some all-purpose mental hygiene clinics operated under private auspices. Their structural alliance with the casework agencies of the community has been limited to referral and occasionally to consultation of one kind or another.

A structural pattern may emerge that will enable the community clinic to travel in both of these directions at once. In fact, those responsible for administering the National Mental Health Act, under which many new local and traveling clinics are being set up, would give the clinic a triple role:

These clinics, whether mobile or stationary, should furnish three broad services: (1) a community clinic; (2) an auxiliary service to the mental hospital; and (3) an agency for community mental health education.

Such a clinic would serve the community by providing out-patient psychiatric treatment or psychological counselling for patients not in need of hospitalization and, most significant, for patients in the early stage of illness, when the prospect for cure is greatest. The accomplishment of this objective would require the active cooperation of other community agencies in carrying out, when indicated, plans for modification of the patient's environment.

It would serve the mental hospital by providing prehospitalization service and by referring those in need of institutional care to the hospital; by providing supervision and follow-up treatment of provisional-discharge or convalescent posthospitalization cases; and by supervising care-and-custody and boarded-out cases.

The mental health education function of the clinic would include dissemination of information about mental health principles and practices, active case-finding programs, and the study and control of mental diseases from an epidemiological standpoint. The clinic cannot do the educational job alone. It needs to coordinate its educational activities with those of the school, the health department and other community agencies.[34]

Future experience no doubt will show whether any single agency can perform all these functions successfully.

FEDERAL-STATE STRUCTURAL ISSUES

The National Mental Health Act, by which the federal government now becomes a participant in the mental health system, was passed in 1946 as a result of a rising public concern over the problem of mental illness. This legislation, which took the form of amendment to the Public Health Service Act, permitted the expenditure of federal funds for the following purposes:

1. *Research*

Establishment of a National Institute of Mental Health, under the United States Public Health Service, to do research and provide training in the cause and treatment of mental disease.

Grants-in-aid for research, which may be made to qualified institutions —universities, hospitals and laboratories—and to qualified individuals.

34 *Ibid.,* p. 7.

2. *Training*

Grants-in-aid to enable non-profit institutions to develop and improve their facilities for training mental hygiene personnel.

Training stipends for graduate students in psychiatry, clinical psychology, psychiatric social work and psychiatric nursing.

3. *Community Services*

Grants-in-aid to the states (up to $10 million annually) to be used for mental health facilities in local communities.

Thus federal funds available to the states for direct services are earmarked specifically for service in the local community; none of the money may be used by them for the operation or expansion of state hospitals or training schools. This by-passing of the institutional program was conscious and deliberate. It stemmed from the public health slant of the Act and from reluctance to invade the state's admitted responsibility for the institutional care of those already mentally ill.

The National Mental Health Act is administered and the funds disbursed by the National Institute of Mental Health of the United States Public Health Service. Funds for mental health are distributed in the same manner as USPHS funds for general health, tuberculosis control, and venereal disease control; that is, the allocation to each state is based upon population, extent of the problem, and financial need.[35] The state has to match the federal funds with one dollar of state and local funds for every $2 it receives.[36]

In order to become eligible for funds the state must designate a mental health authority to deal with the Public Health Service in the development of the program. The Act stipulated that the term "state health authority" meant the state health department ". . . except that, in the case of any state in which there is a single state agency other than the state health authority charged with responsibility for administering the mental health program of the state, it means such other state agency." However, "agencies whose activities in the mental health field are restricted to jurisdiction over mental institutions and their patients do not qualify." [37]

[35] Joseph W. Mountain and Clifford H. Greve, *The Role of Grants-in-Aid in Financing Public Health Programs*, p. 39.

[36] James V. Lowry, "How the Mental Health Act Works," *Public Health Reports,* LXIV, No. 10 (March 11, 1949), 306.

[37] Felix, "The Relation of the National Mental Health Act to State Health Authorities," p. 3.

Actually, about three fifths of the states have designated the state health department as the official "mental health authority." The other states have named a mental hygiene department, a department of welfare, a department of institutions, or some other agency already operating in the mental health field.

Dividing the responsibility for the institutional and noninstitutional program in the mental health structure tends to multiply administrative problems. In Illinois, for example, the Department of Public Welfare, with responsibility for the care and treatment of the mentally ill, already was operating 40 community clinics in various parts of the state, but the Department of Public Health is the recipient of the money to be used for the development of the expanded mental health program.[38] A similar situation is found in California, where the Department of Mental Hygiene is expanding its clinics with money channeled through the Department of Public Health, the official mental health authority. In our experience, such dual responsibility usually leads to confusion rather than to the clarification of purpose.

Whatever the state authority, it must submit a state-wide plan for the development of mental health activities throughout the state, together with budget estimates. The proposed program is sent first to the District office of the Public Health Service for approval, and is then reviewed by the Community Services Branch of the National Institute of Mental Health. Great latitude is permitted to the states in selecting the types of program for which they wish subsidy. During the first year of operation $2,133,358 of the $3 million appropriation was allocated to 46 states. For all the states, these funds were allocated to the various programs as follows: [39]

Program	Allocation (in percent)
Clinics	61
Professional services	16
Training	11
Prevention and educational activities	8
Central administration	3
Special studies	1

[38] Rudolph G. Novick, "Community Organization for Mental Health," *Mental Hygiene,* XXXIV, No. 2 (April, 1950), 213–14.

[39] Lowry, "How the Mental Health Act Works," p. 310.

It may be that the foundation for a comprehensive federal-state mental health structure is in the making. So far, however, the Act is too recent and administrative policies too experimental to warrant any forecast of future trends. It would seem to us that the development of federal influence in this field would depend in considerable measure upon the inclusion of the mental institutions within the scope of the federal program, and further clarification of the role that the clinic should play not simply in relation to the mental health program, but in the total program for preventing maladjustment and protecting the community against its consequences.

THE CASEWORK SYSTEM

The social casework agencies of the country do not constitute a system in any organic sense, even as much as do the mental health agencies. To be sure, the private casework agencies are alike in the fact that they are autonomous, locally administered and financed. Each one also usually belongs to a national agency which represents the particular movement with which it is identified. But the special cement which quite effectively binds all these agencies together is a common orientation, stemming from the philosophy and methods of casework practice as revealed to them by the leaders of the profession. Seldom, however, have the leaders shown much concern over problems of community-wide structure and organization, and when they do discuss these matters, it is without authority for the system as a whole.

TRANSITIONAL EPOCHS

The reader will recall that, historically, the agencies of the casework system originated in the days when a considerable proportion of the community's relief needs were met from private funds. In the last two decades, however, two marked changes have affected the traditional role of the private casework agency and raised perplexing structural issues which have yet to be resolved.

Even before 1930, charity organization societies and their successors, the family agencies, had abandoned their original interest in "organizing" the relief sources of the community. Instead they had begun to concentrate on perfecting the practice of casework as a method for facilitating family and individual adjustments. But to a very considerable degree the community still looked to its constellation of casework agencies for leadership in meeting its relief problems, and most of the cases which came to these agencies came because of a need for financial assistance. From a practical standpoint, therefore, predepression caseworkers had little opportunity to concentrate on the diagnosis and treatment of the type of adjustment problems which require psychiatric understanding, a maximum of professional casework training, and small case loads. Indeed the knowledge and methods of psychiatry were only just beginning to put a deeper content into the thinking of the new profession of social work.

The decade of the 1930s completely changed the position of the private agencies. The public relief programs, first on an emergency and then on a permanent basis, took over the vast bulk of financial assistance cases. Somewhat more recently public welfare agencies in most states have undertaken to provide foster care for dependent and neglected children. As a result of these developments, the private agencies have been concentrating for a decade and a half, or more, on the provision of casework services as their principal objective.

CATEGORICAL COMPLEXITIES

Much of this concentration of casework service has been around certain categories of situations in which troubles tend to appear: the difficulties of transients; of veterans; of unmarried mothers; of dependent and neglected children who require care in foster homes, in day nurseries, in institutions.

Agencies concentrating on the difficulties and circumstances involved in these situations naturally have tended to provide casework for situational or environmental treatment. It will be recalled, however, that in two thirds of the maladjusted families found in St. Paul, there was evidence of behavior disorders which indicated a presumptive need for diagnosis and treatment by some constellation of psychiatric, psychological, and casework skills. Only in one third of these families did it seem that casework assistance was required with respect only to a situational difficulty confronting the family or one of its members.

A very large proportion of services for children traditionally have been organized around categories of dependency and neglect. Early efforts concentrated upon taking them out of bad situations and providing care in institutions. Gradually the emphasis upon providing services in the child's own home, or in a foster home, has resulted in reexamination of the place, and use, of institutions in the total child care program. The present trend of thought is that the institutional setting in this field should be somewhat the same as in the correctional and mental hygiene field—it should be used to provide treatment under the most auspicious circumstances. Authorities generally agree that the institutional structure for this purpose should be on the cottage plan, housing in each cottage not more than twenty children of school age, or twelve under school age.[40] Adequate outdoor play space and indoor recreation rooms should be provided. If necessary, institutions should provide appropriate educational facilities, although whenever possible the schools of the community should be used. In addition to the necessary medical, nursing, and dental services, there should be one or more resident social workers (depending on the size of the institution) and some systematic arrangement for regular provision of psychiatric and psychological services. So called "study homes" which specialize in treatment of seriously disturbed children should have much more intensive service from these three diagnostic and treatment professions.

Although private agencies in the past have carried a very large share of this categorical load, another trend is now well under way. Increasingly, and particularly so within the last decade, public agencies have been employing staff with varying degrees of casework training and experience, to assist people applying for help to adjust to the particular situations within the province of the agencies. The public agencies of St. Paul, for example, were providing four times as much "situational treatment" or "environmental casework" as were the private agencies, and it is believed that St. Paul is a fairly typical community in this respect.

Even in recent years private agencies have carried a substantial share of the responsibility for providing service in connection with several categorical situations in which children find themselves. But as we have seen, this also is changing. In 1947 the United States Children's Bureau estimated that "of the 225,000 children in foster care,

[40] Howard W. Hopkirk, *Institutions Serving Children*, p. 66.

135,000 or 60 percent, are either the direct responsibility of the public agency, or their care under private auspices is being financed from public funds." [41]

Thus the community role of private agencies primarily designed to treat categorical situations is fraught with increasing perplexity. In one direction only has there been a trend toward any structural means of solving the dilemma. It is a traditional theory of both family and children's casework that the child should never be separated from his home if satisfactory arrangements for keeping him there can be worked out. The last decade and a half has seen a practical application of this theory in numerous consolidations of private family agencies with private child placement agencies. This is the standard pattern among Catholic and Jewish Agencies, and the Family Service Association of America reports that over a third of the 250 private agencies in its membership now operate a joint family agency and child placement service.[42]

THE ROLE OF THE FAMILY CASEWORK AGENCY

The family casework agencies of today trace their lineage directly to the charity organization societies, out of which grew most of the present categorical branches of casework service. Perhaps because of this generalized approach, we believe it to be true that these agencies have succeeded better than any other sizable group of private casework agencies in reaching a standard of casework personnel and practice which equips them for the diagnosis and treatment of situations that are complicated by behavior disorders. The statistics collected monthly from the member agencies of the Family Service Association of America consistently show a median case load of about 30 cases per worker. A special inquiry conducted by the Association showed further that two thirds of the agencies reporting had psychiatric consultation regularly available to their staff, and in a substantial number of instances the psychiatrist also interviewed clients whenever this seemed necessary.[43]

The community role of the family casework agency, however, like that of the mental hygiene clinic still needs clarification. In our opin-

41 Mildred Arnold, *Children's Services in the Public Welfare Agency*, p. 5.

42 *Family Service Association of America Directory; 1950.*

43 Information furnished by Miss Anne Shyne of the Family Service Association of America, December 4, 1950.

ion a principal reason for the present confusion is that thought about the role of either of these agencies is bound to be inconclusive unless it is accompanied by thought about the role of the other.

The confusion would be less marked if the services of mental hygiene clinics were integrated with the state institutional program and oriented mainly toward psychotic and psychoneurotic patients. Family casework agencies have shown little ambition to equip themselves for the intensive medical and psychiatric treatment which such cases require.

The situation is different, however, when the orientation of the clinic is wholly or partly toward disorders which manifest themselves in less serious and more varied ways. Under these circumstances the well-equipped mental hygiene clinic can give a case more psychiatric time than the family service agency can make available; on the other hand the latter has more casework time at its disposal. But both agencies have psychiatric and casework talent which they insist must meet accepted standards. The mental hygiene clinic has more confidence and competence in its diagnostic disciplines, and is in a better position to give direct psychiatric treatment. The family service agency has at its command more varied resources for different kinds of treatment. Moreover, at its best the casework agency possesses that extremely important ingredient—experience in dealing with symptoms of disorganization in the total family unit.

Our experience leads us to believe that the existing confusion concerning the respective roles of the generally oriented mental hygiene clinic and the family casework agency will be resolved only by some structural fusion which will preserve the values inherent in the present structure of each agency. Other authorities do not hold this view.

These trends, reflecting various degrees of movement toward a coherent structure within each of the three systems, still leave the community without any pivotal agency or agencies to which to relate all the segments—or even all the important segments—of the present complex structure for providing adjustment services. There is no local agency comparable to the public health department to which agencies participating in the community-wide control of behavior disorders may be related. There is no local agency comparable to the general hospital, to serve as the focal point around which to organize the constellation of services necessary for diagnosing and treating such disorders. There is no pivotal agency comparable to the public welfare department, which consolidates all phases of community responsibility for the problem of dependency.

The adult correctional system is moving toward an ably designed pattern which makes a state authority the pivotal state agency and ultimately would give it administrative control over the various parts of the program. It is a forlorn hope that the first local segment of the correctional structure—the jail—can be incorporated into this consolidated administration at any time in the near future. The second local segment, adult probation, cannot assume local pivotal significance unless it is raised in stature by wider use and by improvement in the quality of its personnel. The juvenile court and its complementary probation service should occupy a pivotal position in relation to the type of juvenile misbehavior which clearly requires authoritative treatment. But the strategic utility of the court is hampered by the confusion of other responsibilities which it often carries. And the design for the integration of this local unit with the state juvenile correctional system is much less clear.

At present the clinic, the local unit of the mental health system, still is likely to be a floating rib. Usually it is not closely integrated with the state institutional system, and it may or may not be used extensively as a resource for diagnosis or consultation. Although those administering the National Mental Health Act would make the clinic the pivotal agency responsible for the several functions of diagnosis, treatment, community-wide discovery, reporting, and systematic control, the practicality of this design is still to be demonstrated. In the casework system the family casework agency, having lost the pivotal characteristics appropriate to the predepression relief setting, has become more and more detached from acceptance of any community-wide responsibility.

The resulting vacuum in the adjustment structure must be filled if there is to develop an effective pattern for a total program to prevent maladjustment and protect the community against its consequences.

Chapter XVI

THE CASE
FOR COMMUNITY
COHERENCE

IN PRESUMING TO MAKE A CASE for a greater measure of coherence among the agencies which deal with the various aspects of maladjustment we may seem to be laboring the point unnecessarily. There is no doubt that intelligent leadership in American communities would welcome any program which served to reduce mental and emotional illness, mental defect, and unsocial, unstable, or irresponsible behavior, and at the same time offered some protection to community citizens against the serious consequences of these difficulties. Only recently, however, have the basic functions essential to such a program emerged with any clarity, and the pivotal units in a community-wide structure have yet to be developed. It may be useful, therefore, to recapitulate certain common denominators in the three systems which, we believe, should impel them toward greater coherence of planning.

THE COMMON DENOMINATORS

To put the matter very simply, the three systems are linked together inextricably, in their interests and in their potentialities for constructive community service, because they draw the disordered persons with whom they deal from the same sources; because the results of their separate failures to prevent and cure ultimately become the same kind of permanent community responsibility; because the essential ingredients for prevention and cure are common to all three systems; and because the meager professional resources necessary to treat and rehabilitate the maladjusted must be husbanded and utilized in a manner calculated to do the most good.

Although state institutions constitute important administrative segments of the correctional and mental health systems, it is well to recall that the great majority of the people served by the two systems reside in the local community and never leave it.

State and federal prisons receive only about one tenth of the number of persons handled locally by the courts and local jails each year.[1] Similarly, only 8 percent of the cases disposed of by 374 juvenile courts reporting to the Children's Bureau were committed to juvenile correctional institutions.[2]

The St. Paul data showed that about four times as many mental defectives were known only to local agencies as were being cared for in the state institutions. National estimates suggest that there are at least ten times as many defective persons at large in the community as are currently under care in state institutions.[3] To be sure, the St. Paul data showed a contrary picture of the mentally ill. There were over twice as many patients from the community in the state institutions for mental disease as there were local persons with a diagnosed psychiatric disorder who were known to community agencies. But the casework and correctional agencies reported some 5,000 persons with symptoms of disorder for whom there was no psychiatric diagnosis. What such a diagnosis might have revealed we do not know. But few will doubt that treatment service should be provided for many cases such as these.

Moreover, evidence is mounting that the families of the maladjusted individuals who come to the attention of any one of the three systems are in high proportion to the families whose members are known to the other two.

We are sure that further research into the significance of this evidence would be extremely fruitful. Meanwhile, on the basis of the St. Paul data, experience in cities maintaining the social breakdown index, and data collected in local surveys, we believe it reasonable to estimate that in most communities a group comprising not more than

[1] U.S. Bureau of the Census, *Statistical Abstract of the United States: 1949*, p. 143.

[2] I. Richard Perlman, "Juvenile Court Statistics, 1944 and 1945," Supplement, *The Child*, XI (November, 1946), 11, Table 6.

[3] Dallas Pratt, *Mental Health Statistics*, p. 2.

5 percent of the total families accounts for more than half the total activity of the casework, mental health, and correctional agencies.

Evidence is also mounting that the various behavior disorders, separately dealt with by the three systems, react on each other in the family setting. Hence failure on the part of any one agency to check these disorders helps to swell the flow of cases toward the terminal agencies for permanent care—state correctional institutions, state mental institutions, and the residual relief load of the public welfare department. The three systems clearly have a joint responsibility to design a local service pattern which will enable them to make the best use of their resources in preventing and reducing the flow of cases to these terminal agencies.

THE COMMON FACTORS IN CAUSE AND CURE

There is now substantial agreement that the agencies in each system should have at their disposal some combination of psychiatric, psychological, and casework service, together with a supporting medical service, in order to diagnose and treat the cases for which they are responsible.

For a long time there has been general agreement that the family plays an important role in the cause and cure of disordered and unsocial behavior. But the practical importance of the family to the organization of the diagnostic and treatment resources of the three systems has been obscured because of undue preoccupation with the behavior of the person. Now the leaders in each system are coming to realize more and more that a family-centered approach is vital to their preventive and rehabilitative efforts.

None of the three systems, however, has designed a complete pattern of diagnostic and treatment service which would combine a family-centered approach with all the essential professional specialties. Nor do we know of any community where the agencies affiliated with any of the three systems provide a generalized family-centered service, equipped to diagnose and treat the complete range of symptoms evidencing disordered behavior. But in a very large proportion of the urban communities known to us, the various services requisite to a well-knit program of diagnosis, treatment, and community protection are available somewhere among the agencies in the three systems.

Within the mental health system are agencies equipped to give direct treatment to *persons* suffering from mental, emotional, and personality defects. Within the casework system are agencies equipped to deal constructively with the disorganization in *families* whose members have mental, emotional, or personality defects. Within the correctional system there are agencies equipped with the authority necessary to control *persons* from such families, whose overt behavior constitutes a community nuisance or menace.

At the risk of some oversimplification we might put the situation in the ordinary urban community even more concretely. Within the mental health system there will be one or more clinics equipped to treat mentally unbalanced persons, but not to diagnose and treat the total family disruption which provides the setting for such disorders. There will be one or more family casework agencies, equipped to deal with the family's total situational troubles, and able also, though only to a limited and as yet undefined extent, to assist the unbalanced persons in the family. There will be the adult and juvenile agencies which exercise authority over a portion of the unbalanced persons from the disorganized families. But only rarely does one find the local agencies of the correctional system equipped with diagnostic and treatment resources.

THE PAUCITY OF TOTAL RESOURCES

To provide the diagnostic and treatment resources needed by the agencies of these three systems, there are an estimated 4,000 psychiatrists, 1,000 clinical psychologists, and 15,000 case workers. Even the most optimistic view cannot expect the potential demand for qualified personnel to be met in any foreseeable future. In their competition for this personnel the agencies of the three systems, handicapped by rapid staff turnover, often have to resort to a thin pretense of competence, which is detrimental to sound treatment as well as to agency policy.

In the interests of all concerned, we believe the three systems should clarify personnel priorities on the basis of joint community objectives and in terms of a pattern of service designed to utilize total available resources in the attainment of those objectives. In our view, the objective to which most communities would give top priority would be the prevention and reduction of the flow of cases into the three terminal agencies—the residual relief load of the public welfare department, the state mental institutions, and the state correctional institutions.

However, in respect to any plan for making better use of present diagnostic and treatment resources, one must recognize that in many communities the private agencies of the casework and mental health systems now have a virtual monopoly of the combination of personnel and working conditions essential to service at the diagnostic and treatment level. In St. Paul, 13.3 percent of the total adjustment service provided during the month of our study was at this level and all of it was provided by a small number of private casework and mental hygiene agencies. The situation would differ in other communities, but everywhere the service of this quality is preponderantly service under private auspices.

There is good reason for this. Private agencies in both systems have pioneered in developing standards of professional practice and training. They have been able to control the size of case loads in relation to staff, thereby assuring the practical ability to diagnose and treat the clients who come to them. Salary ranges are less rigid, and in any short swing of time this fact gives them a practical competitive advantage.

Private agencies have no such advantage over the long swing, however. Experience in other fields has shown that they cannot continue to provide a function which has attained community-wide significance unless they are able to discharge it with community-wide satisfaction. Otherwise, the shift to public service is inevitable. Then, though the structure of the private agency may persist, its function becomes of negligible importance to the total community program.

In our view, placing upon private service in urban communities the principal responsibility for provision of diagnosis and treatment at this level has much to commend it. For some time to come, we shall continue to need the pioneering initiative, the flexibility, and the capacity to develop personnel and leadership which have been regarded as salient characteristics of voluntary welfare enterprise.

Anyone who runs may read that the present concentration of trained personnel in private agencies can continue only if these agencies take their place in a pattern of service designed to achieve new community objectives supported by all three systems. Otherwise the fierce competition to build personnel and resources at all points for all purposes will continue. No agency would profit from such an out-and-out competitive struggle, but in the long run private service would be the greatest loser.

This, briefly, is the case in theory and in practical necessity for the inevitable interdependence of the three systems that minister to the community's adjustment ills. Each system must lean upon the others if it is to serve the community effectively even within the boundaries of its traditional responsibility.

PRINCIPLES FOR A COMMUNITY-WIDE EXPERIMENT

The task of the authors of this book would have been much easier if any city had ever undertaken a considered community-wide effort to reduce the extent and consequences of the maladies which are included under the term "maladjustment." We believe, however, that there is now sufficient knowledge about the causes and characteristics of maladjustment, the functions essential to a community-wide attack upon it, and the structure through which these functions may be organized to warrant experimentation to develop principles and procedures for achieving community-wide prevention and control.

The purpose of the experiment should be to prevent and reduce the ultimate consequences of maladjustment. These consequences may be measured in several ways: by the flow of cases into the three terminal agencies; by the gross volume of behavior disorders, and by family recidivism in behavior disorders; by a combination of these devices; or by others appropriate to the basic purpose, designed with equal or greater precision.

Two factors are essential to the success of the experiment and to its validity: it must have at its disposal certain basic resources in the community, and it must develop basic control procedures as a condition of its continuing operation.

FOUNDATION RESOURCES

Administrative arrangements inevitably would have to vary with the size of the community and the traditional structure of its agencies.

But the following resources should be available and clearly related to the conduct of the program:

Family-centered diagnostic and treatment services.—These should offer treatment of cases involving psychotic and serious psychoneurotic disorders; treatment of cases involving mental and emotional disabilities where the prognosis is fair or good; supportive treatment of seriously disorganized families with complex personality defects, where the prognosis is poor.

Family-centered situational treatment.—This would relieve acute and chronic emergencies not involving personality defects.

Specialized person-centered services.—These should include direct psychiatric treatment, in an institutional setting for psychotic and psychoneurotic patients; casework treatment on the appropriate level in connection with probation, institutional care, and parole for adult and juvenile offenders; foster placement of children, in family homes and institutions; day care for children; single transients; problems of physical illness; institutional and boarding home care for aged and infirm adults.

In broad principle, the specialized services should be used primarily as supplementary resources for family-centered treatment, except under circumstances in which it is clear that the cause of the person's problem is not related to his family, and that his problem is not creating serious complications in his family's life.

CONTROL PROCEDURES

Administrative responsibility for the experimental development of control procedures should be placed in a single unit which might be either the public welfare department, as we have suggested in another connection, or the public health department, or a generalized family diagnostic and treatment agency. A unit might be designed especially for this purpose if none of the existing agencies was considered appropriate. More important than the structural setting of the unit is the necessity that it be staffed by personnel whose professional discipline combines competence in community organization with knowledge about the characteristics of mental and emotional difficulties, behavior disorders, and situational problems, and about the services appropriate to their diagnosis and treatment. Equally important is the need to guard against confusion between the develop-

ment of these control procedures and any diagnostic and treatment
services which the agency might be responsible for administering.

Systematic identification.—Our experience suggests that procedures to identify and discover cases manifesting symptoms of behavior
disorder should be directed toward the various types of cases in this
sequence: the small core of disorganized families which produce such
a large part of the adjustment difficulties now claiming the attention
of agencies in the three systems; families with pathological symptoms
indicative of a trend toward disruption; cases giving symptomatic
evidence of an early stage of unbalanced behavior or family stress.

From a practical standpoint, we believe that procedures for the
systematic identification of the first group of cases have priority in
strategic importance. In every community a high proportion of present agency activity in all three systems is already directed to this
group. We feel strongly that the sum total of this activity is very
wasteful. In order to free the community's diagnostic and treatment
resources for their most constructive use, if for no other reason, the
confused activity now concentrated on these families by many agencies must be organized more economically.

Our experience also suggests three procedures which are useful in
identifying this group of disorganized families. These procedures are
not mutually exclusive, although in certain communities there might
be an advantage in using only one of them during the initial stages
of the experiment. The first is the identification of the group of
multiproblem families, either by the methods used in the St. Paul
project or by some simplified adaptation of them. The St. Paul data
identified a hard core of seriously disorganized families, in each of
which there was some combination of two or more of the three major
problems, dependency, maladjustment, and ill-health. About one-
half of *all* families with maladjustment difficulties and 43 percent of
those with behavior disorders were in this multiproblem group. We
have seen that the dependency and health agencies have as great a
stake in this group of families as do the adjustment agencies. Hence
the health and dependency agencies would have to be full partners
in planning any experimental undertaking which used the identification of this group as its starting point.

A second possibility is to focus upon the identification of families
in which there are mental defectives. In St. Paul persons with mental

defect accounted for about one quarter of all the people with behavior disorders who were known to any agency during the single month of our study. National estimates of the prevalence of mental defect in the general population suggest that this was a substantial proportion of all the defective persons in the community. Our data confirm the well-known fact that the presence of defective persons in a family makes for serious disorganization and often may precipitate behavior that will bring family members to the attention of one or all of the service systems. Consequently, identification of cases of mental defect would produce a considerable nucleus of those families who are responsible for a disproportionately large share of community concern.

A third procedure might involve use of the social breakdown index, designed for the current reporting of families in which there are incidents of crime, juvenile delinquency, child neglect, divorce, and illegitimacy and commitments for mental disease and mental defect. This device has the advantage of including a varied list of symptoms. Recidivism within the categories also would give a fairly precise clue to the seriousness of family disorganization.

None of these devices was invented for the precise purposes of such a demonstration as we have in mind. But experience with them gives us a background for the development of comparable methods for identifying the core of families requiring so much attention from the agencies of the three systems.

We have had less experience with ways in which to identify the group of families who are "once removed" in pathological seriousness from this multiproblem core. But the St. Paul data suggested that there is such a group with characteristics meriting further research. These are families with maladjustment problems and are known only to the adjustment agencies. In such cases the specific evidences of maladjustment were not very different from those found in the hard core of multiproblem families. Mental disease, mental defect, antisocial behavior, and social irresponsibility were found among them in about the same proportions as among the multiproblem group, and there was a similar intermixture of problems. On the other hand, no family in the second group was on relief during the month of our study (although many of them had children under the care of the child welfare division of the Public Welfare Department). Apparently their health was better. They were also younger families and more of their members were young children. These external characteristics seem to suggest potentialities which would make the systematic identification of such families desirable as part of the community program for prevention and control.

There has been relatively little systematic experimentation with case finding procedures aimed to identify either early symptoms of personal mental or emotional disorder, or early symptoms of family disorganization. Our own and other data have shown that the truants of yesterday tend to become the delinquents of today, and the criminals of tomorrow. As we have indicated, there is considerable evidence of family predisposition towards certain of the psychoses and psychoneuroses. Most authorities agree that broken homes produce mental and emotional problems in much greater proportion than do those where the family remains intact. These and other practical "clues" all have significance in the development of procedures for discovering cases at an earlier stage than the one at which they now come to agency attention.

Prognostic, diagnostic, and symptomatic classification.—The progressive development of three different (but by no means mutually exclusive) types of classificational procedures would have to be an integral part of the experiment. Orderly procedures for the reduction and control of maladjustment cannot be based merely on the identification and recording of unrelated symptoms, for such symptoms give little guidance as to the basic types of treatment appropriate to a given case. Conversely, it is neither feasible nor intelligent to assume that every case recorded must be thoroughly discussed by all the agencies and all the experts who might conceivably have a concern with it. To avoid this dilemma, the units responsible for the control procedures, the various agencies which identify and report symptoms, and the agencies responsible for diagnosis and treatment, must have classificational guides to facilitate the orderly handling of different types of cases and their routing to the appropriate community resources.

We have seen that both the mental health system and the correctional system have considerable experience with workable classifications designed to make their institutional treatment more efficient and effective. Certain of the classifications which they use are basically prognostic. Mental institutions make the following distinctions: patients who are acutely ill, and therefore presumably capable of responding to short-time treatment; patients for whom there is at least a fair chance that treatment over a longer period may effect cure or substantial improvement; patients who are convalescent and definitely on their way to recovery; and chronic patients for whom hope of improvement is very poor. Within its more rigid legal framework, the correctional system aims at somewhat the same type of prognostic classification in its assignments to minimum, medium, and maximum security institutions, as well as in its intra-institutional assignments. Orderly and effective use of the different types of local resources will depend, in the first instance, on the development of similar prognostic guides, of a reasonably precise nature, which can be used by all agencies participating in the experiment.

It goes without saying that the better the diagnosis, the more accurate the prognosis. While diagnostic classifications serve primarily to aid the professional specialist in giving treatment, their importance to the community-wide program also is very great. Psychiatry and psychology have classifications of mental illness and mental defect which are subject to a continuous process of refinement and professional debate. But no one as yet has undertaken responsibility for developing diagnostic classifications appropriate for use in the treatment of family disorganization. We believe that some such classificational process is needed in order to provide an increasingly sound basis for prognostic judgments.

A useful step in this connection was suggested by the St. Paul project when it devised an elementary method of distinguishing between situational problems and behavior disorders as components in family breakdown. This distinction was made, with what we believe to be a reasonable measure of accuracy, on the basis of agency records. Whatever its utility to those professionally responsible for family treatment, we think its practical significance as a guide to the more orderly use of different types of community service is considerable.

Psychology long ago developed a fairly precise tool for the classification and detection of the symptomatic evidences of mental defect. More recently there has been experimentation with specific tests designed to detect evidences of personality disorder and emotional deviation. In general, however, little thought has been given to classifying or detecting the early symptoms of family disorganization. Again, we believe that the progressive development of some such tool must be a necessary part of any continuing experimentation with community-wide discovery procedures.

Precision of classification grows with knowledge, research, and experience, especially when tested in practical application. Experimentation with control procedures does not have to wait upon the perfection of prognostic, diagnostic, and symptomatic classifications to a point beyond scientific and professional controversy. Rather, the development of classifications for the purposes of prognosis, diagnosis, and discovery must be an integral part of any experiment to prevent and reduce behavior disorders in the community.

Continuity and appropriateness in family treatment.—It should be clear that methods for the systematic identification and classification of basic types of cases are but a means to an end in any over-all plan. Their purpose is to facilitate the invention and perfection of procedures which will provide each case with such appropriate and sustained treatment as is compatible with the best and most economical use of total resources for preventing and reducing maladjustment.

This is the crux of any experimental undertaking. For at this point it will be necessary to devise policies and procedures governing the action which the community organizing unit should take to assure continuity and appropriateness of treatment for the cases it has identified and classified. Obviously any such action must be based on reasonably up-to-date data. Three principal sources can provide the kind of data needed: periodic reports from agencies currently responsible for service to the family or its members; reports from official or other sources regarding significant incidents which affect the family; reports by the organizing unit's own field staff, when data from other sources are inadequate, or under any other circumstances in which such staff service proves routinely useful.

Policies governing the case-by-case action taken by the organizing unit should emerge in the course of the experiment as a result of increasing skill in:

Making practical prognostic judgments on the basis of reported and assembled facts about the case

Interpreting the significance of successively reported incidents of behavior disorder and situational difficulty

Identifying, through the use of its own or other facilities, those cases which require a more thorough family diagnosis

Making periodic reviews and evaluations of family progress on the basis of the data from all these sources

Interpreting the community-wide policies and practices which evolve from the experiment

Negotiating strategic assignments of community responsibility

Evaluation.—In any such experiment, procedures for evaluation obviously must be set up at three interrelated levels. First, methods which will give clues to family improvement or deterioration must be devised as an integral part of the procedures which guide the case-by-case action of the central organizing unit. Second, there must be additional methods for measuring the results of the total program in preventing and reducing the most serious community-wide consequences of maladjustment. Third, against the background of success or failure reflected by the first two methods, there must be an evaluation of the effectiveness of the procedures which the community organizing unit has instituted.

To repeat, we believe that there is now enough knowledge and enough experience to warrant experimental undertakings with this broad purpose and design. On the other hand, we doubt that the "Case for Coherence" can be translated effectively into a "Community-wide Plan" acceptable to communities throughout the country without the stimulus of such broadly and carefully considered experimentation. Experience with sporadic and casual attempts to bring greater coherence into community efforts to prevent and reduce the separate symptoms and consequences of maladjustment have not been fruitful. It is the growing understanding of the integrity of the problem and the integrity of the services which have grown up to deal with different parts of it, which gives us hope that the next decade will see significant demonstration of the potentials for community-wide effectiveness.

RECREATIONAL NEED

Chapter XVII

ACCEPTANCE OF
RESPONSIBILITY

SINCE THE TURN OF THE CENTURY, public recreational facilities have been provided by an increasing number of communities. The general "need" which has been met in this way requires little exposition. Everyone recognizes his own desire for satisfactory activities in the hours not devoted to work, and knows the feeling of boredom, and even of frustration, which comes when opportunities for recreation are missing.

The complexities of urban life make it difficult for the city dweller himself to provide all the leisure activities and facilities he needs. How many can hope to own a beach or golf course? For those of an older generation "recreation" brings to mind a "nostalgic picture of barefoot boys and faithful Rovers wandering through the woods and over the hills, enticing the canny catfish, snaring the elusive rabbit, finding the mother robin in her nest, or being gorgeously delinquent in some convenient neighbor's melon patch." [1] For a member of a newer generation this picture is replaced by the brick and mortar of his front yard or the street; the hard surfaced playground with its sandpiles, streamlined swings and chutes; organized sports of high school and college; dance halls and bowling alleys; summer camps, and the gang or club with which he spends his leisure time. Even in rural areas, where natural resources may be abundant, the individual and the family need outlets for social activities. Community parks, playgrounds, social centers, gymnasiums, and swimming pools provide these opportunities.

It is difficult to determine with any degree of accuracy for the nation how much responsibility of this kind the communities have assumed. A few studies, made under our own or other auspices, throw

---

[1] Bradley Buell, "Let's Look at the Record," *Survey Midmonthly*, LXXXII, No. 2 (February, 1946), 42.

some light on the proportion of the urban population which now depends in some measure upon public and voluntary community-supported recreation services. Data from our St. Paul project disclosed that persons from about one fifth of all the families in that community were participating in activities of such agencies during the single month of our study. Similar data for a twelve-month period, gathered some years earlier in Dayton, Ohio, showed that members of about the same proportion of families depended on community-provided recreational activities. In Birmingham, Alabama, available data were only for the families which used the voluntary community-supported services; here 11 percent of all families participated in private agency programs during the course of a year.

In St. Paul 7.1 percent of all persons participated in community-supported program groups, and in Ann Arbor, Michigan, during a twelve-month period the proportion was 17 percent. These data, however, include only those who participated in organized activities and do not include the unorganized use of parks or other outdoor or indoor public facilities which constitute a substantial part of the community's public recreational investment.

From a few additional cities we have data showing the proportion of the population depending in some measure for their recreation upon the voluntary agencies: 7.9 percent in Hartford, Connecticut; 15 percent in Waterbury, Connecticut; 8.9 percent in Peoria, Illinois; 8.9 percent in Honolulu, Hawaii; 10.4 percent in Wichita, Kansas. What additional proportions of the population of these cities were utilizing the organized tax-supported services we do not know.

Even such fragmentary data indicate that community-supported recreation is of basic importance to a sizable proportion of the families in urban communities. In St. Paul these services touched 18 percent of the families in the community, as compared with 14.7 percent by the health services, 10.2 percent by its adjustment services and 6.7 percent by its dependency services. It is fair to assume that the "recreation" agencies usually reach a larger proportion of the total number of families in the community than do those which deal with other problems.

Despite very incomplete data, we estimate that annual expenditures for all types of community-supported recreation, exclusive of capital construction, are in the neighborhood of $500 million. In the last decade, moreover, such expenditures have been increasing steadily. A study of 21 urban areas showed an increase of 140.9 percent in expenditures by public recreation agencies (exclusive of park maintenance) between 1940 and 1948, and 110 percent by private agencies in the same period.[2] Community chests throughout the country, which provide a substantial proportion of the income of private agencies, have consistently increased their appropriations to recreation agencies, in recent years.

FOUR COMMUNITY-SUPPORTED SYSTEMS

Even in the midst of complex urban life, the community does not have to provide opportunities for all kinds of recreational expression for everybody. People contrive a great deal of recreation for themselves, in the home and in the family circle, through affiliation with social, professional, church and other organizations and through the purchase of commercial recreation. One of the few attempts to discover how people spend the leisure time available to them was made in Westchester County, New York, nearly two decades ago.[3] It was found that, depending upon economic status, men spent about half their leisure time at home and women from 55 to 65 percent, boys 42 percent, and girls about 50 percent.

Social organizations and commercial recreation enterprises may each be characterized as a "system" in the general sense in which we have used that term. A common denominator of all church, social, fraternal, and civic recreational clubs and organizations, and of cultural and other societies is their intent to offer opportunities for leisure activities and personal associations. The common purpose of all commercial recreation is to make a profit by putting such opportunities at the disposal of people who can and will pay for them. These two systems provide a very substantial part of the leisure and recreational activities in which the people in any community engage.

The study of Westchester County, for example, found that in a well-to-do community 40 percent of the adults belonged to at least one social club, and 15 percent to more than one. In a poorer resi-

---

[2] Community Chests and Councils of America, *Expenditures for Community Health and Welfare, 31 Urban Areas, 1948*, p. 4.

[3] George A. Lundberg, *Leisure, a Suburban Study*, pp. 128, 136.

dential town 36 percent belonged to some club, and 9 percent to more than one. For men in the former community, religious organizations, military, sport, social, and recreational clubs were the most popular. In the less advantaged area, civic and fraternal organizations were most frequently reported. In both areas, religious organizations and women's clubs topped the list for women.

Commercial recreation puts at the disposal of the community a great variety of leisure opportunities. Annual consumer expenditures run into billions of dollars—the amount depending upon what one chooses to classify as "recreation." The various forms of "spectator entertainment" undoubtedly lead: the movies; the theater; sports and athletic contests with either professional or amateur contestants; horse, dog, and automobile races. Amusement parks and a great variety of amusement devices are conducted for profit. So are facilities for certain kinds of individual participation in games of skill: bowling, billiards and pool; less frequently tennis courts and pay-as-you-go golf courses. Bathing beaches, swimming pools, riding academies sometimes are commercially successful. The role played by restaurants, bars, taverns, commercial dance halls may not be ignored. Finally one should note that "vacation" businesses of all kinds aggregate a tremendous sum.

Except for licensing and minimum policing of commercial recreation, the community as such takes no part in directing the activities of these two systems. Little systematic data are readily available about the role which they play in meeting the total leisure needs of the community. Our own research has been insufficient to determine the part which is appropriately theirs in a balanced plan to meet the community-wide recreational needs.

It is against this background of opportunities for leisure activities provided by the family circle, through social organizations, and by commercial enterprises, however, that four community-provided recreation systems have developed. These are the municipal recreation system; the voluntary youth and recreation system; the federal rural youth system; and the system of federal and state parks.

THE MUNICIPAL RECREATION SYSTEM

At last report, some 1,917 different incorporated local jurisdictions throughout the country were making some provision for the maintenance and operation of local parks and playgrounds and for the conduct of organized recreational programs.[4] In specific detail these programs varied greatly but usually included athletics, competitive sports, and social, cultural and educational activities. Most often the responsible unit of government is the municipality; sometimes it is the county or the district. Except in three states, the principal support is from local tax funds, without benefit of either state or federal subsidy. The program is always administered by some unit of local government—a park department, a recreation commission, the school board, or an administrative combination of these. Many of these local units are loosely affiliated, for conference and consultative purposes, through the National Recreation Association. On the basis of available data we estimate that throughout the country public recreation expenditures total $30 million to $40 million annually.

THE VOLUNTARY YOUTH AND RECREATION SYSTEM

In lesser degree than almost any other of the movements which we have characterized as "systems," are the voluntary agencies which serve the youth and recreation needs bound together by organic or professional homogeneity. The general characteristics of most of them are well known: the Young Men's Christian Association; the Young Women's Christian Association; the youth activities of the Salvation Army; the Boy Scouts of America; the Girl Scouts of America; the Camp Fire Girls; the Boys' Clubs of America; local nonsectarian settlements and neighborhood houses which are affiliated through the National Federation of Settlements; local Jewish community centers affiliated through the National Jewish Welfare Board; local Catholic centers and youth organizations affiliated through the National Catholic Youth Council. Other local and national organizations concerned with the leisure interests in different communities and different sections of the country have many characteristics in common with these.

Community support is derived from funds contributed in large measure through community chests. Administration is through a board of local citizens. In almost every instance the board has a great, if not complete, structural autonomy, but direct and indirect ties with the national movement are very strong. With certain exceptions,

4 National Recreation Association, *Recreation*, XLIII, No. 3 (June, 1949), 100.

the national agencies with which they are affiliated have the strength of influence which accrues from large operating budgets, extensive field and supervisory staffs, and national constituencies devoted to promoting their general purposes.

The collective importance of this group of agencies is illustrated by the fact that their total expenditures, in the average urban community, exceed those of the public recreation agencies. In 1948, average per capita expenditures for these private services, in the selected communities for which accurate data are available, was $1.64. For the public recreation agencies in those same communities it was $1.28.[5] Comparable nationwide data are difficult to assemble. Each national agency, naturally, publishes any such information in a form suited to its own purposes, and there is no way to estimate the duplications of membership. Total expenditures by all these agencies probably exceed $250 million annually.

THE FEDERAL YOUTH SYSTEM

Although certain of the national agencies have units which cover small towns and rural areas, their predominant focus is on the urban community. Other programs, however, are organized for boys and girls in rural and agricultural sections by several agencies of the Federal Government. The best-known units in this group are the 4-H Clubs organized by the Extension Service of the Department of Agriculture. The Future Farmers of America, the New Farmers of America, the Home Makers of America, and the New Home Makers of America organized through the United States Office of Education, belong to this "system" also. Although of a quite different nature, we may note here that the Veterans Administration and the Armed Forces also take direct responsibility for organizing recreational opportunities for their special clientele.

THE FEDERAL AND STATE PARK SYSTEM

Agencies of the federal and the various state governments provide for public use of forest preserves, parks, camping and picnic sites, and spots of natural beauty and interest. The National Park Service, the Forestry Service, and the Fish and Wild Life Service are the prin-

[5] *Expenditures for Community Health and Welfare, 1948, op. cit.,* p. 39.

cipal federal units in this system; state agencies develop and control similar facilities.

There is no structural relationship between federal and state agencies which administer parks and areas near large population centers. These also are used extensively. In general the larger outlying areas, under whatever auspices, are preserved in their natural state. In more accessible areas, the state park departments have constructed swimming pools and bathing beaches, boat houses and docks, hiking, bridle, and nature trails, winter sports facilities, nature museums, and areas for games and sports.

Of these four systems, only two—the municipal recreation system and the voluntary youth and recreation system—have a direct bearing upon the programs for the urban community, which is the primary concern of this volume. The programs of the federal youth system are avowedly rural in scope, and the content of their activities is inappropriate to a city setting. Federal and state parks, with vacation and weekend resources, are greatly used by city dwellers. Easy access by automobile, train, or bus has steadily increased their importance to the recreational scheme of the ordinary urbanite. Our research, on the other hand, failed to determine the effect of this availability upon the degree of responsibility assumed by the community for meeting its own recreational needs.

THE MEAGER ROOTS OF PUBLIC POLICY

While precedents can be found in the history of Greece and Rome and even in primitive societies, the modern concept of community responsibility for recreation has developed in the twentieth century.

The settlement movement in this country was well under way as the nineteenth century was ending. Out of the settlements' concern for the economically disadvantaged child of the urban slums came the impetus for public playgrounds which gained momentum during the early years of the twentieth century. Although a number of schools had opened outdoor gymnasiums, and many athletic clubs had been organized in an earlier period, the opening in 1885 of the Sand Garden, an outdoor play center at the Parmenter Children's Mission in Boston, is generally credited with marking the beginning of the organized community recreation movement in this country.[6] The great early expansion of city parks and playgrounds took place after the organization in 1906 of the present National Recreation Association. Recognized as of prime importance in present-day recreation are the programs of the YMCA (organized in 1851) and the YWCA (organized in 1906) ; these were started essentially as religious rather than recreational undertakings. The 4-H clubs were started in 1903, the Boy Scouts and the Camp Fire Girls in 1910, and the Girl Scouts in 1912.

The course of public policy toward public recreation has followed much the same trend that we have noted in regard to hospitals, visiting nursing, and other forms of organized medical care. The original concept of a "charitable" service, designed in this instance to supply playgrounds, opportunities for games and other activities for the "poor," has gradually changed to encompass the provision of similar opportunities for everyone. According to the National Recreation Association, it is now the purpose of the municipal recreation system to see to it "That every child in America shall have a chance to play," and even more comprehensively "That everybody in America, young or old, shall have an opportunity to find the best and most satisfying use of leisure time." Confusion still persists regarding the reasons for this transition from the "poor" to "everybody."

In respect to the agencies of the voluntary recreation system, public policy has been marked by the fact that, in considerable degree, their original concept was neither "recreational" nor "public." The Christian associations were deeply religious in purpose, and social and recreational activities were initiated as the means to further that end. Similarly, the Scouts were dedicated to the building of "character" and "good citizenship." In each case, generalities of purpose were regarded as justification for specific activities. For years the settlement movement was chiefly interested in improving the conditions under which its constituents lived; social and recreational activities were offered as a means to that end. Other agencies provided recreational and social activities in order to preserve cultural or racial homogeneity. In accepting these motives as valid, the public inevitably overlooked a considerable contribution to community recreational life.

Certain agencies of the voluntary system seek and maintain a re-

[6] George D. Butler, *Introduction to Community Recreation*, p. 60.

stricted membership, with attributes of organization morale, member rights, and duties. Thus, although all are supported at least partly by the general public, their restrictive characteristics have tended to obscure their definite contribution to recreational resources.

It is our view that genuine awareness of recreation as a general problem of community concern did not develop in this country before the First World War. Then recreational activities were greatly expanded in more than 600 communities adjacent to military posts and in over 50 industrial centers, under the aegis of War Camp Community Services (promoted and organized by the National Recreation Association). Large campaigns for funds were undertaken. On the military posts the YMCA, the Knights of Columbus, the Friendly Service League of the Quakers, the Jewish Welfare Board, and the Salvation Army conducted programs with the assistance of a coordinating board.[7] Although special religious and other interests were not ignored, recreational and social activities as such inevitably dominated all else in the public mind and in their common plans.

While the end of the war saw the different agencies return to their several ways of operation, stimulus had been given to a greatly increased public interest in recreation for its own sake. That interest found fruitful soil in higher standards of living, more free time, and the growing complexities of urban life. Facilities for municipal recreation expanded, as did the number of employees necessary to supervise and maintain them. So too did the budgets and the activities of the private agencies, many of which participated in the community chest drives first organized for joint financing during this period. This in turn emphasized the contribution made by these agencies to the community's total recreational needs.

The decade of the thirties abruptly changed the soil in which the roots of public policy toward expanding recreation had been flourishing. Private funds were seriously curtailed. Relief and assistance, as we have noted, demanded and received first priority from community chest funds. By 1933 the budgets of private recreation agencies were reduced by almost 50 percent. At the same time, however, public recreation agencies received aid from an unexpected quarter: CWA, FERA, and, later, WPA funds were put at their disposal, not only for the improvement of parks and other facilities, but for the needed addi-

[7] Harold D. Meyer and Charles K. Brightbill, *Community Recreation,* p. 11.

tional personnel. It is estimated that 45,000 full-time recreation workers were added to municipal departments throughout the country in
this period.[8]

In the 1940s, war again demanded the expansion of recreation activities in communities adjacent to military posts and industrial es-
tablishments, this time on a much greater scale than in the First
World War. The principal national private agencies joined together
to form the United Service Organization Inc., which, at its peak,
administered 3,000 different operations in the United States and other
parts of the Western hemisphere.[9] Responsibility for stimulating,
planning, and assisting in the organization of local resources, as distinct from the administrative operation of the USO building units,
was vested this time in a newly created federal agency—the Recreation Division of the Federal Security Agency. Its field staff covered all
sections of the United States. By organizing local communities, giving
consultation, making surveys, developing local and professional leadership, it endeavored throughout the course of its career to lay the
foundation for a continuing community-wide leadership and interest
in recreational matters.

There can be no doubt that at this turning point of the century, it
has become a matter of public policy for communities to provide
adequate recreational opportunities for those who dwell therein. But
the roots of that policy have grown mainly in three short decades. Each
decade has increased public demand for community-supported recreation; each decade has offered newly emergent opportunities for
expansion in the two community recreation systems. The special purposes of each system have been accommodated to the more general
purposes of the whole community. These processes of accommodation
and clarification are still at work. But, regarding public policy on the
provision of recreational opportunities, there remain the questions,
"How much?" "What kind?" and "For whom?"

COMMUNITY-WIDE PROGRAM ISSUES

The elementary requirements for recreation are simple—facilities,
equipment, and leadership on the one hand, and a program of activities on the other. But complications arise when these elements are
translated into specific services for specific groups of people. Facilities

[8] *Ibid.*, p. 15.   [9] *Ibid.*, pp. 18, 19.

range from great parks to little rooms where clubs can meet and art classes can be held. The program ranges from the organization of dozens of athletic teams and hundreds of persons for sports tournaments to specialized services for particular children.

These different enterprises call for different professional training and skills, for different methods of program organization. Some require extensive financial resources, while others can be provided with limited facilities and small outlay. Not all of the ten or twenty agencies in a typical middle-sized city can be equipped to operate them; there must be some division of labor.

Underlying these perplexities is the fact that both public and private recreation service has vastly expanded in these last three decades. Each private agency has developed and extended the program and facilities best suited to meet its own particular objectives. The public agencies with their broader range have reached out in many different directions. Costs have risen steadily and there is a practical question as to how long and how far this trend can continue. There may be, a few thoughtful leaders are beginning to realize, a "saturation point," beyond which the provision of community supported activities is unnecessary and uneconomical.

It is to these issues in community-wide planning that we turn in the succeeding chapters of this section. In respect to some issues there is accepted experience and practice to follow in improving adequacy and efficiency. In respect to others there is much less to go on, and we have been compelled to draw, in so far as it seems profitable, upon our own experience and research.

It seems to us that the formation of sound plans to meet community-wide recreational needs must depend upon:

1. Available knowledge of the nature of the needs and their characteristics of strategical significance to community action
2. An understanding of the basic functions the community service program must fulfill
3. A comprehension of the community-wide agency structure through which the two principal systems now administer these services, and of issues relevant to its simplification and improvement
4. Constructive elements which lend themselves to the development of a more coherent community system and the framework through which it may be achieved

Chapter XVIII

SOME STRATEGIC CHARACTERISTICS OF RECREATIONAL NEED

RECREATIONAL AUTHORITIES assume that recreation is necessary to everyone because of the many and diverse physical, mental, and emotional satisfactions which accrue from it. This is an hypothesis drawn so directly from human experience as to be axiomatic. The easy acceptance of this generality, however, has tended to obscure certain qualitative aspects of the "need" for recreation. About two of these, it seems to us, more precise knowledge is necessary.

The first qualitative aspect derives from the obvious fact that different people need different kinds of recreation at different times. Not everyone needs to play football, to paint, dance, or swim. Knowledge about the "why" of these differences, as well as of their proportionate distribution, has great strategic importance to any community-wide program. The second aspect derives from the equally apparent fact that the community does not have to provide all people with all their opportunities for recreation. As we noted in the preceding chapter, a great many people find sufficient opportunities through the home, social organizations, or commercial recreation. The community needs to plan only for those who are lacking in these resources.

Obstacles to recreation may be presented by the environment, as, for example, by the limitation of space and facilities in modern cities. They may also be presented by the individual. Little attention has been given to why recreational needs vary or to the obstacles which prevent an individual from finding the answer to his own need. The agencies have been preoccupied with expanding their services and improving professional quality, rather than with analyzing the characteristics of community-wide need.

In classifying our own materials and experience for this purpose we have chosen to consider three characteristics of recreational need: (1) characteristic needs for satisfaction; (2) characteristic limitation upon opportunity for these satisfactions; (3) characteristic needs in the life cycle.

CHARACTERISTIC NEEDS FOR SATISFACTION

Psychologists, as well as philosophically inclined recreation authorities, voice the belief that the need for recreation stems from deep instinctive and emotional drives. One of the more recent studies set forth a variety of reasons why people find enjoyment in recreational activities.[1] Briefly summarized, these include:

1) Pure fun and relaxation, the sense of freedom and joy secured through participation in the activity
2) Release of physical and emotional energy
3) A sense of power through control of the whole body, or through control of the hands in such processes as crafts; the sense of power over materials
4) The chance to escape from one's self and from the reality of the moment, to make use of imagination and to express fantasy, to have experiences not possible in real life
5) The opporutnity to find adventure
6) The opportunity to find security
7) The element of sociability, the opportunity to meet new people, to make new friends
8) Pleasant associations gained through past experiences

It is apparent that this list, as would any other, includes general satisfactions achieved in many different settings, in the office or plant, among friends and neighbors, in the home. In forming these lists, social scientists have not precisely related each "impulse" to the particular type of recreational pursuit which would provide the most satisfying outlet for it. Nor, conversely, have recreation authorities precisely related the outlets proffered by them to the impulses and drives which scientists believe us to possess.

Nevertheless, recreation leaders know from experience what people like to do in their leisure time. Much of this knowledge has been gained through trial and error. Together, public and private recrea-

[1] Gertrude Wilson and Gladys Ryland, *Social Group Work Practice*, pp. 212, 213.

tion programs offer literally hundreds of activities from which people may choose those which give them the maximum satisfaction, as "water seeks its own level." Customarily this multiplicity of specific activities is classified either alphabetically or according to administrative convenience.

For our purposes we have chosen a fivefold classification which seems to give a pragmatic indication of major satisfactions: (1) sports and games; (2) social occasions; (3) the arts; (4) informal education; (5) friendship groups. Each of these broad groupings reflects an underlying interest which produces a distinctive type of satisfaction for the average participant. "Sports and games" is a generic term for a multitude of physical activities. Sociability, or friendly association, is the common denominator among the many kinds of social occasion which recreation offers. Outlets for esthetic and creative capacities are found in the opportunities for participation in and appreciation of the arts. Outlets for intellectual interests constitute the common purpose of informal education. Friendship groups meet a special need of teen-age youth. For any one individual a given activity may meet a number of specific interests, and his participation may be due to a complicated mixture of motives. But to put it negatively, a person who dislikes physical activity is unlikely to participate in sports and games; an essentially unsociable person does not seek out social occasions; lack of an aesthetic or creative impulse is not conducive to interest in the arts; opportunities for informal education will not attract persons disinterested in using their minds; older people are not attracted by the forms and patterns of teen-age association.

SPORTS AND GAMES

We have included in this classification all activities which are primarily physical or athletic and which give opportunity for the release of physical energy and of many of the emotional desires closely associated with it. Many of these activities people do, or can do, by themselves—swimming, boating, fishing, skiing, skating, hiking, bicycling, horseback riding, hunting and camping. All people need are the facilities so freely placed by nature at the disposal of our rural forebears.

Of different kind are the competitive games which people play, either indoors or outdoors—tennis, golf, bowling, squash, handball, paddleball, table tennis, archery, quoits, shuffleboard, croquet, and similar activities. Many of these necessitate facilities which the ordinary person cannot supply for himself, and organized assistance may be required to bring competitors together. Popular team activities— baseball, football, softball, basketball, hockey, polo, track and field, and similar sports—all require considerable organization by someone to set up the teams and to arrange the schedule of events. Even "sand lot" baseball requires the facility from which it derives its name.

Unorganized "free play" of many competitive games is characteristic of certain age groups. Boys and girls just get together and choose up sides, or bat a ball around. But the progressive organization of competitive sports requires progressive facilities, promotion, instruction, and coaching.

SOCIAL OCCASIONS

The compulsion for human association may send people in search of many kinds of recreational opportunities, but "social occasions" constitute a direct path toward satisfaction. The need which young people of one sex have for association with the other sex has long received special attention from recreation program makers. But people of all ages desire congenial companionship and social approval. They may find it in social dancing, square dancing, parties of all kinds, club meetings, church suppers, and picnics organized under every kind of informal or formal auspices. Both public and private recreation agencies offer similar activities, under circumstances which seem to create a demand. For these, some measure of promotion and facilities are necessary.

THE ARTS

Among the arts we have included music (vocal and instrumental, both individual and group); the theater; the dance (ballet, folk dancing, tap dancing); graphic and plastic arts (drawing, painting, sculpture, etching, photography and handicrafts); opera and operetta. The common element is a sensuous and emotional experience, and satisfactions of the ear, the eye, and the neuromuscular system which may be contrasted with the common element of physical activity in sports and games. Many people like to sing, play in an orchestra or band, act in pageants and other dramatic productions, engage in interpretative and folk dancing. A similar enjoyment comes through appreciation of the activities of others, as spectators or listeners. Wilson and Ryland characterize these experiences in the following terms with regard to the dance:

The fundamentals of rhythm develop naturally into forms of dance. Throughout the ages, dancing has been a universal mode of expression for human beings. It is a particularly effective medium because it uses the whole body as an outlet for an idea or emotion. It has been described as one of the forms of art to which people turn when words are inadequate to convey the emotional content and overtones of a certain situation.[2]

In addition to the pleasure derived from music itself:

Music is a universal language which needs no translation nor explanation, an ideal medium for facilitating quick contacts among people. It has unique power over the emotions and can sway people toward gaiety or sadness, toward pugnacity and conflict or friendliness and peace. It can be unifying or disrupting: it can promote integration or disintegration.[3]

Dramatics, too, appeal to the eye and ear and carry large emotional content:

Under the heading of dramatics come such forms as games, pantomimes, improvisations, plays, shadowgraphs, puppet and marionette shows, choral speech, festivals, and pageants. All these forms are closely related in that they are means of projecting definite ideas and feelings through action or words, or both. Expression is highly personalized in most forms of dramatics. As a rule, the person himself is the focus of attention, rather than some product of his hands, as in crafts; he plays a special, unique role, instead of participating in common, identical activity with others, as in group singing or dancing.[4]

The creative sense of achievement which comes from any handicraft gives release to many of the fundamental urges identified by psychologists. Two or three generations ago many of those with this special bent were the skilled craftsmen of industry, farmers, or artisans. Today, with the mechanization and specialization of industry and agriculture, outlets for these talents must come in high degree from recreational pursuits.

Opportunity to participate in and enjoy any of the arts requires

2 *Ibid.*, p. 245.   3 *Ibid.*, p. 269.   4 *Ibid.*, p. 284.

facilities, equipment, rooms, audience accommodation. It requires the organization of groups, classes, and performances. Of even greater importance, widespread enjoyment of the cultural arts depends upon the fostering of talented people, who inspire many others by setting the pace for skill and method. From their ranks come teachers and instructors. It is from the work of accomplished artists that audiences draw their greatest satisfaction.

INFORMAL EDUCATION

As good a way as any to distinguish between "formal" and "informal" education is to say that while both may be based on the same interest and serve the same purpose, one is undertaken for academic credit, the other is not.

For some, participation in classes, forums, lectures, or discussion groups may bring recognition of their skill in dialectics, evoke response to their knowledge, satisfy aggressive urges. It may give opportunity for self-dramatization. More often, participation is motivated by a desire to gain understanding, to think out explanations, come to logical conclusions, indulge in expositions, interpret facts, and come to judgments about them.

If there are to be such educational opportunities, some one must provide rooms and facilities, classes must be organized, teachers, lecturers, and leaders must be found.

FRIENDSHIP GROUPS

As we shall see in the next chapter, boys and girls from 9 to 17 years old move progressively from the restricted and protective circle of the home toward the assumption of responsibility for their own social life. It is a period when they put high premium on opportunites for association with young people of their own age; on friendships of their own making; on opportunities to learn self-direction. It is a time, also, when they begin to learn the skills of sports, of the arts, and of their minds, in company with others in whose learning hardships they can find comfort.

For this age group, therefore, active and continuous group association is a peculiarly vital need. The groups to which they belong always engage in many kinds of activities—in sports and games, in social occasions, cultural and educational pursuits. But the underlying motive is not the demand for activity as such. It is the demand for the secure outlets for expression which accrue from intimate, personal, and dynamic association with others of their kind.

Adults of other ages also gain satisfaction from participation in groups in which they have or make close friends. But recreation experience suggests that this compulsion is not so vital, the satisfactions are apt to be more diffuse, the characteristics of the activity more dominant in determining the kind of groups they join. It is during the transition periods of childhood and youth that the need for "group friendship" provides a major common denominator which the recreation program must organize to meet.

If the assumption is valid that people need these five major types of recreational opportunities in order to satisfy basic physical, social, intellectual, aesthetic and creative impulses and interests, then it follows logically that the community-wide program should be balanced in relation to the distribution of these needs. We are of the opinion that the St. Paul project represented the first attempt to get data which would reflect the "weighting" which the total group of recreation agencies actually gives to these principal types of interest. Even those data were not complete.

Sixty percent of the participants in all programs were registered in groups with a varied or "multiple" activity program, one of the criteria used to identify "friendship groups." For the very large number of groups organized around a single activity, information was at our disposal. Almost half of these activities were organized sports and games. Twenty-two percent were concerned primarily with social affairs and activities and about the same percentage was devoted to the arts. Informal education accounted for slightly more than 7 percent.

It is common knowledge that sports and games usually outweigh other types of activities provided by community recreation agencies. Badly needed, however, is the systematic analysis of experience to produce criteria that would indicate whether this distribution does in fact reflect accurately a proportionate "need."

CHARACTERISTIC LIMITATIONS

Some members of the community furnish their own recreational satisfactions; the greater their financial resources the wider the range of possibilities. Their homes will have more space and equipment useful both to old and young for leisure activities. They are more likely to have radios, television sets, cars, boats, summer cottages. If they are in the higher income brackets, they may belong to expensive country clubs or beach clubs. Those with lesser incomes may belong to clubs and associations where the dues are modest and the activities more limited. Those in the lowest brackets (who are often on public assistance rolls) will have little or no money with which to buy recreational extras.

Little systematic analysis has been directed to those who cannot provide for themselves the major types of satisfying activities. Our own research has not added greatly to that already available. Nevertheless, it seems useful to point out three characteristic limitations which tend to make different groups of city dwellers more or less dependent on community assistance. These are: (1) limitations of space; (2) limitations of income; and (3) limitations which are inherent in the nature of the activity.

LIMITATIONS OF SPACE

As we have seen, the public recreation movement had its origin at the beginning of the century in budding community awareness that children in overcrowded sections of cities needed outdoor space in which to play. It was this new experience with lack of urban space which brought home the need for community initiative in recreational matters to a people who had just completed the occupation of a continent. Thus from the beginning, analysis of the "need" for community planned and supported recreational areas has been of prime concern to public recreation and city planning authorities. Standard criteria for use in overcoming this inherent urban obstacle, and in determining what space a city does need to provide, have been worked out systematically and are now widely accepted. In general they call for large reservations, parks and playfields, neighborhood playgrounds, and certain special outdoor resources.

Large reservations of 1,000 acres or more, adjacent to and convenient for the city dwellers' use, should be part of every city's recreational plan. Inevitably their size, distribution, and location will be determined by natural topography.

Authorities believe that space for recreation parks and playfields within the metropolitan area are needed in about the ratio of one acre of space for every 1,000 in the population. These spaces should range in size from 10 to 30 acres. They should be expected to serve the population within a radius of not more than a mile, or a mile and a half. Topography and natural suitability have an important bearing upon the location of these spatial resources.

Playgrounds should be located throughout the city within convenient reach of small children, generally in the ratio of one playground to about five thousand of the population.

In addition, either in the reservations and parks or elsewhere, there should be space for public swimming facilities sufficient to serve 3 percent of the area's population at any one time; for one public golf course of at least nine holes for a population of 25,000, or about one golf hole for every 3,000 of the population; for public tennis courts in the number of one court for each 2,000 of the population; for baseball and softball diamonds, respectively, for each 6,000 and 3,000 of the population. Every community of 100,000 population, it is believed, should have space in its reservation, parks, or elsewhere, for a large outdoor theater. Finally, most cities, regardless of size, should have 5 to 20 acres for a large athletic field or stadium.

LIMITATIONS OF INCOME

Much less precise thought has been given to compensation for the obstacles created by lack of income. Perhaps one reason for this is that limitations of space affect most people regardless of income. Generally speaking, outdoor space is at a premium for almost all urban income classes. The contrary is true of the organized activities offered by the community-supported recreation program. Income affects the kind and amount of recreation that one can purchase for himself. Income has a great deal to do with the leisure facilities that can be provided in and through the home, and through natural social contacts and resources.

A special study of consumer expenditures in three cities shows that the amount of money spent on recreation increases with family income in the following sequence: [5]

[5] Division of Prices and Cost of Living, "Consumer Spending: Denver, Detroit and Houston, 1948," *Monthly Labor Review*, LXIX, No. 6 (December, 1949), 629, 632, 634.

Family Income	Percent of Families in Each Group	Annual Recreation Expenditures
Under $1,000	2.1	$55
1,000–2,000	8.8	64
2,000–3,000	18.7	103
3,000–4,000	25.7	166
4,000–5,000	19.3	212
5,000–6,000	9.9	295
6,000–7,500	6.7	435
7,500–10,000	5.9	520
All under 10,000	97.1	204
$10,000 and over	2.9	$636

According to two studies the home is the locale of about 20 percent of the leisure activities of slum children,[6] in contrast with 40 to 50 percent for suburban children.[7]

We know of no other systematic materials which demonstrate the effect of low income upon the need for community-supported recreational opportunities. Our data from the St. Paul project, in fact, tended to show that whatever their need, the less privileged families actually benefited less from the use of these facilities than others. During the month of our study, it will be recalled, 24,366 families with serious economic, health, and behavior problems were being served by community-supported assistance, health, and adjustment agencies. The recreation agencies served only 7.7 percent of these families, in contrast to 21.1 percent of the other families in the community.

LIMITATIONS INHERENT IN THE NATURE OF THE ACTIVITY

In addition to the "lack of space" and "lack of income," we may note that many activities require facilities and organization which the individual can seldom arrange by himself. Competitive athletic sports, for example, require special outdoor or indoor facilities, someone to promote, arrange, and manage them, perhaps special coaching and instruction. Social occasions of a formal sort need to be promoted and organized, and may need special indoor facilities. The arts require

[6] Reginald Robinson, *Leisure Time Activities of Children on the Lower East Side of N.Y.C.* (Unpublished thesis), p. 60.

[7] George A. Lundberg, *Leisure, a Suburban Study*, pp. 178–80.

rooms where people can work, the organization of classes, with appropriate instructions, larger auditoriums, exhibit space and other audience facilities. So, too, do informal educational classes and activities require both instructors and facilities.

Many recreational activities are not commercially profitable or only at a cost prohibitive to large sections of the population. Facilities and organizing energy are supplied by many of the social clubs, churches, and societies, without support from the general community. But there undoubtedly is a substantial residue of need which the community must meet, if it is to be met at all.

As far as we know, no one has yet precisely determined the effect of these limiting factors upon the need for community-supported recreation. Our own research, of necessity, has been insufficient to aid in this purpose.

CHARACTERISTIC NEEDS IN THE LIFE CYCLE

It is our own view, however, that planning for the community should center around the changing attributes and circumstances of the different stages in the life cycle. There is much practical experience to support this view. The needs of people for self-expression change greatly at different periods in life. Age affects the degree of preoccupation with family-centered activities, the amount of money available to purchase recreation, the kinds of social and other groups with which it is possible to affiliate.

An examination of what we know about the recreational needs of significant age groups in the population should provide a practical base upon which to consolidate all these variables. The following age groupings are generally accepted as having a distinctive relationship to changing interests in the life cycle of most persons:

Group	Age Range
The preschool child	2–5
The school-age child	6–13
Younger 6–9	
Older 10–13	
The adolescent	14–18
The young adult	19–24
The adult	25–59
The elderly	60 and over

THE PRESCHOOL CHILD (AGE 2–5)

Obviously the child at this early age is extremely busy with elementary learnings. He is learning primarily through his senses. His interest span is short, and his self-centeredness makes it hard for him to associate with other children. He is just beginning to achieve the coordination of his faculties. It is not easy to distinguish, in his general growth and development, those particular satisfactions that we think of among older people as coming from recreation.

The family is the natural center for the play of preschool children; by far the greater part of their time is spent in and about the home. In many urban neighborhoods limitations of space and equipment in a small apartment restrict play opportunities. More important, perhaps, is the limited space available for outdoor play. Children of this age may, therefore, be provided with playmates, play facilities, and adult supervision in nursery schools. In our experience the demand for this service comes primarily from two sources. In some families the mother is employed, or has a good many other responsibilities, and wants recreational supervision for her child. In other families, the parents feel that supervised play will be of educational and social advantage to their young children. For those who can afford them, private nursery schools meet this need. For others, community-provided services are in demand.

In many communities modern playgrounds provide some facilities for small youngsters, and these are used under supervision of leaders of preschool groups and of the mothers themselves. A number of private agencies operate programs in their community buildings which may be classified as play groups or as preschool education, depending upon the content of the program.

In St. Paul 390 preschool children were registered in recreation programs. They constituted about one percent of all this age group in the population and 1.8 percent of all persons served by the recreation agencies. About two thirds of these children in St. Paul were served by the public program.

THE SCHOOL CHILD (AGE 6–13)

Now at an age of transition, the child makes his first move from the shelter and protection of his family. In the first part of this period (age 6–9), his experience is still largely home centered, but he is beginning to reach out for friends and companions of his own age, for experiences not found in his home. Wilson and Ryland say, "During the early school-age period relationships within the group are quite loose, almost fluid. The pair relationship is much stronger than the bond of the group as a whole." [8] Although children of this age are still individualists, they begin to work and play with others, and to accept the decisions of the group.

In the latter part of this period (age 10–13), the child makes a major break away from home and family, joins groups of people of his own age and interests. Many of his activities grow out of his need for this association. At this age also he begins to develop rapidly many of the avocational skills so important in his later recreational life, as well as the social skills needed for satisfactory relationships with others. This is the time when he learns team play in its broadest sense. He learns the elementary principles of leadership, the role of the follower, and the give and take of group life. At the same time, it is a period of major growth and change physiologically, and a critical time in achieving an emotional balance basic to his whole life experience.

It is clear, therefore, that the age span from ten to thirteen is a crucial one from many angles and offers great possibilities for learning and development through recreational activities. It is a period in the life of children when they want to move about more freely. In the early part is the age of a good deal of free play outdoors; indoors there are reading, listening to the radio, simple crafts, and, perhaps, some music. In the later period interests and activities range widely, concentrating on sports and games, and social affairs, but also include the arts. A premium is put on "group association" with youngsters of the same age, which may well be more important than any specific activities.

In urban centers, parents can hardly be expected to offer the leadership, the facilities, or the associations required to meet all the varied recreational requirements of the group. On the other hand, the children are not yet at an age when they can take major responsibilities themselves, or on their own find leadership and facilities. Under most circumstances they are unable to purchase the use of facilities.

In practice, in fact, by far the greatest bulk of community-supported

[8] Wilson and Ryland, *op. cit.*, p. 105.

recreation is for this age group. In St. Paul 62 percent of all registrants in recreation agencies were of this age. Corresponding figures from Ann Arbor showed 64 percent to be from this group, and from Los Angeles, 59 percent.

THE ADOLESCENT (AGE 14–18)

During the period of adolescence, definite physical changes take place, children grow at an uneven rate, and girls tend to mature more rapidly than boys. These changes are upsetting and confusing to the young people themselves as well as to adults who are close to them.

The social and psychological characteristics of this age group have equally important meanings for recreation. The further along in adolescence young people go, the more keen is the urgency for self-direction and release from control by parents and the immediate family. Lundberg found in his study of Westchester County that only 5 percent of the boys and 17 percent of the girls of this age group said they had their "best time at home." [9]

Basically, of course, this is a healthy urge. The young people will soon be required to take on the responsibilities of maturity. This reaching out beyond the ties of family results in an opportunity for satisfying relationships with other people of corresponding age and experience. The report of the American Youth Commission states it this way:

The desire to achieve self-direction is closely related to the desire to attain a satisfactory relationship to other young people, which is one of the most powerful driving forces of youth. All individuals experience need for the friendship and respect of their fellows, but this need is most urgent during the initial adjustment to social life outside the family. At this time it is entirely normal for young adolescents to seek the largest possible number of acquaintances and to search for those who are most congenial.[10]

Of adolescents Wilson and Ryland say in part:

. . . they need the opportunity, afforded by the mass activity, to escape for a time from the conflicts within them; on the other, they need the help of the small group in facing reality. Program content should recognize no limitations of media through which the adolescent finds help in working on such problems as emancipation from his family, vocational choice, relationships with the opposite sex, and realization of himself in

9 Lundberg, *op. cit.*, p. 112.
10 American Youth Commission, *Youth: The Future*, p. 107.

relation to society and to his religious beliefs. No one group can provide sufficient testing ground for adolescents as they use their experience in groups to find their way into adult life. . . .

It is essential that [the adolescent] have the support of relationships both with adults and with groups of boys and girls his own age, for through such relationships he can work on the conflict caused by his needs to be both dependent and independent. This imbalance is shown in the way his imaginative plans far exceed his ability to carry them out; the way he fluctuates one minute accepting and carrying through a responsibility, and the next, avoiding or failing to carry the responsibility he has assumed. Groups provide outlets for physical, emotional, and intellectual energy and for the drives through which the adolescent attains his measure of social development. These groups should be as varied and numerous as are the interests and needs of adolescents. The need for the development of skill in the use of the hands and body, so important in the school age, is still a need in adolescence. Interest groups in the arts as well as organized athletics are important types of groups for adolescents. Dancing is the outstanding medium through which teenagers experiment in heterosexual relationships. Mass activities which include all forms of the dance and group games should have prominent places in programs for these young people.[11]

It is during this period of later adolescence that young people seek out the activities in which they can achieve preeminence. For most of us this takes a good deal of experimentation. It calls for dabbling in many different pursuits and indicates a curiosity to explore areas of new experience.

It is therefore not surprising that studies have recorded a great interest in active sports among young people of this age. This is the time when our outstanding athletes are getting their start. Nor should it be surprising that social occasions hold a high place. A pilot study of senior scouting, made by the Boy Scouts of America, showed that social occasions topped even sports and games in interest. This, too, is the age period in which our future concert pianists are developing their talents, and future Broadway stars are playing leads in high school plays. So that interests in the arts and informal education have an important place too in the concerns of these young people.

Although they are entering the period of flowering independence, most young people of this age are not mature enough to organize all their own recreational activities, do not have at their command large areas for sports and athletics, nor rooms for social occasions and

11 Wilson and Ryland, op. cit., p. 108.

parties. They do not have their own swimming pools or beaches. In most instances, they cannot themselves find the talented leadership which will help them acquire new skills. Although they need the anonymity of mass experience, they also need adult leadership which can give them guidance and security. Few of them are financially established so that they can purchase these opportunities for themselves. In St. Paul, 20 percent of all registrants in the community-supported agencies were from this group.

THE YOUNG ADULT (AGE 19–24)

There is less systematic information on the characteristics of young adults than there is on any of the earlier age groups. From the standpoint of physical growth and development, these young people are likely to have reached the acme of their powers.

Both men and women during this period are concerned with their careers, with finding their own place in the productive life of the nation. Many of them are pursuing education, specializing more highly each year in preparation for a chosen vocation. Others have already entered into some vocation and are absorbed in making their way in new and demanding situations. Whether young people are in college or at work, a large part of their time is devoted to furthering their careers, and they are not as free as formerly to take part in recreation activities. Lundberg reported that college students have less leisure time than any other single group.

During adolescence, social relationships were largely experimental and aimed chiefly at learning about themselves and their fellows. During early adulthood, interest shifts toward more personal and definite relationships; young people are beginning to build a stable social role. They may marry during this period, but whether they do or not, they are preparing for more lasting relationships with other people.

These characteristics have deep implications for the recreational needs of this age group. Inevitably there is a strong interest in social occasions which offer an opportunity not only to meet and enjoy the company of friends of both sexes, but also to have a setting in which direct personal relationships can be initiated and furthered. The star college athletes, most of our Olympic team members, and many of the professional athletes are in this age group. These are the exceptional people, to be sure, but the average person is apt to find that his physical powers reach their peak during this same period. Naturally, young people seek ·ways of expression in line with their athletic and sports prowess.

Young people of this age group are also trying to arrive at a better understanding of the world in which they live. Many are trying to find meaning in the complex economic and cultural life around them, and to develop a set of values which will give some stablity to their life patterns. Much of this may not be conscious; it may be no more than a vague groping. Nevertheless opportunities for informal education represent a major field of interest. There may be a deep concern with questions of religion, ethics, politics, and economics. The interest in such questions may be expressed through affiliation in labor unions and political parties and may lead to enrollment in adult education under various auspices.

From young adults as a whole we may expect less demand for community-provided recreation than in the case of younger age groups. First, much of their time and energy are drained off into other major fields of interest, career, and family. People of this age are only starting to earn their living, but in most cases they have money of their own and can pay for the recreation or entertainment of their choice. Some have cars, or have access to cars, and are thus not so dependent upon near-by facilities. Their social interests are more personalized. They prefer occasions which allow them a good deal of freedom of action, and they may resist the controls, rules, and regulations of more highly organized groups. They are generally better able to take care of themselves than younger people, and have less need for outside leadership.

Nevertheless, it seems to us that in several areas community-supported recreation is necessary to meet their needs. This is particularly true of athletics and sports. For these activities, both facilities and leadership are necessary and neither is likely to be accessible except in a community supported program. Furthermore, the management of such enterprises as baseball, basketball, and bowling leagues requires experience and is as necessary as the facilities. For those whose talents and interests lie in the arts and in intellectual activity, schools and recreation departments must provide appropriate programs. It was around the interests and needs of this group that the pioneer programs of the YMCA and YWCA were developed. These and other agencies have served this group for over half a century.

Our St. Paul data showed that only about 4 percent of young adults are enrolled in the community-supported programs. They accounted for 5 percent of all agency registrants. The rate was five times as high for men as for women. We must note, however, that these figures do not include those who used public golf courses, tennis courts, and other general facilities where participation was not recorded.

THE ADULT (AGE 25–59)

For most adults, their jobs and their families are the all-important considerations. During the earlier years of this period young children in the family require continuous care and attention from the mother and father. Leisure hours are often circumscribed. Later on, the family center offers both children and adults the major share of their recreation.

The common family pattern is still that of the husband as breadwinner and the wife as homemaker. Many of the satisfactions sought earlier through recreation, the husband may now get from his work. Almost all occupations involve some kind of social intercourse, and many of them depend on skill in relationships with other people. Many occupations also offer chances to demonstrate skills and abilities which during childhood and youth were found primarily in recreation activities.

Nevertheless, neither the family nor the job satisfy all the basic impulses for which the adult seeks outlet. Lundberg, it is interesting to note, finds that adults spend more time on social occasions than do children and young people. Perhaps this reflects the fact that many jobs are routine and many homes offer fewer social satisfactions than we expect to find there. While interest in competitive sports declines, many adults continue to play tennis and golf, bowl, and engage in other similar activities.

Recreation authorities have for some time felt that a weakness of programs for adolescents and young adults has been their failure to develop skills in "carry over" sports suitable for a mature adult. Evidence suggests that potential interest in participation in the arts is more widespread than has been generally recognized. Certainly many

industrial and white-collar jobs are so routine and involve turning
out so small a part of the finished product that workers derive little
creative satisfaction from them. Evidence also indicates that adults
exhibit about the same interest in opportunities for discussion and
informal education as do high school and college students. The study
in Westchester County revealed what is generally known, an extraordinary interest in club activity among housewives, reflecting a need for
social and intellectual outlets that the home cannot supply.

Generally speaking, adults carry on more of their recreation activities without turning to the community-provided programs than is the
case with younger groups. They usually have money to buy entertainment through the motion pictures, theaters and the like, and are able
to pay the dues required by athletic clubs or the fees charged by commercial bowling alleys, swimming pools, dance halls.

They can exert leadership in organizing and maintaining their own
clubs more readily than is possible for younger people. The more
able among them give leadership to youth groups and recreation activities, direct political parties, school systems, fraternal orders, community agencies, and the whole range of our social institutions.

Nevertheless, there remain facilities and programs which the community should furnish. Parks, stadiums, beaches, and other outdoor
areas for use by adults as well as their juniors must be provided
through public funds. Facilities and leadership for programs in the
fields of music, art, and informal education, otherwise beyond their
financial reach, should be organized on a community basis for a large
number of our adult population.

In St. Paul less than one half of one percent of the adults in this age
range were registered in community-supported activities. They accounted for a little less than 8 percent of all those who were registered.
As with our other recreation data, however, these rates do not include
the unorganized use of parks, playfields, and other public facilities.

THE ELDERLY (60 AND OVER)

For most adults at this age the two great challenges of life activity—
earning a living and raising a family—become less demanding. Work,
while still rewarding, may present a diminishing challenge, and the
time for retirement approaches. In 1940, of the 13,747,654 persons

over sixty, only 3,797,387 were employed.[12] Considerably less than half of the men, and only about 8 percent of the women, were found to be working.

Many of these older people have retired from the active management and responsibilities of a family. Their children are grown and have, for the most part, established their own homes and families. In many instances this has resulted in materially reducing the social contacts and activities of long custom. "In every large city today, there are hundreds of elderly men and women who live alone without any opportunity for normal social contacts. Monotonous days stretch ahead, each one as empty as the day before. The older person becomes self-centered, feels he is the forgotten man. This makes for mental and physical deterioration." [13]

Thus we complete the full circle, started with children, and come to another group of people with time and energy for leisure activities. These older people have long been used to social responsibilities and social contacts. For a long period of years they have utilized their talents and abilities. The absence of opportunities to continue to do so, at a pace commensurate with their strength, leaves a real gap in their lives. The extent of their need for recreation has only recently been recognized in any degree, and not too much is known about it.

From the evidence in hand, it seems clear that as a group they need opportunities to meet the whole range of activity satisfactions we have been discussing. They need active games and sports consonant with their abilities and, particularly, social occasions which give them the satisfactions to which they have been long accustomed. Social and recreation agencies report that older persons participate in drawing, painting, writing poetry, publishing magazines, working at handicrafts. Interest in club membership and participation in discussion and informative programs is a natural outgrowth of experience.

All the existing evidence points to the fact that older folk are unusually dependent on the community for recreation. The lower income groups, especially, no longer have homes and family centers of their own where they can entertain and visit freely. In most cases, in-

[12] U.S. Bureau of the Census, *Statistical Abstract of the United States: 1949*, p. 169, Table 200.
[13] Margaret Wagner, "Meet Yourself at Sixty-five," *Survey Midmonthly*, LXXXII, No. 4 (April, 1946), 110.

PROBABLE PROPORTION OF THE POPULATION NEEDING SERVICE	ORGANIZATION REQUIRED	MAJOR FACILITIES REQUIRED	
		Indoor	Outdoor
Preschool Child (Age 2–5) Proportion unknown; but more from lower income and multiproblem families	Supervised games and play	Playrooms	Neighborhood playgrounds Parks
School Age Child (Age 6–13) *Younger (6–9)* Half the children; more from lower income and multiproblem families	Supervised games	Game room Gymnasium	Neighborhood playgrounds Parks
Older (10–13) Half the children; more from lower income and multiproblem families	Organized sports and games Arts and crafts Supervised friend- ship groups	Game room Swimming pool Gymnasium Craft rooms Club rooms	Neighborhood playgrounds Parks Special areas
The Adolescent (14–18) One third; more from lower income and multi- problem families	Social occasions Organized sports and games Information educa- tion Arts and crafts	Lounge Swimming pool Gymnasium Craft rooms Club rooms or snack bar	Playfields Parks Special areas
The Young Adult (19–24) 5 to 10 percent; more from lower income and multiproblem families	Social occasions Sports and games Arts Informal education	Swimming pool Gymnasium Lounge Craft rooms Club rooms Assembly room	Parks Playfields Special areas
The Adult (25–59) Proportion unknown; more from lower income and multiproblem families	Social occasions Informal education Arts and crafts Organized sports and games	Lounge Assembly room Craft rooms Swimming pool Gymnasium	Parks Playfields Special areas
The Elderly (60 plus) Proportion unknown; more recipients of old age assistance and old age and survivors insurance	Social occasions Arts and crafts Passive sports and games Informal education	Lounge Craft rooms Game rooms	Parks

come is too limited to permit the purchase of many opportunities which they bought as a matter of course during their years of income production. Like others, they need the parks and outdoor recreation areas. Perhaps most important of all, they need social centers where they can engage in activities that will take up the slack in their social contacts, created by withdrawal from vocational and family activities.

Although community awareness of the needs of this group is increasing, attempts to meet it have so far been limited to a few pioneer experiments. In St. Paul the number of people 60 years and over participating in the organized activities of community-supported agencies was negligible—0.2 percent of all registrants.

STRATEGIC INTEGRATION

Thus, it seems to us, changing needs and circumstances at different periods of the life cycle provide a strategic framework within which to integrate the study of other variables which determine for "whom" the community needs to supply recreational opportunities, "what kind" and "how much."

The accompanying chart recapitulates our discussion of the manner in which communities may combine analysis and experimentation in a unified and strategic approach to the special needs at different ages. The proportions of each group needing community-supported recreational opportunities are the best estimates we can make on the basis of the meager data now available. Within the framework of our own classification, we have analyzed and suggested the principal types of organized activity needed by each age group. The facilities required for these activities are consistent with generally accepted recreational classification and principles.

Chapter XIX

COMMUNITY-WIDE
RECREATION FUNCTIONS

LITTLE HAS BEEN DONE to clarify the basic functions indispensable to a complete community-wide program. Professional disciplines required to identify these functions with any degree of precision are still in developmental stages. In the recreation field there are few accepted basic procedures analogous to those of "detection," "diagnosis," and "treatment" in the area of disease control, or of "determination of need" and "provision of maintenance" in the administration of financial assistance.

Different recreation activities, requiring various combinations of facilities, personnel, and organization, traditionally have been viewed in administrative terms by the agencies providing them. While some of the recreation agencies owe their origin to specific recreation objectives, others were established to attain quite different goals and find it difficult to recognize similarities in function. As a result there are as yet no community-wide criteria by which to judge the quality of performance in the recreation field or to allocate labor and responsibility among the community agencies.

Our own experience and research leads us to designate at least three distinctive functions as indispensable to any community-wide, community-supported recreation program, regardless of administrative auspices. These are: (1) the provision of large-scale facilities for public use; (2) the organization of activity interests; (3) the organization of friendship groups.

THE PROVISION OF LARGE-SCALE FACILITIES FOR PUBLIC USE

The origin of much community-supported recreation stems from the spatial limitations inherent in urban life. To offset that limitation, outdoor reservations, parks, playfields, and playgrounds and also large indoor areas must be provided by the community.

In the preceding chapter we gave certain of the accepted criteria which measure the need for different kinds of outdoor space and facilities. Obviously, these serve in turn as precise guides by which to measure the quality and the adequacy of community-wide performance of this function.

Much of the use of outdoor space and large-scale facilities is unorganized. For the most part, individuals and families need only the resource itself; for some of the "organized" activities, both space and facilities are needed. These do not, however, have to be provided by the same agency that administers the activity. This important functional distinction is sometimes overlooked.

Provision of space and large-scale facilities has become widely accepted as a primary responsibility of public recreation units. It is no longer appropriate for private philanthropy to supplement this facility provision except as occasionally a group of citizens contribute to acquire property for transfer to public authorities to operate. This function is appropriately one for tax and bond issue support.

The reasons underlying this principle are quite clear. Public bodies possess certain powers of condemnation which enable them to acquire property needed for development. In many cases location and acquisition of these facilities is an integral part of other public planning programs such as those for highways, schools, industrial development, and zoning. Above all it is now difficult, if not impossible, to finance their acquisition, development, and maintenance through private resources.

THE ORGANIZATION OF ACTIVITY INTERESTS

The organization of activity interests represents a major function of community-wide recreation, in which promotion of a specific activity is the prime organizational objective. In the St. Paul project all agencies which administered "single interest" groups, that is, groups organized for the purpose of conducting one activity only, were classified as providing this function.

Almost all activities such as team sports and games, social occasions, the arts, and information education, require adjunctive equipment, large-scale outdoor or indoor facilities, playing areas, ball diamonds, athletic goods, auditoriums, small class or meeting rooms, benches and tools, and so on. The organizing agency may or may not supply these facilities. It must, however, supervise their use, schedule the programs, and see that equipment for activities is on hand, over and above the basic facilities. It must also, if necessary, recruit and direct the group. Some groups are self-starting and self-directed, and require only the most general supervision to assure success. Others must have skilled directors, instructors, or leaders: swimming instructors, team coaches, teachers of archery and badminton, specialists in the handicrafts, orchestra conductors, drama coaches, must be called upon to instill the proper skills and understanding.

Although different agencies apply various standards in selecting personnel, we know of no common criteria, expressed in precise professional and training standards, for persons who expect to undertake this organizing function. The program pattern, however, is indicative of the general capacities required from qualified staff. Their primary responsibility is to assist the participants to carry on the activities in which they are interested. Major emphasis on staff training and education, therefore, should be placed on developing skill in organization and management and in sports, arts and crafts, and the other special types of activities.

In St. Paul, 57 percent of the registrants in activity-centered groups was reported by public agencies and 43 percent by private agency units. A like count in Long Beach showed 59 percent in the public and 41 percent in the private agencies. Proportions may vary, but it is generally true that both the public and the private agencies undertake to organize activity interests on a substantial scale. There are no generally accepted principles regarding the appropriate division of labor between them.

In our own view this function has increasingly become an accepted public responsibility through school boards, and municipal recreation departments or commissions. As a matter of general principle, it is not a private agency function to organize a general activities program for the community.

A practical reason for this view is to be found in the major responsibility which public agencies now take for providing the facilities necessary to the conduct of these activities. Land must be purchased, expensive plants and equipment provided, all on a scale beyond the resources of private financing in most areas. Many facilities which represent important resources are part of the public school plant—pools, gymnasia, auditoriums, and outdoor areas. In many current plans for replacement and expansion of school plants, community-wide recreation needs are being taken into account and adaptations are being made to accommodate an increased use for leisure time activities. Public schools cover the city and as these plants are modernized, with provision for recreation, there should be less demand for private agency facilities except in especially congested or needy areas.

THE ORGANIZATION OF GROUP FRIENDSHIP INTERESTS

Many persons need assistance in developing secure and satisfying relationships with others. This is particularly true of boys and girls between the ages of nine and seventeen. The cornerstone of this function, therefore, is the organization of groups whose primary purpose is to give opportunities for personal association, in contrast to participation in any single activity. Friendship interest groups inevitably engage in specific activities, but these must first of all further the social interests of the members, and only secondarily serve their activity interests. This is the familiar pattern of activity of the Boy Scouts, Girl Scouts, Camp Fire Girls, the Hi-Y Clubs and the social clubs of the neighborhood house.

Although there are as yet no accepted criteria by which to distinguish precisely between "activity" groups and "friendship" groups, it is generally understood that the latter are marked by certain distinctive characteristics. For one thing most of these groups are friendship groups from the start. The nucleus of the club or troop usually is made up of several people who have known each other in some setting—the school, the church, the block in which they live—and thus constitute a natural group. Community agencies offer them adult leadership to give stability to the group and help its members plan their program.

Another important characteristic is that these groups usually undertake a variety of activities rather than concentrate on a dominant athletic, social, artistic or educational interest. A club or troop will do many things in the course of a year, or a club season. Sports, trips, dramatics, camping and parties all may appear in the annual program records of a friendship group. This range of activities meets a need for new interests and new experiences, and at the same time gives each member an opportunity to excell in his particular field of competence. Through participation in varied activities programs, members of the group develop stronger friendship ties, group loyalties, leadership skills, and an understanding of how to get along successfully with other people.

A final characteristic of friendship groups is that they tend to hold together for longer periods than do activity-centered groups, usually lasting two years or longer. Athletic teams on the other hand tend to be seasonal in character and the group stays together only through a sports season, the fall for football, winter for basketball, summer for baseball. Other kinds of special interest groups may stay intact longer than this. A drama club, for instance, may continue indefinitely, but when this occurs, it often means that the group has in fact become a friendship group, widening its activity range, holding parties, and going on outings together. Here again no hard and fast rule can be applied.

There is, in fact, considerable opinion that the basic distinction between "friendship" and "activity" groups, resides, in the professional qualifications of those who organize, direct, and supervise them. Friendship groups place less premium on the organization of facilities and equipment. They do not require such abundant knowledge about particular activities, neither are they dependent upon specialized coaching, teaching, or instructional skills. On the other hand their direction requires more knowledge of the principles of mental hygiene and group interaction. If young people are to have satisfactory experiences in a troop or club, adult leadership must have sufficient understanding of social behavior to keep in check the overeager members, encourage the shy ones, and see that everyone gets an equal chance. Recognition of the need for this skill on the part of staff is indicated by the requirements for employment in the Girl Scouts: [1] a college degree and "a major in the social sciences, or at least a minimum of twenty semester hours in sociology, biology, psychology, economics, political science, anthropology or related subjects is rec-

[1] Personnel Department, Girl Scouts of the U.S.A., *Professional Opportunity in Girl Scouting*, p. 10.

ommended." Other national agencies with friendship group programs have similar requirements.

The general trend is in the direction of using more of these highly trained workers. As a practical matter, however, qualitative criteria have yet to be developed by which to distinguish clearly the groups whose purpose is the enhancement of personal association from those whose primary purpose is to achieve satisfaction through recreational activity per se. In the St. Paul project we accepted the following as evidence that an agency was organizing "group friendship interest": (1) if it provided groups to serve multiple activity interests; (2) if the group structure was designed for a measure of self-direction and self-determination; (3) if the groups had some continuity, that is, did not automatically disband at the end of an activity season. These criteria give no clue to the qualitative capacity of the group organizer or leader to use these devices as a means of serving the youthful need for association and growth. They are applicable only to structure and activity interest.

In terms of these criteria, however, private agencies now undertake the principal responsibility for this recreation function. In St. Paul it was found that 71 percent of the private agency participants were registered in clubs or troops, and in Long Beach 63 percent were so enrolled. The private agency members in clubs and troops constituted 89 percent of all members in such groups in St. Paul and 90 percent in Long Beach.

It is our own belief that the function of organizing group friendship interests is now more appropriately undertaken by the private than by the public recreation agencies. For some time to come it seems probable that the orderly development of the total community-wide recreation program will be served best by a reasonably clear division of labor which recognizes these basic functional lines.

RECREATION AS THERAPY

Considerable confusion always has surrounded the effectiveness and the appropriateness of using recreation to achieve ulterior objectives. As we have noted, much private agency interest in recreation originated in the belief that activities could be organized in a manner to assist in developing the Christian way of life, in building character, in making good citizens, and otherwise contributing to some such generality of purpose. One may even cite the Hitler Youth Movement as evidence of a strong belief in the effectiveness of recreation in achieving an end, the good of which we would deny. The faith that recreation is a primary antidote for juvenile delinquency has been persistently encouraged, despite the paucity and dubious quality of supporting evidence.

The neglect of scientific efforts to classify the relationship between basic impulses and urges and the principal recreation activities which may satisfy them leaves us in the dark about the exact nature of recreation's impact upon the human personality. Until research can be more definitive about the impulses and drives which urge us on, and the opportunities for their outlet which recreation affords, the truth about the therapeutic value of recreation will continue to be elusive.

Nevertheless, within the last decade or so leaders among the private agencies in particular have begun to rephrase their purposes in terms of "personality, growth and development," and to sharpen their thinking about the professional methodology required to attain that end. The focus of thought has been upon the better use of "friendship groups" to meet the needs of youth, especially those from nine to seventeen. Their needs, it is believed, can best be met by professional leadership whose training puts a premium upon knowledge of the social need of individuals, mental hygiene insights, and the processes of group interplay. With such knowledge more help in personality adjustments can be given to young people than is usually the case from the general friendship group program.

We think it fair to say that while they are interested in the generalities of personality development, in practice the principal recreation systems do not now conceive it to be their task to assume systematic responsibility for the adjustment of young people who show specific evidence of personality disorders or faulty social attitudes. The St. Paul data, as we have noted, showed that the recreation agencies dealt with only a very small proportion of the considerable number of people with such disorders known to other community agencies. Our own surveys elsewhere have shown negligible referrals of persons to recreation agencies, from the casework, mental health, and correctional agencies which deal with such problems. Referrals of persons to casework and mental hygiene agencies for diagnostic and treatment service by the recreational agencies have been equally negligible.

In fact the therapeutic use of recreation activities in connection with behavior disorders and adjustment problems is now being developed primarily, although not exclusively, under psychiatric and medical auspices. The more precise experimentation with this methodology is to be found in camps for diabetic or cardiac patients, or for emotionally disturbed children; treatment groups affiliated with psychiatric clinics and outpatient departments, and hospital inpatient service. In this latter connection special mention should be made of the extensive recreation program initiated by the Veterans Administration for the patients of its hospitals.

THE ROLE OF SOCIAL GROUP WORK

Thought about the group methodology necessary to "personality development" has been considerably influenced by social casework, which early focused upon the processes by which the caseworker assists the individual in making his adjustments. Leaders in the recreation field similarly have focused on the processes by which a skillful leader may use group activities to further the individual growth and adjustment of those who participate in group activities.

During the late 1930's, recreation workers interested in this matter organized the American Association for the Study of Group Work, later to become the American Association of Group Workers, with the general intent to raise standards and improve methodology. Many of the graduate schools of social work now include a "group work" curriculum.[2] Premium is put on the use of psychological and mental hygiene insights, and understanding of the basic principles of the casework process, and the processes of interpersonal relationships within the group itself.

The extent to which this budding professional discipline may help to clarify the basic functions requisite to the community-wide recreation program is as yet unclear. As we have seen, standards for training personnel equipped to undertake the organization of activity interests have not developed to the point of general acceptance.

[2] Harleigh B. Trecker, "Social Group Work," *Social Work Year Book, 1947*, p. 488.

Neither are there accepted standards applicable to the organization of group friendship interests. Furthermore, the use of group activity as a precise technique in the diagnosis and treatment of people with behavior disorders and adjustment difficulties is not now generally conceived to be a recreation responsibility. At present the leaders of the social group work movement hope that its disciplines will be useful in all three directions. A characteristic of practical importance is that the "group worker" does not usually himself deal directly with members of the friendship interest group. Rather, he trains and supervises volunteer leaders who in turn are in direct personal contact with group members. Perforce this limits the extent to which the techniques of professional group work can be applied to particular groups or persons. This also puts a premium on the ability to organize and supervise volunteer workers. Even if a rapid increase in the number of trained group workers takes place it seems that the use of volunteer leaders will continue indefinitely because of the great number of groups to be served.

Similar training is believed to be desirable for those who organize activity interests. But here also in practical operation many of those who direct such particular activities are not "recreation" workers in a generic sense, but rather are specialists in a particular sport, art, craft, or other subject.

As a practical matter, the number of professionally trained group workers is still so small that the concept of social group work at the moment cannot be expected to have a significant impact on the recreation programs of most communities. Underlying this is the further fact that it is not yet clear whether there is developing a generic recreation professional discipline, or a specialized discipline pointed more sharply toward the adjustment of personality difficulties and disorders through the use of group processes. Until this point is sufficiently clarified so that criteria for the quality of personnel and the supervision required by each of these functions can be established, an important and basic consideration for distinction of functions will be lacking.

Chapter XX

COMMUNITY-WIDE STRUCTURE

AS WITH OTHER COMMUNITY PROBLEMS with which this volume deals, the basic recreation needs of people are much the same in all communities; the variation is in their intensity and distribution. The same program functions are necessary to meet these needs; the number and kinds of agencies which provide these functions for the community vary greatly. Local agency administration depends largely upon the quality of personnel and the soundness of internal agency policy. In neither of these respects is the situation in two communities ever the same.

In the ordinary community there are fewer different administrative units for recreation service than there are for either maladjustment or health. In St. Paul, 16 agencies providing recreation programs contrasted with 45 responsible for problems of maladjustment, 30 for problems of ill-health, and 17 dealing with dependency. In contrast to these other fields also, no part of the recreation structure is administratively integrated into a state or federal system, although the local private agencies in particular have strong ties with national bodies. As in dependency, however, the number of public units is small—seldom more than three, the private agency being in considerable numerical superiority. As in most of the other fields, more thought has been given to the structural simplification of the community's public units than has been the case for the voluntary service units.

Although the number and identity of particular agencies differ from community to community, basic patterns are recurrent. In recreation, as elsewhere, it is possible to find principles and trends which have significance to any community desiring to improve the over-all structure through which its services are administered.

THE MUNICIPAL RECREATION SYSTEM

In almost every community three principal public bodies play, or should play, the major role in providing public recreation service: the park administration, the recreation administration, and the school system. Together these carry the major burden of providing the facilities needed for the public program and in organizing the activities which it offers. The park administration and the recreation administration commonly are units of the municipal government. The school system, on the other hand, usually is independent. In either case, these administrations are dependent for their powers upon state enabling legislation.

ADMINISTRATIVE PRINCIPLES

Opinions differ as to the structural design for these three units that will best serve the purpose of an integrated community-wide program. Considerable agreement exists, however, regarding the administrative principles which should guide their joint operation. The main purpose of these principles is to facilitate the organization of a varied recreation program; they are calculated to implement adequate provision for, and maximum use of, all the available facilities.

A long-range master plan for the development of outdoor space and of both outdoor and indoor facilities is regarded as essential to the guidance of all three public bodies. The selection of needy areas, the design of the areas, buildings and equipment for them, and study of their relationship to land use in the community should all be prepared systematically well in advance of action. Leadership for this frequently resides with the City Planning Commission, if there is one. In making realistic plans, however, it needs to build upon the resources of the park department, recreation unit, the school board, and the private recreation agencies. Plans must reflect systematic regard for the city's natural topography, population concentration, relative area needs, and potential growth.

In most communities the park department, the school system, and the recreation unit will each own some facilities. The park department maintains large outdoor areas and installations. The school system owns the school plant and outdoor areas including playgrounds and athletic fields. The recreation units may own playground and playfield areas and community center plants of its own. In most cities, each of these units is expanding its holdings. Park areas are being developed more and more for recreation purposes. The newer school plants are being planned and built with a view to providing both outdoor and indoor recreation resources. Community centers and outdoor areas are being furnished by the municipal recreation unit. Whatever form the public agency structure assumes, it should be one that provides for an adequate and balanced set of basic facilities— parks, playfields, playgrounds, and indoor centers.

Definite policies governing the full use of all physical resources for activity purposes is regarded as essential. Park areas, playgrounds, indoor centers may be maintained by one unit, while the activities requiring the utilization of these facilities will be organized by another. Duplication of expensive facilities and waste in their use will result unless clear policies are worked out to give the program organizing units ready access to all available facilities. Many authorities believe that these policies should be in the nature of contractual agreements so that the arrangements may be definitive and stable.

This is particularly true in relation to the use of school plants when the responsibility for organizing the community-wide activity program is vested in some other unit. School properties represent a large public investment in buildings and grounds which lend themselves to recreational activities when school is not in session. Their full use for this purpose is assuming great importance in sound public recreation planning. We know of at least one community where the recreation department takes over full responsibility for the operation of the school plant from 4 o'clock on. More often modified plans are worked out by which schools make available their properties at specified times, under prescribed circumstances.

The same general principle applies to the use of park facilities, when a separate recreation division is responsible for the organization of activities. Authorities are generally agreed, also, that school, park, and other public facilities should be available to groups organized by private agencies, under similar contractual policies covering the arrangements.

A qualified personnel naturally is stressed by all authorities, as is the use of the merit system, in these no less than other public service appointments. Park administrators need knowledge of engineering and landscape architecture, and the technicians on the staff should include specialists in land use and maintenance.

The recreation director is the key to the program of organized activities, whether he is in a separate administrative unit, in the park department, in the school board, or some structural combination of them. In many respects, he occupies a strategic community-wide position comparable to that of the public health officer and the public welfare director in their respective fields. His program is limited to no one constituency and has the intent to serve all groups regardless of age, sex, nationality, geographical location or other special circumstances. He has or should have direct access to the principal and most expensive physical resources which are necessary to the organization of activity interests. In organizing to meet community-wide needs, these characteristics rate high in strategic value.

Unfortunately personnel standards applicable to his office are still couched in terms of general administrative competence and experience. Facilities for training are meager and stress principally intra-agency administrative duties and procedures. Local public recreation directors have been concerned primarily with expansion of activities under their own administrative direction. But in more recent years an increasing number have begun to use their key positions for community planning leadership. They have developed a broader view about the basic objectives of the total program and accompanied this by seeking to understand other services in the community and their essential purpose. They have shown a willingness to shape the policies of the public agency in the light of this understanding. One may hope for the continued development of training resources to better prepare public recreation personnel for the assumption of a broader leadership for which their strategic position offers great opportunity.

A clearer prescription is equally needed for the training of the public recreation staff whose primary task is the organization of activity-centered interests. For this is, and we believe it should be, the principal function of the public recreation unit.

About the role of citizen boards or commissioners there is less general agreement. Some authorities place great stress upon them, and many communities have commissions appointed by the chief municipal officer with administrative control over the recreation or the park department. In other cities, the custom is to give full authority to the executive officers of the park or recreation department, but to appoint an advisory board of citizens to consult and advise with the executive director on major policy questions. In still others the policies of the departments are determined wholly by the staff and executive officers of the municipality. This is usually the tendency under the city manager form of local government.

STRUCTURAL ALTERNATIVES

Opinions differ about the type of community-wide structure best suited to implement general administrative principles such as these. A major reason for this lies in the fact that the organization of activity interests depends to such a large degree on the use of outdoor and indoor facilities. The question is how best to make these available.

The community which is impressed by the need for a close tieup between the recreation program and the areas maintained by the park department may have set up its recreation administration within the park department. Another city, more aware of the desirability of using the available resources of the schools for activity purposes set up its recreation program under the school board. Or a city may be fully aware of the necessity for close relationship between both the parks and schools but feel that not sufficient attention will be given to the organization of activities if responsibility is placed in some agency which has another major function. In this case, it may be considered advisable to have an independent recreation authority in the city government with an arrangement for close working arrangements with both parks and schools.

THE CASE FOR CONSOLIDATED STRUCTURE

Recreation authorities are in general agreement that responsibility for the organization of activities should be consolidated in a single unit, whether that unit be located in the schools, the park department, or in a separate structure. They do not believe, in other words, that the school system *and* the park department, *and* a separate recreation commission all should be organizing activities on properties at their disposal. They point out that the organization of recreation activity has been accepted as a major public responsibility, that it should have

unity of purpose and planning, and that this is best achieved under a
unified administration. Otherwise, confusion, duplication of effort,
waste of facilities and money, inevitably result.

Some authorities also make a strong case for a consolidated park
and recreation structure as the pivotal unit around which to organize
the total activity and facility program. Several large cities are operating under such plans, in which there are numerous apparent advantages. This park and recreation department is, of course, a major unit
of the city government, comparable in importance to the public welfare and public health departments. The administrative chart calls
for an administrative division, a division of grounds and buildings,
and an activities division.

The administrative division makes for economy and efficiency by
combining all business, financial, and clerical operations in a single
unit.

The division of grounds and buildings makes for a unified development of all recreation properties. Planning, expansion, and maintenance are integrated through this operation. Unified architectural
engineering and construction resources can be brought to bear upon
all properties used for whatever purposes.

The activities division is responsible for operating the recreation
program on all the properties of the department. The central staff
carries specialists in various program fields, and staff workers are
placed in the indoor and outdoor centers owned and managed by the
department and in other major facilities which the department arranges to use for program purposes.

This structure does not incorporate the administration of the school
plant and facilities. Obviously it would be impractical to do so. Education is the primary business of the school system and has the first
call upon its physical resources. But it makes clear that the recreation
role of the schools is to share their facilities in so far as this is feasible
and desirable. Furthermore, it simplifies the necessary contractual
arrangements.

The schools operate their own physical education programs, such
special interest groups in sports and cultural subjects as may directly
supplement the curriculum, and such social affairs as the school students wish to carry on as part of their school activities. Under this

plan, the schools can make arrangements with a single administrative unit for the full use of their facilities on behalf of broad community-wide recreation.

THE VOLUNTARY YOUTH AND RECREATION SYSTEM

As we have seen, the private agencies differ in philosophy, aims, traditions, and ties with their own national bodies. They typify the American practice of developing institutions to express and put into action convictions held by different groups of private citizens. In this lies much of their strength and value. At the same time it poses a difficult problem in planning an integrated and smoothly functioning community-wide recreation program. Not only does the multiplicity of units make for a complicated administrative structure, but the variety of purposes and auspices make for difficulties in getting a clear-cut division of labor in the performance of recreation functions.

We know of no current thought which is being directed to the simplification of this pattern. But we believe it would be useful to distinguish between two principal types of agencies. First, those whose activities are largely centered in buildings which they maintain and operate for activity purposes; and second, non-institutional agencies which use facilities not under their own management. This is a generally recognized distinction, in respect to which certain current trends and issues have community-wide structural significance.

BUILDING-CENTERED AGENCIES

The local YMCA, YWCA, settlement houses or neighborhood centers, Jewish Community Center, Boys' Club, if any and perhaps a scattering of other local units all have in common the fact that theirs are indoor facilities. Their total expenditures greatly exceed those of the non-building units, as might be expected, because of requirements for plant operation. This expenditure is offset to some extent by fees paid by members for the use of plant and equipment.

Some buildings, notably the YMCA and YWCA, are for city-wide use in the sense that they draw people from many parts of the city. Others, such as the settlements, Boys Clubs, and community centers, are primarily for neighborhood use. They are in the particular section of town the agency wishes to serve. The buildings themselves range from the large plant with many resources to a small neighborhood office or activity center.

A recent study [1] by the National Council of the YMCA classified the type of buildings used for different aspects of the "Y" program into three major groups. These classifications are generally appropriate to the different types of buildings used by other agencies:

Non-Equipment Buildings. Rented quarters or small buildings used for office headquarters and leadership training.

Activities Buildings. This type ranges all the way from small social headquarters, including offices, club rooms, refectory and kitchenette for use of small groups only, to office and club headquarters with limited physical recreation facilities, such as one all-purpose room to be used for social events, banquet service, and athletic games, with a locker and shower room ensemble.

Comprehensive Buildings. These have most of the following: social and office headquarters with Junior and Senior lounges, game room, general-purpose room, and an adequate athletic department including a gymnasium, swimming pool, and locker rooms. This type may also have various enlargements and additions, such as two gymnasiums, hand-ball courts, health-service department, and food-service equipment. In the YMCA they may be constructed with or without dormitory facilities.

Some of the agencies which operate buildings, the YMCA and the YWCA especially, run extension programs in which they organize groups whose activities are centered outside of the agency's buildings in churches, homes, schools, and public recreation centers. But traditionally the nature of the programs of these agencies depends to a great extent on the kind of facilities in the building. Obviously, a building with a gymnasium or swimming pool will have an appropriate program and staff. A different kind of program and staff will be found in a unit operating a social recreation or informal education program.

As we have seen, we are now in a period of great expansion of public recreation plants. With the remodeling of school and recreation buildings, and the addition of new units, many new facilities under public auspices have become available. At the same time it has become more difficult to secure private funds for new capital plant and improvements. There are signs, too, that the upward trend in contributions

[1] David F. DeMarche, *The Relative Effectiveness of Y.M.C.A. Branches with Various Types of Buildings*, pp. 1, 2.

to current operations cannot continue indefinitely. Recent increases have not been commensurate with increased costs of operation, and this financial picture is requiring careful review. Therefore, shifts in the private agency structure seem inevitable.

At the very least, it seems to us that plans for new private agency building should be made in conformity with a community-wide master plan for all physical facilities. A modest "activities building" makes it possible for an agency to offer its constituency a whole range of activities if it is located adjacent to a larger public facility to which it has access. If its program is coordinated with the public recreational activities in a school, it will have at its disposal the gymnasium, perhaps a swimming pool, an auditorium, classrooms, rooms for dances, and perhaps some outdoor facilities. If near a park or playfield, use of these resources augments its own. Concentration of private effort on the organization of "friendship" rather than activity groups, which seems logical to us, lends itself to more modest building requirements. If these are located with due consideration to a master plan, on or adjacent to more comprehensive facilities under public auspices, private agency groups still will have available a variety of opportunities. Central downtown buildings, such as the YMCA and YWCA, may still be necessary to serve older age groups, but their branch buildings in larger cities might well conform to this general policy.

NON-BUILDING AGENCIES

In this group fall the Boy Scouts, the Girl Scouts, Camp Fire Girls, possibly the Catholic Youth Organization, a number of the 4-H Clubs, and units of local origin and sponsorship. These maintain no program plants of their own, but organize groups in connection with schools, churches, settlements, recreation centers. Their administrative characteristics reflect this kind of program structure. Their staffs are concerned with the recruitment and organization of groups, the training of volunteers, the promotion of activities. They carry no responsibility for operation and maintenance of a plant, except for possible camping facilities. In one sense the program of these agencies is more flexible. On the other hand, it is highly dependent on others for resources for meetings and other activities. They find it harder to conduct groups in sections of the community where they do not have easy access to churches, schools, settlements or some natural facilities.

The organizational structure and the nature of the constituency of each of these non-building agencies is determined primarily by the characteristics of the national movement with which it is affiliated. From a community-wide standpoint the principal weakness is in the fact that such a completely separate structure is not conducive to the equitable extension of services to the different sections of the city. Some areas tend to be well supplied with troop and club opportunities, others largely neglected. Individually each agency may have good reasons for its selection of areas in which to work, but the result in community-wide terms is an imbalance in opportunities for recreation. The obvious remedy is cooperative planning. Our experience includes some communities where this has been done, but experimentation so far is insufficient to mark a national tendency in this direction.

Chapter XXI

FRAMEWORK FOR COHERENCE

IN THE PRECEDING CHAPTERS we have seen that at the present stage of community planning for recreation, many fundamental questions are still unanswered. The nature of the need for community-supported recreation requires clarification. Precise criteria by which to distinguish the basic recreation functions, as well as to judge the quality of performance, must still be developed. For the present at least, simplification of the complicated voluntary agency structure seems impractical.

Nevertheless a practical framework is emerging within which communities can make substantial progress toward more coherent planning. The foundation for it rests on the fact that the recreation activities of most people are carried on within striking distance of home. This is true of children and adolescents almost without exception, and true to a considerable extent for young people and adults.

These more or less circumscribed areas correspond to the "natural areas" of the city, long identified by sociologists as a significant characteristic of urban life: the downtown section where business and stores are centered; industrial districts; slums; the "gold coast." On the outskirts of town are the new developments of small homes as well as the more pretentious residential areas. Each of these sections has its own particular set of common characteristics. Most of the people are in the same general economic class; they have much the same educational and cultural backgrounds; children attend the same schools; housewives do their shopping in the local markets.

Most of these natural areas are communities in the technical sense of having some social unity, achieved through their own political groups, churches, schools, parent teacher groups, merchants' associations, and the like. Main traffic arteries, rivers, hills, railroad tracks, and other physical features help separate them from each other.

Public recreation agencies in many cities are increasingly following natural lines in the location of outdoor and indoor facilities and in organizing activity programs. District recreation patterns are commencing to develop, partly as a result of pressures for facilities from people living in the areas, partly by happenstance, and increasingly by thoughtful local planning.

THE DISTRICT PATTERN

Few cities, in our experience, have defined the boundaries of their natural areas for purposes of recreation planning, although this is not difficult to do. Those familiar with special aspects of the city's history, topography, lines of communication, commercial, industrial, social and population distribution, usually will come to easy agreement regarding the boundaries of its most distinctive sections. Not all of these areas will be of the same geographic size, nor are their population totals entirely comparable. For example, we found that Hartford, Conn., naturally divided into thirteen areas. The populations varied from about seven thousand in the smallest to almost 22,000 in the largest. Sixty-five districts in Metropolitan Los Angeles ranged from a population of 9,000 in a community in the San Fernando Valley to 85,000 in a downtown district. In St. Paul the smallest of twelve areas had a population of 15,000, the largest 47,000.

Regardless of size, however, our experience suggests that the plan in each district should center around facilities and activities at six focal points: (1) a park; (2) a playfield; (3) properly spaced and distributed playgrounds; (4) a general indoor activity center; (5) a youth social recreation center; (6) a joint noninstitutional club and troop program plan.

THE PARK

The facilities of a park, authorities agree, constitute a necessary foundation for any district pattern. If possible the park should be within the boundaries of the district itself or at least adjacent to it. Under any circumstances, it should be not more than a mile from the district boundaries. Its major role is to enable the residents of the area to enjoy the outdoors at their leisure, in both summer and winter. This is especially important when the district is crowded with multiple dwellings and there is little open space except the street and sidewalks. People in other types of districts should have access to parks too, but priority should be assigned to the congested areas.

Meyer and Brightbill describe as follows the characteristic contribution of the park to city recreational life:

The pleasant, natural environment of the recreation park provides opportunity for the city dweller and his family to escape the turmoil of urban living.

It is evident that such parks cannot be of standard design, nor even incorporate standard facilities. Such areas should include woodlands and lawn, hills and meadows, and if possible, streams and other natural water areas. An effort should be made to retain as much of the areas as is practicable in a primitive condition. Roads are necessary to make facilities accessible, but should be kept to a minimum.[1]

Hiking trails, bridle paths, gardens, bird sanctuaries, perhaps winter sports facilities, all should be well prepared for spontaneous and unorganized use by the individuals and families who live in the district. These facilities should be available also to organized groups, under both public and private auspices, for nature study, picnics, outings, and so on.

Administration and maintenance of the park, of course, is the responsibility of the city-wide park authority.

THE PLAYFIELD

A district playfield may be in a park that lies within or near the district boundaries. Another good place for it is on or adjoining high school property. But authorities are agreed that a minimum of ten acres, and a maximum of twenty, should be available to serve the population living within a radius of a mile to a mile and a half.

Meyer and Brightbill describe the facilities for which the playfield should make provision as follows:

Playfields commonly provide for baseball, football, softball, soccer, and other field games; multiple-use areas which can be used for basketball, volleyball, badminton, shuffleboard, paddle tennis, roller skating, occasionally ice skating, and social events. There are lawn areas for croquet, bowling on the green, archery, and the like. Sometimes, space and natural features permitting, it is wise to include picnic areas, outdoor theaters, and band shells. Many playfields include a children's play lot and/or play-

1 Harold D. Meyer and Charles K. Brightbill, *Community Recreation*, p. 447.

ground and not infrequently swimming and wading pools. Often playfields are used for junior and senior high school physical education and
sports programs.[2]

Like the park, the playfield is most important for crowded districts. Even outlying areas of most cities now are being built up so
that informal baseball and touch football played in vacant lots is becoming rare. It is quite conceivable that except for those fortunate
enough to belong to a country club, citizens living in most of the districts of the city will eventually be without basic facilities for organized outdoor activities unless there is a public playfield nearby. For
this reason, although the playfield originally was thought of as serving primarily youth and adults, it is now conceived to be a resource
for the whole family.

Administration of the playfield as such, as well as primary responsibility for organization of the activities which its facilities make possible, must be the responsibility of the city-wide public recreation
unit. The field should be freely available to voluntary agencies for
use by groups supervised by their own staff or volunteer leaders. For
this is, and should be, the main resource for all large-scale outdoor
district activities. Systematic arrangements for its use by friendship
groups under voluntary auspices, and for inter-city leagues and tournaments greatly enhance its district utility.

Authorities agree that a playfield usually requires a staff of two full-
time people to supervise organized activities, use of the equipment,
and to give leadership to those engaging in sports and other activities.

PLAYGROUNDS

There should be playground facilities within the district for each
neighborhood of approximately five thousand people. These should
be located within easy reach of small children and will be their main-
stay for outdoor play, especially in the warm weather months.

Meyer and Brightbill describe as follows the facilities needed for
these playgrounds and the uses to which they may be put:

This is the chief outdoor play area for neighborhood children from approximately six to fourteen years inclusive. Originally this term was used
for a children's area alone. In more recent years, however, the thought is
increasingly accepted that children and adults need not necessarily be

[2] *Ibid.*, p. 444.

served at entirely separate centers. The neighborhood playground should include a simple variety of activities for the short daily leisure periods of the entire family.[3]

A playground is a requisite in any family residential district, to serve about the same population as does the elementary school; authorities agree that there is great advantage in combining the two facilities. Indeed, the principle is now generally accepted that each elementary school should have attached to its plant a space of from three to seven acres for playground purposes. Where this arrangement is impossible, or where topography or traffic arteries prevent school playgrounds from giving coverage to the entire area, the recreation authority may provide additional playgrounds. In Los Angeles, for instance, in addition to approximately 190 available at the schools, the recreation authority operated 38 playgrounds on separate open spaces.

Administration of the playground as such and organization of most of the activities on it are the logical responsibility of a city-wide public recreation unit, which may make it available to private agencies for use by organized groups under their own supervision. The regular program on a well-supervised playground, however, will fill up most of the schedule and will leave little time available for use by other agencies.

Part-time supervisors usually are employed during the school year and full-time workers during the summer when children use the area throughout the day.

Indoor recreation center.—During warm and fair weather the playfield and the playground are the centers of organized recreational activity programs in the district. In southern states this holds true for a greater part of the year. For other parts of the country there are many months in which much of the recreation activity must be carried on indoors. Each district, therefore, needs at least one indoor recreation center, to serve as the counterpart of the outdoor areas providing facilities and activity programs for all age groups. If it is a very large district there may be need for more than one.

In many areas the school plant is the key to this operation. An elementary school with a gymnasium, assembly, and other facilities may well be adapted for this purpose. A junior or senior high school, if

[3] *Ibid.,* pp. 443, 444.

present in the area, may offer still better facilities, larger gymnasiums and frequently a swimming pool. Indeed designs for the "community school" now call for a combination of facilities for education and recreation, although few such units have yet been completed.

Where school plants are poorly located or equipped, it may be necessary to erect a center designed especially for recreation purposes. For many years, in many communities, neighborhood settlement houses under voluntary auspices constituted the only centers available for indoor recreation purposes. Substantial use was made of their facilities by neighborhood groups and other agencies. In some instances this is still the case, although the tendency has been to build up special constituencies and activities which have a prior claim upon the facilities of the building. When one or more settlements are located in a district without other suitable indoor facilities, however, our own experience indicates the wisdom of examining the cooperative potentialities before undertaking new construction.

Whether the indoor center be publicly or privately owned, it is important that other agencies have access to the gymnasium and swimming pool or to the equipment for activity programs, as well as to rooms where friendship groups may meet. In Long Beach, one third of the private agencies' clubs and troops met in schools or community centers.

While the indoor recreation center can serve all ages, in practice the program tends to be dominated by the age group from ten to fourteen, the group which makes the heaviest total demands on the community-supported program. The older adolescents and youth, whose activity interests are somewhat different, are not easily served at the same time in the kind of indoor center usually provided by the local school.

The administration of the center, as such, will usually be the responsibility of the city-wide public recreation unit, if the facility used is a school, a special community center, or other publicly owned building. In this case, authorities generally agree, the organization of varied activity interests require a full-time staff of two workers, with special assistants, depending on the size and variety of the program.

The same kind of staff will be required for activity purposes, should realistic planning indicate the use of a settlement or neighborhood house as the focal indoor recreation resource for the district. Under these circumstances the division of responsibility between the settlement and the city-wide public unit must be worked out and agreed upon with equal realism.

YOUTH SOCIAL RECREATION CENTER

The spontaneous organization of "youth canteens" which swept the country during the war years, gave practical evidence that the older adolescent group requires a program of its own. For one thing, their recreation interests are different from those of the youngsters. For another, much of their sports activity is centered in the school. They use the general outdoor and indoor centers, of course, but their chief desire is a meeting place which can serve as their hang-out. They need to have facilities for special social occasions, for club meetings, for dances, dramatic productions, and musical affairs. Many of them belong to friendship groups organized by the different agencies, and a common meeting place for these has many advantages. Every district needs to provide a social recreation program for this group.

Whether a district needs a special facility for the program depends on how well the other facilities and leadership are suited to serve the youth group. If there happens to be a high school located in the area, with an extracurricular recreation program and a plant adapted to recreation, another unit may be superfluous. If the downtown YMCA and YWCA are within easy reach of residents of the district, these units may fill the need. A public recreation center may have the facilities and staff to serve the youth group as well as the younger children.

In most cities, however, there will be areas where no such resources exist, and a special facility is indicated. Such districts may be lower income areas where young people's own resources are limited and local commercial recreation of an inferior quality. Or there may be better residential areas where families and young people have resources but where some focal point and skilled leadership are needed to help realize the potentialities that already exist.

Administrative provision for this facility seems to us a logical voluntary agency responsibility. In one city plans are being made in three districts to adapt available private facilities for this purpose. In two of these, settlements have lost the general constituency for which they were originally intended. Their outworn plants are being replaced and remodeled to serve the special needs of young people. To serve a third needy district, a private unit now located elsewhere plans to relocate.

In contrast to the general indoor center, the physical requirements for youth centers are relatively modest and inexpensive, easily within the bounds of voluntary financing. Their location near the general indoor center, with its gymnasium, swimming pool, auditorium, or near the outdoor playfield or park with its facilities, can avoid unnecessary expenditures for such activities. Private agencies have had more and longer experience in working with this age group. There is, however, no basic reason why the public recreation unit should not assume responsibility for the provision of this facility and the conduct of its activities. But here as with the other focal points in the district pattern, it is highly important that the youth center be freely available to all agencies for use by the various groups and activities under their direction.

JOINT CLUB AND TROOP PLAN

In every community the Boy Scouts, Girl Scouts, Camp Fire Girls, YMCA, YWCA, often other agencies, recruit and supervise friendship clubs, troops, and groups on a city-wide basis. The focal point for each group is its meeting place in the district where the young people live—a church, private home, the American Legion Post, the school, a settlement, or some other center. Although the groups carry on many activities, their focus is the weekly session at the meeting place. Most of the members are youngsters under fifteen, although there may be a few groups of older adolescents and young people. Activities are determined by group interests, and these depend upon the age and sex of the members, not upon some focal point outside the group.

The number of these groups within a particular district depends on the separate organizational and promotional activities of half a dozen or more different city-wide units. The result in most cities has been a haphazard development in the different sections. There were, for example, 4,326 such groups in the sixty-five natural districts of Metropolitan Los Angeles. The average was 18 groups per 10,000 of the population. Coverage ranged from one district in which there were only 7 groups per 10,000, to another with an approximate 35.

Among the 65 districts, 14 were classified as especially "needy" areas. Among these, five showed relatively high ratios of groups to population—but three showed very low ratios.

In respect to this type of friendship group, therefore, the district focal point cannot be the administration of a facility. Rather, the focus must be a *joint plan*. Los Angeles affords a noteworthy example of a joint approach in certain areas, through its Youth Project. Some other cities also have had experience in joint planning to meet the group service needs of particular districts. A systematic district-by-district scheme for allocating and promoting group coverage, however, seems to us the only way to assure attention to it on a par with the other five.

BALANCING NEEDS AND SERVICES

In reviewing our own materials about community-supported recreation in the different natural districts of three cities, Los Angeles, Hartford, and Long Beach, we find evidence of considerable practical provision for these focal points. Public recreation agencies have distributed parks, playfields, playgrounds, and indoor recreation centers so that these facilities were available in most districts. Park, playfield and playground space frequently did not conform to accepted standards, but the use of these standards as a general guide to spatial development was apparent. The location of indoor centers was more haphazard, but they were available in many districts, and the public recreation intent to give the city suitable coverage was also evident. Social recreation centers for youth were rarer; at the time of our studies only in Los Angeles was there experience with joint planning for friendship groups on a district basis.

To bring about real coherence in community-wide planning, however, these six focal points must be used primarily as a point of departure from which to plan and organize services to meet different needs in different districts. Except in the allocation of space, our experience affords much less evidence of attempts to differentiate between district needs and to match services against them. Playgrounds would be understaffed and underequipped in certain sections, as compared with others. Playfields in one area would be busily engaged by many groups in a great variety of activities, meagerly used for limited purposes in others. Indoor centers in some sections provided an apparently varied program for boys and girls at different age levels; in others, facilities and staff were directed to limited activities for a particular age group. Club and troop programs in some districts had wide coverage among boys, and a very small coverage among girls.

Part of this apparent disparity no doubt is due to over-all shortages of facilities and organizing personnel. But this merely puts a greater premium on the need to establish district priorities in order to make the best community-wide use of available resources. The disparity is due in great part to the lack of procedures (again excepting requirements for space) for appraising relative district needs and evaluating the adequacy of service in relation to them.

At present, common sense and general experience constitute the principal sources of guidance for procedures. This wisdom should not be neglected. The most under-privileged areas of any community are easily identified. If they are teeming with children, a prior emphasis on facilities and activities appropriate for this group is logical. The contrary would be the case in sections predominately occupied by transient adults. A high proportion of older people may mean that more space is required for shuffleboard or quoits, and more attention should be paid to the organization of activities which will particularly appeal to older persons.

Certain cultural groups have special interests in music, the dance, and in particular sports and games. General knowledge about church activities, affiliation in cultural, racial, and fraternal societies in the district give clues regarding the importance of activity programs for adults. We have seen that the few studies which throw light on this matter indicate that considerably more leisure is spent in the family circle among the higher income brackets than is the case among the lower income groups.

Reliance on common sense is subject to considerable limitations. Our own experience suggests that three kinds of information about each district help take the guesswork out of the "needs-to-service" equation. Accurate data about the total number of individuals participating in the programs of the community-supported agencies, by age and sex, make it possible to analyze the characteristics of that part of the population in the district that does receive service. Data about the main types of activity in which they participate make it possible to analyze the degree to which different types of recreational needs are being met. Information about the social, physical, and other characteristics of the district gives a background for some judgments regarding the relative adequacy of what is being done.

More is needed, however, than procedures for collecting these data. Research is required to establish valid criteria to appraise the need for community-supported services, in each district as well as in the community as a whole. The appropriate materials, it seems to us, should come from uniform studies in a number of communities representative of different parts of the country, different population characteristics, and typical variations in emphasis on community-supported recreation offerings. Our own experience suggests that the data for each city and for each natural area of the city should follow the lines just suggested.

The results of this research would show first the actual rate of participation in community-supported recreational activities by sex and by the different age groups discussed in Chapter XVII—the preschool child, the schoolchild, the adolescent, the young adult, the adult, the aged. As we have indicated in preceding chapters, pieces of this information have been secured in a few cities, but not on a strictly comparable basis. Nevertheless, the findings suggest that broad norms of "need expectancy" can be established for different age segments in the life cycle.

Second, the data would reveal actual participation by age, sex, and district, in the different types of activity listed in Chapter XVIII: sports and games; social occasions; the arts; information education. As far as we know, the St. Paul project represented the first attempt to compile this information on a community-wide basis. It was not complete, but the results were suggestive. They indicated that nearly 50 percent of participation was in sports and games; that a little over 40 percent was divided about equally between the arts and social affairs; that a very few participants were concerned with informal education. Uniform data from a number of cities should throw light on whether or not "norms of expectancy" are similarly applicable to these major interests. The data should also help establish the extent to which participation is dictated by genuine interest in a specific activity and how much is due to availability.

Third, uniform studies should be made of certain conditions presumed to affect the need for community-supported recreation. One set of conditions, it seems to us, include: population density, income status, and the degree of family disorganization. Another set would relate to the availability of noncommunity supported resources, including the principal types of commercial recreation, and the activities of churches, societies, clubs, and other organized groups.

Our own experience leads us to believe that the analysis of comparable data from a selected sample of urban cities would give a foundation for the creation of working norms. These should prove extremely useful in appraising the need for the principal types of community-supported activities, among the principal age groups in the different natural districts of the community. Not only the criteria themselves, but the precise thought attendant upon the research necessary to their establishment, seem to us the *sine qua non* of further coherence in community-wide recreation planning.

FINDINGS

Chapter XXII

SIGNIFICANCE OF
THE FINDINGS FOR
COMMUNITY-WIDE
PLANNING

THROUGHOUT THE PRECEDING PAGES we have assumed that inherent in the culture of America is a belief in a progressively better way of life which would minimize continuously and realistically the ancient hazards of poverty, disease, social abnormality, and of unrewarding leisure.

Our purpose has been to show what now is involved in better methods of preventing and protecting the community against the consequences of these hazards. Throughout, we have been guided by the fact that when both problems and services are seen from a community-wide vantage point, compelling reasons appear for establishing a carefully planned interrelationship between the principal fields of present service. One value of this approach has been the identification of many gaps in knowledge and experience; wherever we have felt qualified to do so, we have indicated directions for the research and experimentation needed to fill them.

Our materials make it quite apparent that the services as now organized and rendered to the people of our communities do not offer a purposeful, comprehensive, well-integrated program. Certain segments have behind them a tradition of community-wide objectives and of functional integration. Others do not have such a tradition. Many of the agency systems, or movements, through which these services are provided have interests and objectives not easily accommodated to a unified community plan.

It is our expectation, however, that the trend toward coherent community-wide planning, within and among the major fields, will accelerate in the years immediately ahead. Therefore, it seems useful to summarize our materials from the standpoint of two principal factors that will affect this trend. The first has to do with the basic ferment necessary to real progress. The second concerns the realistic elements in the present status that have special significance for the task ahead.

STRATEGIC FERMENT

We believe that the preceding pages make it clear that the pace of integrated community planning depends upon (1) a greater unity of purpose, (2) better scientific and professional disciplines, and (3) more coherent national leadership in terms of community-wide guidance and stimulation.

UNITY OF PURPOSE

Up to a certain point, each of the agencies and services directed to the problems of dependency, ill-health, maladjustment, and recreational need can stand alone. Each is based upon the characteristics of the problem to which it is directed. Each has distinctive functions considered necessary for the protection of the community. Each has developed structural patterns through which these functions are administered.

We believe the evidence is clear, however, that there is a point beyond which none of the four principal programs can stand unaided. That point is where the major problems in all four areas converge in some combination to destroy effective family life.

The St. Paul project provided dramatic data about the complex manner in which this comes about. Inasmuch as evidence of pathology is always seen with greatest clarity in its most serious manifestations, the facts about the group of multiproblem families in that study will bear repeating.

There were 6,466 families in that group, 6 percent of all the families in the community. Over 5,000 families were dependent; in over 5,000 there was evidence of serious maladjustment; in nearly 5,000, serious ill-health. In more than one third, persons were chronically ill; in more than one quarter, chronically handicapped; in nearly one third, there was an official record of antisocial behavior on the part of one or more family members; mentally defective persons were found in about one fifth. Caseworkers reported persons who were failing to meet major social responsibilities in 40 percent.

Over one third of the mentally defective persons in this group of multiproblem families were heads of families, as were a quarter of those who exhibited antisocial behavior. Altogether nearly half the persons with reported behavior disorders were at least titular heads of families. In this group of 6,466 families there were 1,940 persons with both behavior disorders and physical illness, and half of these were family heads. Less than 10 percent of this group of families, however, participated in any of the community's organized recreation activities.

Our general experience makes us quite sure that this picture is not unique. In every community there is a similar small group of families whose ills are compounded of dependency, maladjustment, and disease. They usually receive little organized recreation attention. They absorb a large part of the time, service, and money expended by assistance, health, and adjustment agencies. Even to achieve its own ends, each of these agencies must cooperate with the others at many points. Despite meager evidence regarding the ill effects of insufficient recreation upon family life, our own premise has been, and will continue to be unless evidence proves the contrary, that lack of satisfying recreation must have some precise crippling effect upon family capacity.

Implicit in the totality of these separate programs is the common purpose to prevent and protect the community against the consequences of family breakdown. But implicit though this seems to us, the realistic exploration of its unifying values will not come easily. The necessity of increasing specialization creates greater and greater barriers. Organizations built upon interest in particular needs and symptoms of individuals tend to disregard the family as the dynamic setting in which these problems have their being.

These barriers are very real. They have impeded study of the strategic relationships of the dynamics of family life to the specific difficulties with which the different agency systems are concerned. Awareness that such study is needed, however, is growing steadily.

We have seen that the residual dependency load results from constellations of disabilities, the net result of which is to destroy the family's ability to produce income. Health authorities are beginning to see that the family must play a vital role in protection against the hazards of chronic disease and physical disability. Understanding is growing that the cause of much behavior disorder is rooted in family incompetence. Moreover, the fact that the family circle is the natural setting for a great portion of leisure activities warrants greater consideration in determining the extent of the need for community-supported recreation.

In the preceding sections we suggested three systematic procedures by which to add to knowledge about the strategic relationship of the family to all these problems.

The first of these procedures is inherent in the St. Paul project, which was started with the assumption that the family should be the unit for any integrated study of community needs and services. Here, for the first time, the family was used as a statistical unit in tabulating data about all the specific problems presented to, and the particular services rendered by, every agency in the community. This made it possible to consolidate and compare data heretofore subjected only to separate and unrelated study. The values accruing from this procedure have been liberally illustrated in the four sections of this volume. We believe that increasing use should be made of the family as the basis for statistical reporting and analysis of different segments of the organized community program.

The second procedure which we have suggested also grows out of our experience in the St. Paul project. We are sure that in every community there is a relatively small group of families in which these agencies now concentrate a high proportion of whatever is being done about dependency, chronic illness, chronic handicap, mental illness, mental defect, antisocial behavior, and, in general, about all those who are in trouble. There can be no doubt that there is a very great deal of waste in the totality of their joint endeavor.

We believe there is pressing need for experimental development of systematic procedures which will assure:
1. Early identification of these families and continuous, systematic recording of data about them
2. Integrated diagnosis of the total range of problems which confront each family unit
3. Classification of the rehabilitative potentialities of families as well as of individuals

4. Coordinated organization and direction of the specialized services needed to achieve these potentialities

5. Periodic review and objective evaluation of the continuing agency programs which are related to this group of multiproblem families

A high percentage of the families are dependent upon public assistance. They account for a large part of the residual load, the reduction of which is one of public welfare's aims. As we have seen family characteristics have an important bearing on the course of chronic disease, on chronic handicaps, and on behavior disorders. The same general types of procedures need to be developed by the principal systems concerned with these disabilities, and by the most highly qualified leaders in each system.

The procedures in each case must be designed to make full use of the appropriate community resources. The resulting methodology will be significant for special programs for the control and reduction of dependency, for special programs for the control and reduction of chronic diseases and conditions, and for special programs for the control of behavior disorders. Each program is inextricably related to the prevention and control of the denominator common to them all, the breakdown of family competence and self-sufficiency.

The third procedure is closely related to the second. The family is a group of individuals. As a group it is capable of giving constructive support to members who may be ill, mentally unbalanced, unable to work, or in any trouble. It is this competence to function as a group which in turn may be adversely affected by the disability of any of its members.

The professions of social casework, especially family casework, and of medicine and psychiatry, know a good deal about the disorganizing influences which affect this basic social group, as well as the dynamic processes out of which emerge its principal assets and liabilities. Each professional worker must judge the strengths and the weaknesses in families with which he deals. As yet the accumulated experience has not been analyzed and classified to provide tools for systematic use. Agencies operating in these different fields badly need such tools to sharpen diagnostic practice, to accelerate the pace of treatment, to provide definite means of communication from one to the other, and to introduce economies and efficiencies in case-recording. They need classification aids, in short, to help perfect the disciplines directed to the diagnosis and treatment of family breakdown.

The community-wide program needs classification aids likewise, but for another purpose. Total diagnostic ánd treatment resources, as well as financial support for them, are limited at best. In a similar setting of restricted resources the best mental hospitals, to cite one example, use their maximum diagnostic talent to classify patients in accordance with their basic needs and their potentiality for response to treatment. A full battery of treatment specialists is brought to bear on those with acute mental diseases when the chances of rapid recovery are good. Disposition of professional talent is of a different character for those needing a long period of treatment. Decent care, with medical and other attention as required, is the primary prescription for arteriosclerotic and senile cases, where prognosis seldom indicates much hope of recovery. For the protection of the community, tuberculosis and certain other types of illness require special treatment of the patient regardless of prognosis.

A community-wide program should be designed to utilize available services with the maximum of effectiveness and economy. Much of the present waste is due to misdirection. In most communities within our knowledge, a disproportionate amount of time and effort is spent upon families discovered too late and for whom the prognosis is bad. In consequence, too little is available for those in which hopeful elements are more readily discernible. Community Research Associates, Inc., is now engaged in a two year project directed to this purpose, in cooperation with the St. Paul Family Service and the Greater St. Paul Planning and Research Council.

Other procedures inevitably will suggest themselves to those with an experience different from our own. But it is through such studies of the precise significance of family life that there may emerge a more realistic understanding of the purposes common to community agencies. Here, in the long view, is the focus for the creation of strategic over-all coherence out of the multiplying specialties of modern welfare programs.

SCIENTIFIC AND PROFESSIONAL DISCIPLINES

For fifty years, more or less, the manner in which communities, and the greater society of which they are a part, have dealt with the troubles of human beings has gone through a great transition. It has proceeded from complacency, brutality, and indifference toward man's suffering, through the high motivations of humanitarian impulse to improve his lot, to the realism of scientific concern about the precise causes of conditions and effective remedies for them. We are still in this process of transition. Its different phases meet in a confusion of ideas which at times seem to block the achievement of strategic coherence in the community's attempt to promote the common welfare.

The first two decades of this century were years of great humanitarian leaders and great humanitarian movements. In a very real sense humanitarian impulses outran scientific knowledge about the troubles they tried to alleviate. One may hope that they always will. Nevertheless, it should be clear that scientific knowledge about cause and cure is of the essence of true coherence in community welfare.

Present knowledge about the cause, prevention and cure of disease greatly exceeds that about the other major problems with which this volume is concerned. Not until the turn of the century did scientific thought make the basic distinction between the causes of dependency due to imperfections in the economy and those due to personal disability. It was not until 1935, when the first social security legislation was enacted, that this distinction became firmly embedded in public policy. Many kinds of maladjustment are still surrounded by mystery, fear, and traditional dogma. It is mainly during the last quarter century that the impact of psychiatry has begun to have a practical effect upon the community services which deal with behavior disorders. Even now there is little scientific knowledge about the precise needs for self-expression and satisfaction which can best be met by recreation and leisure time activities.

But it is our conviction that progress depends as much upon the disciplined application of what is known as upon advancement in scientific knowledge and understanding of cause and cure. These disciplines of application are of two types and must be clearly distinguished one from the other. First are the disciplines concerned with the solution of the problems of a particular individual or family. Second are the disciplines directed to community-wide prevention and protection against the hazards and consequences of these individual and family problems.

Solution of individual and family problems.—Clues to practical progress toward creation of the first set of disciplines are to be found in the degree of precision and authority attached to standards of practice in the professions.

For the physician these are exacting and rigid. His medical education and experience are prescribed in detail, and are designed to qualify him for the diagnosis and treatment of disease. He must be licensed, and the continuing conduct of his practice is subject to authoritative rules and ethics of the medical profession.

The discipline of the nurse equips her for a more limited role in the care of patients, but requirements are defined with no less precision and authority.

Professional requisites for the diagnosis and treatment of adjustment problems are less precisely and authoritatively established. The basic discipline of the psychiatrist is the same as that of the physician, psychiatry being a branch of medicine. His further prescribed education and experience are concentrated on equipping him to diagnose and treat personality disorders.

For social casework the diagnostic and treatment objectives are still in the process of being defined. Accredited schools prescribe the course of study requisite to a degree or certificate, but many persons in community agencies now classified as caseworkers do not meet these requirements.

The disciplines of the psychologist are at present limited primarily to testing and classifying mental capacity and aptitudes. Standards which would require prescribed clinical experience and which would more precisely define objectives have been adopted, but as yet relatively few psychologists qualify under them.

The precise objectives for which a specialized discipline is needed in the administration of public assistance are not yet clear. If the primary purpose is to ensure the efficient determination of need and provision of maintenance, sharper standards for training and performance will have to be devised. The fact that these standards may be less rigorous than for the diagnosis and treatment of physical and mental maladies does not lessen their importance.

It is impossible as yet to predict with any authority the characteristics of a generic discipline applicable to the comprehensive field of recreation.

The discipline of mind and method, the exacting evaluation of performance which comes from schooling in precise application of appropriate knowledge to the solution of an individual or family problem, is of slow growth. But it is indispensable to coordinated progress on the major fronts of community welfare.

Community-wide prevention and protection.—Only the public health system has developed a recognizable discipline for the organization of processes to this end. The essential requirements include the competence: (1) to see the processes by which diseases or disorders affect the whole community rather than specific individuals or families; (2) to understand the statistical and research techniques for analysis and evaluation of the effect upon the community of different diseases, disabilities, and conditions; (3) to know the causes and methods of prevention and control of disease and disability; (4) to understand diagnostic, treatment, and prognostic practices; (5) to put into effect measures which will prevent the onset of diseases and reduce their consequences for the community as a whole, and to promote a state of complete physical well-being, not merely the absence of disease or infirmity.

Awareness of the importance of similar disciplines in each of the major fields is increasing. In the last fifteen years the public welfare movement has assumed community-wide responsibility for the care of dependent families. While, so far, no precise discipline has developed, attention is beginning to be focused on ways and means of preventing and reducing the size of the residual relief load. The public welfare department is thus the pivotal agency for dealing with this problem.

In recreation, the public department or commission stands in a somewhat similar position. Public recreation leaders have long been concerned with the community-wide promotion of their own activities. Many now see that this must be accompanied by a more accurate analysis of the total recreation needs of the community and of the functions and facilities which voluntary agencies offer in meeting these needs.

In the field of maladjustment as a whole, no pivotal structure has as yet emerged around which to develop a discipline appropriate to the organization of all the processes for prevention and protection. But psychiatry, grounded in preventive medicine and conditioned to the solution of family and individual problems, is beginning to recognize the need for experimentation and research as the basis for a community-wide attack upon the problems of mental health.

During the past quarter century community chests and councils of social agencies have been widely established throughout the country. These central bodies have helped greatly in increasing community awareness of the number and variety of local agencies. They conduct financial and other useful common services for their member agencies; they have provided a forum for professional discussion and have assisted in bringing into being many new services. They have many noteworthy achievements to their credit in bringing about reorganization and improved administration within particular local units. Structurally they are representative of all four of the major problem and service areas; the councils include both public and private agencies among their members. But to the present time there has not developed an authoritative discipline competent to guide comprehensive community-wide planning for prevention and protection. Our own experience suggests that among the basic requirements for such a discipline should be:

1. Thorough understanding of what is known about the cause and cure of the principal problems toward which the total community program is directed
2. Equal understanding of the objectives, purposes, and stages in planning, of the four principal segments of the program
3. Command of the research and statistical techniques needed to analyze the community-wide characteristics of the problems in these different fields and the strategic relationships between them
4. Precise familiarity with the different disciplines and techniques which provide the functional foundation for the total program, and of standards and criteria applicable to their performance
5. Equal familiarity with principles and purposes useful in guiding the simplification of the community-wide structure
6. Competence to aid in developing systematic procedures for the community-wide control of problems in which services from more than one of the principle fields is required
7. Familiarity with present procedures for evaluating the results of different sections of the program and competence to aid in developing others of over-all significance

8. Competence to organize community forces for effective community action, which includes facility in working with groups

COHERENT NATIONAL LEADERSHIP

Whatever may be the community's will and strength, coherent
progress in its total welfare efforts cannot come through local leadership alone. This is inevitably a shared responsibility. Sometimes the
degree to which it is shared is quite clear. For example, the state
operates and finances correctional and mental institutions for the
benefit of the whole state. Each community shares only indirectly in
financing and in the control of these programs. Or again, part of public assistance is financed through a federal state system. Obviously, in
such circumstances administrative policy must be determined in
some measure at each level.

But there are more subtle forms of sharing that have to do with ideas
about objectives, and the methods of their attainment. The formation
and dissemination of these ideas take place through many different
public and private nationwide service systems. Each has its own national leadership and constituencies, each represents a particular
broad general purpose which is variously reflected through the community agencies. The ideas created and promoted within these systems permeate nearly every community in the country, through conferences in which local people participate, through the exchange of
professional personnel, through varying degrees of direct affiliation.
National responsibility for the practical course of local policy is very
great indeed. The true significance of the dynamic processes of
national-state-local interaction through which it is discharged, however, is little understood.

It is well to remember, moreover, that during the past three decades
nationwide welfare activities have expanded with great rapidity. Both
national and local agencies have multiplied. Services have been extended to more and more people, and money has been spent more and
more liberally. Even in the local community, within whose restricted
boundaries expansion is tightly and obviously compressed, these years
have not been conducive to coherent thought about the totality of
endeavor. They have been less so at the national level.

The decade of the twenties was the great heyday of expansion for
voluntary activity. The community-wide fund raising methods of

newly created community chests spread rapidly throughout the country. The amount of money made available to agencies in different communities often doubled and tripled. New service agencies came into being, many of them made possible by money from this new outpouring. In 1920 there were 39 chests which raised a total of $19,651,-334. By 1930 there were chests in over 350 cities and they raised $76 million.[1]

The decade of the thirties was the heyday of expansion for the governmental agencies of communities. The great depression sky-rocketed public expenditures for relief and multiplied the number of emergency agencies through which the relief was administered. The basis for a permanent national public welfare system was established. The greatly increased personnel put at the disposal of public recreation and other agencies during this period was an important by-product of WPA. The foundations were laid, too, for substantially increased governmental expenditures in the interests of public health.

In the decade of the forties, both voluntary and public services continued to expand. War fund appeals unlocked fresh wellsprings of private generosity and by 1950 over 1,300 local community chests raised almost $200 million. Recreation and mental health became wartime necessities. The burden of relief expenditures due to outright unemployment fell off rapidly in the forties, but relative expenditures for others in need of financial assistance went up. Governmental expenditures for health and for recreation also rose. The upward trend of the price level offsets some of this expansion, but the increase in dollars is overwhelming to the citizen who remembers 1920.

Of the changes which have taken place in the past three decades, the rise in responsibility, leadership, and power of the federal government has commanded the most attention. In many respects this has constituted a revolutionary break with 175 years of American tradition. The tradition of complete local responsibility for dependency was strong until it was shattered by sudden realities of the depression which made relief a national responsibility. The tradition of local and state responsibility for public health and mental health is equally strong. This has not been shattered by a great emergency requiring

---

[1] Community Chests and Councils, Inc., *Yesterday and Today with Community Chests,* p. 16.

sudden national action, but the infiltration of federal money and influence in relation to these problems has greatly increased in the past fifteen years.

Facts about the federal share in the over-all financing of local services are available from a small but fairly representative number of urban communities, whose total population is 19,312,200.[2] Their data do not cover certain services with which this volume is concerned; especially the insurance payments of the federal insurance systems. But they do cover the cost of the great bulk of direct services provided in these communities to families with problems of dependency, maladjustment, ill health, and recreational need.

In these 29 cities, federal money met 12.1 percent of the total of $814,033,349 expended on behalf of their populations. For dependency, the field in which the federal government is most heavily engaged, 35.5 percent of all funds expended were federal funds. For adjustment services the proportion from federal subsidies was much smaller, only 3.3 percent, and for local health services an even smaller proportion, only 1.2 percent. For recreation the amount received from federal sources was negligible, being less than .01 percent.

These local expenditures included a substantial sum, $238,247,654 (or 29.3 percent of the total); this was met by payment from persons who received hospital, recreation, and other services from agencies which made some charges to those who could meet them. When these funds are excluded, federal funds met a somewhat higher proportion, 17 percent, of the "community subsidy" provided from tax funds, voluntary contributions, income from investments and other miscellaneous sources of income.

These figures do not, of course, include federal funds expended at state levels for administrative and other purposes which may not be reflected in local community expenditures for service. Of particular note is the fact that at present approximately 20 percent of the total expenditures of state and local health departments come from federal funds, and that while federal funds in the hospital field are limited to construction purposes, many state-wide plans for hospital construction have been made on the assumption that roughly one third of the cost will be met from federal grants-in-aid. Most of the money

[2] Community Chests and Councils of America, Inc., *Expenditures for Community Health and Welfare, 1948*, p. 39.

available under the comparatively new Mental Health Act, also, is too recently appropriated to be reflected in the figures quoted, which cover the year 1948.

With due regard for the sheer power which may accompany the control of the purse strings, this proportionate assumption of responsibility by the federal government does not seem to us alarming, even in relation to dependency. Within each of the principal areas of dependency and health, moreover, federal policy is helping to bring out integrated administration of services at state and local levels. In many states and local communities a single local public welfare department now administers all public assistance functions. Federal funds for both public health and hospital construction are administered through the Public Health Service at the national level and by the state health department in a majority of the states. This is true also of the federal funds appropriated for the promotion of mental health.

Uncertainties about the intrinsic nature of the processes of national-local interaction in such a large democratic country as ours is well illustrated by opposite federal policies in these two principal areas. Obviously the Congress and the administrative agencies have yet to decide: whether they wish primarily an integrated, albeit flexible, federal-state system; a policy of federal appropriation to 51 state and territorial systems; whether funds should be given for particular purposes to those states believed to be most in need; whether they wish to subsidize all states on a uniform basis.

At present the structure of the assistance program approximates an integrated federal-state system. All state plans have to meet basic federal requirements as to the eligibility of applicants, uniformity of coverage, basic investigational and budgetary procedures, application of the merit system to employed personnel, and so on. Within limits, federal funds match those expended by the states. Congress has steadfastly refused to adopt a policy of variable grants. There is great variation and flexibility in the state plans and in state expenditures, but the categorical assistance program is essentially a national program, the broad purposes of which are defined by Congress and jointly administered and financed by the federal government and the states.

The pattern of federal participation in health affairs is not so clear. Two different federal administrative units distribute the federal money, the Children's Bureau and the Public Health Service. The latter appropriates mainly on a "needs" rather than a "matching" basis. Allocations for both public health and hospital construction take into consideration size of population, financial resources, and the intensity of the problem. The Children's Bureau distributes money both ways; half of it on a uniform matching basis, half on a needs basis. Both require states to submit a plan as a basis for their request for funds.

In the main, the distribution of federal money for public health, including child hygiene, for mental health, and for hospital construction, is basically an allocation of particular funds to particular states for particular purposes. The allocation procedures reflect the theory that funds are to supplement and improve state systems rather than to implement a federal-state plan with basic uniformity.

The Social Security Board, the Public Health Service, and the Children's Bureau all are units within the Federal Security Agency. Thus we have in a single federal agency practical expression of two different ideas or philosophies about how to guide the interaction between federal and local influence in health and welfare matters.

Innumerable variations of philosophy and policy affecting this process are represented among the voluntary national agencies with local community affiliates. The relative impact of their power and authority is difficult to measure. With few exceptions, it does not reside in direct administrative or financial controls. Rather, it rests in processes which embrace the power to articulate philosophies and objectives; to set standards; to recommend for position; the power of national prestige; the control of methods of communication within the movement. Community chests have long realized that the policies of their member agencies are not guided wholly by local community influences, despite the wholly local sources of their support.

In a country of the size and complexity of ours, the dangers from greatly centralized national power are always very real. So too, is the possible stultification of initiative and creativity, usually described as "bureaucracy," and the epidemiological characteristics of this truly dread disease are by no means wholly governmental. Equally real is the danger of local self-complacency, of the inherent limitations of local capacity and resources. Our experience is overwhelming that local services without effective national connections, governmental or voluntary, will be found to be the poorest services in the community.

The unknown quantities involved in creating coherent national-local leadership are many. They go far beyond the problem of devising formulae for appropriating and matching funds, of budgetary and administrative directives. The prerogatives and processes of leadership may seem intangible, but they are no less real on the national scene than in the local community.

Maturity of thought usually emerges after great periods of pioneer expansion, rather than during the process. Our preceding sections have given evidence that within each of the separate national systems there is a growing concern for greater coherence of purpose and the perfection of scientific disciplines. One may hope for an acceleration of this pace. For, if we may repeat, "the responsibility of national leadership for the practical course of local community policy is very great indeed."

PRESENT STATUS

Whatever constructive ferment may come from more purposeful unity, scientific progress and community-minded national leadership must work upon the practical ingredients at hand. In organizing the materials of the different sections of this volume, we conceived the following to be essential to progressively better community planning: strategic knowledge about the community-wide characteristics of the problem; clarity and competence regarding the functions indispensable to a program for prevention and protection; a community-wide structure for the administration of these functions, designed with a rational regard for efficient relationships between the various parts; awareness of basic forces and trends that should move the principal agency systems toward greater coherence in their approach.

In the following pages, we recapitulate briefly the present stage of progress, or lack of it, toward these four essentials in the four major problem areas with which our community services are concerned.

STRATEGIC CHARACTERISTICS OF PROBLEMS

1. Disciplined analysis of the strategic community-wide characteristics of dependency is in its infancy. Consolidated public welfare departments, however, now have data about almost all families in the

community who become dependent. Especially needed is the application of procedures such as those used in St. Paul to distinguish between dependency caused primarily by family disabilities, and that caused primarily by the unavailability of employment. As in St. Paul, the utility of continuous dependency rates for the whole population needs to be explored. So too, does the breakdown of rates for special occupational, industrial, racial or other significant population segments. Very little is now known about the backlog volume of economically handicapping disabilities. Neither is there enough known about the constellations of disabilities most often recurrent in the families comprising this backlog who eventually become dependent.

2. Development of data important to the community-wide control of communicable disease and the hazards of maternity and infancy has been a signal contribution of the public health system. Disciplines requisite to this purpose are at the command of the public health officer and his staff.

Procedures for the disciplined analysis of the community-wide characteristics of particular chronic diseases are only beginning to emerge. Needed are better means of establishing community priorities within the general classification of chronic diseases and disabilities. Particularly important is the determination of the relative value of early detection of these; prognostic variables at different stages of each of the diseases; and other characteristics of significance to planned community action. The utilization of data available from hospital inpatient and outpatient records for purposes of community-wide analysis has not yet been adequately explored. Especially needed are procedures for the disciplined analysis of the family characteristics of chronic diseases in relation to the processes of detection, control through treatment regimes, social and occupational rehabilitation.

The public health system has not assumed responsibility for the disciplined analysis of the strategic characteristics of physical handicaps. State-wide data about prevalence, degree of impairment, employability and other characteristics of importance to planned action are developed and used by state agencies for the blind, and to a lesser degree by state agencies for crippled children. Needed, however, are procedures for over-all analysis of the community-wide characteristics of blindness, orthopedic handicaps, disabling deafness, and speech defects. As with the chronic diseases, especially needed are procedures for the disciplined analysis of the family characteristics of these conditions and their relationship to social and occupational rehabilitation.

3. Properly speaking, beginnings have yet to be made in the analysis of data pertinent to a community-wide program for prevention and protection against the consequences of maladjustment. We believe, however, that disciplined experimentation with such procedures is of first importance. Our own experience shows that the family unit is a useful base for consolidating data about specific evidences and symptoms of maladjustment. The St. Paul project demonstrated the importance of distinguishing between those maladjusted families in which there is evidence of behavior disorders and those in which there is not. The social breakdown index lends itself to systematic detection as well as to analysis of the concentration of disorders. Other evidence, as well as our own, makes it quite clear that mentally defective persons represent a greatly disproportionate share of the community's problems in relation to maladjustment.

4. Disciplined analysis of the strategic characteristics of community-wide need for community-supported recreation so far has been limited almost exclusively to determining the need for outdoor space and large-scale facilities. Equally needed are procedures for the analysis of the need for different types of community-supported activities. We have suggested two complementary bases from which to develop these procedures. The first is by realistic reference to the relative needs of the principal age groups which reflect changing recreation characteristics in the life cycle. The second is by equally realistic reference to relative recreation needs in the different natural districts or neighborhoods of the community.

OF INDISPENSABLE FUNCTIONS

1. The principal functions necessary to the community-wide care of dependent families are well established in good public welfare administrative practice. The determination of need involves a systematic estimate of requirements for the principal items in each family's budget, and an examination of its available resources, if any. Provision of maintenance should be by cash grants which are equal, theoretically, to the difference between the total budgetary requirements and total current resources. In many states, in practice, public fiscal policy does not accept the living standards on the basis of which these itemized

needs are estimated. Better procedures are needed for reconciling expert and public judgment regarding the income minimum below which families in the community should not be allowed to fall. Needed also is a more precise and authoritative definition of the content of the specialized professional discipline required for the performance of these functions.

Consideration of functions and procedures necessary to the prevention of that part of dependency caused by instabilities and frictions in the economy has been outside the competence of our research. The St. Paul data, however, as well as more general evidence, indicate that in periods of high employment a great portion of the residual dependency load arises from disabilities that limit family income. We have suggested that the public welfare movement assume leadership in the experimental development of procedures for the systematic identification, classification, and continuous analysis of the circumstances found in these families. We believe the results will lay the foundations for a better coordinated program for community-wide prevention and control of dependency.

2. The development of a functional discipline applicable to the community-wide control of communicable disease, and of the hazards of pregnancy and infancy, has included systematic procedures for the reporting of individual cases and special techniques for their discovery at earlier stages than would otherwise be routinely reported. The specific procedures applied in cases of communicable disease to assure maximum protection to the affected person, his family, and the general community, are determined by precise knowledge about the strategic characteristics of a particular disease. Similarly, procedures invoked during the course of the maternal and infant cycle assure instructive diagnostic, treatment, and other services in relation to the known hazards. For tuberculosis, which is both chronic and communicable, the maintenance of a continuing register of all patients is essential to determining progress or retrogression, the appropriate execution of plans for care, treatment, and rehabilitation, as well as the over-all evaluation of the community-wide program for the prevention and reduction of the disease. Requisites for the disciplined conduct of this function by the public health officer, the public health nurse, and other specialized personnel are precisely and authoritatively established.

The initiation of similar procedures appropriate to the known characteristics of chronic diseases is now being undertaken experimentally in certain areas. We hope that the pace and spread of that experimentation may be accelerated and that it will give due regard to family implications in these diseases. Broadly speaking, assurance of the appropriate detection, diagnostic, and treatment services is more necessary to the control of chronic diseases than to those of the infectious variety. Because of these facts, in common with many others we believe that development of procedures in this area depend on close collaboration between public health and hospital authorities.

Similar procedures are now in effect in some places for the state-wide control of blindness, crippled children, and of potentially employable handicapped adults. Control, however, is under separate auspices; the community-wide application to the prevention, reduction, and rehabilitation of the composite of disabling physical conditions has not been attempted. In theory, at least, this seems to us a logical function of the public health system.

The function of medical diagnosis and treatment is the exclusive prerogative of the physician; its performance is increasingly dependent upon organized association of specialists from the different branches of the medical profession in the interest of the patient, and the use of specialized ancillary equipment and facilities. Assurance of the availability of specialized facilities and of specialized personnel through the community-supported general hospital has become an indispensable attribute of this function. In the past decade especially, more precise standards have developed with respect to hospital facilities, medical staff composition and organization, and medical policies affecting the treatment of the patient. Group medical practice by physicians associated in private practice under various types of auspices has also been increasing, but the community as such has taken no direct responsibility for promoting this form of medical practice.

Bedside and public health nursing, the two main divisions of the nursing function, are the exclusive prerogative of the nurse. The one is an important component in medical treatment under the direction of a physician; the other in community-wide disease control under the over-all supervision and direction of the public health officer. The standards for training and professional performance essential to this discipline are precisely and authoritatively established.

3. The principal functions indispensable to community-wide pre-vention and protection against the consequences of maladjustment are less well established. The diagnosis and treatment of behavior disorders is shared jointly by the professions of psychiatry, social case-work, and psychology, and there is general agreement that all these disciplines are needed in some combination in many types of disorder. Standards applicable to appropriate combinations should be based upon comprehensive classification of the disorders; at present any such existing standards are in terms of administrative units. This needs to be much more precisely explored in order to give a sound basis for the community-wide provision of this diagnostic and treat-ment function. The form and content of these three professional dis-ciplines are in different stages of perfection, and the requisites for training and standards of performance vary considerably in precision and intensity.

The broad distinction between diagnosis and treatment of behavior disorders and that of social treatment of situational difficulties by so-cial caseworkers has long been recognized. But we lack the definitive and authoritative standards by which to determine the competence of community agencies to undertake social treatment.

Practically speaking, no attempt has yet been made within this field to develop procedures appropriate to the community-wide control of behavior disorders. The correctional system has made great strides in improving and directing the processes by which cases flow through the successive stages of apprehension, adjudication and disposition, probation, institutional correction, parole, and discharge. Best prac-tice in the institutional programs of the mental health and the cor-rectional systems calls for careful prognostic classification before as-signment, discriminatory release, parole, and follow-up supervision. In segments of the voluntary casework system there is a measure of community-wide control over the processes by which children are separated from their own homes and placed in boarding homes or institutions.

There has been no significant experimentation with the systematic community-wide detection and reporting of disorders, diagnostic and prognostic classification, periodic review of progress or retrogres-sion, analysis of the appropriateness of care and treatment, and basic evaluation of results. We believe that sound experimentation with such procedures would make a signal contribution to clarifying the confusion in this field and would lay foundations for eliminating much of the present waste. We have emphasized sufficiently, we trust, our reasons for believing that the family unit is the keystone for the perfection of these procedures.

4. The indispensability of space, and both outdoor and indoor facilities, to much recreation enjoyment and activity has made this a dominate concern in the recreation plans and programs of all public, and many private, agencies. As we have indicated, standards applicable to community-wide needs, especially for outdoor space and facilities, have been carefully worked out and authoritatively established. We believe that the provision and maintenance of these facilities should be a primary function of the public agencies.

Criteria by which to distinguish between the function of organizing activity-centered interests and group-friendship interests are not so clearly established. Both have in common the fact that the activities must be organized. The prime objectives are presumed to be different, and we believe that in fact they are. The major objective of activity-centered interests is the degree of satisfaction derived from engaging in a particular activity. The main objective of the friendship group is the satisfaction which comes from association with persons who make up the group. Under certain circumstances each may produce the essential satisfactions of the other.

Different skills are required for leadership and direction of these two major types of groups. In neither case has there yet emerged the form and content of a special discipline with precise and authoritative standards.

Considerable informed opinion holds that the organization of activity-centered interests should be a primary responsibility of public recreation agencies and that private agencies should concentrate on group-friendship interests. Precise clarification of the essential differences between them is needed for sound long-range community planning.

COMMUNITY-WIDE STRUCTURE

1. Authorities are unanimous in the opinion that administration of all forms of public home relief and institutional care should be consolidated in a single public welfare department, preferably county-

wide. Such an agency should plan and execute all phases of the community-wide program in this field.

Except in two areas, the need for voluntary agency service in the field of dependency is of negligible significance. Settlement laws of many states restrict public relief to persons who meet state and local residence requirements. All expert opinion concurs in the belief that these should be abolished, but progress in so doing has been extremely slow. Where restrictions exist, private agencies perforce must fill the gap. The need for institutional care of persons with chronic disabilities suggests that homes for the aged under private auspices, like public county homes, offer economical opportunity for conversion to meet this problem.

2. In urban communities a single public health department has long been considered the pivotal agency in the administration of the program for the community-wide prevention and control of disease. Authorities believe that in most instances a county-wide setup is preferable, and that in sparsely settled areas its jurisdiction should be extended to cover a population of at least 50,000 persons. There are precise standards as to the budget required for public health nurses and other personnel in the administration of this unit.

Principles governing the relationship of the public health nursing services to the public health program for the control of communicable disease, and the hazards of maternity and infancy, also are well established. Preferably the administration of these services should be by not more than two separate units—the public health department itself, and a voluntary visiting nursing association, combining both public health and bedside nursing care of the sick. Serious experimentation is now being undertaken with the combination of these services into a single unit.

National and local leadership in many fields of service subscribe to the principle that private agencies should experiment with procedures and services that eventually can be turned over to, and strengthen, the program of the public unit. This has long been a cardinal plank in the platform of voluntary agencies concerned with the communicable diseases and with maternal and infant and child health. Authorities generally agree that this principle should be applied to the programs being developed by an increasing number of voluntary agencies concerned with special aspects of chronic illness and disability.

The pivotal agency in the community-supported program for the diagnosis, and treatment of illness is the general hospital, with both inpatient and outpatient service. With the possible exception of the largest cities, hospitals specializing in particular diseases or conditions are now considered unnecessary. Generally accepted, also, is the principle that special clinic service should be consolidated in the administration of generalized hospital outpatient departments. Increasingly accepted is the principle that both public and private general hospitals should not only be equipped to serve all types of diseases and conditions but all income groups as well, on a full-pay, part-pay, or free basis. The trend is to link together, within prescribed geographical areas, through contractual or administrative arrangements, the resources of large general hospitals with smaller hospital units and health centers.

Unrealistic though it may be in many sections, we have registered our conviction that community-wide responsibility by the public welfare department for the determination of need for free or part-free hospital and medical care and payment of its full cost offers the only practical solution for the present great confusion and economic waste.

Voluntary insurance against hospital costs has spread with extraordinary rapidity in the past decade. A substantial proportion of families in the middle and higher income brackets are now covered, and the principle has the support of all important groups. Voluntary insurance against the cost of physicians' services, within as well as outside the hospital, has made slower progress, primarily because of different schools of thought regarding arrangements to provide it. In our own view, the policyholders' selection of a doctor from a panel of physicians associated on the medical staff of the same hospital offers a constructive solution for the need to preserve the individual doctor-patient relationship in a setting which assures the availability of a composite of specialized services and facilities.

To date, proposals for national governmental insurance against the cost of hospital and physicians' services have made no practical progress in Congress. It seems to us unlikely that they will do so until the opposing schools of thought regarding administration are more nearly reconciled.

3. It is impossible to identify with assurance any agency which occupies an unquestioned pivotal relation to the community-wide pro-

gram for prevention and protection against the consequences of maladjustment. We predict with some confidence that such an agency, or agencies, eventually will emerge. In our view the pivotal agency should be family-centered. Its disciplines should synthesize the disciplines of psychiatry, social casework, and psychology and should be equipped to serve as the focal point for the generalized diagnosis of behavior disorders in the community. The types of cases to be carried for treatment should be planned carefully in terms of prognostic knowledge about relative community-wide needs and the availability of specialized treatment resources. Also in our view, there is needed an agency equipped to organize community-wide procedures for the continuous identification, recording, classification, and over-all review of families manifesting the more important evidences of maladjustment. Perhaps this can, and should be, the same agency, although the professional disciplines requisite to the performance of these two functions need to be clearly distinguished.

We have not attempted, artificially, to create such a pivotal agency or agencies. The present trends within the several systems are too obscure. Responsibility for these functions might be lodged with equal logic within the public welfare department or the public health department, or in a community outpost of a well-integrated correctional or mental health system. Or the service might be conducted under private auspices, or under joint sponsorship of some appropriate type.

Within the correctional system some leaders are moving in the direction of a state adult correctional authority which would consolidate the administration of local jails, state institutions, probation, and parole. Systematic diagnostic, and prognostic, classification prior to and during custody is considered the cornerstone of this proposal. The State Youth Authority is designed for much the same purpose for juvenile and youthful offenders, although a countertrend is to incorporate the detention, probation, institutional, and parole services under the administrative aegis of state or local public welfare departments.

Within the mental health system, the administration of the state institutions and of local community clinics traditionally has been divorced. A countertrend is to be noted in a few states. The intent of the federal Mental Health Act seems to be to continue this separation, lodging responsibility for expansion of community clinics, in most instances, in the State Health Department. Within this system a state-local structure appropriate to both mental disease and mental defect, designed to provide suitable diagnostic screening and classification prior to assignment to different types of care, and equally designed for follow-up supervision after release, seems to us to be of great importance indeed.

For both public and private agencies dealing with children, a key point in operations centers around the decision to separate, or not to separate, the child from his family. The increasing integration of public foster home services with the family services of the public welfare department, and with responsibility for investigating cases of child neglect for the juvenile court, provides a sound structural design for better consideration at this point. We have noted the trend, locally, toward the consolidation of the voluntary family casework and children's casework services.

4. In many respects the public unit responsible for the organization of recreation activities is the pivotal agency in the community-wide program for meeting recreation needs. Particularly is this true if administration is consolidated with either of the two public agencies which provide space and large facilities—the park department and the school system.

Our own view tends toward a consolidated park and recreation department which would make clear and definite arrangements with the school system for use of its indoor and outdoor facilities. In practice, however, authorities agree that the best structure locally is the one which most readily assures to the organizing unit the use of these principal resources.

The structure of each private agency is designed for its own purpose, usually after the pattern of the national movement with which it is affiliated. While most communities probably would welcome some simplification of the present composite pattern, any hope for movement in this direction in the near future is generally understood to be unrealistic. On the other hand, if communities continue the present trend to place responsibility for provision of large scale building-centered activities upon public departments, in all probability voluntary agencies which provide similar facilities will find it strategic to shift their own structural focus.

FOR COHERENT PLANNING AND ACTION

1. Beyond question the trend toward consolidated local administration of all public assistance services has helped greatly to make for more coherent thought and action in respect to the community's program for dependency. Needed, however, is a leadership more clearly aware that solutions for this problem do not lie simply in more adequate relief grants to individual families; in wider and higher insurance coverage; or even in greater budgetary provision for casework and medical service. Solutions lie also in the disciplined analysis of distinctive community-wide causes of dependency; in the systematic marshaling of community forces, including available technical services, to prevent and reduce the consequences arising from recognized causes. Especially since the end of the Second World War, there has been increasing evidence of a realistic acceptance, among public welfare leaders, of the necessity for moves in this direction. The years that lie immediately ahead call for concentration on the development of practical ways and means.

2. Particularly in the last decade, the clear emergence of four trends in the field of health holds great hope for a more coherent attack upon the totality of diseases and conditions which affect the community's health. The public health movement has been assuming more aggressive leadership in the community-wide control of chronic disease. The role of the community general hospital as an instrument through which to assemble the constellations of medical specialties and facilities now necessary to serve the needs of the patient, has become increasingly clear. This, in fact, is merely the complement of an increasing recognition among physicians that a major problem of modern medicine is how to put at the disposal of the patient the composite wealth of specialized medical knowledge and method. Finally, the steady expansion of insurance against medical costs is of aid in solving the problem of finance.

The fusion of these trends into coherent plans for practical community-wide action is still to come. The catalytic agent most needed, it seems to us, is greater knowledge about the strategic community-wide characteristics of the principal chronic diseases. For this knowledge is essential to the development of procedures for detection, assurance of diagnostic and treatment resources, and the continuing supervision and review of status of patients with which all must be concerned. Knowledge, discipline, and methods to this end, it also seems to us, must be contributed from both the public health and hospital fields. Leadership in these fields, in turn and in truth, represent those segments of the medical profession itself which have the greatest community-wide experience and concern.

3. We have stated our case for the need for greater coherence in community planning and action to prevent and protect the community against the hazards and consequences of maladjustment. It rests, in the first instance, on the fact of increasing knowledge about the characteristics of disordered and irresponsible human behavior. It rests in the second, on increasing competence in the three professions with responsibility for diagnosing and treating these disorders—psychiatry, social casework, and psychology. It has behind it the pressures which arise out of great community confusion about the application of this knowledge, and the most effective use of the professional disciplines.

Realistic trends toward more coherent community planning and action, however, are not now readily discernible. The most clear-cut is to be found in recognition that organization for diagnosis and treatment requires some combination of the three services. This in turn is engendering a more general awareness of mutual concern and relationships between the systems of correction, mental health, and social casework than was true even so recently as a decade ago.

What is most needed to stimulate the realities of coherent thought, it seems to us, is planned experimentation in certain areas, with the avowed, and concentrated, intent to prevent and reduce the community-wide manifestation of maladjustment in its various forms. Experimentation of this kind in a number of communities three or four decades ago crystallized the objectives and laid the foundations for precise procedures for similar measures in the prevention and reduction of disease. Specific evidences of maladjustment are steadily increasing. So too are expenditures for specific care and treatment. But only out of experience can the form and content of a coherent pattern of functional processes for precise control begin to take shape.

4. Of greatest strategic significance to community-wide recreation planning is the fact that people spend most of their leisure within

striking distance of their homes. Attention is now given to the balanced distribution of space and large-scale facilities to meet the relative needs of the "natural" areas. But these districts should also provide a framework within which to assure a better distribution of all community recreation activities. Recreation agencies are accustomed to think in terms of their own programs and constituencies, on both a city-wide and area basis, instead of thinking about how their services would fit into the requirements for each district: a park, a playfield, playgrounds, a large indoor center, a youth center, and a noninstitutional group plan.

These provide a manageable design around which to fill in the composite picture of a district's recreation services in comparison with other districts. Better tools must be devised by which to measure and judge variable needs of districts which possess different age, economic, social, and population characteristics. Better tools are needed to distinguish between the functions appropriate to these needs. But in the local community, a systematic framework within which to plan for district needs and services gives a most effective stimulus to coherent thought about community planning and action.

The pages of this volume have been concentrated upon a great community enterprise, built by our people for the common welfare. A tribute to a cherished and uniquely American tradition, this enterprise has been constructed in a spirit of optimism, ingenuity, generosity, and mutual responsibility. Today, drawing upon increasing resources of progressively competent scientific and professional personnel, the community pours forth a great volume of service to troubled people. The demands are tremendous, and to a great extent have been well met.

This enterprise of service is too precious a possession, too useful a community asset, to take for granted. It requires and deserves the thoughtful attention of the professional and layman alike in the interests of realizing its rich potentialities for more meaningful performance. Complex and baffling as its patterns are, it holds, at its core, the possibility for prevention as well as remedy of the more serious problems which occasion human suffering. The task of discovering the precise nature of these possibilities, and working to free them for practical expression calls for disciplined thought, courage, and patience. Indeed, the authors of this book have acquired a very healthy respect for the amount of discipline and forbearance requisite to the fruitful realization of these potentialities. They offer their findings for whatever they may be worth to people who wish to do a more purposeful job of planning for the common welfare.

SELECTED BIBLIOGRAPHY

Aaronson, Franklin and Hilda Rosenbloom. "State Aid to Veterans." *Social Security Bulletin,* VIII, No. 2 (February, 1945), 18.

Acee, Alfred. "State Workmen's Compensation Legislation in 1947." *Monthly Labor Review,* LXV, No. 4 (October, 1947), 417.

—— "Workmen's Compensation Legislation, 1948." *Monthly Labor Review,* LXVII, No. 3 (September, 1948), 280.

Administrator of Veterans Affairs. Annual Report for Fiscal Year Ending June 30, 1948. Washington, Government Printing Office, 1949.

Alexander, Franz. "The Accident-prone Individual." *Public Health Reports,* LXIV, No. 12 (March 25, 1949), 357.

Alt, Herschel. "Juvenile Behavior Problems." *Social Work Year Book, 1947,* New York, Russell Sage Foundation, 1947, pp. 266, 272.

Altmeyer, A. J. "Old Age, Survivors and Disability Insurance." *Social Security Bulletin,* XII, No. 4 (April, 1949), 4.

—— "People on the Move: Effect of Residence Requirements for Public Assistance." *Social Security Bulletin,* IX, No. 1 (January, 1946), 3.

American College of Surgeons. Manual of Hospital Standardization. Chicago, 1946.

American Hospital Association, American Medical Association, American Public Health Association and American Public Welfare Association. Joint statement: "Planning for the Chronically Ill." *American Journal of Public Health,* XXXVII, No. 10 (October, 1947), 1256.

American National Red Cross. Handbook of Information Concerning Servicemen and Veterans. ARC 207 revised. Washington, 1947.

American Nurses Association. 1949 Facts about Nursing. New York, 1950.

American Prison Association, Committee on Classification and Casework. Handbook on Classification in Correctional Institutions. New York, 1947.

American Prison Association, Committee on the Model State Plan. Manual of Suggested Standards for a State Correctional System. New York, 1946.

American Public Health Association. The Control of Communicable Diseases. 6th ed. New York, 1945.

American Public Health Association, Committee on Administrative Practices. What's the Score? New York, 1949.

American Public Health Association, Subcommittee on Medical Care. "The Quality of Medical Care in a National Health Program." *American Journal of Public Health,* XXXIX, No. 7 (July, 1949), 898.

American Public Welfare Association. "Local Council Notes." *Public Welfare*, I, No. 3 (March, 1943), 93.

American Public Welfare Association, Committee on Medical Care Report. Chicago, 1938.

American Public Welfare Association, Welfare Policy Committee. "Objectives for Public Welfare Legislation—1947." Chicago, 1947.

American Youth Commission. Youth and The Future. American Council on Education, New York, 1942.

Arnold, Mildred. "Children's Services in the Public Welfare Agency." *Child Welfare Reports*, No. 3 (May, 1947), 2.

Barnett, M. Robert, and Helga Lende. "The Blind." *Social Work Year Book—1951*, New York, American Association of Social Workers, 1951.

Bellows, Marjorie T. "Case Registers." *Public Health Reports*, LXIV, No. 36 (September 9, 1949), 1148.

Bengs, Hilding. "Department of Public Welfare Approach to Mental Deficiency." *American Journal of Mental Deficiency*, L, No. 3 (January, 1946), 644.

Berman, Jules H. "State Public Assistance Legislation, 1949." *Social Security Bulletin*, XII, No. 12 (December, 1949), 6.

Beveridge, Sir William. Social Insurance and Allied Services. New York, The Macmillan Co., 1942.

Bolduan, Charles Frederick, and W. Nils. Public Health and Hygiene. 4th ed. Philadelphia, W. B. Saunders Company, 1949.

Britten, Rollo H. "Receipt of Medical Service in the Different Urban Populations." *Public Health Reports*, LV, No. 48 (November 29, 1940), 8, Table 6.

Browning, Grace. "Public Administration and Human Welfare." *Social Service Review*, XXII, No. 1 (March, 1948), 11.

Buell, Bradley. "Let's Look at the Record," *Survey Midmonthly*, LXXXII, No. 2 (February, 1946), 42.

Burns, Eveline M. The American Social Security System. Boston, Houghton, Mifflin Company, 1949.

Butler, George D. Introduction to Community Recreation. New York, McGraw-Hill Book Company, 1940.

California, Assembly Interim Committee on Crime and Corrections. Partial Report. Sacramento, 1949.

Canadian Youth Commission. Youth and Recreation. Toronto, Ryerson Press, 1946.

Chapin, Robert Coit. The Standard of Living in New York City. New York, Russell Sage Foundation, 1909.

Chapman, A. L. "The Concept of Multiphasic Screening." *Public Health Reports*, LXIV, No. 42 (October 21, 1949), 1311.

Cianci, Vincentz. "Home Supervision of Mental Deficients in New Jersey." *American Journal of Mental Deficiency*, XLI, No. 3 (January, 1947), 519.

Clark, Dean A., and Katharine G. Clark. "Medical Care." *Social Work Year Book, 1947.* New York, Russell Sage Foundation, 1947.

Colcord, Joanna. Cash Relief. New York, Russell Sage Foundation, 1936.

—— Your Community—Its Provision for Health, Education, Safety and Welfare. New York, Russell Sage Foundation, 1947.

Commission on Hospital Care. Hospital Care in the United States. New York, The Commonwealth Fund; Cambridge, Harvard University Press, 1947.

Community Chests and Councils of America, Inc. Community Chests and Appropriations to Their Member Agencies (Bulletin 71). New York, 1932.

—— Expenditures for Community Health and Welfare, 31 Urban Areas, 1948. New York, 1949.

—— Yesterday and Today with Community Chests. New York, 1937.

Community Surveys, Inc. A Survey of the Florida State Welfare Board. New York, 1949.

Cronin, John W., *et al.* "Hospital Construction under the Hill-Burton Program." *Public Health Reports,* LXV, No. 23 (June 9, 1950), 744, Table 1.

Crutcher, Hester B. "Family Care of Mental Defectives." *American Journal of Mental Deficiency,* LIII, No. 2 (October, 1948), 345.

Darley, Ward. "Denver Rheumatic Fever Clinic." *Public Health Reports,* LXIV, No. 51 (December 23, 1949), 1631.

Davies, Stanley P. Social Control of the Mentally Deficient. New York, Thomas Y. Crowell Co., 1930.

Davis, Michael M. "Outpatient Service in the United States." *Administrative Medicine,* ed. Haven Emerson. New York and Edinburgh, Thomas Nelson and Sons, 1941.

Dawson, Marshall. Problems of Workmen's Compensation Administration in the United States and Canada. Department of Labor, Bureau of Labor Statistics, Bulletin No. 672, Washington, 1940.

DeMarche, David F. The Relative Effectiveness of Y.M.C.A. Branches with Various Types of Buildings. New York, Association Press, 1947.

Deming, Dorothy. "Visiting Nurses Service." *Administrative Medicine* ed. Haven Emerson. New York and Edinburgh, Thomas Nelson and Sons, 1941.

de Schweinitz, Karl. England's Road to Social Security. Philadelphia, University of Pennsylvania Press, 1947.

—— People and Process in Social Security. Washington, American Council on Education, 1948.

Dimock, Hedley S. Rediscovering the Adolescent. New York, Association Press, 1937.

Division of Prices and Cost of Living. "Consumer Spending: Denver, Detroit and Houston, 1948." *Monthly Labor Review,* LXIX, No. 6 (December, 1949), 629, 632, 634.

Dorn, Harold F. "The Relative Amount of Ill-Health in Rural and Urban Communities." *Public Health Reports,* LIII, No. 28 (July 15, 1938), 1181–1195.

Eggers, Carl. "Education of the General Practitioner." *Trends in Medical Education.* New York, The Commonwealth Fund, 1949.

Ellingston, John R. Protecting Our Children from Criminal Careers. New York, Prentice-Hall, Inc., 1948.

Emerson, Charles Phillips, and Jane Elizabeth Taylor. Essentials of Medicine. 15th ed. Philadelphia, J. B. Lippincott, 1946.

Emerson, Haven. Administrative Medicine. New York, Thomas Nelson and Sons, 1941.

Emerson, Haven, and Martha Luginbuhl. Local Health Units for the Nation. New York, The Commonwealth Fund, 1945.

Evans, J. W. "The Facts in the Case." *Survey Graphic,* XXXVII, No. 3 (March, 1948), 109.

Evans, Louis. "Providing Institutional Care for Recipients of Public Assistance." *Public Welfare,* III, No. 11 (November, 1945), 250.

"Extent of Workmen's Compensation in the United States." *Monthly Labor Review,* LXXI, No. 4 (October, 1950), 487.

Falk, Myron. Settlement Laws. New York, American Association of Social Workers, 1948.

Farman, Carl, and Catherine Perrins. "The New British System of Social Security." *Social Security Bulletin,* X, No. 2 (June, 1947), 9–22.

Federal Security Agency. Annual Reports. Washington.

—— Handbook of Public Assistance Administration. Washington, 1946.

—— Social Security Year Book, 1946, 1947, 1948. This is an annual supplement to the *Social Security Bulletin.*

Federal Security Agency, Bureau of Public Assistance. Families Receiving Aid to Dependent Children, October, 1942. Washington, 1945. Part I, pp. 25–27.

—— "Personnel in State and Local Public Assistance Agencies, June, 1949." *Social Security Bulletin,* XIII, No. 4 (April, 1950), 12.

—— "Public Assistance Supplementation of the Income of Old-Age and Survivors Insurance Beneficiaries." *Social Security Bulletin,* XII, No. 10 (October, 1949), 18.

Federal Security Agency, Children's Bureau. Services to Children (Fact Sheet). Washington, 1950.

Federal Security Agency, Office of Education. Bulletin No. 5: Education in Training Schools for Delinquent Youth. Washington, 1945.

Federal Security Agency, Social Security Administration. "A Comprehensive Social Security Program." *Social Security Bulletin,* XIII, No. 1–2 (January–February, 1950), 4.

—— Compilation of the Social Security Laws. Washington, 1947.

—— "Current Operating Statistics." *Social Security Bulletin.* Washington.

—— Public Assistance Goals, 1947. Washington, 1946.

Felix, Robert H. "The Relation of the National Mental Health Act to State Health Authorities." *Public Health Reports,* LXII, No. 2 (January 10, 1947), 6.

Fisher, Ruth, and Margaret Lovell Plumley. Development of a Combination Agency. New York, National Organization for Public Health Nursing, 1947.

Fitzgerald, Gerald B. Community Organization for Recreation. New York, A. S. Barnes and Company, 1948.

Foote, Franklin M. "Milestones in Sight Conservation." *Yale Journal of Biology and Medicine,* XIX, No. 4 (March, 1947), 595.

—— "Public Responsibility for an Eye Health Program." *The Sight Saving Review,* XVII, No. 4 (Winter, 1947), 232.

Garrison, Fielding H. An Introduction to the History of Medicine. 4th ed. Philadelphia, W. B. Saunders Company, 1929.

Gentile, Felix M., and Donald S. Howard. General Assistance. New York, American Association of Social Workers, 1949.

Gillin, John Lewis. Poverty and Dependency. New York, D. Appleton–Century, 1937.

Gilmartin, Richard T. "From Planning to Action: New York State Integrates Its Welfare Services." *Public Welfare,* IV, No. 6 (June, 1946), 133.

Glassberg, Benjamin. "Rent Policies under Emergency Relief." *Social Service Review,* XI, No. 3 (September, 1937), 419–433.

Girl Scouts of the U.S.A., Personnel Department. Professional Opportunity in Girl Scouting. New York, n.d.

Glueck, Sheldon and Eleanor Glueck. Later Criminal Careers. New York, The Commonwealth Fund, 1937.

Goldmann, Franz. Voluntary Medical Care Insurance in the United States. New York, Columbia University Press, 1948.

Gunn, Selskar, and Philip S. Platt. Voluntary Health Agencies. New York, The Ronald Press, 1945.

Hamilton, Gordon. Theory and Practice of Social Case Work. New York, Columbia University Press, 1940.

Hamilton, Kenneth W. Counseling the Handicapped in the Rehabilitation Process. New York, The Ronald Press Co., 1950.

Hamilton, Samuel. "Public Institutions for Mental Defectives, Their Organization and Equipment." *American Journal of Mental Deficiency,* L, No. 3 (January, 1946), 452.

Hansen, A. H. Economic Policy and Full Employment. New York, McGraw-Hill, 1947.

Heller Committee for Research in Social Economics. Quantity and Cost Budgets for Three Income Levels, Priced for San Francisco, and Budget for Dependent Families. Berkeley, University of California Press, 1946.

Henderson, D. K., and R. D. Gillespie. A Text-Book of Psychiatry. 6th ed. New York, Oxford University Press, 1944.

Hill, John G. "Great Britain's New Social Security." *Survey Midmonthly,* LXXXIV, No. 8 (August, 1948), 243–245.

Hilliard, Raymond M. "Basic Principles in Public Assistance." *Public Aid in Illinois,* (March, 1948), p. 9.

—— "Chronic Illness Major Cause of Dependency." *Survey Midmonthly,* LXXXIII, No. 11 (November, 1947), 307.

—— "The Emerging Function of Public Institutions In Our Social Security Structure." *Social Service Review,* XX, No. 4 (December, 1946), 481.

Hiscock, Ira V. Community Health Organization. 3d ed. New York, The Commonwealth Fund, 1939.

Hoehler, Fred A. "What is UNRRA Doing?" *Survey Midmonthly,* LXXXI, No. 4 (April, 1945), 99.

Hoge, Vane M. "Hospital Survey and Construction Program in the United States." *Public Health Reports,* LXIV, No. 32 (August 12, 1949), 991, 994, 995.

Hollingshead, August B. Elmtown's Youth. New York, John Wiley and Sons., Inc., 1949.

Homan, Paul T., and Fritz Machlup, eds. Financing American Prosperity: a Symposium of Economists. New York, The Twentieth Century Fund, 1945.

Hopkirk, Howard W. Institutions Serving Children. New York, Russell Sage Foundation, 1944.

Howard, Clive. "Every Doctor's Office a Cancer Detection Center." *Readers' Digest* (December, 1950), 108.

Howard, Donald S. The WPA and Federal Relief Policy. New York, Russell Sage Foundation, 1943.

Hunt, G. Halsey. "Medical Group Practice in the United States." *New England Journal of Medicine,* CCXXXVII, No. 3 (July 17, 1947), 72, 73.

Hurlin, Ralph G., et al. Causes of Blindness among Recipients of Aid to the Blind. Washington, Federal Security Agency, Bureau of Public Assistance, 1947.

Hurwitz, Abner. "D.C. Income in Relation to BLS Family Budget." *Monthly Labor Review,* LXVI, No. 6 (December, 1948), 622–23.

Kaiser, Raymond F. "Proposed Elements of a State Cancer Control Program." *Public Health Reports,* XLIV, No. 37 (September 16, 1949), 1171.

Kassius, Cora., ed. Relief Practices in a Family Agency. Family Welfare Association of America, 1942.

Kellogg, Lester S., and Dorothy S. Brady. "The City Worker's Family Budget." *Monthly Labor Review,* LXVI, No. 2 (February, 1948), 133–70.

Kempf, George A. Laws Pertaining to the Admittance of Patients to Mental Hospitals. Washington, U.S. Public Health Service, 1944.

Kessler, Henry H. Rehabilitation of the Physically Handicapped. New York, Columbia University Press, 1947.

Lebergott, Stanley, et al. "Labor Force, Employment, and Unemployment,

1929–39: Estimating Methods." *Monthly Labor Review,* LXVII, No. 1 (July, 1948), 51.

Lemkau, Paul V. Mental Hygiene in Public Health. New York, McGraw-Hill Book Company, Inc., 1949.

Limburg, Charles C. Patients in Mental Institutions, 1947. Washington, National Institute of Mental Health, 1950.

Lowry, James V. "How the Mental Health Act Works." *Public Health Reports,* LXIV, No. 10 (March 11, 1949), 306.

Lundberg, George A. Leisure, a Suburban Study. New York, Columbia University Press, 1934.

McGibony, J. R., and Louis Block. "Better Patient Care through Coordination." *Public Health Reports,* LXIV, No. 47 (November 25, 1949), 1501.

Major, Ralph H. Fatal Partners in War and Disease. New York, Doubleday Doran and Company, 1941.

Marquard, Elva. "Dependents in Social Security Systems of Great Britain, New Zealand, Australia, and Canada." *Social Security Bulletin,* XI, No. 9 (September, 1948), 3–15.

Matschek, Walter. "Railroad Social Insurance." *Survey Midmonthly,"* (December, 1946), pp. 316–318.

Menninger, Karl. The Human Mind. New York, Alfred A. Knopf, 1947.

Meyer, Harold D., and Charles K. Brightbill. Community Recreation. Boston, D. C. Heath and Company, 1948.

Monroe County [N.Y.] Board of Supervisors. A Study of The Public Welfare Program in Monroe County. Rochester, N.Y., 1950.

Moorman, Edgar M. "Public Institutions and Public Assistance." *Public Welfare,* V, No. 6 (June, 1947), 131.

Morgan, John S. "Some Recent Developments in Social Service in Great Britain." *Social Security Bulletin,* X, No. 6 (June, 1947), 3–10.

Morrison, Lawrence D. "The Police and the Delinquent Child." *Redirecting the Delinquent Child* (1947 Year Book, National Probation and Parole Association). New York, 1948.

Moss, John. "The New English National Assistance Scheme." *The Social Service Review,* XXII, No. 2 (June, 1947), 194–198.

Mountain, Joseph W. *et al.* Ten Years of Federal Grants-in-Aid for Public Health (Public Health Bulletin No. 300). Washington, 1949.

Mountain, Joseph W., and Evelyn Flook. Guide to Health Organization in the United States. Federal Security Agency, U.S. Public Health Service. Reprinted, 1948.

Mountain, Joseph W., and Clifford H. Greve. The Role of Grants-in-Aid for Public Health (Public Health Bulletin 303). Washington, 1950.

Muller, Gulli Lindh, and Dorothy E. Dawes. Introduction to Medical Science. 2d ed. Philadelphia, W. B. Saunders Company, 1948.

National Cancer Institute, Cancer Control Branch. Services and Facilities for Cancer Control in the United States, January 1948 (Supplement No. 208 to the *Public Health Reports*). Washington, 1948.

National Office of Vital Statistics. Deaths and Death Rates for Selected Causes, 1948. National Summaries, March 6, 1950.
—— Special Report, November, 1948.
National Organization for Public Health Nursing. Public Health Nursing Program and Functions. New York, 1944.
—— Desirable Organization of Public Health Nursing for Family Service. New York, 1947.
National Recreation Association. *Recreation,* XLIII, No. 3 (June, 1949), 100.
National Resources Planning Board. After the War; toward Security. Washington, Government Printing Office, 1942.
—— Security, Work, and Relief Policies (Report of the Committee on Long Range Work and Relief Policies). Washington, 1942.
New York Academy of Medicine. Institute on Medical Education. New York, The Commonwealth Fund, 1947.
New York City Department of Welfare. "Comparison of Monthly Estimated Needs." *The Welfarer,* II, No. 1 (December, 1949), 12.
New York State, Department of Mental Hygiene. 57th Annual Report. Albany, 1946.
New York State Health Preparedness Commission. A Program for the Care of the Chronically Ill in New York State. Albany, The Williams Press, 1947.
"1949 in Review." *Social Security Bulletin,* XIII, No. 3 (March, 1950), 1.
Norman, Sherwood, and Helen Norman. Detention for the Juvenile Court: a Discussion of Principles and Practices. New York, National Probation Association, 1946.
Novick, Rudolph G. "Community Organization for Mental Health." *Mental Hygiene,* XXXIV, No. 2 (April, 1950), 213–14.
Nutt, Alice Scott. "The Responsibility of the Juvenile Court and the Public Welfare Agency in the Child Welfare Program." *Redirecting the Delinquent* (1947 Yearbook, National Probation and Parole Association). New York, 1948.
—— "Juvenile and Domestic Relations Courts." *Social Work Year Book, 1947,* p. 276. New York, Russell Sage Foundation, 1947.
Ostertag, Harold C. "New York Revises and Simplifies Its Social Welfare System." *The Social Service Review,* XX, No. 1 (March, 1946), 14.
Pearse, Innes H., and Lucy Crocker. The Peckham Experiment. London, George Allen and Unwin, Ltd., 1947.
Pense, Arthur W. "Trends in the Institutional Care for the Mentally Defective." *American Journal of Mental Deficiency,* L, No. 3 (January, 1946), 453.
Perlman, I. Richard. "Juvenile Court Statistics, 1944 and 1945." *The Child,* XI, Supplement (November, 1946), 11, Table 6.
Pierson, John H. G. Full Employment. New Haven, Yale University Press, 1941.

Pigeon, Helen D. Probation and Parole in Theory and Practice. New York, National Probation Association, 1942.

Pratt, Dallas. Mental Health Statistics. Philadelphia, National Mental Health Foundation, 1947.

Pratt, George. Your Mind and You. Rev. ed. New York, The National Committee for Mental Hygiene, Inc., n.d.

Public Welfare Council. Needs of Neglected and Delinquent Children, a Report to the 1947 Connecticut General Assembly. Hartford, 1946.

Randall, Ollie A. "The Aged." Social Work Year Book, 1947. New York, Russell Sage Foundation, 1947.

Rennie, Thomas A. C., and Luther E. Woodward. Mental Health in Modern Society. New York, The Commonwealth Fund, 1948.

Robinson, Reginald. "Leisure Time Activities of Children on the Lower East Side of N.Y.C." Unpublished thesis.

Rusk, Howard A. "Rehabilitation in Operation." Southern Medical Journal, XLI, No. 1 (January, 1948), 57–62.

Schwasheimer, Waldemar. "Common Ear Troubles." Hygeia, XIX, No. 9 (September, 1941), 690, 691.

Shortley, Michael. "Vocational Rehabilitation." Social Work Year Book, 1947. New York, Russell Sage Foundation, 1947.

Shryock, Richard H. The Development of Modern Medicine; Interpretation of the Social and Scientific Factors Involved. New York, Alfred A. Knopf, 1947.

Sinai, Nathan. Introduction to Public Health Economics. University of Michigan, School of Public Health, 1946.

Slavson, S. R. Recreation and the Total Personality. New York, Association Press, 1948.

Smilie, Wilson G. Public Health Administration in the United States. New York, The Macmillan Company, 1947.

Smith, I. Evelyn. "Adoption." Social Work Year Book, 1947. New York, Russell Sage Foundation, 1947.

Social Legislation Information Service. Bulletin, Nos. 56, 85. Washington, 1950.

Social Security Act Amendments of 1949. Hearings before the Committee on Ways and Means, House of Representatives, 81st Congress, on H.R. 2893.

Sorenson, Roy, and Associates. Recreation for Everybody. Los Angeles, Welfare Council of Metropolitan Los Angeles, 1946.

Spencer, Sue. "Great Success in Professional Education." Survey Midmonthly, LXXXIII, No. 6 (June, 1947), 167.

Stern, Bernhard J. American Medical Practice in the Perspective of a Century. New York, The Commonwealth Fund, 1945.

Stewart, Estelle M. The Cost of American Almshouses (Bureau of Labor Statistics, Bulletin No. 386, Miscellaneous and Series). Washington, 1925.

Sturges, Gertrude. "Home Medical Care." *Administrative Medicine,* ed. Haven Emerson. New York, Thomas Nelson and Sons.

Sudhoff, Karl. "History of Medicine." *Encyclopedia of the Social Sciences,* X, 283–287.

Thorman, George. Toward Mental Health (Public Affairs Pamphlet No. 120). New York, Public Affairs Committee, 1946.

Tracy, Margaret A. Nursing, an Art and a Science. St. Louis, C.V.S. Mosby, 1949.

Trecker, Harleigh B. "Social Group Work." *Social Work Year Book, 1947.* New York, Russell Sage Foundation, 1947.

Truesdell, Dr. Leon E. Patients in Mental Institutions, 1945. Washington, Bureau of the Census, Department of Commerce, 1948.

U.S. Bureau of the Census. Historical Statistics of the United States 1789–1945. Washington, 1949.

—— 1950 Census of Population. Preliminary Reports, Series PC-7, No. 2. Washington, April 11, 1951.

—— Statistical Abstract of the United States: 1949. 70th ed. Washington, 1949.

U.S. Bureau of Labor, United States Employment Service. Selective Placement for the Handicapped. Rev. ed. Washington, 1945.

U.S. House of Representatives, Committee on Labor. Aid to the Physically Handicapped. Washington, 1946.

U.S. Public Health Service. National Health Survey: Sickness and Medical Care Series, Bulletin No. 1. Washington, 1940.

—— Summary, U.S.P.H.S. Surveys of California's Mental Institutions and Mental Hygiene Clinics. Sacramento, 1949. Mimeographed.

U.S. Public Health Service, Mental Hygiene Committee. "Conclusions Concerning Psychiatric Training and Clinics. Reprint from *Public Health Reports,* LXI, No. 26 (June 28, 1946), 14.

U.S. Senate Advisory Council on Social Security. "Unemployment Insurance Recommendations." *Social Security Bulletin,* XII, No. 1 (January, 1949), 16.

—— "Proposed Changes in Old-Age and Survivors Insurance." *Social Security Bulletin,* II, No. 5 (May, 1948), 22.

Upjohn Institute for Community Research. Full Employment in Your Community. Chicago, Public Administration Service, 1947.

Upham, Frances. A Dynamic Approach to Illness. New York, The Family Service Association of America, 1949.

Van Horn, A. L. "Crippled Children." *Social Work Year Book, 1947.* New York, Russell Sage Foundation, 1947.

Wagner, Margaret. "Meet Yourself at Sixty-five." *Survey Midmonthly,* LXXXII, No. 4 (April, 1946), 110.

Wandel, William H. "Insurance against Unemployment in the United States." *Monthly Labor Review,* LXX, No. 1 (January, 1950), 11.

White, R. C. Administration of Public Welfare. American Book Co., 1940.

Wilson, Gertrude, and Gladys Ryland. Social Group Work Practice. New York, Houghton Mifflin Company, 1949.

Winslow, C.–E. A. "Preventive Medicine and Health Promotion—Ideals or Realities?" *Yale Journal of Biology and Medicine,* XIV, No. 5 (May, 1942), 444.

World Health Organization. Manual of the International Statistical Classification of Diseases, Injuries, and Causes of Death. Geneva, 1948.

Wyers, R. E., and George Tarjan. "Administrative Practices to Provide Better Psychiatric Care of Mental Patients." *American Journal of Mental Deficiency,* LIV, No. 1 (July, 1949), 31–37.

Yoder, Dale, and Donald G. Paterson. Local Labor Market Research. Minneapolis, University of Minnesota Press, 1948.

Zimmer, V. A. State Workmen's Compensation Laws as of June 1, 1946 (U.S. Department of Labor, Division of Labor Standards, Bulletin No. 78). Washington, 1946.

INDEX